10/06

R. Amith

D0916581

AMONG THE
LOWEST OF
THE DEAD

Law, Meaning, and Violence

The scope of Law, Meaning, and Violence is defined by the wide-ranging scholarly debates signaled by each of the words in the title. Those debates have taken place among and between lawyers, anthropologists, political theorists, sociologists, and historians, as well as literary and cultural critics. This series is intended to recognize the importance of such ongoing conversations about law, meaning, and violence as well as to encourage and further them.

Series Editors: Martha Minow, Harvard Law School
Elaine Scarry, Harvard University
Austin Sarat, Amherst College

AMONG THE LOWEST OF THE DEAD

The Culture of Capital Punishment

DAVID VON DREHLE

The University of Michigan Press

Ann Arbor

St. Louis Community College
at Meramec
LIBRARY

Copyright © by the University of Michigan 2006
First published in 1995 by Times Books, a division of Random House, Inc.
All rights reserved
Published in the United States of America by
The University of Michigan Press
Manufactured in the United States of America
⊗ Printed on acid-free paper

2009   2008   2007   2006   4   3   2   1

No part of this publication may be reproduced, stored in a retrieval system,
or transmitted in any form or by any means, electronic, mechanical, or otherwise,
without the written permission of the publisher.

A CIP catalog record for this book is available from the British Library.

Library of Congress Cataloging-in-Publication Data

Von Drehle, Dave.
     Among the lowest of the dead : the culture of capital punishment /
     David Von Drehle.
          p.   cm. — (Law, meaning, and violence)
     First published in 1995 by Times Books, a division of Random House, Inc.
     Includes index.
     ISBN-13: 978-0-472-03123-8 (pbk. : alk. paper)
     ISBN-10: 0-472-03123-6 (pbk. : alk. paper)
     1. Executions and executioners—United States.   2. Death row—United States.
     3. Death row inmates—United States.   I. Title.   II. Series.

HV8699.U5V66   2006
364.660973—dc22   2005046667

To my mother

And I Tiresias have foresuffered all

Enacted on this same divan or bed;

I who have sat by Thebes below the wall

And walked among the lowest of the dead . . .

T. S. Eliot, The Waste Land

PREFACE

Ten Years Later

A book about a subject as contro-
versial and fluid as the death penalty is inevitably a bucket pulled from a
moving stream. No sooner is it published than readers—and the author—
begin to wonder whether the water in the bucket still represents the whole
river.

Has this book about a "slow, costly and inefficient" system—an
"arbitrary," "chaotic . . . merry-go-round," in the words of one of the
central figures—become outdated by the frequency with which Texas has
carried out executions in the past ten years and by the burst of executions
in states like Virginia, Oklahoma, and Missouri? (Indeed, a twenty-first-
century "death belt" now runs north from Texas through Oklahoma and
into Missouri. These three states regularly account for more than half of all
executions each year. The former "death belt," which ran from Florida to
Texas across old Dixie, has been outdone, at least for now.)

Because of these few states, more men (and a handful of women)
have been executed in the past decade than I expected when I wrote, in
the closing pages of this book, that "a random few dozen" executions per
year "is still the limit of possibility." I remember wondering to myself how
many executions the modern death penalty system could produce in a
year and guessing that the limit would probably be around fifty. Five years
later, in 1999, the states put ninety-eight people to death. Nor was that an
aberration. In 2002, Texas alone executed as many people (thirty-three) as
were put to death in Florida during the entire span of this book. I imagine
a year with a hundred or more executions nationwide—a rate unmatched
in more than half a century in America—remains possible.

A whole book, or maybe a shelf of them, could be written exploring
the reasons for these higher rates in Texas and the new death belt. A fact

alluded to in these pages is that Texas wrote a death penalty law in the 1970s that was unique, closer to a mandatory penalty than the elaborate weighing system upheld by the U.S. Supreme Court for other states. The Texas law is simpler and apparently less open to interpretation than laws like Florida's that are premised on "guided discretion." A special Texas "death court"— the state Court of Criminal Appeals—expedites capital cases, showing scant appetite for parsing the law. And the key federal court for Texas inmates— the Fifth Circuit Court of Appeals—has turned a cold eye on death row issues. At the same time, Texas has done little to provide strong advocates for its death row inmates; it is likely that Justice Ruth Bader Ginsburg had Texas at least partly in mind when she recently observed that she had never seen a death penalty case, in nearly ten years on the Supreme Court, in which the inmate had received a good defense at trial. Her colleague former justice Sandra Day O'Connor echoed this assessment in a 2001 speech, having weighed capital cases on the Supreme Court for twenty years. Citing statistics showing that capital defendants in Texas with court-appointed attorneys were 28 percent more likely to be convicted than those who hired their own counsel—and 44 percent more likely to be sentenced to death if convicted—O'Connor ventured: "Perhaps it's time to look at minimum standards for appointed counsel in death cases and adequate compensation for appointed counsel when they are used." O'Connor gave this speech not in Texas but in Minnesota, which does not have the death penalty. "You must breathe a big sigh of relief every day," O'Connor told her audience.

Texas is the perfect storm of the American capital punishment enterprise, a state in which inmates receive minimal representation, judges mostly refrain from tinkering with the system, and appellate courts take a dim view of complaints from the row. Even in Texas, however, there are more prisoners living under unresolved death sentences today than there were a decade ago—about 450—despite a plunging crime rate that has helped to drive down the number of capital trials. In other words, even in Texas, the executioner cannot keep up.

Nationwide, the clanking, spluttering, unreliable machine described in these pages is running just as badly a decade later. As I was writing this book, experts were predicting a wave of executions in California. That has not materialized: the death row population there is now well over six hundred, while California executes just one or two prisoners each year. In the face of these numbers, it is hard to imagine an emptier or more craven government promise than a California death sentence. Several states, amid growing doubts that the system is working reliably, have imposed a moratorium on executions lasting months or even years—a development that I would never have imagined, given the political power of capital punishment a decade ago.

Take Illinois, for example.

According to a special commission appointed to study that state's death penalty, "serious questions about the operation of the capital punishment system in Illinois . . . were highlighted most significantly by the release of former death row inmate Anthony Porter after coming within 48 hours of his scheduled execution. . . . Porter was released from death row following an investigation by journalism students who obtained a confession from the real killer in the case."

Northwestern University journalism professor David Protess and his students documented to the satisfaction of virtually everyone that there were innocent men on the Illinois death row—a total of fifteen men, in the recent past and present. The reaction to their investigation was a moratorium on executions that was still in effect more than five years later. A specially appointed Illinois Commission on Capital Punishment conducted an exhaustive examination of the death penalty system. The commission's report in 2002 ran to more than two hundred pages, diagnosing nearly one hundred distinct problems with the system, from inadequate defenses to insufficiently skeptical cops. My cast of characters in Florida would recognize just about all of them. The Illinois legislature followed up with sweeping reforms of the state's death penalty laws. Ultimately, then-governor George Ryan, a lame-duck Republican, commuted more than 170 death sentences to life in prison.

The commissioners split on the question of whether the system was worth overhauling again. The renowned author and former prosecutor Scott Turow was a member of the commission. He began his work with mixed feelings about the death penalty but was startled by what he found. "Capital punishment has been one of the most notorious train wrecks of American politics," he concluded.

This same realization—that the system is a train wreck and may not ever work well—has continued to dawn on public officials closest to the issue. The frustration and resignation expressed by judges and prosecutors in the closing pages of this book have spread across the country, as capital punishment continues to snarl the justice system nearly three decades after the Supreme Court declared that a constitutionally acceptable death penalty had been devised. Capital punishment is "by far the most difficult, time-consuming, frustrating and critical joint problem [courts] have to grapple with on a daily basis," according to Judge Gilbert Merritt of the federal Sixth Circuit Court of Appeals, which covers the Upper Midwest. In Arizona, Stanley Feldman, the senior state supreme court justice, called on the state to consider doing away with the system entirely: "There is no way really to do it right," he said. Moses Harrison, a chief justice of the Illinois Supreme Court, put it this way: "Despite the courts' efforts to fashion a death penalty scheme that is just, fair and reliable, the system is not work-ing."

The U.S. Supreme Court, after a relatively hands-off period, is once again showing itself willing to reopen various legal controversies related to the death penalty, taking cases to decide whether electrocution and certain lethal injection procedures are cruel and unusual punishment; whether trial judges or juries should weigh the evidence for and against death sentences; whether execution is acceptable for the mentally ill, the mentally retarded, and juvenile offenders; what constitutes adequate defense counsel, and so on.

On balance, the picture of delay, caprice, and confusion painted in *Among the Lowest of the Dead* continues to represent the death penalty in America. When the book was published, there were about three thousand prisoners on death row across the country. Today, despite the higher execution rates, the emptying of the Illinois death row, the sharply reduced murder rates across the country, and a decline in the frequency of death sentences, that number is even higher—about thirty-five hundred. Capital cases continue to clog courts from coast to coast, and if the problem is not metastasizing as quickly as before, the main reasons have little to do with the death penalty machine itself. There are fewer violent crimes today, more alternatives to death sentences in the form of "life without parole," and, perhaps, a growing sense among prosecutors that the expense and complication of a death penalty trial are often not worth it, given the slim chance of an eventual execution. Nationwide, the frequency of death sentences has dropped by half from a decade ago—a trend matched by the once gung-ho people of the state of Florida.

If this book continues to have value—and I hope readers agree that it does—it is because it tries to show the death penalty system from all sides and through many eyes. The project began fifteen years ago without my even knowing it. An editor at the *Miami Herald* showed me some powerfully intimate photographs from the early years of Florida's modern death row. The pictures were taken by a young man named Bill Wax. Bill was a college student at the University of Florida when John Spenkelink was approaching his weird destiny as the first man to be executed against his will in a dozen tumultuous years. The row was a relatively open place in those days; reporters and photographers came and went rather easily. Bill met Spenkelink, visited death row, and recorded it all with his camera—access I could only envy when I began to delve into the death penalty ten years later. His pictures were like passports for me across a stern, search-lit frontier to a place where men sit sullenly, wash socks in sinks, stare, doze, and wait decades to die.

The editor chose me to write an essay to accompany Bill's pictures—I suppose because I had written several pieces about how and why the death penalty had failed to deliver on its promises. Death row in Florida then housed more than 250 inmates, yet executions were comparatively rare. Everyone complained about the endless and expensive appeals process, but nothing seemed to change. I set out to understand why. Along the way, I caught the assignment, along with scores of other journalists, to cover the execution of Ted Bundy—the most notorious murderer of a generation—from a cow pasture near the Florida State Prison.

As I tried to interpret Bill Wax's pictures, it dawned on me that Bundy's execution had come almost exactly ten years after Florida had begun its modern death penalty experiment with the electrocution of John Spenkelink. And that span, from the pointless execution of a faceless drifter, to the circus execution of a truly diabolical killer—with years of anguish and fiasco in between—seemed to gather up the whole mixed bag of frustrations and stratagems and sorrows that the death penalty had to offer to American life.

Five years, thousands of documents, scores of interviews later, I told the story of those ten years in *Among the Lowest of the Dead*. The book was my best effort to show, from every perspective—prosecution and defense, politicians and judges, victims and killers, survivors of every type—what the death penalty in contemporary America *is actually like.* In the course of my research, I read many books by highly skilled thinkers and writers designed to persuade readers. This book has a different purpose: to examine, describe, report.

Now it is more than twenty-five years since Spenkelink's death. Everything and nothing has changed. The same David Kendall who sped up and down the pine-bordered highways of North Florida in his desperate effort to save John Spenkelink went on to defend President Bill Clinton against articles of impeachment in the U.S. Senate. He now has two historic events on his resume: the first involuntary execution in the modern era and the only impeachment trial of the twentieth century. The second time, Kendall won—thanks in part to the votes of juror Bob Graham of Florida. Kendall's silent nemesis in the fight for Spenkelink's life had become a U.S. senator voting on impeachment. Ray Marky, the relentless prosecutor, lost his larynx to his endless chain of nervously puffed cigarettes and now visits Tallahassee schools to warn against the dangers of smoking. Warden David Brierton moved into management of the Florida prison system and ultimately found himself back on the row, investigating botched executions. Robin Gibson, the governor's right-hand man, returned to a prosperous small-town law practice in Central Florida. Millard Farmer is still in Atlanta, throwing monkey wrenches into the courthouse machine. Reverend Joe Ingle, in Nashville, no longer has to leave Tennessee to carry on his ministry to the condemned; the death row in his state has become one of the busiest in the country.

The decision to focus on one state's experience, rather than skimming across the entire death belt, was partly driven by an author's imperatives. Simply to sketch the tale in a single state required me to introduce dozens of figures and to trace a tangle of legal and political strategies. Additional states would have compounded the complications. But the choice of Florida was not accidental: during the period covered in this book, the formative decade of the modern death penalty, Florida led the way in reinstating capital punishment. It was the first state to pass a new death penalty law after the U.S. Supreme Court struck down the old punishments in 1972. It was the first state to execute a man against his will, the first to make a routine of executions, the first to confront the crisis of hundreds of inmates in need of adequate appellate counsel. True, there are now larger death rows, in California and Texas, and more inmates die in the execution chambers of several states. But Florida remains a microcosm of the system nationwide. If you sketched a range of state experiences with capital punishment, with a state like Minnesota on one end—no death penalty at all—and Texas on the other, Florida would lie in between: a place where sentences are imposed with stern regularity, where condemned prisoners are housed by the hundreds, where millions are spent to litigate appeals year after year after year. But in the quarter-century since Spenkelink's execution, this apparatus has produced, on average, barely more than two executions annually.

The tinkering never stopped.

There was a long fight over Old Sparky, the aged oak electric chair. You can see the first salvo of the battle near the end of this book, where I tell the story of Jesse Tafero, whose head caught fire when the chair malfunctioned in 1990. Over the next ten years, other inmates were burned or bloodied in other malfunctions—enough that in 2000 the U.S. Supreme Court agreed to look at the question of whether electrocution was cruel and unusual punishment, an issue that had supposedly been settled more than a century earlier. Faced with this prospect, the Florida legislature mothballed the chair and adopted lethal injection as the state's execution method.

But this method, too, has had its imperfections. Bennie Demps was one of the first Florida inmates to die by the poisonous cocktail, in which an anesthetic is followed by a paralytic drug to halt breathing, after which comes a drug to stop the heart. The protocol at the Florida State Prison called for two intravenous lines, one in each arm, so that a second round of drugs could be quickly administered if the first round failed to work. The IV went easily into the prisoner's left arm, but when technicians moved to install the second line, they jabbed twice without hitting a vein. They tried again in the prisoner's groin—no luck. Exasperated, a technician pulled out a scalpel to attempt a procedure known as a "cut-down." After making a small incision in the prisoner's thigh, a crew member tried to pull a vein to the surface. Another failure. They tried again near his ankle. No luck.

Bennie Demps was wheeled into the execution chamber more than half an hour late, well after his 6 P.M. date with death. (For the first time in modern memory, the execution was not scheduled at dawn; prison officials had decided there was no point in everyone getting up so early.) Demps used his final statement to demand an investigation of his execution. "They butchered me back there. I was in a lot of pain. They cut me in the groin, they cut me in the leg," Demps said in an angry tirade some seven minutes long. "This is not an execution, it is murder."

"Eyes bulging and voice quavering," the *Miami Herald* reporter wrote, Demps "said the medical examiner would find 'a wound on my leg that they sutured back up. I was bleeding profusely.'" After the speech, the executioner depressed a plunger, and the drugs began to flow. At 6:53 P.M., on June 7, 2000, Bennie Demps was pronounced dead.

Lawyers for the next inmate slated to die, Thomas Provenzano, raised Demps's botched execution in hopes of winning a stay, with no success. In the long history of legal executions, an almost unimaginable range of methods have been employed: stoning, burning, flaying, dismembering, beheading, starving, shooting, hanging, electrocuting, gassing, and so on. In that context, lethal injection looked almost peaceful. Provenzano won no votes on the issue of the execution method, though two Florida Supreme Court justices voted to stay his death warrant out of concern that Provenzano had lost his mind. "He suffers from a delusional belief that he is Jesus Christ and that this is the real reason he is being executed," wrote Justice Leander Shaw. Provenzano was killed by lethal injection two weeks after Demps, on June 21, 2000.

One of the running sagas in this book concerns the ragtag band of lawyers recruited by a chain-smoking, wisecracking, hard-drinking dynamo named Scharlette Holdman to defend the men of death row. Over time, even the pro-execution government of Florida concluded that taxpayers should replace Holdman's makeshift operation with a centralized agency for capital appeals, called—a triumph of stupefying bureaucratese—the Office of Capital Collateral Representative.

As it played out, no one was entirely happy with the result.

Initially, CCR lawyers worked themselves half to death—it must have been the only state agency that kept roll-away beds in the office for employees who couldn't, or wouldn't, go home. Over time, the responsibility of defending literally hundreds of lives began to grind down the CCR staff. One of the office pioneers, Michael Mello, has since written his own accounts of the confusion, chaos, and insanity of Florida's death penalty project in such memoirs as *Dead Wrong, The Wrong Man* (which tells the story of Mello's successful effort to free Joseph "Crazy Joe" Spaziano from death row), and *Deathwork*.

Gradually, many of the founders of CCR drifted away. Mello migrated north to teach law and write books in Vermont. Holdman ultimately headed west, winding up in California, where she remained one of the finest death row investigators in the country. One of the best of the CCR lawyers, Mark Olive, remained in Florida and kept fighting. If someone were to write this book today, Mark Olive would be the mainstay.

A decade or so was enough to see that CCR, by itself, fixed nothing, and Florida authorities began taking the agency apart. Democratic governor Lawton Chiles, elected in 1990, embraced a plan to divide CCR into three regional offices. But the changes made little or no difference. Despite the latest overhaul, the machinery of capital punishment stubbornly refused to hum. Late in his second term, Chiles died in office, and the Florida death penalty was still failing. A short time later Jeb Bush was elected governor, and the system was overhauled again. Now it came full circle: the Florida legislature created a statewide "registry" for capital defense lawyers. And so, after some fifteen years and scores of millions spent, Florida returned to a bureaucratized version of Scharlette Holdman's pencil-scratched ledger, in which she tracked death penalty cases and tried to match the condemned with lawyers. Several years into the registry program, Florida's execution rate remains about the same—between two and three prisoners per year on average.

Other schemes have been hatched and debated. In 2001, one of the leading authorities on the Florida death penalty, editorialist Martin Dyckman of the *St. Petersburg Times,* summarized the state of affairs in a column that suggested little has changed since this book was first published. "The Florida Supreme Court spends about half its time on the tiny fraction of its cases that involve the death penalty," Dyckman began. "Knowing this, some legislators offered competing proposals last year to 'help' the court, either by expanding the bench from seven seats to nine or by creating a separate supreme court just for criminal appeals. What they really wanted was to change the outcomes of those death cases that pile up in Tallahassee, so that more inmates would die, and die faster.

"Cooler heads deflected the court-wrecking schemes by creating a Supreme Court Workload Commission, which was expected to report, as in fact it recently did, that there is no good use for either 'reform.'

"A larger Supreme Court would slow things down, not speed them up," Dyckman continued. "Nine people need more time to argue and exchange draft opinions than seven do. As for the other, two courts of last resort would bring utter confusion to the rules of evidence."

The writer wound up with some data: "There were 856 first-degree murders [in Florida] in 1999, 741 arrests, more than 1,000 convictions for all degrees of murder and manslaughter combined, yet only 21 death sentences. That suggests the death penalty is nothing but a costly, capricious symbolism which serves no purpose—other than to enable politicians to posture about it—that couldn't be served just as well at much less expense by simply throwing away the keys" through life-without-parole sentences.

It is almost stunning to find courts and lawmakers still sifting and resifting these issues three decades after the law was written.

There was a time when I could shock people by telling them that some Florida prisoners would soon be marking their twentieth anniversaries on death row. Twenty-year legal battles seemed like something from Dickens's *Bleak House*—not the routine business of a major American state. I used to wonder what might happen when inmates started hitting twenty-five years, which was then the minimum a first-degree murderer sentenced to life in prison had to serve before being eligible for parole. (Since then, Florida and a number of other states have adopted true life-without-parole sentences.) Would it be fair to execute a man after he had already served the minimum alternative sentence? Wasn't that weirdly close to paying double: a life sentence *and* a death sentence? Some version of that idle speculation is now an element in dozens of death row appeals, and someday the courts might find merit in it.

Meanwhile, Florida's senior death row inmate, Gary Alvord, passed the thirty-year mark in April 2004.

Thirty years. And there is nothing especially complicated about his case—no disputes over guilt, or accusations of racial prejudice, or evidence withheld. Alvord was a violent twenty-five-year-old living in a mental hospital when he escaped and went on a murderous rampage, assaulting and strangling three women. He arrived on death row about four months after John Spenkelink got there, when the population of the row was barely enough to fill out a football team. He watched it grow into a small town.

According to a personal advertisement written by Alvord and posted by his supporters on the Internet, he is now "55 yrs, 6'0, 200 lbs . . . fairly intelligent, able to empathise. I miss normal people/life and . . . enjoy reading [and] caring about others." The prisoner hasn't always sounded so reasonable. In the early 1980s, Alvord was so clearly insane that he wasn't fit even for death row, where raving pedophiles and mumbling psychotics managed to fit in. He was moved for several years to the state hospital for intensive treatment. In time, Alvord was rendered sufficiently sane to resume his place on the row—which has moved, since this book was written, to a new facility across a creek from the older prison at Starke.

Gary Alvord is not the only man growing old in the tiny cells of Florida's death town. In an average year, old age takes as many lives as the gurney. Alvord has only a few months of seniority on Thomas Knight, who continues, as of this writing, to survive *two* death sentences—one he received in 1975 for the murders of Stanley and Lillian Gans and another handed down six years later for the death row slaying of prison guard Richard Burke. There are now five members of Florida's thirty-year club, soon to be six, soon to be more.

In 1994, as I was putting the last touches on *Among the Lowest of the Dead,* Jeb Bush was coming down to the wire in a hot, hard campaign against Lawton Chiles. In a final grab at victory, Bush aired a controversial television ad in which Wendy Nelson, the grieving mother of a murdered little girl, looked into the camera and said: "Fourteen years ago, my daughter rode off to school on her bicycle. She never came back. Her killer is still on death row, and we're still waiting for justice." Wendy Nelson blamed the incumbent for the delay. Some said a backlash against the ad helped to reelect Chiles.

Almost a dozen years later, Larry Mann, the kidnapper-killer of gregarious little Elisa Nelson, is still on death row. His lawyers say he is no longer the self-loathing, drug-addled, violent pedophile dispatched there so long ago. Supposedly he has found God in his prison cell and studies ancient Greek to better understand the New Testament. Mann survived four more years of Chiles and now nearly eight years of Governor Bush. He has been sentenced and resentenced and resentenced again. At one hearing, Wendy Nelson filled the courtroom with supporters from the victim rights group she founded out of her frustration with the dysfunctional death penalty system. The presence that day of so many grim-faced members of the League of Victims and Empathizers was recycled into yet another ground for Mann's appeals.

I often think of the morning I spent in the company of Wendy Nelson, hearing her story. We talked in the presence of a photograph of her adorable ten-year-old daughter. She spoke movingly of the pain that sharpened with each birthday. She had imagined Elisa as she might have been at age sixteen or twenty-one. That was a lot of birthdays ago, and I'm sure Wendy Nelson has pictured a wedding day that Larry Mann prevented and a baby's birth. "I try to imagine what she would be like . . . but I only ever knew the child," Wendy said.

The inability of the death penalty system to resolve a case like Larry Mann's, given fourteen years of trying, led me to declare that capital punishment was "a cruel hoax" for families like the Nelsons. That was one of the most salient, powerful truths I was able to learn about this troubling subject. And it is even more true today, when those fourteen years have turned to twenty-five.

I mentioned Dickens a moment ago. Recently a leader of the fight to end capital punishment in America described today's situation as the best and worst of times. After a generation in which public opinion hardened steadily in favor of executions, Gallup polls suggest that the trend has reversed, albeit slightly. From a high of 80 percent in favor of capital punishment at the time this book was first published, the number has fallen to about 65 percent—still very strong. But if people are given the option of life without parole, the public is evenly split.

The steady stream of inmates released from death row has led Congress to the brink of passing major legislation to improve the defense of capital prisoners. In 2003, ten inmates nationwide were freed due to doubts about their guilt—tying the 1987 record. That number included two Ohio prisoners exonerated more than twenty-five years after their arrest.

Rudolph Holton was released, having served sixteen years on Florida's death row, thanks to DNA and other evidence that pointed to another man as the killer.

Yet capital punishment continues to serve one function quite well: it inoculates politicians from charges of weakness or coddling of criminals. Most leaders in both parties continue to support the death penalty. President George W. Bush presided over more executions than any modern governor yet was able to run for election on a platform of moderation. There is little reason, beyond the hopes of abolitionists, to imagine that the death penalty won't be with us another ten years down the road, and ten years after that.

So once again I offer this picture of the system from the inside, as seen through many eyes and many perspectives. It is the story of a particular time and place, yes—but it remains true for Florida and for America. The death penalty machinery pictured here is the same perplexing, frustrating, and costly rattletrap we live with today.

David Von Drehle
Washington, D.C.
March 2006

CONTENTS

PART I

LOOSE THE
FATEFUL
LIGHTNING

On Florida's death row, in the bloom time of spring, grimy windows beyond the cell bars glow with the beauty of freedom, and reminders of the living world stream through in a ceaseless taunt. Sunshine teases but doesn't touch the men of death row. You can tell just by looking at them, especially the white guys, whose skin, after a couple of years, goes as pale and doughy as a lump of mozzarella. Blue skies and sunshine beyond the prison's windows set a caged man to thinking, and the inhabitants of the row live lives that don't bear much thinking about. There's the ugly past that got them to that place, the miserable present, and the future they don't want to come.

May 18, 1979, was a glorious spring morning, the sun warm in a Wedgwood sky: heaven to the tourists on their beach towels, paradise to the retirees along their neat green fairways. A postcard Florida day. Perhaps John Spenkelink reflected that morning on the fact that he would be inching up on parole—if only he had been smart enough to cop a plea. Some six years earlier, John Spenkelink had killed a man in a Tallahassee motel room. Spenkelink was a bad young man, but the victim was at least as bad, and arguably worse. The prosecutor and the defense attorney danced around the matter of a plea bargain to second-degree murder, and it seemed like a good solution to most everyone involved—except Spenkelink. He thought he could get on the witness stand, explain why he did it, and talk his way out of the whole lurid matter. As with most men on death row, thinking was not Spenkelink's strong suit.

What ultimately happened was that the prosecutor filed first-degree murder charges, and the jury convicted. The jurors thought so little of Spenkelink's testimony that they recommended the death penalty, and the judge took their advice. So there he sat on that fine May morning, taunted by the view, in a cell the size of a bathroom on

Florida State Prison's R-wing, home to 134 condemned men, the largest death row population in America at the time. And there, at about 9 A.M., a guard arrived, handcuffed Spenkelink, and walked him to a nearby office to meet with the warden.

"I have something to read to you, John," said the warden, David Brierton—but the piece of paper on the warden's desk spoke for itself. It was bordered with a quarter inch of black. A death warrant is a curiously bloodless government document, one dry "whereas" after another, culminating in a businesslike "therefore." A busy governor signs thousands of papers much like it every year, so the black border was added to avoid confusion.

Not that the black border was really necessary in this particular instance. The death warrant Brierton read to John Spenkelink was, from a legal standpoint, the most important one in many decades in the United States; a mix-up was hardly likely. Executions had slowed to a drip, then stopped completely in the 1960s. In 1972, the U.S. Supreme Court struck down every capital punishment law in the country as unconstitutionally vague. New laws were quickly passed in many states, but no criminal had been put to death against his will in a dozen years. John Spenkelink's death warrant would test whether executions would resume.

The governor had signed it that morning, and the document was hand-carried to Brierton by Louie Lee Wainwright, czar of Florida's vast prison system. Its preparation had been painstaking and wrapped in secrecy. A secretary so utterly discreet she was known as "The Sphinx" had typed and retyped it in the middle of the night. Every letter, comma, and period had to be perfect. Her botched versions were gathered by a government lawyer and disposed of miles from the capitol building. For all that caution, though, there was something strange about the finished draft. This man's death warrant was a test of great national significance; his portrait had appeared in *The New York Times Magazine;* his story would be judged the most important of the year by Florida newspaper editors. But the governor's staff was not sure how to spell his name.

Their uncertainty was as old as Spenkelink's six-year odyssey through the courts. Most legal papers, beginning with the arrest warrant in 1973 and continuing through half a decade of appeals, referred to the defendant, incorrectly, as "Spenkellink," with two *l*'s. His prison shirts were stenciled "Spinkellink," with an *i* and a double *l*—also wrong. The correct spelling was "Spenkelink," with two *e*'s and one *l*. His death warrant listed all three versions, connected by the words "also known as," which is law enforcement lingo typically used for listing aliases, not spelling errors. But here the lingo diluted any impression that the state was going to kill a man without troubling to learn his exact name.

Spenkelink seemed shaken as the warden read the warrant. Afterward, he was permitted to telephone his lawyer. Then he was ushered out of the office and a second inmate, Willie Jasper Darden, was led in. There was a warrant for him, too. Brierton read this one just as carefully, but deep down he did not take it as seriously as the first. Knowledgeable lawyers in the state attorney general's office had put out the word that Darden was not likely to be executed. Not this time. His appeals were not as far along as Spenkelink's; some court somewhere would probably block Darden's electrocution for some indefinite time.

Apparently Darden believed this too, because he took the news more easily than had Spenkelink. He asked that his phone call be placed to a woman friend named Mary, and while the switchboard operator dialed the number, he passed the time chatting idly about his wives, who were several and far flung. Eventually, Mary came on the line and Darden told her what had happened. There was a long pause. Mary must have collapsed in grief, because Darden shouted into the phone: "Get up, woman! They signed the warrant on me, not you!"

The reason the Supreme Court briefly abolished capital punishment, in a 1972 case called *Furman v. Georgia,* was that the system made no clear sense. Some six hundred prisoners awaited execution on America's death rows, but only a comparative handful had been hanged or gassed or electrocuted in the decade before the *Furman* decision. Discretion to impose the death penalty lay mostly in the hands of local judges and juries, with little guidance given by the law as to how this power should be used. In a disturbing number of cases, this undisciplined process had allowed racial prejudice to taint the process—and beyond racism the process was infected with caprice. One person would be executed while the next one, whose crime might seem much worse, would not. "Under these laws no standards govern the selection of the penalty," wrote Justice William O. Douglas. Justice Potter Stewart compared the irrationality of the death penalty to being struck by lightning.

Following the *Furman* decision, Florida was the first state to draft a new law aimed at eliminating flukes of chance from the death penalty. The lawmakers were so eager they held a special session for just that purpose; the session was a three-day whirlwind resulting in a complicated legal contraption for weighing shades of evil. Florida's new law provided for several layers of review in each capital case and promised certainty in place of the old caprice. In 1976, that law—along with laws from Georgia and Texas—was upheld by the Supreme Court, which concluded that the new death penalty would be rational.

In view of this history, many people familiar with John Spenkelink's case were perplexed that his should be the test case. He wasn't a serial killer or cop killer or homicidal child molester, and there were plenty of all three on death rows across the country, and plenty of all three serving lesser sentences. Spenkelink had killed a career criminal. His case "shoulda been . . . murder two," a prosecutor later allowed. But as Justice Byron White predicted in his opinion upholding the new death penalty laws, "Mistakes will be made and discriminations will occur which will be difficult to explain." Thus, the Spenkelink test was an apt beginning, and anyway, the battle over his life really had less to do with the particular inmate than with a much larger question: Would the individual states be allowed to carry out their lawful punishments or not?

On the day of the death warrants, in Washington, D.C., a lean young lawyer named David Kendall arrived at work feeling a little ragged, his mouth dry, his head aching. He had overindulged a bit the night before at a swank fundraising party for the NAACP Legal Defense and Educational Fund, Inc., his previous employer. The occasion was the twenty-fifth anniversary of the Legal Defense Fund's great triumph: *Brown v. Board of Education,* the monumental U.S. Supreme Court case that ended school segregation as a legal policy in America.

From that early victory, the LDF, known to insiders as the Inc. Fund, persevered and sometimes prospered through years of voting rights litigation, fair housing lawsuits, and struggles to end capital punishment. Its stature as the nation's premier civil rights law firm was cemented by the appointment of its first director, Thurgood Marshall, to a seat on the Supreme Court. The Inc. Fund attracted lawyers of the highest caliber, lawyers who could, if they wished, easily find work in offices furnished in leather, dark wood, and brass. Kendall was such a lawyer when he joined the Inc. Fund in 1973; he had the sort of credentials that would arouse any blue-chip law firm. He was a Rhodes scholar, a graduate of Yale Law School; he had clerked for a Supreme Court justice and been commissioned as an officer in the U.S. Army. But he also had certain values acquired during a Quaker boyhood in a small Indiana town. As a college student, those values took Kendall to Mississippi to register black voters during the Freedom Summer of 1964. Arrested and thrown in jail, he was bailed out by Inc. Fund lawyers. Later, during his term as a clerk for Justice White, Kendall marveled as the great legal scholar Anthony Amsterdam persuaded the Supreme Court to empty the nation's death rows in *Furman v. Georgia,* an Inc. Fund case. For Kendall, the Inc. Fund became the epitome of legal acumen marshaled to the service of righteousness, and so he spurned the oaken offices for a metal desk in an Inc. Fund cubicle.

He had intended to practice all manner of civil rights law, but soon found himself consumed by the firestorm that followed the brief victory over capital punishment. Across the country, state legislatures joined Florida in the rush to restore the death penalty, and America's death rows steadily refilled. Like water in a hydraulic press, the rising tide of newly condemned inmates squeezed everything else from David Kendall's portfolio, until all his clients were people under a sentence of death.

His cubicle contained a strange barometer of his burgeoning, macabre practice. Early on, Kendall discovered that many death row inmates, locked in their cells some twenty-three hours a day, play chess to pass the time. He made it his custom to challenge each new client to a friendly game through the mail. When the challenge was accepted, as it nearly always was, Kendall would buy a cheap chessboard with plastic pieces and set it up in his office to keep track of the game. He would move a piece on the little board, note the move in a letter along with any legal developments, then wait for his client's move by return mail. Soon, Kendall had half a dozen boards going, then a dozen. Ranks of pawns fell to advancing bishops while queens clashed with crusading knights in battles that ranged over Kendall's bookcases and file cabinets. The profusion of chess pieces was silent testimony to the expanding battlefield on which Kendall fought his life-and-death war.

And it was quite a war. In 1976, the Inc. Fund lost the critical U.S. Supreme Court cases restoring—at least in theory—capital punishment. The following year, with Kendall leading the way, the Fund had struck back, persuading the Court to abolish the death penalty for rape. It was all-consuming work, exhausting both physically and spiritually, and after five years Kendall had his fill as a general in the war. In 1978, he had joined a blue-chip firm with spacious offices, the influential Washington partnership of Williams & Connolly. But he took with him a pile of his most important death penalty cases. At the top of the pile, the most important of all, was the case of John Spenkelink.

"I need coffee," Kendall thought, as he shrugged off his suit jacket. Bleary and befogged, he left his office and trudged, mug in hand, toward the kitchenette down the hall. Halfway there, he heard the soft, elegant voice of Williams & Connolly's receptionist paging him for an urgent call. Kendall, his cup still empty, made his way back to his office, striding more purposefully now. For several weeks, he had been hoping for word from the Florida governor's office that Spenkelink's sentence would be commuted to life in prison. Maybe this was it.

One word from the caller, though, and Kendall sagged. The thick, gravelly drawl was unmistakably that of Mary King, switchboard operator at the Florida State Prison. Prisons don't ring with good news. "I have a phone call for you from John Spenkelink," said the operator. "He's with the superintendent." After a short pause, Dave Brierton came on the line. He quickly turned the phone over to Spenkelink. The prisoner's flat midwestern voice was tense and strained.

"The governor signed a death warrant."

Kendall sighed. "Have you got it there? Can you read it to me?" Spenkelink began reading his own death order. When he got to the date—the coming Wednesday, May 23—Kendall stopped him.

"What are we gonna do?" Spenkelink asked. Kendall tried to be soothing. He said he had been combing the case and had found some new issues for an appeal. "I think we've got some strong arguments for a stay of execution."

"You really think I got a chance?" Spenkelink sounded relieved.

"I think we have a good chance."

Kendall didn't like to lie to a client, but the circumstances demanded it. The lawyer promised to call Spenkelink's mother and give her the bad news. He said he would fly to the prison the next day. Then the warden came back on the line. Spenkelink would be moved to Q-wing, Brierton said, to an isolation cell near the execution chamber. The prisoner would be allowed one legal visit per day, and Kendall should plan accordingly. There was a pause, as if Brierton were pondering. Then he said, "Let me tell you just one more thing. This is not going to turn into a circus. I won't allow it. Not in my prison."

Kendall cradled the receiver. His headache was gone, swallowed up by a feeling much worse than any hangover. For a dozen years, no American lawyer had lost a fight to keep his client alive. Now he, David Kendall, was facing checkmate.

The signature on the death warrants belonged to Daniel Robert Graham, brand-new governor of Florida. A youthful man from an uncommon family, Graham was wealthy, ambitious, and—at that particular moment—had a blank slate for a future. Signing the warrants was a significant step into that future.

Graham had astonished voters, politicians, even his friends (everyone, it seemed, but himself) by winning the election the previous November. No one had expected him to survive the Democratic primary, where the favorite was the state's law-and-order attorney general, Robert Shevin. So strong was Shevin's line on crime that even the panhandle Dixiecrats and conservative farmers of Central Florida seemed willing to put aside the fact that he was a Jew from Miami.

They cheered Shevin's speeches as if he were Baptist. Graham, by contrast, was a little-known state senator with a liberal record. What small fame he possessed was as a leader of the legislature's "Doghouse Democrats," whose progressive platform, frequently championed by Graham in long, righteous orations, kept them perpetually in the doghouse with the conservative party leadership. In the state senate chamber, it was common to see Graham speaking earnestly on behalf of one reform or another, then taking his seat, followed by a panhandle Democrat rising to make a wordless gesture plainly visible throughout the chamber: thumbs down. And another of Graham's causes would die a quick death.

Given this record, professional pols viewed Graham's candidacy as a darkly amusing blood sport, like feeding a bunny to a pack of starving dogs. His physical appearance did not help matters: Wide-eyed and dumpling-cheeked, with a high-pitched voice, Graham struck a lot of people more like a teddy bear than a governor. One capital insider recalled having a sumptuous dinner with Graham one evening some months before the election. After the plates were cleared, Graham popped the question: I'm running; how would you like to join my campaign? The dinner guest admired Graham's courage, but he had a career to think of and did not relish a trip through the Shevin buzz saw. He declined.

What he, and nearly everyone else, failed to perceive was Graham's protean genius for discerning the public's wishes, and his capacity to shape himself to their desires. The key to Graham's victory was a brilliant gimmick he called "workdays." One hundred times during the campaign, he spent the day toiling alongside voters, actually doing their jobs while discussing their dreams. He hauled fishing nets and picked oranges and waited on tables and emptied bedpans. It made great television, giving millions of voters their first glimpse of Bob Graham. For Graham, it was an education, a chance to meet and understand the people he wanted to lead.

He reinvented himself. As a Doghouse Democrat, Graham made no secret of his Harvard Law degree and his capacious brain. In a capital full of Billys and Franks and Docs and Jims, he was identified as "D. Robert Graham." By Election Day, it was just Bob. Known for years as a wallflower in Tallahassee, blossoming only when the conversation shifted from sex and quail hunting to, say, teacher certification, Graham learned to slap backs and chew the fat. One journalist, sizing up the governor several years into his term, wrote: "The transformation of Bob Graham was a triumph of personal and political image-making, and more. Graham actually taught himself to be governor, painfully, step-by-step, against the most difficult of burdens: his own insufficiencies."

The raw material for this act of creation was fertile. Graham came from a family that bespoke the American dream, both the shining side and the dark. His father, Ernest "Cap" Graham, was a rough and decisive character, a pioneer who prospected the West for gold, then settled on another frontier, the watery savannah of South Florida. He ran the Pennsylvania Sugar Company's experimental sugar cane plantation, and when the devastating hurricane of 1926 was followed by the Depression, Cap Graham assumed ownership of the plantation from the chastened company. With his customary grit he built his stake into a prosperous dairy empire.

Cap Graham fathered two boys and a girl by his first wife, who died of cancer. He married again, but only after Hilda Simmons agreed they would have no children. By then, the offspring of his first marriage were nearly grown, and the elder Graham was not eager to begin again. He had his eye on the state senate, and beyond that, the governor's office. Cap was in the midst of a successful senate campaign when the last of his four children was born, contrary to plan, in 1936. That was Daniel Robert.

If Cap Graham's story was something fit for Horatio Alger, the progress of his sons was material enough for F. Scott Fitzgerald, an only-in-America story of ascent and angst. The eldest Graham boy, Phil, rose from his boyhood home on a houseboat in the mosquito-infested South Florida wetlands to the inner circles of the American elite, taking the helm of *The Washington Post* from his father-in-law in the 1940s. As a law student, young Bob Graham sometimes slipped away from Cambridge for an evening at his half brother's grand Georgetown home, where the guests were people like Adlai Stevenson and Joseph Alsop. Phil Graham was a brilliant man, a Harvard protégé of Justice Felix Frankfurter. The media empire he assembled grew to rival even the great New York Times Company for glory and influence, and eventually piled up magnificent annual profits from its flagship newspaper, a string of television stations, and a feisty magazine called *Newsweek*. But Phil Graham never witnessed most of this triumph. A man of great bursts of energy countered by deep bouts of depression, he shot himself to death in 1963, leaving his widow, Katharine, to consolidate, and even surpass, his achievements.

The second Graham boy, William, took a portion of the family's real estate holdings and built a town, Miami Lakes. It was a conceptual masterstroke, a little slice of normalcy in a region on the verge of disintegration. While much of Dade County spun headlong into a crazy future as America's new melting pot, Bill Graham made Miami Lakes a niche of Middle America. The more Miami became known for shady characters and high-rise condos, Cuban exile terrorists and Brooklyn retirees, the more Miami Lakes cultivated its wide streets, tidy baseball diamonds, and fresh-faced children. Like many Florida developments, the name of the town had no link to reality: Miami Lakes was the antithesis of Miami, and its lakes were man-made. It was pure invention, and a lasting commercial success.

Bob Graham was playing golf at the Miami Lakes Country Club when the course manager rushed up with the news that his half brother Phil had killed himself. The future governor thanked the man politely. He possessed, at twenty-seven, all the steely self-control that observers would comment on with increasing frequency over the next quarter century. From the beginning, the littlest Graham was hard-driving. He was president of his high school student body. At the University of Florida, he earned a spot in the prestigious Blue Key society, launching pad to state government. In college, friends recall, Graham read *Time* magazine while they were reading *Playboy*—and not just because he found *Time* more stimulating. As he told his future wife, Adele, when they were both undergraduates: He was going to be governor one day. A head full of knowledge might come in handy. George Bedell, one of the governor's closest friends, once said to a newspaper reporter: "I don't know anyone as driven as Bob Graham. He is driven toward political power."

But having become governor, Graham had trouble wielding the power he sought. His administration got off to a weak and indecisive start. Graham chalked this up to "inexperience," but many Tallahassee pols believed they had a patsy on their hands. The legislature was uncooperative, the editorial boards of the Florida newspapers were unimpressed. The governor's closest advisers quickly grew convinced that Graham needed to show some spine, flex some muscle.

Enter the death penalty. In his campaign against the fire-breathing attorney general, Graham had promised he would sign death warrants, but there was a lingering suspicion among those who knew Graham as an idealistic liberal that he would not actually preside over the electrocution of a human being. This suspicion deepened when one of his first acts as governor was to schedule formal clemency hearings for ten of the inmates who had been on death row the longest. Though the new governor's staff said he was moving quickly to choose a pioneer case for the resumption of executions, some people believed Graham was more interested in undoing death sentences. The clemency hearings ended in April; Graham said nothing. Days dragged by, then weeks. Graham remained silent. Secretly, however, he began making preparations. He dispatched his general counsel, a boyhood friend named Robin Gibson, to the state prison to begin planning an execution.

Choosing Gibson, a meticulous lawyer from a small town in Central Florida, was astute, for Gibson was dogged about details, and in this instance every detail had to be perfect. Gibson knew that the attention of the whole country would be fastened on Florida, and he knew that this act would be a defining moment for Bob Graham. A single foul-up could ruin his friend's career just as it was ready to blossom. At the prison, Dave Brierton led Gibson on a tour of death row, ending up in the tiny chamber where the worn wooden electric chair was housed. Gibson wanted to know what they would do in case of a last-minute stay. How could they be certain that the execution would be stopped?

Brierton pointed to a telephone on the wall chamber. "We'll have a direct line from here to the governor's office," he said. Gibson studied the phone, wondering: How secure was it? Protesters from all over the country would try to stop this execution. What if someone managed to tap into the governor's line? At last he said, "We need a password"—a word, a phrase, for the governor to utter that would let Brierton know the call was for real. Gibson stood quietly and thought.

The moment demanded something distinctive, something to make Graham's piece of history purely his own. Gibson's mind drifted back to his earliest memory of the man. They were student body presidents at rival high schools, Gibson at Edison High and Graham at Miami High. The mascot at Graham's school was something called a Stingaree. That would be a distinctive password. But no . . . he remembered a Miami High cheer: "Sting 'em, Stingarees!" In the matter of an electrocution, that seemed in rather bad taste.

Gibson thought some more, and his thoughts turned to milk. The Graham fortune was founded on dairy cows. He smiled and said to Brierton, "The password will be 'Louis Pasteur,'" the French scientist whose process for purifying milk made dairy fortunes possible. Brierton should wait for the words "Louis Pasteur."

The machinery began to move, but Graham remained mute, and the odor of weakness surrounding the new governor intensified. At last, in mid-May, the governor called Gibson into his office, closed the door, and said that he intended to sign warrants on John Spenkelink and Willie Darden. According to Gibson, the governor did not explain his reasoning, nor did he give any indication of the emotional burden involved in his decision. Actually, Graham's inclination had been to start with Spenkelink all along. Soon after his election, he had discussed the matter with his popular predecessor, Reubin Askew, and Askew advised him that Spenkelink's case was ripest. Spenkelink was white, so his case was not haunted by the old specter of the lynch mob. He had confessed his guilt, which streamlined the legal issues. Graham had found no reason to conclude otherwise.

Gibson was simply relieved that Graham had finally made a decision, and he was ready with the details: The death warrants, he told the governor, would have a life span of one week. If either prisoner won a stay of execution lasting more than a week, his warrant would expire and a new warrant would have to be issued in order to kill him. The best day for signing would be a Friday, Gibson said. If the case went down to the last tick of the clock—and they all expected that it would —it would be best if the crucial last days were weekdays: Judges would not have to be hunted down on a weekend to hear last-minute appeals. Gibson would take charge of the execution. As much as possible, Graham would remain above the fray, aloof.

Folks in North Florida joke that when they die they'll have to go to heaven by way of Atlanta. Every airplane they board seems to stop there, and the link is psychological as well as physical. The air routes through Atlanta connect the plain, small-town citizens of upper Florida to the mainland, to terra firma. South of them, the pendulous Florida peninsula seems to fall away, in terms of spirit as well as geography. People in North Florida share a strong sense of vertigo, a feeling that they are dangling over the abyss, the sucking black hole, the pandemonium of the lower latitudes. North Florida is Dixie, or at least aspires to be, and the populace thinks of the state's southern half as tugging and beckoning in a direction that smells of perdition. The state is strongly divided, North and South, and the route south is, to North Floridians, a Dantesque penetration of the successive circles of Hell, a perilous journey in which one encounters sunburned tourists in mouse ears, blue-haired New Yorkers thigh to thigh in Seminole Indian bingo parlors, chubby men with hair transplants flaunting their gonads in neon bikinis, and homosexuals oiling one another on beaches. And—at the very end of that netherworld—Miami, that sweaty Babel of Cubans and Nicaraguans and Salvadorans and Haitians and Puerto Ricans and Venezuelans and Chileans and Dominicans and Bahamians and Jews and Yankees and Damn Yankees and Goddamn Yankees, all seething and teeming and yammering and cohabitating. Decent North Floridians are suspended by a thread above this Inferno, and the thread depends on Atlanta—their sustaining hub.

On Saturday, May 19, David Kendall's early morning flight from Washington touched down in Atlanta, and the young lawyer hustled to transfer to a flight departing for Jacksonville. There, Kendall rented a car and drove west on Interstate 10 through pine forests and mossy hardwoods. As the car raced along, sunlight glinted and flashed in the trees. Half an hour from Jacksonville, Kendall steered onto U.S. 301 and headed south along the busy four-lane.

Each mile was that much farther along the road from somewhere to nowhere. By noon he was nearing the middle of nowhere, and shortly thereafter he rolled into a hamlet called Starke. At the central intersection along the town's main drag, he made a right and drove another ten minutes until the pines suddenly vanished and he entered a vast clearing. In the distance he could see the low, spare rectangles of Florida State Prison, surrounded by concentric wire fences. A blacktop led to the guard tower, where Kendall shouted his name into a squawk box and got approval to pass. He parked in a space reserved for visitors and walked to the administration building. After a brief exchange with an assistant superintendent, he was ushered through a series of gates, doors, and sliding bars to the room where he would meet with his client.

John Spenkelink, thirty years old, entered the room with his hands cuffed before him and a guard hovering just behind. He smiled quickly at his attorney through the thick glass that separated them. Spenkelink was about six feet tall, lean, flat-bellied, and stringy, and possessed what one female admirer called simply "a good build." From the neck up, he was striking. It was a long pedestal of a neck, and his face was oval with full, feminine lips, high cheekbones, and a mousy little nose. His eyebrows were thick and dark, and there were dark circles under his eyes, which were also dark, and piercing—giving him the aspect of someone gazing from a cave. He had a high forehead and his dark wavy hair was combed straight back, and—most memorable of all—the hair had gone white in a skunk stripe at the middle of his head. The stripe, combed back the way it was, suggested an angry wave cresting at his crown, or a tongue of flame. It was a shocking head of hair, made no less disconcerting by the punkish sideburns he wore, so long out of fashion. Descriptions of him ranged from "gorgeous" to "weird."

There was a voice-activated microphone in the glass between them, which permitted a tinny, irregular communication. Talking through "The Wall," as the partition was called, could be terribly frustrating, like trying to have an intimate conversation with the ticket seller at a movie theater. Kendall could see his client talking, but the voice through the tiny amplifier sounded a million miles away. The lawyer was prepared to talk about his client's appeals; the condemned man was in no mood that sunny Saturday to discuss his prospects. Instead, Spenkelink took control of the conversation and directed it backward in time and outward in place, back before he had been sentenced to die, out beyond the prison walls, beyond the pines and bogs of Florida, backward and outward to a few happy relics of his sorry biography. He spoke as if sifting through random snapshots in an old shoebox.

Kendall mostly listened. He already knew the outlines of Spenkelink's life from trial transcripts and clemency pleadings; now he got some shades and contours. John Spenkelink was born on an Iowa farm to a Dutch immigrant with a drawer full of military decorations and a debilitating drinking problem. Like a lot of farm-country fathers, Bernard Spenkelink taught his son early to drive a truck; unlike most of them, he was cultivating his own taxi service. By the time Johnny was nine, he was ferrying his drunken father home from benders at the local bar.

When the benders finally broke him, Bernard Spenkelink decided to start over in Southern California, in a little suburb called Buena Park, one of a hundred booming towns of postage-stamp yards erupting emerald from the dusty desert. "The promised land," Bernard called it. He started a business installing sprinklers, which was hard work, digging trenches in the hot sun, but if there was such a thing as a sure bet in Greater Los Angeles circa 1960, it was lawn irrigation. The region was in the process of sucking the mighty Colorado River dry to grow its gardens and fairways and lawns. But Bernard continued drinking, and by 1961 he had lost his business. Neck deep in debt, living on his wife's income as a schoolteacher, he peddled vacuum cleaners door to door.

"He was a war hero," John Spenkelink said, leaning toward the microphone and gazing at Kendall. "Army paratroops. He helped liberate Holland." The prisoner dragged on a cigarette. For several minutes he recounted tales of his father's exploits against the Nazis that had held him spellbound as a boy. Happy memories.

He did not talk about May 3, 1961. On that day, Johnny Spenkelink came home from school to find his dog, Skippy, whining at the garage door. He hoisted the door and a wave of bad air came out. The family's '53 Chevy panel truck was idling inside. The hose from an unsold vacuum cleaner ran from the tailpipe to the interior. Bernard Spenkelink was dead on the front seat, his cheeks red as cherries from the carbon monoxide.

Years later, friends and neighbors of the Spenkelink family wrote letters to Governor Bob Graham marking this gruesome discovery as the turning point in John Spenkelink's life. "He was 11 years old and was a paper boy on our street," wrote Regina Newkirk, whose sister Jenny was briefly married to John. "I am sure that anyone who had found someone dead, especially someone you loved, is very hard . . . it must have made an important mark on him. John had to help out financially," she continued. "He had his paper route, odd jobs, and did all the repairs on his house. He did as much as any young boy could. . . . But John needed someone there, and there was never an adult male for him to learn from." Mr. and Mrs. Robert Eggert wrote with recollections of Johnny Spenkelink "helping his mother with newspaper routes and other odd jobs. Together they would deliver newspapers, do babysitting, do yardwork, etc. to earn money and keep the family together . . . although he was too young to assume all the responsibilities of the 'man of the family.' He always tried so hard to help with everything."

And so forth. Whatever the cause—perhaps there was no cause but cussedness—this faithful boy with the paper route deteriorated into an endless source of trouble. He sniffed glue and drank liquor and popped pills; at fourteen, he was arrested for stealing a car. He ditched school and picked fights. His mother, a plain woman who put a lot of stock in the curative value of fresh air and fishing for a troubled boy, blamed John's problems on his shiftless friends and sent him to live with a relative in Iowa. On death row, Spenkelink would speak wistfully of his Iowa hiatus, "sliding down the hill on a snow slide in back of a barn, that big white horse, smoked meat . . . that farm was paradise to me." But that was a doomed man's nostalgia talking. At the time, the exiled boy begged his mother to let him return to California.

She did, and things were as bad as before. John was a pothead and a thief, but in spite of it all there was something charming about him. The youthful delinquent played out Robin Hood dreams—once, he stole a car to take a friend's parents to the grocery store. Jenny Jones, a cute blond Catholic schoolgirl, fell for the wayward boy and remained devoted for many years, like a character in a Broadway musical. Eventually, they were married. "John is the gentlest person there ever was," Jones once said.

Spenkelink's probation officer had a clearer view. In his judgment the only positive thing you could say about the man was that, up to age twelve, he was a "wonderful paperboy." Within a year of his wedding, Spenkelink was doing five-to-life for robbing a fast-food joint, five gas stations, two young lovers, and a grocery store, all at the point of a .357 magnum. He was not a model prisoner. Over the first four years of his term, he earned fourteen disciplinary reports for infractions like throwing cups, loitering, and making tattoos. So when word leaked through the prison grapevine that he was not going to be paroled anytime soon, Spenkelink paroled himself: On October 15, 1972, he simply strolled off the grounds of the minimum-security prison at Slack Canyon, California, stole a blue Camaro, and headed north.

His days on the run were some of his happiest memories, an unencumbered time of absolute freedom. As Kendall listened, Spenkelink's disembodied voice described the magnificent forests and cool autumn air along the highway from California into Canada. So vivid was the telling that Kendall could almost see the snowcapped mountains, taste the rain, hear the tires on the road. It was clear that Spenkelink had savored these images many, many times in his cell. The fast car, the open spaces, the sweet liberty—if only the next part had never come.

Spenkelink drew another lungful of smoke. "Do you think this thing is bugged?" he asked, pointing to the microphone between them.

"I imagine so," Kendall answered.

A grin spread across the inmate's face. "Well, then, fuck you, whoever's listening." Both men laughed. It would become a running joke between them in the coming days: "Fuck you, whoever's listening!" A motto of absurd defiance.

As Kendall's hour with Spenkelink ran out, he wondered if his client fully comprehended his predicament. The talk of freedom was so passionate; he did not sound like a man who expected to be dead in a handful of days. Kendall did not press the point. Instead, he asked what books Spenkelink was reading. The prisoner always had several books going at once. Spenkelink mentioned a volume by the German writer Hermann Hesse, *Siddhartha,* and a prison novel entitled *On the Yard.* He was also reading something titled *Life After Life,* a guide to reincarnation. As Kendall knew, reincarnation is a very popular subject on death row.

The guard signaled that their time was up. "See you soon," Kendall said.

Spenkelink gave him a thin smile. "I'll be here."

Outside the governor's mansion in Tallahassee, eight men drew lengths of chain and padlocks from their bags and shackled themselves to the iron fence in front of the pillared home of Bob and Adele Graham. They called themselves People Against Executions—PAX, Latin for peace—but they were not an organized group as much as eight individuals loosely connected through mutual friendships and shared causes. Most of them were ordained ministers or seminary graduates who had devoted themselves to working with prison inmates. Some months earlier, the men had agreed to drop everything when the time came and do their damndest to stop the first involuntary execution in contemporary America, wherever it might be.

The press had been notified and was there in force. Reporters interviewed the shackled men and took note of their signs, which had been hastily painted that morning. THOU SHALT NOT KILL, one said. NOT IN OUR NAME, said another. It was a splendid day for shorts and T-shirts, but the men of PAX wore pressed shirts buttoned to the throat and carefully knotted ties. They wanted to make a favorable impression in front of the television cameras—ideally, while being arrested.

Two hours passed, though, and nothing happened. Robin Gibson had foreseen a demonstration like this and ordered police to let it proceed. He knew how it would look to have a group of ministers dragged away by burly lawmen, and he did not take the bait. Gibson watched from the governor's study inside the mansion as the camera crews grew bored and settled onto the grass under a cluster of shade trees across the street. This was precisely what he wanted.

But now Graham was growing restless at the sight of all those television cameras, worried, apparently, that his silence might be misunderstood. Abruptly, he said: "I want to go out and talk to them."

Gibson tried to talk him out of it. Remember the plan, he said. I'm the public foil. You have to stay above it all. It was a good plan, devised when their heads were clear and emotions ran cool. Just because eight guys fastened themselves to the fence was no reason to change course. "I think I can talk to them," Graham insisted. Gibson turned for support to Steve Hull, the governor's press secretary. Too risky, Hull said. Think of those cameras: Every word, every gesture, recorded for posterity and exposed to the entire country. Political careers had been ruined by extemporaneous missteps. The governor headed for the door. When the bored reporters and lolling camera crews saw Graham striding down the path—his aides rushing behind— they scrambled for their gear. Along the fence, the stunned protesters held a frantic caucus. What to do? Someone said, "Let's hear him out."

"No way," urged another. "As soon as we talk to him, we're coopted." By then Graham was upon them. In a friendly tone, he asked the men to unchain themselves and step across the street into the shade. One by one, the protesters complied. As the cameras pressed in, John Lozier, director of the Southern Prison Ministry in Nashville, demanded to know how Graham could order the execution of two men and still profess to be a Christian.

Graham answered calmly. "I do not consider the responsibility of carrying out a duty which is mine to be inconsistent with Christian values." The reporters scribbled furiously. "There are other values of life involved here," he added, "including the values of the lives which were taken."

But executions don't prevent crime, another of the protesters said heatedly. They just heap brutality on brutality. No, the governor answered. "I believe this course will result in the least brutalization of society." Graham affirmed his faith in the deterrent value of the death penalty, and said, in the long run, "the total loss of life will be less."

"In the name of God," cried Larry Cox, an official with Amnesty

International, "isn't there *some* way we can at least open your mind and ask you to reconsider? How can you distinguish what you're doing from Pontius Pilate?"

Graham's expression, serious yet friendly, never wavered. "In the cases we're discussing," he said softly, "we have two individuals who have committed very serious offenses, individuals who have had all their rights afforded to them. I've determined that in their cases there is not a basis to grant clemency."

Gibson and Hull watched the governor with growing awe; they realized they were watching a masterful flanking maneuver. The protesters were hoping to stake out the high ground, eager to have the government roll brutishly over them. They wanted their nobility to dominate the evening news. Instead, the protesters looked almost shrill, while Graham was the picture of calm and reason. When Floridians switched on their sets or opened their Sunday papers, they were going to meet a strong, temperate governor who remained cool even when he was being called Pilate. One of the protesters, a photographer named Doug Magee, also perceived the governor's victory. As he snapped pictures, he felt a strange mixture of anger and wonder at what he saw through his viewfinder. "Graham's too smart," he thought to himself. "We're not going to be arrested; we're not going to get the bloodthirsty redneck treatment. This guy knows all the angles."

When it was clear there was nothing else to say, Graham gave the protesters a solemn and magnanimous look. "I respect very deeply the values you share and the depth of your feelings," he said. "I hope God will look out for and care for us all." And he extended his hand to Larry Cox.

For a tense moment, the governor's hand just hung there, frozen in the air. Then Cox drew back, as if the hand were leprous. "I can't shake your hand, Governor. It's got blood on it," he said.

Graham didn't react. He turned and headed back toward the house. The protesters returned to their vigil. The reporters drifted off to prepare their stories. The peace was disturbed only briefly, when a pickup truck full of beery and belligerent teenagers roared up the street. "Fry the bastards!" they screamed as the truck passed the mansion. "Fry

YOU bastards!'' Some beer cans clattered to the sidewalk, and the men of PAX struck up a hymn.

A few blocks from the protest, at a desk in a state office building, Ray Marky—junior partner in the unofficial firm of Georgieff & Marky, prosecutors unto death—was reviewing his work. Marky was a man who left nothing to chance, especially now. It was his job, as assistant attorney general, to preserve John Spenkelink's death warrant, no matter what David Kendall and the Inc. Fund tried. Marky was not handsome, he was not a Rhodes Scholar, and he never had any grand law firms bidding for his services. He was a tiny man with thick glasses and a degree of intensity that fatigued everyone around him. He was a damn terrier, always sinking his teeth into some little nub of the law and shaking it, gnawing it, fretting over it, talking it to death. He could be, frankly, a pain in the ass. And he was a very good lawyer. With his partner, George Georgieff, Marky was Florida's most important prosecutor of capital appeals. Local lawyers working for elected prosecutors handled death penalty cases at trial and through the first appellate level, but given the sentiments of Florida judges and juries, that was fairly easy work. With the crime rate rising steeply, juries overwhelmingly favored the death penalty, and local judges—who had to answer every few years to fear-stricken voters—freely pounded the gavel of doom. The justices of the Florida Supreme Court, court of first resort for inmates facing the electric chair, were solidly in favor of capital punishment. But when the cases shifted to the federal courts, it was a whole different matter. Though judges and juries across the country dispatched men to death row by the hundreds, the federal courts had permitted only one execution in a dozen years. That was the case of a Utah murderer named Gary Gilmore, who filed suit demanding his right to be shot through the heart by a firing squad. The law in these matters was murky and untested; prosecuting appeals was a peculiar and maddening art. Marky and Georgieff were artists.

They made quite a pair. Georgieff, chief of the attorney general's criminal division, was a banty rooster, clever and profane. The son of a Bulgarian immigrant in East Chicago, he grew up with a single-minded goal of finding a well-paid job in a warm climate. Following a stint in the Army Air Corps, he enrolled at the University of Miami's law school, mostly for the weather. After graduation, Georgieff tried private practice but it didn't take. He landed a job with the Florida attorney general.

Georgieff was an unforgettable figure. Against a background of drab government lawyers in short-sleeved shirts and crew cuts, Georgieff was loud, rude, flamboyant. His suits were Hickey-Freeman, tailored at the best Tallahassee shops. His shirts were two-toned, with starched white collars and monogrammed cuffs. On trial days he wore a fresh carnation in his lapel, and there were rumors—which Georgieff did nothing to dispel—that he had his shoes shined three times a day. The only stain on his dandification was the condition of his teeth. He hated dentists, and as a young man declared that he would never visit another one. He kept his word, and it showed.

Georgieff considered it a waste of time to pore over law books and polish briefs; he preferred to spend that time playing poker and telling stories. His mind was so quick, and facts stuck with him as though his brain was tar; he could afford to cut corners. In court, he was more scrapper than scrivener: He liked liquid oratory and a bare-knuckle fight. And so it pained Georgieff to no end to watch Ray Marky at work. For every ounce of swagger in the older man, Marky had a pound of insecurity. Georgieff got the job done on strut and brains; Marky relied on sweat and diligence. In law school, Marky read every textbook three times: once when he bought it, again as it was assigned in class, and a third time at the end of the semester. Marky approached his own mind like a storage closet requiring constant rearranging. Mastering information seemed, for Marky, an endless labor of adding new shelves and drawers and hooks—now and then hauling everything out and replacing it in some new configuration so the details he most needed would be closer to hand.

His willingness to go through these labors was testimony to Marky's passionate desire to be a lawyer. Like Georgieff, Marky came from a modest background; born in Buffalo, he spent his earliest days moving from one town to another as his father pursued work with the WPA. When Marky was sixteen years old, his father died and his mother moved them to Florida, where they settled with Marky's aunt, the wife of a prosperous West Palm Beach attorney. In that house Marky found his calling, in the formidable example of his uncle, Harris Drew. Drew was a presence unlike any the boy had encountered before: confident without arrogance, ambitious without selfishness, wealthy without ostentation. Drew struck Marky as one of the noblest figures imaginable. A few months after the Markys arrived in Florida, Harris Drew was elected to the Florida Supreme Court and Ray and his mother moved to a little house on Drew's estate in Tallahassee. Marky sat rapt at the jurist's dinner table, drinking in the loving discussions of the law.

Harris Drew was rich, but money wasn't what attracted Marky to his uncle's profession. It was a combination of more ephemeral things. Integrity, for example. Around Drew's table, there was a lot of talk about doing the right thing—and not just talk. Drew was a man who, three months before he was to stand for reelection, wrote a ringing dissent from his colleagues' decision to bar black students from Florida colleges. That was no way to win votes in Florida in the 1960s, but it was the right thing to do. Marky also saw the law as a fixed thing, systematic and well organized. Right or wrong, he never considered himself especially bright, but he did value his own determination and believed that he could, through force of will and self-discipline, get the better of anything that would hold still for him. The nature of the law was to be permanent, reliable; or if it changed, to change gradually, in measured and sensible steps.

Lastly, the law represented a level field, which especially appealed to Marky. Undersized, jug-eared, and four-eyed, the teenaged Marky was eaten up by a need to compete with the taller, prettier boys. It wounded him to love basketball as he did, and to work so hard at it—thump-thumping the ball up and down the court, first with his right hand, then with his left, practicing his jump shot through countless solitary hours—only to be cut from the team in favor of boys who never had to work for anything. Law was different. Appearance meant nothing to the lady with the blindfold. Marky read and reread his law books, preparing for the day when he would stand up in court, all five feet four inches of him, and "kick the shit out of a six-footer."

When that day came, it was everything he had hoped it would be. "I walked into court and there was this guy, tall and pretty and wearing a nice suit," Marky recalled years later. "I could tell he was laughing at me. He was just like any other tall guy I ever saw. I could tell he never had to work for anything. Well, I said, 'You're on my turf now, man.' And I beat his ass up one side and down the other." But the sting never went away. There was always something to bring it back—real or imagined. Marky often recounted the story of his first appearance before the U.S. Supreme Court. There was no prouder man in the world that day. Yet when he rose to speak, Chief Justice Warren Burger leaned toward his microphone and said (with a smirk, as Marky recalled it): "Mr. Marky, do you need a podium assist?" In other words, did he need something to stand on.

Marky remained cool, though his blood was boiling. Here he was, representing the People of the State of Florida before the highest tribunal, and the chief justice was making a joke about his height. He forced a grin. "Being from Florida," he said, "I'd love an orange crate to stand on. But mostly I don't care if you can see me, as long as you can hear me." And before Burger could answer, Justice Hugo Black—tiny Hugo Black—drawled: "Oh, yes. We can hear you just fine." The chief had no clever comeback. Marky lost that case, but he liked to believe that he and Hugo Black had put another six-footer in his place.

Marky reckoned that David Kendall was six feet tall. And in this landmark case, he intended to kick the shit out of his adversary. He spent the weekend reading and rereading the Spenkelink file in preparation for Monday morning, when the courthouse doors would open.

The prison staff prided itself on its military air. In keeping, the day the death warrants were issued was designated "Execution Day—Minus Five (5)." After Robin Gibson's visit to the prison, a detailed schedule had been prepared by warden Brierton's staff to guide this execution and all that would follow: day by day, then hour by hour, and finally minute by minute as the critical moment approached. On Execution Day—Minus Five (5), the schedule called for the naming of an execution squad, choosing witnesses, staffing checkpoints, notifying the medical staff, briefing top prison guards, and testing the generator, the telephones, and the chair. Trouble was anticipated. The sheriffs of Union and Bradford counties, the Highway Patrol, the Department of Law Enforcement, and the National Guard were alerted.

Saturday was Execution Day—Minus Four (4). "Measure inmate(s) for clothing," the schedule dictated, among many other tasks; the State of Florida provided a new suit of clothes in which the executed prisoner was to be buried. The schedule also called for the first rehearsal of the execution squad. With a prison guard playing John Spenkelink, Dave Brierton led his handpicked crew through the long-forgotten ritual.

> The Superintendent, Assistant Superintendent for Operations, and Correctional Officer Chief IV will escort the condemned inmate to the execution chamber.

The team entered the small white room. Though it was just practice, they were solemn and workmanlike. They were Brierton's best, and remained intent throughout the exercise.

> The Assistant Superintendent for Operations and Correctional Officer Chief IV will place the condemned inmate in the chair. [Spenkelink's stand-in sat down.] The Superintendent and Asst. Superintendent for Operations will secure back and arm straps and then forearm straps.

Their hands fumbled with the heavy buckles on the thick leather straps. After years of disuse, a new set had been installed on the oaken chair known as Old Sparky. It took several attempts to master quick fastening of the straps.

> When the inmate is secured, the Asst. Superintendent for Operations and Correctional Officer Chief IV will remove the restraint apparatus [here, Spenkelink's stand-in was released from his handcuffs] and then secure lap, chest, and ankle straps [nine straps in all]. The anklet will then be laced and the electrode attached.

Old Sparky worked by pouring electricity in through the inmate's skull and out through an electrode wired to the lower right leg. The ankle electrode was made from a metal plate fixed to the top of an old leather boot and was secured by a cat's cradle of shoelaces. Tightening the laces could be tricky under pressure. This was practiced repeatedly.

> The Superintendent will permit the condemned inmate to make a last statement. The Supt. will then proceed to the . . . open telephone line to inquire of possible stays. The electrician will place the sponges on the condemned inmate's head [to improve conductivity and reduce burning], secure the head set and attach electrode. [Certain steps, like the wet sponges, were omitted in rehearsal.] The Assistant Superintendent for Operations engages the circuit breaker. The electrician in the booth will activate the Executioner Control Panel. The Superintendent will give the signal to the executioner to turn the switch and the automatic cycle will begin. . . .

No one on the team had ever done this before. Everyone was nervous. But Brierton had met privately with each member of the team and offered them the chance to decline this duty, no questions asked. These men were willing. Speed and smoothness were the keys, so they practiced several times. They would rehearse again Monday, and again Tuesday.

David Kendall worked that day, Saturday, on a yellow legal pad in a dreary room of the Best Western motel on Highway 301 in Starke. Inside, it smelled of mildew; outside, of diesel fumes. Starke was an appropriate name for this place. More than once, Kendall paused to marvel that he was doing this work at all. He had been so confident in his appeal to the governor for mercy. Shortly after taking office, Graham had announced that he would give every condemned inmate a clemency hearing. If he decided in the prisoner's favor, the approval of three of the state's six elected cabinet members was legally required to formalize the grace. That's what clemency was: an act of grace, exercised for undefined reasons, according to unstated standards.

Spenkelink's clemency hearing had been held a month before the death warrant was issued, in a nondescript meeting room of the new state capitol building. A bank of theater seats faced a dais where the governor and cabinet sat in high-backed chairs. Spenkelink's mother was there, resting heavily on a cane. She was a large, white-haired woman, and she wore a sleeveless dress with a pattern on the placket. In one hand she held a handkerchief, and she dabbed often at her eyes as she listened to men in dark suits deciding whether her son should live or die.

Anthony Guarisco, chief prosecutor at the Spenkelink trial, spoke first. "Why," he asked by way of beginning, "should John A. Spenkelink be granted clemency and avoid the death sentence?" He scanned the seven faces at the long table before him. "Basically, I'd like to review some facts regarding this case. On February 4, 1973, Joseph J. Szymankiewicz was murdered in a motel room here in Tallahassee, Florida. Subsequently, his body was found in the room, about a day later. After an investigation—which began in Florida, went into California—this culminated in the arrest of John Arthur Spenkelink and a codefendant by the name of Frank A. Brumm. . . .

"On November 28, 1973," Guarisco continued, still in a Joe Friday monotone, "during the trial of this matter, the jury came back with a guilty verdict, first-degree murder against John Arthur Spenkelink, and acquitted the codefendant, Frank Brumm. On December 20, 1973, based on an advisory opinion rendered by the jury, John Arthur Spenkelink was sentenced to death by the Honorable John Rudd, Circuit Judge."

The pedigree of his case concluded, the prosecutor fell into a more informal tone—still tinged, though, with the rhythms of a police procedural, and reverberating with the defendant's triple-barreled name. John Wilkes Booth, Lee Harvey Oswald, James Earl Ray—there is something vaguely menacing about first, middle, and last names. Guarisco loved to say "John Arthur Spenkelink."

"John Arthur Spenkelink, at the time, was a twenty-four-year-old career criminal," he said. "Twice-convicted felon, escapee from a California correctional institution. At that time, he picked up an individual by the name of Joseph Szymankiewicz—who's the victim in this case—while traveling in the Midwest. They traveled around the country and finally ended up here in Tallahassee, Florida. While in Tallahassee, Florida, John Arthur Spenkelink decided to depart company with Joseph Szymankiewicz because, as Spenkelink testified at trial, Szymankiewicz allegedly relieved him of some money. . . .

"While in the motel on the day of the murder, Spenkelink leaves the room, goes and washes the car . . . and it was at this time, on the way back to the motel after washing the car, that he picks up the codefendant, Frank Brumm, who was hitchhiking at the time. Apparently, it was brought out in testimony, Frank Brumm wanted to go to New Orleans and Spenkelink agreed to take him to New Orleans. But Spenkelink told Mr. Brumm—again from his testimony—that he must go back to the motel room. And he told Brumm that he would leave him off a little ways from the motel room. And then further Spenkelink testified that, 'If you hear a shot, that I am at the Ponce de Leon Motel, room number four.' Now this, to me gentlemen, indicates that he was beginning to form his premeditated design to murder Szymankiewicz."

Guarisco moved to the climax of his story. "Spenkelink went into the room, into the motel room, and shot Szymankiewicz, who was at that time asleep, as we contended at trial. In the bed, he shot him to death. He was shot in the back of the head, a bullet entering behind the left ear. He was shot in the back, the bullet striking the spine and fragmenting and rupturing the aorta, wherein the victim drowned, in essence, in his own blood. And he was struck in the head by what was determined at the time as an unknown instrument. But there were several blows to the head.

"I have photographs, gentlemen"—Guarisco brandished a set of color glossies—"if you would like to observe these photographs, if it's permissible to, at this time." No one on the dais made any move to take the gruesome pictures. So Guarisco laid them on the podium and resumed.

"Spenkelink, during the trial, alleged that the killing was the result of self-defense. He was defending himself from an attack, supposedly that Szymankiewicz had violent tendencies. There was no evidence to indicate that there was a struggle in that room. And the photographs that we introduced at trial—I have copies here—prove that there was no evidence of a struggle in that room. So what we have is an individual sneaking up on the victim, who is asleep, and shooting him. Shooting him in the back of the head! Shooting him in the back! Bashing his head in with some unknown instrument! So this is really not a case of self-defense."

Guarisco paused to let the depravity sink in. Then, with a weary note in his voice, he reminded the panel of the many appeals John Spenkelink had raised, and lost. "Now gentlemen, this case has gone on for six years. It's been in and out of the Florida Supreme Court, it's been in and out of the federal appellate courts, it's been in and out of the Supreme Court of the United States. The Florida Supreme Court has upheld the conviction, has upheld the sentence, and this has been affirmed by the appellate courts in the federal areas and the United States Supreme Court." Again, the prosecutor paused.

Next he reeled off the litany of Spenkelink's youthful offenses, his armed robberies, and his escape from prison. "It's a step," he said, "from juvenile to adult, where he graduated from petty crimes to serious felonies to murder. This is the type of individual we're dealing with. There's no doubt in my mind that this crime was an evil crime," Guarisco intoned. "A wicked crime. A heinous crime! A cruel crime! Brutal crime—Szymankiewicz being shot in the back of the head, being shot in the back, drowning in his own blood." With a flourish, the prosecutor held up a copy of a recent front-page article from *The Miami Herald,* a detailed account of Spenkelink's life and crimes by a young reporter named Barry Bearak. Somehow, Bearak had gotten an interview with Frank Brumm, who never testified at trial. Brumm's story, told publicly for the first time, did little to help John Spenkelink.

"Spenkelink directed—this is from Brumm's statement in *The Miami Herald*—'Here's a hatchet, hit him in the head.' Which Brumm said he did, in this article. Now, this is Spenkelink directing Brumm to participate in this murder," Guarisco emphasized. "Then Spenkelink, according to Brumm in this article, took the hatchet and hit him in the head some more, about four times. . . . So we have evidence here in this article that Szymankiewicz, when Brumm walked in there, was alive, gasping for breath, and then finished off. Also in this article, Brumm stated that while they were awaiting extradition from California to Tallahassee, they concocted the self-defense story.

"Gentlemen, in conclusion . . ." Guarisco shuffled his papers, and decided to try once more with the gruesome pictures. "I have the photographs," he said. "If it would be permissible, I would be glad to show the cabinet."

Still, no one moved to take them.

"These are photographs depicting the wounds of the victim and also the condition of the room, which the members of the cabinet could readily see shows no signs of a violent struggle as indicated by the defendant, John Arthur Spenkelink." At last someone took the pictures from the prosecutor's hand and passed them down the dais. Satisfied, Guarisco resumed.

"In conclusion, I think the facts of the murder, the criminal record of John Arthur Spenkelink—he's a career criminal. He has shown no signs of rehabilitation. His prison record leaves a lot to be desired, participating in escapes, participating in riots, and then escaping himself. . . . All this clearly establishes that John Arthur Spenkelink is not entitled to clemency, and I urge the governor and the members of the cabinet to carry out their duties and sign the death warrant of John Arthur Spenkelink.

"Thank you, gentlemen."

Seated in the front row of theater seats, David Kendall weighed his opponent's performance. It was rough—men don't go to death row for jaywalking—but no worse than he'd expected. Guarisco's job was to show why Spenkelink, among all the thousands of murderers in Florida, should be electrocuted, and Kendall didn't feel the prosecutor had done so. After all, he had introduced the charge that Szymankiewicz had stolen Spenkelink's money (which had to count as some kind of provocation), and he had raised the idea that Brumm—Mr. Free-and-Clear—had delivered several blows to the still-breathing victim. Kendall was pleased to see Ralph Turlington, the liberal commissioner of education, lean forward to question Guarisco.

"Have you read the statement of Justice Ervin?" Turlington asked, referring to a retired Florida Supreme Court justice who had written of

Spenkelink. "In his case I believe it will be found that on a comparison basis with other murder cases where Florida courts have imposed life sentences, Spenkelink is being discriminated against . . . largely the result of local prejudice against drifters."

"Yes sir, I have," Guarisco responded.

"And I'd like you to comment on that," Turlington said. But before Guarisco could respond, he pressed further. "I understand that you offered a plea of second-degree murder."

"That's not true, sir," the prosecutor countered. "A plea of second-degree murder was proposed by defense counsel. The State of Florida rejected that plea as evidenced by the fact that we went to trial on this crime of first-degree murder." It was a fine point, and Guarisco was dancing on the edge of the truth. Spenkelink's trial attorneys, following the customary steps of that delicate minuet called a plea bargain, had asked if the State would agree to second-degree murder. The prosecutors indicated they would. Only after Spenkelink nixed the deal did the prosecution "reject" the plea and proceed with the first-degree trial.

Turlington pushed on. "Next, to the record of the defendant. Do you have any knowledge or do we have any knowledge as to the—not the record of the defendant, but the record of Szymankiewicz? What kind of person was he?"

"That record, sir . . ." Guarisco stammered briefly. "He did have a very long criminal record himself. And his crimes constituted fraudulent crimes, forgeries, prostitution. He admitted, according to John Spenkelink, that he had murdered or killed an inmate. Yes, he had a record."

Turlington: "Well, now, thinking back over your own presentation of a few moments ago . . . would you think it appropriate to take into account this record and to evaluate that individual as to how he might have actually threatened in some manner, at least mentally, the security of those that might be with him?"

Guarisco: "I'm not going to say that as a prosecutor I do not consider the record of the victim. I think it does have bearing. But also, you've got to take into consideration the facts of the case. . . . And when you look at the facts of the case, it's clearly evident that this man

—and from the photographs, and from the evidence that was introduced—there was no violent struggle in that room. Does that give John Spenkelink the right, just because he thinks that Szymankiewicz is violent, does it give him the right to come in and shoot him in the back?"

"No, of course not."

"Okay."

"But does it make a difference in terms of how you would, perhaps, consider the element of clemency . . . life imprisonment versus the death penalty? Would you not take that into account?"

"No sir, not in this case. No sir . . ."

"Would you say there's not a mitigating circumstance if someone, perhaps, may have you in physical threat? . . ."

"No sir. This case is a classic death penalty case."

Turlington sighed. "I have heard ten cases up here and I have ten classics," he said sardonically. "Now, tell me, don't you think there's something there in the way of mitigation?"

"No sir."

"Wouldn't you consider that the victim and the relationship between the victim and murderer in this case have some distinguishing characteristics?"

"No sir."

"You wouldn't consider that at all?"

"No sir, I would not, not in this case."

Turlington gave up trying to budge Guarisco. At the center of the dais, Bob Graham leaned toward his microphone. "Mr. David E. Kendall is here on behalf of the defendant, Mr. Spenkelink."

Kendall spread out his papers on the podium. He wore a well-cut suit that showed just the right amount of his starched white cuffs. His hair was neatly trimmed, although as he spoke his boyish bangs fell, strand by strand, across his forehead. Through large, black-framed glasses, he fixed his gaze on the governor.

"The question before you," Kendall began, after he had introduced himself and his client's family, "is how John Spenkelink should be punished for the crime of first-degree murder. I'm not going to go through the facts in detail. Mr. Guarisco has laid many of them out.

There are a few corrections I'd like to make that I think the record will support. But clemency is essentially a matter of grace, a matter of mercy, not something anybody is legally entitled to. It's a means of curing imperfections in the criminal justice system. I don't say legal errors, and I'm not going to make a legal argument to you. But imperfections, because the criminal justice system is administered by human beings and it is not perfectly infallible.

"Now, I'm going to try and tell you why John Spenkelink's life should be spared, why he should be punished with life imprisonment. Since 1935," Kendall said, turning to his notes, "about one-third of all condemned inmates, whose sentences have been affirmed by the courts, have been spared through the executive clemency process by previous governors, previous boards. I am not suggesting that is in any way binding. . . . But it does show Florida's tradition of using clemency to correct imperfections of the judicial process. . . .

"I think that a man's past history is relevant to the decision whether or not to grant clemency," he continued. "But I don't think that his history as a child, as an adolescent, as a teenager, should determine absolutely whether he lives or dies right now. I think you've got to take a look at the man in the present—because I could tell you that John Spenkelink was in trouble between ages twelve and nineteen. He didn't have a father, he didn't have a lot of economic security. He had a mother who loved him but couldn't control him. He had two sisters who cared about him but couldn't keep him out of trouble. And he had a lot of bad friends. He was in trouble, the record reflects. . . . But it was at age nineteen that in a one-day spree—I think Mr. Guarisco correctly called it a spree—he was charged with six armed robberies in a three-hour period."

Kendall noticed disgusted looks on several faces. "I think if you want to execute a bad kid, then this is the case," he said. "But I don't think that's what you want to do. I think you're interested in assessing where John Spenkelink is now, today. Where he is morally, emotionally, spiritually. What kind of an inmate is he? Is he an animal or is he a person, who, given the harsh punishment of life imprisonment, can contribute something to the community whose laws he has broken, even while he's in prison?"

A deep breath.

"Now, I'd like to begin talking about John Spenkelink today. I'll move to the crime secondly. We have collected . . . a number of representative letters from prison officials, from ministers, from friends and relatives. There are many more in the governor's office. There are more that have been sent to you individually. But I think these letters show that John Spenkelink has evolved. He has changed. I think if you compare his time in the California prisons with his time in the Florida prisons, I think you can see that evolution."

In the months leading up to the hearing, Kendall had collected more than two thousand signatures in favor of reducing Spenkelink's sentence to life in prison. He had testimonials to Spenkelink's good behavior as an inmate. The city council and the PTA in Spenkelink's hometown of Buena Park, California, had passed resolutions calling for mercy. Now the lawyer touched on the highlights of this campaign.

"B. J. Leverette, the former superintendent of the Florida State Prison, calls John a 'positive leader' who helped settle a hunger strike, helped restore trust and confidence between the inmates and the administration. . . . He writes that John was never a troublemaker. He worried about the burden on his family caused by his imprisonment. His attitude in the prison in Florida was one of 'acceptance and respect.' 'I feel,' Mr. Leverette writes, 'that John could serve a life sentence in prison in a productive manner.' "

Kendall paused to allow the former warden's endorsement to register. "The second representative document is from Mr. S. R. Johns, who's a middle-level prison official. He was for many years a death row counselor, charged with monitoring and evaluating death row inmates. He, in his twenty years at Florida State Prison, has seen hundreds and hundreds of inmates. Now, he notes that John was in trouble as a juvenile. . . . But nevertheless, Mr. Johns goes on—and here I'm quoting: 'During the time I was acquainted with him, I sensed a clear evolution in his character and felt that he was definitely maturing and changing for the better. I think he's come to know himself much better in the past few years. I feel he could make a definite contribution to society in the future. I think that John has learned from the experiences he's undergone, has accepted the fact of his guilt and the necessity of his punishment and has both the potential and the inclination to put his past behind him.'

"Finally," Kendall continued, "on the lowest level of the prison hierarchy, we have a letter from a guard, Mr. Dwight Murphy—or an affidavit—who notes that John was friendly and cooperative. He wasn't abusive and back-talking. He broke up fights. He helped cool down younger inmates. He read to inmates who were illiterate. He wrote letters for inmates who were illiterate. He ministered to a defendant in the cell next to him who had sickle-cell anemia. Murphy's affidavit states, 'Of all the inmates I knew during my time at Florida State Prison, John seems to be one of the most deserving to have his death sentence changed to life imprisonment. John is a very good influence inside the prison.'

"I think from those documents you do get a sense of the evolutions and change," Kendall said. And, deviating briefly from his notes, he held up a letter he had received only the previous night, from the chairman of the prisons and parole committee of the state house of representatives. Kendall read the letter, emphasizing the phrase "this young man should not die." Then back to the notes.

"Dwight Murphy, the guard, says that John Spenkelink seems to him to be a Christian. Now . . . I'm not suggesting that a sudden death row conversion to religion is a very weighty reason to grant clemency, because such conversions are, I'm sure, very common." There were nods from some of the cabinet members. "John Spenkelink's religion, I think, is different. He hasn't flaunted it like the Pharisee praying in the temple. We've collected letters from three ministers who have not only written to John frequently, but who also visit him at the prison. And these show—not by any means that he's a saint, nobody is suggesting that. . . .

"I mention all this," Kendall continued, "simply to show that John Spenkelink has the kind of human ties that nurture him and can sustain him through a prolonged period of imprisonment. . . . He's not a man outside the human community. He's a man who—he was a bad kid. . . . But I think the point is to try and assess the progress that he's made, the transformation in his character by age thirty."

Now the lawyer turned to what he hoped would be his most

telling argument: the fact that the victim was a low character who may have provoked his own death.

"We have included," Kendall said, "some documents that speak to where this crime, how this crime compares to others. I start with the character of the deceased, Joseph Szymankiewicz . . . not because John Spenkelink had a right to kill him . . . but simply for reasons of comparison. Because when, I think, when you compare this case to the other capital cases on Florida's death row, there are strong elements of provocation here, as established by the record. . . . The deceased here was different than the deceased in most other capital cases. Not because he had any less right to live. I'm not making that argument. But different because the prior relationship between the deceased and John Spenkelink engendered—*produced*—this homicide in a way that I don't think you find in any other capital case that I know of.

"In no other case, for example, that I'm familiar with has the Florida Supreme Court written of the deceased—and this is the majority opinion—'Admittedly, the evidence clearly shows that the deceased was an individual of vicious temperament.' Joe Szymankiewicz was not the innocent victim of an armed robbery, of a rape, or a burglary. He was not a police officer acting in the line of duty. He was not killed pursuant to a contract, or for hire. . . . Szymankiewicz had been in prison almost twenty years continuously. These were for adult felonies. He was twenty years older than John. As Mr. Guarisco noted, he bragged of killing a guy in prison. John Spenkelink was afraid of him. He robbed John Spenkelink. He forced him to commit a perverted sexual act at gunpoint. He made him play Russian roulette. He took all of his money. John Spenkelink was afraid of him! I think properly and with good cause."

Kendall's time was running out, so he hurried to make two final points. The first had to do with the enigmatic Frank Brumm. Had the courts really arrived at a fair result? If both men had participated in the crime—as the prosecutor had alleged a scant half hour earlier—was it fair for one to go free while the other paid with his life?

"Now the State originally charged, Mr. Guarisco pointed out, Frank Brumm with first-degree murder. A grand jury found cause to indict him. At trial, the State proved . . . that Brumm was in the room. His fingerprints were all over the place. Now, at that point, the lawyers' trial strategy differed. Brumm did not take the stand. John Spenkelink did. John Spenkelink was convicted of first-degree murder. Frank Brumm was acquitted. Mr. Guarisco mentioned *The Miami Herald* story. And if I could, I'd like to direct your attention to that. Because Brumm has admitted not only to me, personally, but to *The Miami Herald* reporter that he struck Joseph Szymankiewicz on the head. . . .

"It's hard to know how much of what Brumm says is true. He didn't take the stand. . . . What I think happened here, what Brumm originally told me, although what he now denies, is that he and John Spenkelink together went back into the motel room. That there was a fight between Szymankiewicz and John. Both of them apparently thought Brumm was on their side. Both of them yelled at him for help. Brumm struck Szymankiewicz on the head with something and John shot him two times. John has never denied shooting him. He has contested the circumstances under which the shooting took place. I think that this disparity in treatment . . . can only be corrected by clemency."

The last point on Kendall's agenda was the plea bargain. "It was the State's position up until trial that this case was disposable of by a second-degree murder plea. They weren't going to offer it. But plea negotiations, I think I know and I think all lawyers know, are not things like the entry into a contract. They involve bargaining. They involve finding out what would be acceptable and what not acceptable. In retrospect, it would have been wiser for John Spenkelink to have said he would plead guilty to second-degree murder. My point here is not that the clock should be turned back, that he should be allowed to accept a second-degree murder plea. My point is only that this is not a case in which the State implacably sought death from the very beginning. It is a case that could have been disposed of earlier, not with the death penalty. . . . This is not a case which from the beginning is one of those cases where the State recognizes, the newspapers recognize, everybody recognizes that this is a death case."

Now it was Kendall's turn to be questioned. Insurance Commissioner Bill Gunter wanted to know more about an incident at the prison the previous Thanksgiving. A death row inmate named Bobby Lewis had gotten his hands on a guard's uniform, and when visiting hours had ended, had changed clothes in the bathroom and walked out of the prison.

In the aftermath of the escape, death row visits were summarily canceled. Spenkelink asked permission to call his mother, to alert her not to come for the holiday. When this request was denied, he protested by refusing to return his tray after dinner. A group of five guards (known to inmates as the "goon squad") was dispatched to retrieve the tray. By the time it was over, Spenkelink had been knocked unconscious and one of his ribs was broken. The episode was terribly confused. Spenkelink claimed he was savaged; the guards said he attacked them. Whatever the truth, it did not help Kendall's argument that his client was a model prisoner. Kendall argued that the episode had arisen from the good-hearted desire to "tell his mother not to drive . . . to the prison."

The second query came from the new attorney general, Jim Smith. By a quirk in the Florida law, the man charged with opposing the appeals of death row inmates also had a vote on their clemency petitions. Smith's was a plain-sense question that cut to the absurdity of the crime itself. "Wouldn't you think a reasonable person would have just gotten in the car and left?" Though Kendall tried, fumblingly, for a satisfactory response, the question defied any winning response. Killing a thug in a motel room was not a reasonable thing to do.

The governor leaned toward his microphone and ended the presentations. "On behalf of the board I wish to commend the participants—attorneys, and the audience—for the decorum, demeanor, that has existed . . . in this meeting," he said. Afterward, reporters gathered around a weeping Lois Spenkelink, who said: "I hope God will be with Graham and give him a hand."

Kendall gathered his papers and headed for the door. The session had gone well, he thought. He felt he had answered the prosecution's strongest points. It seemed so plain to him that the case was too murky, too muddled by questions of fairness and culpability, to stand as the test case for Florida's return to the electric chair. So many cases were worse.

But he had missed one detail: a particular weak spot of the governor's. Unbeknownst to all but his closest friends and family, Bob Graham could not stand the sight of blood. Those pictures the prosecutor had insisted on passing along the cabinet table—they were drenched in blood. A corpse, facedown on a cheap motel bed. The mattress caked red-brown. The spread darkened by a ruddy blossom. And, worst of all, the battered, oozing skull.

With all the impassioned speeches and the questions back and forth, hardly anyone noticed when Bob Graham went pale, then left his chair and hurried through a side door from the room. He had gone to throw up.

Saturday night, May 19. In an isolation cell on Q-wing, a few steps away from the execution chamber, John Spenkelink sat on his bed and chain-smoked Marlboros. Beyond the bars, a guard watched constantly, jotting notes every few minutes on the prisoner's moods and activities. Spenkelink's possessions were piled outside his cell, beyond his reach; whenever he wanted a book or a toothbrush or any little item he had to ask for the guard to pass it to him.

The keeper was as restless as the kept. Warden Dave Brierton listened to soulful music on his stereo when his mind was troubled. Bach on a harpsichord, perhaps. Or Prokofiev's score to the film *Alexander Nevsky,* especially the haunting song of the dead sung by the mezzo-soprano after the battle on the ice. "This may tell you more than you want to know about me," Brierton once said, "but every New Year's Eve, I open a bottle of wine from my cellar and I listen to Verdi's *Requiem* with Toscanini conducting." A requiem is a Mass for the dead. "I get all broken up during the "Dies Irae," and then, after a good cry, go on with the year." The "Dies Irae," according to the official version promulgated by Pope Pius V in 1570, says:

A day of wrath, that day,
it will dissolve the world into glowing ashes . . .
What trembling there will be
when the Judge shall come to examine everything in strict justice!

. . . .

So when the Judge is seated,
whatever sin is hidden will be made known.
Nothing sinful shall go unpunished. . . .
What shall I, a wretch, say at that time?
What advocate shall I entreat to plead for me
when scarcely the righteous shall be safe from damnation?

. . . .

Just Judge of vengeance,
grant me the gift of pardon
before the day of reckoning.

Brierton was an uncommon man. Visitors to Florida State Prison who came expecting a warden out of *Cool Hand Luke* instead found one who collected Chinese art and practiced gourmet cooking. Dave Brierton could bench-press a quarter of a ton and had a certificate in management from Harvard. He could quote Camus and rip a shank from the hand of a cold-blooded killer. He counted among his greatest moments at Starke the day he had discovered leeks growing wild in a remote corner of the prison property.

It was odd that he was in Florida. For some fifty years, the state's prison system had been largely the domain of a few dynastic families— Brierton, characteristically, compared the management to the inbred reign of the Spanish Hapsburgs. But by the late 1970s, Florida State Prison had become such a stinkhole of violence and corruption that its warden hardly dared venture from his office into the cellblocks. Florida required a formidable replacement, and found one in Brierton, an Illinois outsider.

Right away, Brierton got a feel for his new place of business when one prisoner stabbed another over a biscuit. As warden, he had a simple rule for prison management: Either he ran the show, or the inmates would. So he cracked down hard. When he noticed a prisoner wearing rings on every finger, fifteen in all, Brierton issued an edict limiting each inmate to two rings, maximum: a wedding band and one other. Why? Because the only way an inmate gets fifteen rings is by stealing them from weaker men. Fifteen rings is a display of power, a sign of violent intent. Brierton also banned gold chains. "A man will kill for a gold chain," he said simply.

Stories about the muscle-bound warden spread quickly through the prison. One held that Brierton had beaten a man to death with his bare hands in Illinois. Another said he once took on six inmates single-handed, and whipped 'em all. In private, Brierton scoffed at the tales, but he was perfectly happy to have his prisoners believe them. Brierton walked the cellblocks day and night, alone, and pumped iron in the yard with the big bulls. He invited his captives to tell him whatever they had on their minds, and anything that couldn't be said in front of other inmates, a prisoner could raise in a private session. Brierton held weekly "call-outs," during which any man who wanted a word in confidence was ushered to the warden's office. Sometimes, the inmates had complaints; other times, they wanted to snitch. Once a burly killer from death row, a motorcycle gangster, visited Brierton's office with a confession, something too terrible to admit in front of his compatriots: He had developed a liking for poetry. What should he read? Brierton recommended Nikos Kazantzakis's *The Odyssey: A Modern Sequel.*

His office was dominated by an uncanny desk that he'd made himself, during a phase of his life when he'd taken up metal sculpture as a hobby. The base was a stout piece of farm machinery, a seventy-five-year-old corn planter Brierton discovered rusting away on an Illinois farm. He had scraped and repainted the machine, and balanced a thick sheet of glass on top of it. Brierton liked his creation because he found people were generally uncomfortable in the presence of a 300-pound prison warden, and this desk was a good way to break the ice, a real conversation starter. A number of his visitors liked what the desk said about its owner: It was a sturdy, transparent, unusual workplace for a unique individual with nothing to hide.

As he prepared for the Spenkelink execution, Brierton was stalked by a ghost—the ghost of Gary Gilmore, the Utah crackpot. Sentenced to death by firing squad for the murders of a motel clerk and a gas station attendant, Gilmore had shocked the world in 1977 by demanding to be put to death. The spectacle that ensued was as ridiculous as it was pathetic. At first, Gilmore was dismissed as a lunatic—there had been no executions in America in nearly a decade—but as his campaign gained momentum, reporters and film crews, activists of every stripe, publicity hounds, gawkers, and assorted wackos all flocked to Utah State Prison. Hollywood dealmakers scurried from one Gilmore friend to another, from relative to relative, flashing cash and brandishing contracts for exclusive rights to the sad, loopy saga. A few days before the scheduled execution, Gilmore's girlfriend smuggled a cache of pills into the visiting room, and that night the lovers attempted a mutual suicide —she gobbled her pills outside the prison, he swallowed his in his cell. Both survived, but the prison officials looked like fools. To make matters worse, the night before Gilmore was to be shot at dawn, the visiting room filled with friends, family, and hangers-on. They carried with them ample supplies of booze. Gilmore reveled at his own wake.

It was disgraceful, in Brierton's opinion—the ultimate example of an inmate running the show. The prospect of another Gilmore fiasco constantly shadowed Brierton's thoughts. He made this clear on Sunday afternoon, May 20, 1979, when David Kendall came for a visit. About 1 P.M., Kendall took a seat before Brierton's desk and said, "We need to talk about visits for John with his family and friends."

The warden answered quickly. He wasn't sure he was going to allow any visits, except through the glass partition. Security reasons. Kendall started to protest, but Brierton cut him off. "Listen, I don't have to tell you what happened with Gilmore. It was a circus. Well, I'm not going to have a circus in my prison. We're not going to have anyone bringing psychotropic drugs in to the prisoner. We're not going to have any suicide pacts. If that means no contact visits, then that's the way it will be."

"I think you've got things mixed up," Kendall countered. "I can assure you, no one intends to help John kill himself. John doesn't want to die. We're trying to keep him alive. It's the State that wants him dead. Not us."

That's not what the newspapers say, Brierton answered. Several articles had suggested Spenkelink had no intention of giving the government the satisfaction of killing him. But Kendall repeated, "I'm telling you, I don't think there's a problem." Surely Brierton could not mean what he was saying. How could he deny Spenkelink a chance to hug his mother before he died?

"His mother—we'll do what we can for his mother," Brierton said. "We want to be reasonable. But you've got to understand our point of view. This is not an everyday occurrence."

What about Spenkelink's girlfriend?

"I don't think you should plan on it."

"You're telling me that John's going to be executed without a chance to kiss his girlfriend good-bye?"

"I'm telling you we're not going to have a circus."

The negotiation continued. "What about a clergyman? We want the minister of John's choice to be with him." Brierton responded that the prison had a chaplain on staff. "That's crazy," Kendall said. "You can't deny a man the right to take his last Communion from his own clergyman."

Brierton knew, however, that any kook with a Bible could call himself a preacher. "Tell me how we're supposed to know anything about these 'clergymen,'" he said. "How are we supposed to know what's in the Communion wine?"

David Kendall considered this rampant paranoia. "We're going to have to discuss this later," he said finally. "I've got to see my client."

"I'm trying to be reasonable," Brierton repeated. He rose to usher Kendall out. "Don't think," he added, "that this is easy for any of us."

Later, inside the cellblock, Kendall related the story to Spenkelink through the microphone in the glass. "They're worried somebody's going to bring you something to kill yourself with."

Spenkelink swore. And then, leaning closer to the glass, he raised his cuffed hands toward the metal amplifier and pressed his fingers to the device—all very slowly, so that he wouldn't draw the guard's attention. Kendall watched admiringly. Still pressing with his fingers, Spenkelink gave the microphone a slight counterclockwise twist, and a narrow space formed between the metal and the glass. A space about the width of a cyanide capsule, the length of a razor blade. The prisoner pointed to the aperture and shrugged. The message was clear. If he wanted pills, he'd get them through the glass, contact visits or not. A moment later, the gap was closed and Spenkelink's hands were back in his lap.

"I saw in the papers they got a vigil going at the governor's

mansion," Spenkelink said. "You know, I appreciate what they're doing. You tell 'em that." He pulled on a cigarette. "Do you think it will
do any good?"

"It can't hurt."

"I've been thinking," Spenkelink said. "Maybe I should give a
press conference. Let 'em hear my side of the story."

Kendall frowned. He did not think much of the idea—last-minute
appeals are a tricky business, he told Spenkelink. A judge might resent
having the case tried in the press. Also, the problem with a press conference was that you never knew how the words would look in print.
"Besides," he said, "I don't think the prison would allow it. Listen. If
you want to do something, why don't you write out a statement?
Then, if the time comes, you can let people know what's on your
mind. That way, you can be sure it says just what you want."

The inmate seemed disappointed, and smoked quietly for a minute. "You better check the phone line to the governor's office," he said
at last. "If I know those clowns, they'll probably leave it off the hook.
Or short the damn thing out."

Kendall explained what he planned to do in court the next day.
He intended to approach the Florida Supreme Court with a legal version of his emotional appeal at the clemency hearing a month before.
He would argue that the evidence presented at trial was insufficient to
justify a first-degree murder conviction. The State hadn't proved pre-
meditation and it hadn't proved, beyond a reasonable doubt, that the
killing was unprovoked. The Inc. Fund had also developed some broad
attacks on the fairness of the death penalty in general. If they failed in
the state court, they would appeal upward through the federal courts.

"So what happens if we win?" Spenkelink asked.

"A new trial."

"Man, that's what I need. You'd be my lawyer?"

"Sure."

"What would you do? I mean, different from the guys I had
before?"

"I can tell you one thing, I'd work with you for days getting your
testimony straight. We wouldn't just set you up there and see what
came out of your mouth."

Spenkelink pondered that briefly. "Well," he said, "I sure couldn't do any worse with you."

"John," Kendall answered quietly, "that's not exactly a ringing vote of confidence."

"Aw, you know what I mean."

When the guard signaled that the visit was almost over, Spenkelink took a page from a box of papers he had brought from his cell. He had hoped to give these to Kendall—they were mostly messages to friends and supporters—but Brierton had forbidden the exchange. Kendall immediately recognized the paper as one of the man's letters. A letter from John Spenkelink was unmistakable. He wrote in meticulous script, using a ruler to keep the lines perfectly straight. He punctuated sentences that made him happy with little smiling faces, and irritating news was noted with tiny scowls. For example, from a letter written in the summer of 1978:

> These blood-thirsty politicians have now got my attorneys rapidly preparing another appeal to the U.S. Supreme Court. I was told yesterday that the U.S.S.C. can refuse to hear my arguments. [Scowling face.] Now that would not be very nice. [Smiling face.] I'll handle anything they dish out. [Smiling face.] It'll be interesting how this situation turns out. [Smiling face.] Patience. [Smiling face.]

Spenkelink held the paper to the glass. "I've changed the way I end my letters," he told Kendall. "You know how I used to say, 'Yours truly'? Well, now I write: 'Capital punishment—Them without the capital gets the punishment.'" As Kendall laughed, Spenkelink said, "Fuck you, whoever's listening," and they both laughed some more. Then the guard stepped over and Spenkelink was led away.

Before leaving the prison, Kendall remembered one more piece of business. Combing the law books, looking for a miracle, he had come across an old statute providing for the unclaimed bodies of executed inmates to be delivered to the University of Florida's medical school for dissection. He was damned if he was going to let that happen to his client. He stopped back by the warden's office. Brierton was out, but his assistant, Richard Dugger, was available. Dugger listened politely to Kendall's concern, and though he found it a bit insulting—they weren't ghouls, after all—he assured the lawyer that "if the time comes," Spenkelink could have a proper burial.

Spenkelink had already specified his epitaph: "Man is what he chooses to become. He chooses that for himself." During five years living under the fiercely disciplined conditions of death row, John Spenkelink had begun to make something of himself. He chewed through books, improved his writing, and began to take an interest in the real world. That Robin Hood charm, revealed in flashes as a boy, ripened into a full-fledged personality. Spenkelink was a con—but he was a well-liked con, respected even.

Tom Feamster, a priest who counseled death row inmates, said, "John was not a good kid. He was not at all ready to get out of prison. But I do believe he was working in that direction. John was macho. He was tough. Definitely a leader type. But he was also a good conversationalist—he engaged in back-and-forth; he listened, he was responsive, he didn't overwhelm you. You might say that John was the perfect candidate for rehabilitation, except that he didn't need rehabilitation. He needed habilitation. He needed to start over from childhood and do the growing up he'd never done. From the time he started sniffing glue at twelve years old, until he reached death row, I don't think he ever drew a sober breath. My contention is that before he got to prison John was not even in this world. Yet he became a person who was very thoughtful, considerate, concerned about people's feelings."

One time, Spenkelink was meeting with a lawyer and the lawyer concluded that the prisoner's handcuffs were too tight. The lawyer began shouting at the guard to loosen them—but Spenkelink cut the lawyer off, saying, "Don't do that to him. He's a good man. He just has his orders." Another time he offered to take the cell next to the most loathsome and annoying man on death row, a child molester named Arthur Goode. Spenkelink thought he might be able to help the guy adjust to prison life, and though he failed, the gesture touched Dave Brierton.

Since his first death warrant in 1977—and especially during the last six months—Spenkelink had become a cause célèbre. His portrait was on the cover of *The New York Times Magazine* (WILL HE BE THE FIRST? asked the headline) and his case was debated as far away as the European Parliament. And though some men on death row were irritated by his high profile, Spenkelink was plainly improved by it. He spent hours every day answering his mail, and kept up on the newspapers and magazines so he could talk intelligently with the visitors who flocked to his cause. With his head clear for the first time since boyhood, he latched enthusiastically onto every passing whim, and his mind grew sharp, by death row standards, though utterly inconsistent. He dabbled in Christian theology at the same time that he pondered reincarnation. He developed into a pretty fair artist. He met regularly with a screwball white supremacist preacher, and spent a lot of time talking about the guy's racist theories, but at the same time his best friend on death row was a black man, Doug McCray.

"I'd heard he was a racist," McCray said years later, "so for a long time I never talked to him, even though we were next door. In the exercise yard, he played volleyball and I played basketball. One day his volleyball lands at my feet. I just looked at it. 'What's your problem?' he says.

"And I said, 'You expect me to walk this over to you?'

"Well, he gave me this grin and said, 'You ever heard of the forward pass?' And I tried not to laugh, but something about it was so funny I wound up on the ground, I was laughing so hard." After that breakthrough, Spenkelink and McCray were always talking, about life and death, about sports and politics. They shared the belief that Bob Graham's election would be good for them, that he was "a wimp" who would not pursue the death penalty with any vigor, and they shared the shock when they realized their mistake. McCray was an earnest man who frequently burst into tears; he enjoyed Spenkelink's dry sense of humor. "Oh, John!—he could be funny," McCray remembered. "He hated that his hair was prematurely going gray, and I had this great big Afro back then. He used to say, 'Man, let's change hair.' And I'd say, 'What would Mrs. Spenkelink think about that?' "

It's hard to know what attracts a woman to a man under sentence of death, but it happens often, and it happened with Carla Key. She was a single mother from Jacksonville who read about Spenkelink and began visiting regularly. For a while, she called herself Spenkelink's girlfriend; eventually, they spoke of themselves as married. And this odd relationship made the biggest change of all in the prisoner, according to Dave Brierton.

"I saw a real change in John," the warden said. "I think he finally grasped The Dream. He had Carla, and as time went on, she started acting like his wife. Eventually he started getting letters from Carla's daughter addressed to 'Daddy.' John used to stop me on my rounds and show them to me. 'Hey, Dave, come see the pictures of my family!'

"He had it. He finally had The Dream," Brierton repeated. "And it was like something from a past life had got him where he was, and if he could just get beyond that, he could live The Dream. See, I think John was a guy who one day woke up and realized he would like to be a normal person. But there was no way back."

David Kendall was drained by his day at the prison, counseling his client and haggling with the warden—exhausted already, and the ordeal had hardly begun. He would file his appeal at the Florida Supreme Court first thing in the morning; for tonight, he had a reservation at the Driftwood Motel in Tallahassee. He steered his rental car down the prison road, past the guard tower and onto the highway for the two-and-a-half-hour drive to the capital. As he drove, he rehearsed the presentation he planned to make to the state high court. For years, Kendall had been arguing in courts across the country on behalf of prisoners sentenced to death. This time, though, it would be different. This time it truly was life or death.

The farther he drove, the more impassioned he became, orating over the roar of the engine and the whine of the tires. The more impassioned he became, the harder he pressed on the accelerator. This is not a death penalty crime! he cried. This case proves the unfairness of the death penalty! This just can't be allowed to happen!

Blue lights erupted in the rearview mirror. Kendall looked down at the speedometer: He was doing over eighty. The ticket cost him twenty-six dollars.

He reached Tallahassee about the time Lois Spenkelink was leaving it. The mother of the condemned man had traveled to the capital that day to join the protests against her son's execution. She was a simple woman, naïve even; she believed that the sheer force of a loving request might stop the process that had been set in motion. The more savvy protesters understood the power of her innocence—her deeply lined face and her unadorned language reached out and grabbed hearts; her pain was obvious and her need was vivid. She was her son's best advertisement, but this placed a heavy burden on her, emotionally and physically. Lois Spenkelink was not practiced at pleading for mercy, yet here she was begging for her son's life. A private figure, she had to steel herself to face television cameras. Without status or pull, she had to confront the governor.

At the governor's mansion that Sunday afternoon, Lois Spenkelink had taken her place alongside the men of PAX and demanded to speak to Bob Graham. When she was told that Graham was away at a college commencement, she asked for a meeting with the governor's wife. A "mother-to-mother appeal," she called it. She wanted to ask Mrs. Graham "not to let your husband kill my son." And she wanted to explain a bitter truth she had learned over the years: "You never know what your children will do when they grow up."

She sat down on a folding chair and waited. The protesters sang "Amazing Grace" and recited prayers. Nearby that day were about twenty supporters of capital punishment—drawn by news reports of the vigil, they had gathered for a counterprotest. They carried signs reading: HE WHO SPILLS BLOOD WILL HAVE HIS BLOOD SPILLED. Like the PAX men, these folks knew their Scripture, and the two sides fired Bible verses back and forth in support of their respective positions.

Inside the mansion, the governor's aides watched nervously, worried not so much about violence anymore, but about Lois Spenkelink. She was sixty-seven years old, overweight, and leaned on a dark wooden cane when she stood. The sun was high and hot overhead. The ordeal could kill her, and the governor's aides didn't want that—

not for her, and certainly not on the evening news. For nearly an hour they tried to gauge her condition as she waited in vain to see Adele Graham.

Eventually, Lois Spenkelink left the mansion fence to attend a larger rally on the plaza of the state capitol, and by the time she got there, the strain was showing on her face. Several hundred people were clustered in the heat. The ranks of the truly committed had been inflated by curious townspeople enticed by reports in the morning newspaper that the event might be stocked with celebrities. Actor Alan Alda, comedian Carol Burnett, cartoonist Garry Trudeau, and singers Joan Baez and Peter Yarrow were mentioned—but when the time came, the most famous face in the crowd was a former governor, Leroy Collins. Collins was a hero to Florida liberals for his brave stand against segregation. His courage ultimately cost him his political career. As governor, he signed the death warrants of twenty men—"It was my duty," he said—but he had come to oppose the death penalty fervently.

After a prayer and a few speeches, Lois Spenkelink mopped her brow and struggled to her feet. She wore a patterned shift and white church-going shoes. A hint of slip showed at her knees; sadness and confusion marked her broad face. She spoke only a few labored words, but the simple sight of her moved many in the audience to tears. "We're all in society," she said, "and if we let a person be killed, we're all guilty."

The rally ended peaceably, and Lois Spenkelink, worn out by the day's events, returned to Starke to be near her son. It was dark by the time she got back. The red neon cross on the Starke water tower glowed in the night. As the car she was riding in approached the home of a kindly family that had taken her in, the headlights caught a small white placard on the lawn across the street.

FRY JOHN SPENKELINK, it said.

∴

Florida State Prison. Execution Day—Minus Two (2). The schedule:

1. Execution squad drill.
2. Asst. Supt. Operations tests telephone.
3. Electrician tests equipment.

Monday, May 21. Forty-eight hours to go. Ray Marky met the sunrise over the rim of a coffee cup, through a blue cigarette haze. But what he smelled was victory. In nearly seven years spent laboring in the abstract fields of death-penalty law, he and George Georgieff had seen incremental successes—but no close-the-book, slam-the-gavel, trip-the-switch triumphs. Now he felt himself on the verge.

What did Spenkelink's lawyers have? Nothing. Marky had been over the case file again and again, sifting and resifting in his painstaking way, and he saw nothing to support a last-gasp appeal. So he was eager for the day to begin. He was going to kick some butt today. Marky had good reason to feel confident. The Spenkelink case had always gone his way. At the first appellate level, in the Florida Supreme Court, the prosecution won a solid endorsement of the death sentence, despite the ambiguities surrounding the murder. Soon after that, in 1977, then-governor Reubin Askew signed a death warrant on Spenkelink. It was (for reasons that have never been entirely clear) the only warrant Askew signed during eight years in office.

Pushed into the federal courts, David Kendall filed an impressive appeal attacking the death penalty as fundamentally unfair. His brief was a mass of statistics showing that people who killed white victims were significantly more likely to get the death penalty than killers of blacks. At the end of 1976, only five of more than one hundred victims murdered by the men on Florida's death row were black—even though blacks, statistically, were far more likely to be murdered than whites. This, Kendall argued, was proof that capital punishment was still arbitrary and racially biased, placing more value on white lives than on black lives. In other words, the flaws the U.S. Supreme Court identified in the *Furman* case had not been eliminated. The appeal was potential dynamite, because if Spenkelink prevailed, the courts might conclude that capital punishment was irretrievably unconstitutional. Marky stood to lose everything he and his colleagues around the country had been fighting for.

"I went crazy," Marky recalled. "I was asking Georgieff, 'What are we going to do?' Finally, we decided to get Askew to order every state attorney in Florida to compile information on every first-degree murder case since 1972. We wanted to know the race of the bad guy, race of the victim, the disposition of the case, and the reasons. We hit the panic button. I remember Askew summoning one state attorney from a fishing trip in the middle of the Gulf of Mexico."

Across Florida, an army of lawyers, paralegals, and secretaries— 112 in all—was pressed into duty, working overtime to gather ammunition to stop Kendall. They had to show that Kendall's statistics did not prove racial prejudice in any particular case. As expected, the warrant signed by Askew expired before the matter was decided. John Spenkelink was spared for a time. Eventually, though, Marky prevailed. And every lawyer and paralegal and secretary involved received a grateful letter from Governor Askew. "We are aware of the many long and tedious weekend hours that were consumed in assimilating this important information," the governor wrote. Mountains were moved for the death penalty.

While that issue was pending, Kendall had come up with another avenue of appeal, courtesy of the U.S. Supreme Court. Ruling in an Ohio case, the court declared that defendants on trial for their lives must be allowed to present any evidence that might help them show why their lives should be spared. This was a refinement of the reforms that rescued the death penalty from oblivion. Under the redesigned capital punishment laws, death sentences could be imposed only after a careful weighing process. On one side of the scales were the "aggravating circumstances" of the case—certain facts that, in the eyes of the law, made a particular murder worthy of the death penalty. On the other side were the "mitigating circumstances" —qualities of a defendant and his crime that might call for mercy. The Supreme Court ruled in the Ohio case that it violates the Constitution to limit the evidence that can be offered on the side of mitigation.

Florida's law set just such limits; the state supreme court specifically said so in a 1976 opinion. Heartened by the Ohio ruling, Kendall
rushed into the Florida Supreme Court with a new petition to have
Spenkelink's sentence thrown out as unconstitutional. Again Ray
Marky felt a panic attack, and again he scrambled for data. This time he
combed every death penalty case weighed by the Florida Supreme
Court since 1973 and found several examples in which courts had, in
fact, considered mitigating evidence that went beyond the boundaries
set by state law. He argued that it didn't matter what the law appeared
to say; what mattered was how the law was applied. Marky argued that
the Florida system, in practice, had never actually limited mitigating
evidence. The dry letter of the law was not important.

The Florida Supreme Court was happy to agree with Marky, and
ruled in another case that its way of doing business was foursquare with
the U.S. Constitution. It was a vindication of Marky's favorite theory
about how to win in appellate courts: "First, you make the judges want
to rule in your favor, and then you give them an argument to stand
on."

By 1978, Spenkelink's case had made it to the Fifth Circuit Court
of Appeals—the next-to-last rung on the ladder. Its implications were
so important that Kendall had stepped aside and allowed Anthony Amsterdam to handle the presentation. This was a simple decision: Amsterdam was the best. His oral argument in the landmark *Furman* case was
described by one U.S. Supreme Court justice as the finest presentation
he had ever heard. Even so, he wasn't able to save Spenkelink. In
August 1978, a three-judge panel unanimously upheld the death sentence. Soon afterward, the panel's opinion was certified by the circuit
court as a whole. Kendall appealed to the U.S. Supreme Court, re-
newing the arguments he had used in the lower courts. On March 2,
1979, the high court refused, without comment, to hear the case,
which opened the way for Bob Graham to sign a death warrant.

To a layperson this might seem like a tortuous process, but to
Marky it was clean as a whistle. It was, in fact, about the simplest capital
appeal he would ever prosecute. Kendall had gone to every court available, and Marky had won every time. Now Kendall's only resort was to
try the same courts one more time. When the Florida Supreme Court

opened for business that morning, briefs were immediately filed from Marky and Kendall. Copies disappeared into the offices of the seven justices.

In an office across the street, the governor's morning mail arrived in huge canvas bags. Pick one from the multitude: a cheap greeting card of a very sentimental genre. On the cover is a bright pastel rendering of a plump little girl with sausage curls and chubby fingers; she is hanging laundry out to dry on a warm and sunny day. "Just a line . . ." says the cheerful message.

Inside:

Dear Gov. Graham,
    I'm Gerri Vander Velde, a 12 year old from Rock Valley, Ia. I just want to say that I would like to see John Spenkelink (my cousin) have a less drastic sentence. Put yourself in John's shoes. (Not very fun, Huh?)
    Sincerely,
    Gerri V.V.

Another notecard, this one pink, decorated with flowers and butterflies, unsigned:

Please—please sign that death warrant—Let's get on with it! Give the poor victims a break!

The prospect, and now the reality, of death warrants signed by the Florida governor had caused a worldwide sensation, and a tidal wave of reaction came crashing into his correspondence office: telegrams, mailgrams, handwritten notes, neatly typed letters on corporate stationery. Hundreds in favor and hundreds opposed. A roiling wave of anger and outrage, pleading and peroration. The mail was rather evenly divided between supporters and opponents of the death penalty, but Graham's aides were quick to notice that most of the Floridians who wrote were in favor. "Let the word go out to all criminals across the land that

Florida is tough and will get even tougher," wrote a businessman from Coral Gables.

Letters asking mercy for Spenkelink arrived from England, Germany, Canada, Sweden, Australia, Spain, Italy, Abu Dhabi, France, Switzerland, Austria, Denmark, Norway, and Holland. Amnesty International, the Nobel Prize–winning human rights organization, had made Spenkelink's survival a worldwide cause. A careful study of the international mail suggested the outlines of an orchestrated campaign. Letters came in clusters from AI chapters, most obviously copied from a single model. Because many authors were not fluent in English, a mistake in spelling or grammar might be repeated in a dozen missives. A batch of letters from Sweden all began the same way: "I am deeply chocked . . ." National stereotypes showed through. The mail from England invariably expressed a dignified reserve; British writers began with solemn deference and considerable throat clearing about their reluctance to poke their noses into another nation's business. The French proudly refused to translate their letters, assuming that anyone who had risen to the rank of governor of Florida would surely know how to read French. These were collected and sent to foreign-language students at Florida State University for translation.

An especially intense outpouring came from the Netherlands, much of it from the province of Pwentse on the German border. In town after town of the province, local phone directories were filled with Spenkelinks—a name as common in that part of Holland as it was rare in North Florida. A distant relative of the condemned man was interviewed by all the major Dutch newspapers, and his distress over the impending execution provoked additional barrages of mail to Bob Graham. Still more mail followed a resolution by the European Parliament calling for mercy. Europe had all but abandoned capital punishment in the decades following World War II, and the Continent now found a chance to flaunt its advanced morality. In Great Britain, where a bill was pending in the House of Commons to reintroduce the death penalty, the events in Florida added new weight to the opposition.

From across the United States, religious leaders preached forgiveness, while other ministers wrote to commend vengeance. Each side marshaled Scripture: Chapter 13 of St. Paul's Epistle to the Romans was a favorite of the pro-death-penalty pastors. "Let every person be subject to the governing authorities. For there is no authority except from God, and those that exist have been instituted by God. Rulers are not a terror to good conduct, but to bad. . . . If you do wrong, be afraid, for he does not bear the sword in vain; he is the servant of God to execute his wrath on the wrongdoer." Opponents of the execution preferred to quote Jesus speaking in Matthew, Chapter 5: "You have heard that it was said, 'An eye for an eye and a tooth for a tooth.' But I say to you, Do not resist one who is evil. But if anyone strikes you on the right cheek, turn to him the other also."

A fistful of letters arrived from Tupelo, Oklahoma, where folks had been agitated to learn of the sexual proclivities of Spenkelink's victim, Szymankiewicz. "Please commute Mr. John Spenkelink's sentence," one woman wrote. "He did not do wrong by killing that homosexual the people like that are worthy of death." Another Tupelo woman said: "He does not deserve the electric chair. Iran killed off alot [sic] of Homosexuals and America should do the same. God bless John." She closed her letter, "For God and Justice."

Political figures petitioned Graham, too. Former South Dakota governor R. F. Kneip cabled a simple message from his post as ambassador to Singapore: "Please reconsider."

A letter arrived in the quaking, meticulous penmanship of an elderly woman:

> As the kindergarten teacher of John Arthur Spenkelink in Whiting, Iowa, I am pleading with you to please spare his life. . . . As I know John Arthur I can't think of him as being a murderer.

It was signed Miss Aurilla Mustard. The penmanship was almost identical on a letter from Miami:

> In executing one cold-blooded, vicious killer you will hopefully save the lives of thousands of innocent persons.

Responsibility for the flood of mail fell to Sue Tully, Graham's regal and unflappable correspondence secretary, a title that may not convey the importance of her job. A person who takes time to write is a person who takes time to vote. Mishandling their letters is something they won't forget. And they'll likely tell their friends. Successful politicians are extremely careful about their mail. Tully understood: Every letter required a response. Her staff had scarcely begun to slit the envelopes on Monday morning's mail when a second, even larger shipment arrived shortly after lunch. The next day's shipments were even larger, and still more came the following day. So much mail poured in that capable, efficient, unflappable Sue Tully would need the rest of the year to answer it all.

When Bob Graham left the governor's mansion for work at the capitol that Monday morning, the men of PAX went, too. They took up places on the well-polished floor, blocking the tall double doors to Graham's office, and refused to let anyone pass. They brought with them a neatly typed petition.

Dear Governor Graham,

We are here today in your office because we believe in life—because we believe that no human being has the right to take the life of another. And we are here today because you have announced your intention to kill two men, John Spenkelink and Willie Darden, on Wednesday morning, May 23rd.

We have come from around the country to appeal to you as a fellow human being and a child of God. We have written to you. We have spoken with you. We have prayed for you. But your heart remains hardened. Your intention to commit murder has remained firm.

And it is murder you will commit. You continue to hide from this horrible truth. You hide behind the theory of deterrence. However, studies show that capital punishment does not deter violent crime and may even increase it. According to the

U.S. Supreme Court, there is no conclusive evidence that the death penalty acts as a deterrent.

You hide behind the courts and the legislature. Yet the law gives you the power to stop these killings, to save these lives.

You have refused to speak with Lois Spenkelink, the mother of one of the men you will kill, saying you do not want emotionalism to influence your decision. But society has always considered those murders carried out without emotion to be the most heinous and barbaric.

We cannot—we will not—allow you to make killing a routine affair of government. There can be no business as usual as long as you refuse to stay the executions of these two men.

We must all listen to and follow the words of God, the only giver of life: "I am now giving you the choice between life and death, between God's blessing and God's curse, and I call heaven and earth to witness the choice you make. CHOOSE LIFE." (Deuteronomy 30:19)

PAX (People Against Executions)

Predictably, the television cameras arrived soon after the protesters, and at the sight of the cameras, the protesters began staging mock executions. One donned a black hood while another was dragged, shouting and struggling, to a chair. The hooded man pantomimed pulling a switch, and the man in the chair stiffened as if dead. When they weren't performing, the demonstrators sang hymns and hoped they would be arrested.

Robin Gibson continued to insist that no one would be arrested. Reporters demanded to know what was going to be done, and all morning Gibson repeated his stock answer: "The governor respects the fact that these people are very committed to what they believe." Meanwhile, the governor's staff spread the word to lawmakers and lobbyists and government executives that business should be conducted through a little-known side door to the governor's suite. After several hours, Gibson decided to face the protesters, and walked through the blue-carpeted foyer to the big double doors.

"I'm Robin Gibson, the governor's general counsel," he announced. He was met by a chorus of voices: "Choose life!" "Stop this madness!" Someone pressed a copy of the petition into his hands. Gibson glanced over it, then said, "I wish you would respect the rights of the people who have business in the governor's office."

"We can't respect the business of murder," one of the PAX ministers retorted, and explained that they intended to stay right where they were, night and day, until the governor changed his mind. Gibson considered the prospect.

"All right," he said at last. "The bathrooms are down the hall, and the cafeteria in the basement opens at seven each morning."

David Kendall chewed nervously on a sandwich in his room at the Driftwood Motel in Tallahassee. It was noon and still no word from the Florida Supreme Court. He had hoped for a chance to argue his case before the justices that morning, but now the day was half over and still he had no idea when—or even if—the court would hold a hearing. He checked his watch, saw that fifteen minutes had passed, and dialed the number for the court's clerk, Sid White. "There's still no word," said the voice at the other end of the line. "We have your number, Mr. Kendall, and we'll call you when something happens."

But Kendall phoned again fifteen minutes later, and fifteen minutes after that, and so on all through the afternoon. He was worried the court might call and his phone would be jammed; it rang incessantly with reporters, with worried friends eager for news, and with dozens of strangers calling to offer advice. For the reporters Kendall had a polite but firm "No comment." He didn't want to rile any judges by appearing to conduct his case in the press. For friends, Kendall had an exasperated "Still nothing!"

Anyone who called with advice received a patient hearing, however, because Kendall could use all the help he could get. Unfortunately, none of the advice was of much use. One serious man said he had discovered a legal loophole: If Spenkelink filed for personal bankruptcy, the man offered earnestly, the courts would be forced to stay the execution. Kendall marveled at the man's thinking, and wished it could be so simple.

A team of Inc. Fund lawyers stopped by the motel room on their way to the federal courthouse downtown. They had a hearing before U.S. District Judge William Stafford where they planned to argue that a recent Georgia case should be applied to John Spenkelink. In that case, the U.S. Supreme Court had ordered a new trial because prosecutors had not informed the defense of the "aggravating circumstances" they would attempt to prove. Kendall wished them luck and began pacing.

He picked up the phone and called Betty Steffens, the lawyer in the governor's office who handled clemency pleas. "Betty, this is no way to handle a case of this magnitude," he said. Here he was dangling while the state supreme court decided whether to hold a hearing, and his colleagues were already in federal court. Proper procedure had gone out the window. In the next twenty-four hours they would all be rushing to the federal circuit court and on to the Supreme Court in Washington. It was chaos, and a man's life was at stake. "We need a stay from the governor," he pleaded. "Nobody can make good decisions under all this pressure."

Steffens listened politely, even sympathetically. Many of her associates believed that, deep down, she opposed the death penalty; at the very least she felt it was her duty to make sure that every possible argument was weighed. "Look," she said. "If you have any new evidence that would change the facts of the case, something new since the clemency hearing, the governor will be willing to hear it. But I have to tell you, he's not interested in rehashing what he has already heard. What do you have that's new?"

Inc. Fund investigators had been trying all weekend to locate the elusive Frank Brumm, who had vanished since his interview with *The Miami Herald*. They hoped for some new insight into the fatal episode at the Ponce de Leon Motel. So far, Kendall acknowledged ruefully, they had nothing.

"If you get something, call me," Steffens said. Kendall cradled the phone, then snatched it up again. Another call to the clerk's office. Still no word.

At 3:40 P.M., the Inc. Fund lawyers returned from federal court, looking whipped. Judge Stafford had denied everything—the stay of execution, the petition for a hearing on the Georgia case, even Spenkelink's petition to proceed *in forma pauperis*. The last was normally a routine matter, granted to prisoners who have no money to pay court costs or lawyers' fees. Judge Stafford would not even give them the crumbs. But there was no time to sulk: In thirty-six hours, the head cook at Florida State Prison was scheduled to begin preparing Spenkelink's last meal. The lawyers conferred quickly with Kendall, then scooped up their papers and headed for the airport, bound for the Circuit Court of Appeals in New Orleans.

At 5:15 P.M., the phone rang. "This is Sid White at the Florida Supreme Court. You may want to come on over because the court is about to publish an opinion." Kendall sped to the white marble courthouse, across Duval Street from the capitol, and shouldered his way through a crowd of reporters and photographers into the clerk's office. Someone handed him a depressingly brief document. As he skimmed frantically through the pages, Kendall's heart sank. He had lost on every point. He had never gotten a chance to make his passionate speech.

For the first time, it really hit him: John is going to die. I'm going to lose this case, and my client is going to die. What were the chances in New Orleans, after all? The same court had affirmed Spenkelink's sentence less than a year earlier. After that, the only thing between Spenkelink and the electric chair was the U.S. Supreme Court, the same nine men who had refused to consider Kendall's pleas in March. Beyond that, only a change in Bob Graham's heart could save him.

Kendall searched for a phone and dialed Robin Gibson. "The governor has got to reconsider," he pleaded when Gibson came on the line. "I'm telling you in good faith, I've handled dozens of capital cases over the past six years and there is no way this is a death case. I guarantee that in two years' time it will be clear to everyone that this never should have happened. It's a mistake!"

"Look," Gibson answered. "We were handed this warrant."

Kendall understood this cryptic remark to mean that Graham could not back down from a case that his predecessor had pursued. "It doesn't matter," he said. "What matters is that it's Graham's responsibility now."

"We already gave you another clemency hearing," Gibson countered. "We didn't have to do that, you know."

Kendall's business in Tallahassee was finished; he could think of nothing else to try. He checked out of the Driftwood and pointed his car back toward Starke. He had a promise to keep there. He had promised John Spenkelink that—if and when the time came—he would watch him die.

Tuesday morning. Execution Day—Minus One (1). The phone rang in Kendall's room at the Starke Best Western. "David," drawled the caller, "this is Millard Farmer." The voice was mud-thick, sorrow-laden, singular, unforgettable. Not just basso profundo, but unremittingly world-weary, as if the woes of the ages had scarred his vocal chords. It never mattered what Farmer was talking about; he always sounded as if he was trying to break the news that your child was dead.

Farmer got straight to the point. With all due respect, he said, Spenkelink's lawyers had screwed up the defense. Farmer wanted to take over the case. Of course, this was hardly the sort of thing Kendall wanted to hear; ordinarily, he would have told Farmer to get lost. But this was not an ordinary situation, and Farmer was no ordinary lawyer. He was God's angry man against the death penalty, a tall, skeletal figure with a halo of blond, graying curls atop a head that was little more than skin stretched tight on a skull. He was mysterious, prophetic, awesome.

Scion of one of middle Georgia's wealthiest families, Millard Farmer had grown up in a Tudor-style mansion on a bluff and ridden to school in a limousine. His family owned just about everything in the town of Newnan: the cotton gin, the fertilizer plant, the coal supply, the Phillips Petroleum distributorship, thousands of acres of peach orchards, and the plant where the peaches were processed. His mother's family owned a neoclassical mansion on the same bluff, and when Farmer's parents were married, it was a consolidation of wealth and influence in the style of European duchies.

Educated in segregated schools, Farmer studied business at the all-white University of Georgia, where he pledged the conservative fraternity of Kappa Alpha. But over time he began to bridle at the burden of his heritage. Out of college, running the family fertilizer business, he studied law at night school, and when he passed the bar, he scandalized the town by bringing a suit against the Coweta County jury system. He maintained that it discriminated against blacks.

In ways that the people of Newnan could hardly understand, Millard Farmer ached at the thought that his family's wealth had been wrung from the sweat of black men. "I began realizing," he once said, "how everything I had—everything my family has—had been exploited from blacks. For years, we paid them slave wages. I was part of a system taking from the poor. . . . I had to do something about it."

What Farmer did was establish, in 1976, a small nonprofit law firm devoted to fighting the death penalty. He called it Team Defense, and its tactics were cynically subversive. In Newnan, Farmer had become convinced that American justice was simply one more face of political power, and power, he believed, was closely held by white hands. He decided to make his stand in the place where that power was greatest—in capital cases, in which courts actually decided who would live and who would die. He believed that the system survived on the willingness of lawyers to play by the rules. To Millard Farmer, playing by the rules was the same thing as selling a client down the river: The only way a poor man, a black man, could get a fair trial was by breaking the rules. Farmer kicked out the jambs. In his first big Team Defense trial—the so-called Dawson Five case—Farmer whipped up a media event unlike any Georgia had seen since the civil rights upheavals of the 1960s. Later, representing a black man on charges of killing a white police officer, Farmer filed forty separate motions, dragging the case out over two years. He disqualified six judges from that case; one he eviscerated, forcing the man to admit that he had opposed school integration, joined two all-white clubs, refused to have blacks in his home, and, as district attorney, instructed his assistants never to call black defendants "Mister."

That last point was a favorite of Farmer's. He cringed each time a black man was called by his first name in court. During one trial, he demanded that the prosecutor and judge call the defendant "Mister." Judge Elie Holton declined. Farmer protested; the judge persisted. "Your Honor," Farmer finally drawled, "do you object to me calling you Elie?" That earned him jail time for contempt of court.

A deputy sheriff once slugged him in the mouth during a murder trial. Another time, a county prosecutor called a press conference on the courthouse steps and burned a law book—illustrating, he explained, Farmer's contempt for the rules. "He doesn't practice law," the prosecutor said. "He's a damned idealist. . . . And what makes our American system work is that there is no room for ideals—just the rules."

"I am the cutting edge," Farmer told an Atlanta newspaper not long before Spenkelink's death warrant was signed. At this, the last possible moment, he was asking David Kendall for a chance to prove it.

Kendall knew Farmer's record, and considered him the best "monkey-wrench thrower" in the business. This was not Kendall's style, but he had to admit that sometimes it worked. With the machinery grinding relentlessly toward John Spenkelink's death, maybe a wrench in the works was their only hope. Kendall listened, then, as Farmer told him that Inc. Fund lawyers had played too much by the rules. Farmer said Kendall had spent too much time on the high road, arguing the broad issues, relying on the federal courts to hold the line against executions. The real battle was down and dirty, case by case, life by life. It was political, not theoretical. Farmer's proposal was as simple as it was outrageous: He wanted to go into court with a lawsuit claiming that Spenkelink's attorneys—beginning with the trial lawyers and continuing through Kendall and the Inc. Fund team—had performed inadequately. "I've been through the court file, and I think there's some things y'all missed."

David Kendall weighed the alternatives. It would hurt—no doubt about it—to have another lawyer stride into court to argue that he had failed John Spenkelink. And he knew the case file cold; he hadn't missed anything. Kendall genuinely believed he had done everything possible. There was this fact, though: He had lost. Spenkelink would be killed come morning. How could he think about his own pride at a time like this?

"What do you need?" he asked finally.

"John's going to have to sign something designating me as his attorney," Farmer responded.

"We'll get it for you this morning."

Millard Farmer had his case, and there was no telling what he might do.

The case of John Arthur Spenkelink was full of riddles and a lot of plain craziness. Millard Farmer's late entry was just one example. Following Bob Graham's encounter with the protesters at the mansion, the governor had become an enigmatic figure, disappearing into a cocoon from which—in keeping with Robin Gibson's strategy—he never commented on the case. The law itself was a riddle to millions of Americans watching the case; it promised a harsh finality, but only after a hundred obscure hurdles were crossed.

Alongside those mysteries, the paradox of a weight-lifting, metal-sculpting, gourmet-cooking, art-loving prison warden was easy to understand. Just because a man makes his living in a cesspool doesn't mean he has to like the smell. Dave Brierton yearned to elevate himself and his condition, as if art and culture could inoculate him against the diseased environment in which he worked. He naturally took the same approach to the execution. His way of preparing himself was to read a book on death and dying by Elisabeth Kübler-Ross, the distinguished authority on the subject.

Kübler-Ross theorized that people facing death go through stages in their reaction: denial, anger, bargaining—ultimately leading to acceptance. Brierton was fascinated with her ideas, and in them he found a way of raising this frantic and sordid ordeal to a higher, academic plane. He studied Spenkelink for signs of each Kübler-Ross stage, and wondered how he might help him along the path. Sometimes, Brierton felt that he was the only one who truly cared about John Spenkelink as a person, not as a cause. The warden worried endlessly about preserving the man's dignity.

This got him into trouble with the scores of reporters who flocked to his twice-a-day press conferences, held at 10:30 A.M. and 2:30 P.M. in a pasture across the highway from the prison. The press wanted to know every minute detail of the procedure: voltage, amperes and cycles of electricity, the last meal, the final walk, and so forth. Brierton refused to discuss the procedure. "I was trying to maintain some dignity about this, if that makes any sense when you're talking about killing a man," he said later. The press figured he had something to hide, and their reports grew increasingly critical.

No one knew the pressure he was under. Brierton was in a vise, and every few minutes it seemed that someone turned the screw. Police agencies were picking up tips by the bushel, and dumping them all on him. Riots were being planned, they reported. A scheme was being hatched to bomb the prison. There were plots to kill the warden. Exactly what the hell was Brierton supposed to do about any of that? Who was he, Dick Tracy? "Look," he finally told the lawmen. "You take care of things outside the prison, and I'll take care of things inside."

In his office, Brierton's phone rang constantly, and when he got home each day, exhausted in body and spirit, a stack of messages awaited him. Up to now, he had been a little-known man in a tiny Florida town; there was no reason not to list his phone number. Callers shouted "Murderer!" and hung up, but he got no more pleasure from the callers who said, "We're behind you," or "Fry the sumbitch!" There were calls with phony stays of execution, people claiming to represent the governor or the U.S. Supreme Court. One message supposedly came from Brierton's boss, Louie Lee Wainwright, but when Brierton dialed the number, some anti–death penalty nut answered the phone. "Listen, you lying bastard," Brierton exploded, "don't you ever, ever, pull something like that again!"

That weekend, hoping to escape for a few hours, he had taken his wife to dinner at a restaurant in town. But as the Briertons crossed the parking lot, a man approached them and stuck out his hand. "Great job!" he said by way of a greeting. "Fry 'em!" The warden and his wife turned and went home.

He couldn't pick up a newspaper or turn on the television or tune in the radio without hearing Spenkelink's name. By Tuesday morning, Dave Brierton was beginning to wonder what terrible sin he had committed that, of all the wardens at all the prisons in all the land, this was happening to him. And then there was the endless negotiating with Spenkelink's friends over details of the final hours. At 9 A.M. on Tuesday, another delegation entered Brierton's office. David Kendall was there, along with Joe Ingle, a quietly intense Church of Christ minister who headed the Southern Coalition on Jails and Prisons; Susan Cary, a lawyer from nearby Gainesville who frequently pleaded for better conditions on death row; and Tom Feamster, the Episcopal priest from a local parish who had begun counseling Spenkelink two years before.

The meeting got off to a rocky start when Brierton cited some Kübler-Ross. "John's in his anger stage," he announced. It was the wrong way to begin.

"Maybe John's angry because you are trying to kill him," Ingle said.

Brierton let that pass. The rest of the agenda was, by now, tiresome, and the session quickly became snagged on two familiar points: contact visits and a last Communion. Brierton said he would allow one contact visit and one only. Spenkelink could choose who it would be. When Susan Cary started to object, the warden cut her off. It was his prison, he said, and his mind was made up. But Cary persisted. The warden's ruling would force Spenkelink to choose between embracing his mother or his girlfriend before he died. What kind of a choice was that? Cary chose her words gently and diplomatically, which Brierton greatly appreciated. Gradually she wore away at him until he relented. Spenkelink could have thirty minutes with his girlfriend and forty-five minutes with his mother.

Kendall pushed on to the second sticking point. "We have been doing some research," he said. "And we've found it was customary in the past to allow a man to spend the last hours with the clergyman of his choice."

I don't know anything about that, Brierton said. "You have to understand," Feamster offered, "John is a Christian. The sacrament of the Holy Eucharist is the greatest symbol of his life in Christ. You can't deny him that."

And Brierton snapped: "You don't have to tell me about Communion. I'm a good Catholic. I grew up with the Jesuits at Loyola Academy."

"Then you understand."

"What I understand is that I have no way of knowing what psychotropic drugs might wind up in the Communion wine. No offense. But that's my concern. I'm not going to let this thing get out of hand."

Brierton considered telling them about a conversation he had once had with John Spenkelink. As Brierton recalled it, the prisoner had said, "You will never execute me. If worse comes to worst, I'll kill myself. But you will never put me in the electric chair." The moment passed, however, and Brierton said simply, "That's how it's gonna be."

"You can test the wine if you want," Feamster offered. "You can provide the wine, it's fine with me."

Brierton wasn't budging. "There's no way I'm going to get involved in messing with Communion wine," he said.

Everyone was edgy. When Kendall spoke, his voice was low, but there was a ragged edge to it. "I'm going to have to call the governor's office on this," he said. "You can't deny this man his choice of clergy."

"You call," said Brierton. "I'll listen to the governor's people. But I don't think they can say anything that will change my mind."

"There's the press tent right outside," Feamster said. "I've got no problem with going right out there and telling the whole world that you won't let John take a last Communion."

"Do what you have to do," Brierton answered, and the meeting was over.

Kendall went to a nearby office; there, he placed another call to Betty Steffens, the governor's aide, to complain about Brierton's decision. As always, Steffens listened politely but was noncommittal. The governor's staff didn't want to interfere with the warden's prerogatives.

As he left the prison administration building, Kendall passed the switchboard where Mary King was working frantically over a chirping, blinking console. Stepping into the brilliant sunshine, he paused to study the scene. The prison grounds, normally empty and forlorn, were filled with bustling lawmen. Traffic was backed up along the narrow highway—cars full of journalists and protesters and government officials and gawkers. In the distance, Kendall saw tents and awnings, some pitched by news crews, others by devoted citizens—a few supporting the execution, many more opposed to it—who wanted a bit of shade as they kept their vigil. Helicopters *whup-whup-whup*ed overhead. And at the very edge of the lawyer's vision, cattle grazed, contented, surreal.

Kendall recalled Brierton's frequent refrain: "I won't let this turn into a circus." What was this?

And then he realized that he had heard nothing about Willie Darden. Everyone was so certain that the courts would block the other execution. Kendall had hardly given it a thought.

Robert Augustus Harper knew he had been forgotten, and it burned him up. Scandalous: the NAACP's Inc. Fund pouring everything into saving Spenkclink, a white man, while he was left almost alone to stop the execution of coal-black Willie Darden. Harper was a dashing young Tallahassee attorney who looked as if he had just finished posing for a statue to honor the Confederate dead. He had the piercing eyes, the angular nose, and the neatly trimmed beard of a rebel cavalry officer, and diction and rebelliousness to match. He was a man to flutter the heart of Scarlett O'Hara, in every respect but one. His cause was defending black criminals. A dozen times or more, Harper strode into courtrooms and unleashed his fiery rhetoric to save a defendant from a death sentence, and he'd won every time. Now he had picked up Darden's case on appeal. Where David Kendall's tactics centered on civility and politesse, Harper approached his cases ablaze. When the call came alerting him to Darden's death warrant, Harper launched himself on a seventy-two-hour binge of drafting briefs, combing law books, and searching old records.

Monday morning he was at the county courthouse in Bartow, Georgia, waiting for the doors to open. When they did, he went straight to the clerk's office to file his appeal. Quite deliberately, he asked a black man to carry the supporting files into the building; as Harper expected, sheriff's deputies stopped the man at the front door.

Harper then flew on a chartered plane from Bartow to Tallahassee, where he filed papers with the Florida Supreme Court. The appeals in Bartow and Tallahassee were mere formalities in Harper's mind; both the trial court and the state supreme court had already considered and denied appeals from Darden. But they were necessary steps between Harper and the federal courts. From Tallahassee, he flew to Tampa, and he was waiting at the federal courthouse when the state courts denied him again. He immediately filed his federal appeal.

On Tuesday morning, U.S. District Judge Terrell Hodges took the bench to hear the matter. The judge appeared to be in a bad mood, glowering from his lofty perch. Couldn't help noticing the protesters on the courthouse steps, said the judge. The ones waving signs and chanting, "No death!" Hodges focused on the defense table. Mr. Harper, he asked, do you know who is responsible for this? Are *you* responsible?

"No, Your Honor," Harper drawled sweetly.

The judge seemed skeptical but moved on. Harper explained that he wasn't seeking an immediate decision on Darden's appeal. These are important issues, he said; they shouldn't be decided in a few hours under such horrific pressure. What he needed was for Hodges to take the appeal under consideration and stay the execution until he could hear all the evidence and properly weigh the arguments.

Hodges listened impassively, as judges do. When he had heard enough, he rose and swept from the courtroom. Drained by days of frantic research and frenzied typing and wild flights back and forth across the state, Harper suddenly could do nothing but wait. At 5:15 P.M., less than fourteen hours before the appointed execution, Hodges published his judgment. Darden's appeals, he ruled, deserved a full hearing in federal court. For the time being, Darden was saved.

Twenty hours from Old Sparky, John Spenkelink was sassy and buoyant as he met at The Wall with a stream of friends and supporters. Through the thick glass, Spenkelink joked with Joe Ingle about the guard keeping watch on his isolation cell. The guy's a nervous wreck, Spenkelink reported. Why should he be nervous? I'm the one they want to kill.

After lunch, he met with Kendall, who told him about Millard Farmer and his wrench-throwing mission. Kendall tried to convey with his voice an optimism he lacked in his heart. There was still no word from the circuit court in New Orleans, but he anticipated bad news. Through a guard, Spenkelink passed over the statement he had drafted for the press. Kendall took the pages and read them. Most of the statement dealt with Spenkelink's wish to speak to the governor. All things considered, the tone was reasonable and calm. Kendall approved. And the prisoner said: "There's one other thing I want to ask Brierton for. I'm sure he won't deny me a favor." There was a glint in Spenkelink's eye.

"What's that?" Kendall asked.

"I want him to hold my hand when they throw the switch."

The visit ended about 4 P.M., when Kendall was summoned to the assistant warden's office. Richard Dugger's tone was businesslike. He wanted to lay out some rules. They might seem cold, Dugger conceded, but they were necessary, and they were final: Carla Key—Spenkelink's girlfriend—would meet with John from 7 to 7:30 that evening. Lois Spenkelink would visit immediately afterward, from 7:30 to 8:15. One embrace and one kiss would be permitted at the beginning of each visit. Visitor and prisoner would be allowed to hold hands, but only above the table, in view of the guards. Another embrace and kiss would be allowed at the end of each visit. Was that clear? "And the superintendent has decided against your request for Communion," Dugger said.

Kendall was stunned. He had assumed his phone call to Betty Steffens would settle the Communion issue in Spenkelink's favor. He stormed from Dugger's office to a nearby telephone and began trying to reach the governor's office again. Before he made contact, however, a call came for him on another line. It was the news from New Orleans. The Circuit Court of Appeals had denied all of Spenkelink's claims.

A man thinks he's prepared for bad news, but then it comes. Kendall felt sick. They would file an appeal with the U.S. Supreme Court, and maybe a liberal justice would give them a brief stay, but he could see no way they could get five votes to make the stay last. The high court had already washed its hands of this case. Oh God, Kendall mumbled. It's over.

Ray Marky exhaled a lungful of smoke and let a tired grin crawl across his face. "This guy is gone!" he thought to himself. He heard the verdict from New Orleans within minutes of the call to Kendall, and he shared his opponent's analysis of the situation. Marky could hardly believe it. After nearly seven years of pressing the death penalty, after digesting literally tons of paper, converting that knowledge into hundreds of legal briefs—after all he and Georgieff had been through—the "pussies" were finally gonna let it happen.

The pussies, in Marky's view, were politicians who talked tough but had no guts. Marky and Georgieff were surprised, frankly, that Bob Graham was standing up to the pressure so resolutely. They'd had him pegged for a wimp. The media, too, campaigning to make heroes of the scumbags on death row. And the judges. The judges were worst of all in Marky's mind, wringing their hands, stroking their chins, but never biting the bullet to let a man die. They were sworn to uphold the law, weren't they? Well, the death penalty was the law of the land. How many times had Marky and Georgieff, the odd couple from the attorney general's office, stood up in court and said, basically, "Jesus, Judge, let's get on with it!" Only to learn that the judge was a pussy. Well, Marky had dreamed of the day that the wavering would finally end, and now that day had come. Spenkelink was a goner.

The bone-deep fatigue Marky felt after three nearly sleepless days gave way to a giddy rush. This case was making history. Ray Marky's case! He could have gone home right then and hit the sack, but he was goosed on adrenaline and high on victory. Or he could have put on his black leather jacket and gone for a ride on his motorcycle—people laughed behind his back at little Ray on his big bike, trying to be a tough guy. They wouldn't laugh now. He had won his biggest case— and the victory was not just his; it belonged to all law-abiding people. There was a principle at stake. A sovereign state like Florida must be allowed to enforce the laws passed by its duly elected legislature. The people of Florida demanded the death penalty and now they would get it.

He could have gone home, or gone roaring down some long, straight road with his bike rumbling between his legs . . . but instead he decided to wait around the office for the final word from Washington. What a sweet moment that would be.

∴

As night came on, the horizon went blue to orange to red to black, and the pine shadows crept onto the empty scar of the prison grounds. Harsh vapor lights gathered strength within the fences, illuminating the no-man's-land where darkness never settled. Red and blue emergency lights strobed wildly as police cars came and went on unknown missions. The prison yard, the road leading to the prison, and the highways funneling to the prison road were watched by hundreds of troopers, deputies, and guardsmen. A roadblock at the foot of the prison road was designated Checkpoint Bravo, and no one passed without prior approval.

The pasture across the highway was filled with protesters who joined hands and sang folk songs, slowly swaying back and forth. Between songs they chanted, "Death row must go! Death row must go!" Television lights glared on one face or another, recorded it, then returned it to the dusk. One young woman, apparently trying to express her love of freedom, stripped off her clothes and ran naked. On the other side of the road, the prison administration building was crowded with cops loitering over coffee and cigarettes; the little building was cloudy with smoke and buzzing with gossip. SWAT team members strutted in their stenciled windbreakers, while the weekend warriors of the National Guard wore camouflage pants and drab green T-shirts.

It was eight o'clock. Somewhere in the bowels of the prison, John Spenkelink was saying good-bye to his mother. In half an hour, David Kendall would see his client for the last time. He waited in the administration building, watching the lawmen come and go. His gut was in a knot, his blood was pounding, his nerves were jangling. Dave Brierton entered the building, headed for his office, and Kendall shouted, "What's it gonna be?" as he moved toward the warden. Would Spenkelink's ministers, Feamster and Ingle, be allowed into the prison or not?

Brierton stopped, turned, and said he had already given his answer. Kendall snapped, for the first time all week. All the frustration of this, the worst experience of his life, spilled into the smoky air. He began yelling at Brierton, protesting the decision to bar the clergymen. The more he yelled, the higher his voice got, and his face went red.

The cops and guardsmen and prison officers stopped buzzing and stared as the lawyer ripped into the warden. Kendall's tirade was a furious mix of rant and legalisms. Prison tradition, he repeated over and over, dictated that a doomed man could enjoy the consolation of his chosen pastor through his last night on Earth.

Brierton was as frayed as Kendall, and began shouting back. Get this straight: I'm running this prison! I've made my decision! No more changes!

"You're violating years of practice!"

"Your history is all wrong!"

"I've heard it from your own people!"

"I don't give a damn where you heard it."

Brierton's face reddened to match Kendall's. Their voices, rough with fatigue, hoarsened at each syllable. Kendall crowded in toward Brierton but the warden wouldn't back down. For one crazy moment, Kendall thought they were on the verge of throwing punches. And though he knew the huge warden could beat him bloody, he no longer cared. He felt his hands balling into fists . . . but then he became aware of the cops and soldiers staring at him. Christ! They were grinning. His nightmare was their sideshow.

He drew a long breath, and when he spoke again, his voice was low and tight. "You're giving me no choice," Kendall said. "We're calling a press conference for nine o'clock. The whole world is going to know about it. This will have to be on your conscience."

Brierton's voice dropped and tightened, too. "My conscience can handle it," he answered.

"I'm sure it can," Kendall spat.

Twenty minutes later, as Joe Ingle prepared the press conference, Kendall sat in a prison office waiting for a call from Millard Farmer. Dave Brierton appeared in the doorway of the office and motioned wordlessly. Kendall followed him outside. The night sky was filling with stars. A breeze freshened over them, a welcome caress. Brierton spoke calmly, as if the screaming match had never happened. Tell me something about these ministers, he said. What made Kendall think they were reliable?

Kendall chose his words carefully; he did not want to let this olive branch slip away. For what seemed like the hundredth time, he tried to explain that Spenkelink's supporters would not abet a suicide. "I'd like you to see this from my point of view," Brierton said. He wanted to do what was right, but he was determined to keep control of events that were spiraling wildly beyond anyone's ken. The threats, the protests, the chaos. Whether John Spenkelink lived or died was far beyond the warden's control—that question was in the hands of politicians and judges he would never meet. Brierton could not stop it, he could not change it. If he refused to carry out their orders, in the blink of an eye they could find someone to take his place. His only power was over the tone of the proceedings. For the dignity of a man on his way to death, Brierton was not going to allow any stunts, any headline grabbing, any debacle.

He offered a compromise: One minister would be allowed in, and it would be Tom Feamster. The priest had made a favorable impression at the meeting that morning. Brierton recognized that Feamster was strongly opposed to the death penalty—but he seemed to have a better grip on reality than some of the others. Certainly, Feamster was noth-ing like the Episcopal stereotype: no bumbling vicar out of an English novel or thin-lipped headmaster of a Connecticut prep school. In fact, Tom Feamster was one of the rare men who actually towered over Dave Brierton.

A hulking six feet eight inches, the priest had hands the size of an ordinary man's feet and feet the size of serving platters. Tom Feamster had been a star defensive end at Florida State University, drafted by the Los Angeles Rams in 1956 and quickly traded to the Baltimore Colts. He spent his first NFL training camp blocking against the legendary Big Daddy Lipscomb, who greeted the rookie by lining up opposite him and growling, "You scared, white boy?" The next thing Feamster heard was the sound of Lipscomb's forearm smashing into his head like a baseball bat. He played both ways during the '56 season, tackle on offense and end on defense, and even kicked the Colts' extra points. His football future seemed golden. There was just one problem: At the end of his rookie year, Feamster realized that he hated football.

"I played football because people told me how wonderful I was," he once said. "I reached the point where I wanted to know, 'Hey, without football, what am I worth?' " So he quit, and wandered from one job to the next, restlessly searching for something with meaning. One morning in 1965, he walked into the office of Rev. Jim Hardison, Tallahassee's best-loved Episcopal priest. "Jim," Feamster said, "why am I here? Not here in this office. Why was I born?" Hardison helped him find his answer.

In 1969 he entered seminary, and half a dozen years later Reverend Feamster was assigned to a small parish not far from Florida State Prison. He began weekly visits with various lifers and men on death row, offering advice and compassion. But Feamster was unlike many of the other well-meaning Christians who visited the prison: He knew a con when he saw one. Among the lifers he counseled was Jack "Murph the Surf" Murphy, infamous beachboy, jewel thief, and cold-blooded killer, a man with an angle on everything. When Murphy arrived for one of their sessions wearing a cross on his prison uniform and saying he had "accepted Jesus in his heart," Feamster concluded it was just another con. And a good one, given the number of devout Baptists on the parole board. "You know, Jack, you're going to get yourself out of here with that act," Feamster said. (And he was right. In 1986, Murph the Surf was paroled after serving sixteen years of his double-life-plus-twenty. He announced he was becoming an evangelist, and said, "Sometimes, God has a sense of humor.") Feamster met John Spenkelink in 1977, after his first death warrant was signed, and the relationship they built was like a troubled kid's with his tough-but-hip uncle. Spenkelink never tried to con him, Feamster said. "He was like a little boy in so many respects."

Tom Feamster could stay the night with the prisoner. That was Brierton's offer, and Kendall quickly agreed to convey the compromise to Spenkelink. The prisoner accepted. The threatened press conference was canceled.

Half an hour later, the prison erupted. It started with a few scattered inmates shouting threats at the guards. "Kill one of ours, we'll kill some of yours!" The shouting spread.

Bang! Bang! Bang! The prisoners began pounding on the bars of their cells. *Bang! Bang! Bang!* in cacophonous rhythm. A chant took shape. Save John Spenkelink! Save John Spenkelink! *Bang! Bang! Bang!* Save John Spenkelink!

Someone threw a book. It thudded on the floor. Another thud. Another. Guards trying to quiet the protest found themselves dodging a fusillade of books, shoes, juice cartons, bars of soap. Then a wad of flaming newspaper was added to the barrage. Within seconds, scores of fires were set. Prisoners stripped the sheets from their beds, snatched up towels and T-shirts, shredded old magazines, and put matches to everything. The tiers of cells quickly filled with smoke. Trapped inmates lurched to their sinks to soak shirts and washcloths, then gasped for breath through the wet filters. Still the banging and shouting and chanting continued. Save John Spenkelink!

Outside the prison, this outburst was faintly audible but brilliantly visible as the burning missiles flickered behind the distant windows. An inmate managed to loft a flaming bedsheet through two banks of bars and out an open window, and it trailed sparks like a comet as it drifted to the ground. Cheers went up from the execution opponents; a low groan came from the scattered death penalty supporters. The opponents saw this outburst as a moment of heroic bravery, the inmates expressing solidarity with a doomed brother. The supporters feared any disruption at such a fragile moment, so close to their goal of the death penalty's return.

To Brierton, it was a damned nuisance. He was not a big believer in romantic notions of brotherhood among prisoners. In his experience, prisoners would do just about anything for a little excitement, and this was nothing more than a welcome excuse. But the nuisance was also very dangerous; few things are as menacing to a prison as fire. In the claustrophobic guts of a maximum-security prison, a little fire is all it takes to suffocate a man in a cage. With the first alarm, he rushed from his office into the center of the prison, where he met a squad of officers in riot gear, their shields and batons poised.

Richard Dugger, the assistant superintendent, was already inside, commanding the operation. Earlier that evening, Dugger had ordered all prisoners locked in their cells. It was a night made for trouble, and he figured they couldn't do much harm from their cells. He hadn't counted on fire. Dugger called for the hoses, only to learn that they were stowed away in closets. Long minutes passed as the hoses were located, fixed, then rushed into the flaming corridors.

At last the water came on, and within minutes the fires were out. Up and down the cellblocks, prisoners coughed and swore. A few still chanted. *Save John Spenkelink!* But the protest was over. As the smoke crept along the ceilings and drifted from the windows, guards began storming the cells of the instigators, one by one, roughly stripping them of their possessions. And Richard Dugger put out the word: The next time a fire broke out—at the first sign of a flame—the guards had instructions to soak the offender in his cell, along with everything he owned. Safety first.

John Spenkelink was with David Kendall during the eruption, and the lawyer left the prison alongside the riot squad. They scarcely registered on his worn emotions. Everything was unreal. Spenkelink's reaction to the inmate protest is something Kendall has never discussed —the meeting was so draining and difficult, and the lawyer balked at reliving the ordeal. He said only that Spenkelink was sapped by the visits with his mother and girlfriend and had asked edgy questions about the progress of the case. Kendall had tried to give encouraging answers. Millard Farmer was still working, somewhere.

But Kendall knew that once he left, guards would lead Spenkelink back to his death-watch cell. Tom Feamster would join him for the long hours of the night. Around 5 A.M. they would feed him. Then they would kill him. Unreal.

At the Best Western, Kendall paced and fretted. What was Farmer doing?

With fewer than twelve hours left, Millard Farmer was in his Team Defense office, atop a parking garage in Atlanta, surrounded by a legal team scraped together in the space of a few hours. Young lawyers rifled through law books and fed citations to a woman hunched over a chattering IBM Selectric typewriter.

Margery Pitts Hames was one of those who had agreed to help. She had made her name as a skillful civil rights litigator while trying the case of *Doe v. Bolton,* a companion case to *Roe v. Wade,* the abortion-rights landmark. Professor William Bowers of Northeastern University pitched in too. Author of a massive tome on the death penalty, *Legal Homicide,* Bowers was one of the nation's leading authorities on the emerging disparity in death sentences between criminals who killed whites and criminals who killed blacks. Though he had testified in Spenkelink's earlier, losing, appeal, Bowers remained convinced that racial discrepancies in death sentences would one day render capital punishment unconstitutional across the board.

And then there was Farmer's ace in the hole—Ramsey Clark, former attorney general of the United States. Few lawyers could outdo Farmer at pissing people off, but Ramsey Clark was one of them, in a league of his own. The son of a conservative Supreme Court justice, Clark appeared cut from the same plain Texan mold as his patron, Lyndon Johnson. Clark tended toward high-water trousers and short-sleeved dress shirts and kept his hair slicked down and cut high above the ears. He spoke slowly, in a soft Texas twang. And his demeanor was so homespun that, even at the height of his power and influence, he could easily be mistaken for a lawyer who handled wills, property disputes, and the occasional divorce in some small town, probably out toward Austin.

When Clark left government in 1969 and threw himself into opposing the Vietnam War, he became a darling of the Left, but his fame turned to infamy when he visited Hanoi, the enemy capital. He was unique: a man who had reached the top law enforcement post in the country, only to conclude that his country's government was an evil to be thwarted. The death penalty was, to him, just one more odious abuse of power.

Farmer agreed, and figured it couldn't hurt to have an attorney general by his side, regardless of politics. So when he learned that Clark was arriving in Florida to join the protesters at the state prison, he left a message at the Starke motel where Clark was registered. The message was relayed to Clark at a gas station pay phone. Clark returned the call and Farmer drafted him to his team.

Because of the late hour, every court in the country was closed, and none would reopen before the appointed hour of Spenkelink's

death. Farmer's plan was to find a single judge from the Fifth Federal
Circuit, go to his home, and plead for an emergency stay of execution.
Even though the New Orleans Circuit Court of Appeals had denied
Spenkelink earlier that day, Farmer believed each judge retained the
power to issue a stay. It would be a grievous break with decorum, but
what did Millard Farmer care about decorum when a man's life was in
the balance? A stay from a single judge would be legally binding, and
that was all that counted.

In approaching the Fifth Circuit, Farmer had reason to be hopeful. During the agonizing years of the civil rights struggle, the Fifth
Circuit had emerged as a potent force on behalf of equal rights. After
the U.S. Supreme Court had decided *Brown v. Board of Education,* the
burden of enforcing desegregation had fallen mostly to the Fifth Circuit. Judges of the circuit had literally risked their lives to bury Jim
Crow; the leading lights—John Minor Wisdom, Robert Rives, John
Brown, and Elbert Tuttle, known as "The Four" to their enemies—
stood up to death threats, bomb scares, burning crosses. During the
ugly years of the 1960s, civil rights leaders came to think of these
judges the way a sailor thinks of a hurricane hole: If they could only
guide their causes through the raging storms to the Fifth Circuit, they
would be safe. Now Farmer and his ad hoc team had decided to turn to
one of those legendary judges for help. As the typewriters rattled in the
outer office, Ramsey Clark placed a call to the home of the Honorable
Elbert Parr Tuttle.

"Those who think Martin Luther King desegregated the South
don't know Elbert Tuttle and the record of the Fifth Circuit Court of
Appeals," a veteran reporter of the civil rights movement once said.
Tuttle, a retired general in the National Guard and a reformer of Georgia's Republican Party, served the Fifth Circuit as chief judge through
the roiling years of desegregation. He had retired to "senior" status,
which had reduced his workload but left much of his legal authority
undiminished. After eight decades of life, Tuttle remained the same
formidable figure who had once commanded his National Guard troop
to fix bayonets in defense of a black man about to be lynched. Precise
but fearless—never a stickler over the letter of the law—Tuttle made an
art of finding the grounds to do the thing he felt needed to be done.

He believed judges should lead, when necessary, not just wait until the dust had cleared to adjudicate over the ruins. This was exactly the sort of man Farmer needed: a judge who would take the lead and let the niceties be damned.

Some would charge, in the aftermath, that Ramsey Clark had called Tuttle because he was owed some sort of favor, but Clark and Farmer forever denied it. They insisted that Clark had called Tuttle simply because he knew the judge would be aghast at the suggestion that a racially tainted law might send a man to the electric chair, and because he trusted that Tuttle, if persuaded of an injustice, would not hesitate to try to stop it. Besides, Clark figured, the government frequently went "shopping" for friendly jurists; why shouldn't a defense team look for a potential friend?

On the phone, Clark asked if he could come to Tuttle's home with an emergency petition. Quietly, the judge said yes. Farmer's team took two cars to the Tuttle home in suburban Atlanta. Professor Bowers waited outside while the lawyers went to the door. The judge's wife greeted them and ushered Farmer, Clark, and Hames into Tuttle's study. It was now after 10 P.M., past the judge's bedtime; still, he commanded the study like a courtroom.

Tuttle asked why they had come to him. Ramsey Clark explained his belief that politics had come to overshadow the progress of justice, that the rush to resume executions was snowballing through the courts. John Spenkelink, he said, had become a mere token. Someone needed to stem the avalanche. Tuttle had the jurisdiction, and he had the will.

The judge nodded, and asked about the issues involved. Farmer quickly outlined his case: Spenkelink had not been competently represented, at trial or in his appeals. His court-appointed lawyer had waived his chance to make an oral presentation in his original hearing before the Florida Supreme Court. "A stunning course of action," Clark interjected. Farmer concurred. Potentially critical points were forfeited by that decision, he told the judge. "This," said Farmer, in his sorrowful drawl, "is a tragedy of justice."

Then Clark resumed. Briefly, but passionately, he made the case that Spenkelink was facing execution for purely political reasons: He was a white man, whose death would inoculate Florida from 150 years of racial discrimination in capital cases; he was a drifter with a foreign-sounding name on trial in a Deep South town; he was a pretty boy who had raised the specter of homosexuality during his trial. Lastly, Clark summarized the data Bowers had collected, suggesting that racial discrimination still shadowed the death penalty. He insisted that, even though the courts had passed on the issue, the full implications of these statistics had not been considered. This case, Clark concluded, has no business being a death case. Someone must step in and stop it. Given a stay, Clark argued, cooler heads would prevail.

Judge Tuttle listened solemnly. Several times during the speeches he had interrupted with questions, probing at the facts, but more importantly probing the sincerity of his visitors. When Clark finished, the judge took a deep breath. For a time, he said nothing. Then: "It seems to me this needs to be heard. Society has a right to have this matter heard. Did you bring an order for me to sign?"

Farmer was, frankly, amazed; but his amazement evaporated into chagrin when everyone turned to him for the necessary document. He didn't have it. "We were like a congregation gathered to pray for rain and nobody brought an umbrella," he said later. It dawned on Farmer that he had no idea what a stay of execution in a Florida case should say. He wasn't even licensed to practice in Florida. Stammering apologies to the judge, he picked up the phone and called David Kendall in Starke.

"This is Millard Farmer," he said.

Kendall wanted news; the suspense was nearly unbearable. But Farmer cut him off. "Now David, I'm not in a position to tell you anything right now. I just have a question. Supposing we were to get a stay, how would it read?"

"Millard, don't play with me. What's happening?"

"I can't say right now. I'm just asking your legal advice. What should a stay of execution have in it?"

Nervously, eagerly, Kendall dictated a stay of execution over the phone. On a yellow legal pad, Farmer took it down, frantically, unevenly, as if a moment's delay would give Judge Tuttle time to change his mind. His writing alternated wildly between capital letters and lowercase; in places, the letters ran off the edge of the page. There were

cross-outs and write-overs and misspelled words. As usual, the condemned man's name was misspelled: JohN SpeNKlinK. But it was a
legal order, "that a stay of execution of the sentence of death imposed
upon John Spenklink [*sic*] scheduled to be carried out at 7:00 AM
Wednesday May 23, 1979 is hereby stayed until futher [*sic*] notice of this
court."

At 11:30 P.M. it was signed.

Elbert P. Tuttle
Judge Court of Appeals
Fifth Circuit.

Kendall waited impatiently for Farmer to call again. What was
happening? He had dictated a stay of execution. Could Farmer possibly
have found a judge to sign one? That was the obvious explanation, but
it seemed too much to hope for. Time crawled, like a child's time
awaiting Christmas; time stretched, like the horrific instant before a car
wreck. At last the telephone jangled. Farmer had just left Tuttle's house
and rushed to the nearest pay phone. The news was good, better than
good, excellent, it was stunning.

Unbelievable! Somehow, Farmer had lodged a wrench in the machinery. John Spenkelink would live. Relief surged through Kendall
like a drug, poured into the numb parts of him and set them tingling.
He felt the rich, simple joy of a sleeper who wakes, trembling, to
discover that the nightmare is not real. He felt the sweet luxury of an
answered prayer.

They had to get word to the prison. It seemed that half the world
was ringing the prison switchboard that night, so Kendall decided to
drive out to see Brierton in person while Farmer contacted the governor's office in Tallahassee. Before hanging up, he asked Farmer to
dictate the stay order back to him; he wanted to have something official
to present to the warden. As Kendall started out the door, the phone
called him back. This time it was Joel Berger, an Inc. Fund lawyer in
Washington. More good news: U.S. Supreme Court Justice Thurgood
Marshall, unaware of Tuttle's action, had granted a stay of his own. This

was a tenuous gesture; they all knew it—as soon as the entire Court convened, the justices could, by majority vote, dissolve Marshall's order. Most likely, they would. Still . . .

Incredible! Not one stay, but two. The sun would rise on a living, breathing John Spenkelink. Word spread quickly through the motel. Joe Ingle grabbed Deborah Fins, another Inc. Fund lawyer, and spun her in a wild dance across the parking lot. They hopped into a car and headed off to tell the protesters outside the prison. Kendall was about to follow when, on impulse, he snatched up the phone and tried the prison number. He expected a busy signal, but instead heard one ring and then the voice of Mary King. She patched the call through to Brierton.

"We've got a stay! We've got two stays!" Kendall exulted. Brierton had already heard of Tuttle's action. Kendall quickly read the order from Thurgood Marshall. "Obviously, you should stop everything," he said.

"Until I hear different," Brierton answered, "the execution is off."

The protesters hugged and cried and laughed and cheered as word of the stays spread through them. "Thank you, Jesus!" a woman wailed, and another, the mother of a man on death row, broke down sobbing, her shoulders shivering under the weight of emotion. "It's a miracle," said Susan Cary, the anti-death-penalty lawyer.

Minutes later, another cheer went up, far away, inside the prison. The news had broken on television.

John Spenkelink sat chain-smoking in his death-watch cell, his butt on a rolled-up mattress, his back against the wall, idly watching a television set just beyond the bars. Tom Feamster sat on a folding chair outside the cell.

Johnny Carson was on. Several beeps interrupted the chitchat, and a string of letters began crawling across the bottom of the screen. An urgent bulletin: The execution was off. Both men let out a long breath, and Feamster pumped Spenkelink's hand through the bars. Spenkelink smiled broadly, plainly relieved, and said, "Thank God!" But he didn't seem surprised. It was as if he had been expecting precisely this.

Feamster had his doubts that the stay would last, but he kept them to himself, and simply echoed the prisoner: "Thank God." Then a guard announced that the minister would have to leave. Spenkelink was just another prisoner now, with no special rights to a visitor.

In Washington, rain fell softly, steadily, on the white marble grandeur of the U.S. Supreme Court, and on a small group of protesters across the street keeping a vigil against the death penalty. There were perhaps fifty of them, religious leaders, civil rights workers, a member of the District of Columbia City Council. They had been there since early evening. At half past midnight, a man burst from the building, running wildly. "Marshall stayed the execution!" he shouted, and a voice called back, "Amen."

Tears of relief mixed with rain on their faces as the protesters shouted and clapped their hands. A sweet, soulful voice began singing:

Paul and Silas bound in jail
Had no money for their bail.
Keep your eyes on the prize,
Hold on, hold on.

Ray Marky was in his office, the glow of victory burning down like a candle in his gut as he savored the prospect of a well-earned sleep. Near midnight, he began gathering his things, sure there would be no news until morning.

"He just got a stay from Marshall!" The face of a young lawyer appeared at Marky's door, then disappeared. Marky sagged back into his chair. *My God—the pussies.* He rolled the bulletin through his brain. Marshall. That wasn't so bad. They would have the justices polled and the majority would surely dissolve the stay. Marshall was a fanatic.

Another face appeared at the door. "They got a stay out of Judge Tuttle."

Tuttle? Jesus! Now Marky was confused. Elbert Tuttle was retired, serving on "senior judge" status; he had no business on this case. What in the name of Christ was going on? And now George Georgieff was in the doorway, looking as angry as Marky felt. "Forget Tuttle," he said. "He's probably senile. Forget about him."

"Yeah," Marky answered. "But what are we supposed to do about it?"

"That's what I'm trying to tell you," Georgieff said. "Ignore him. He has no jurisdiction. Just tell the governor to ignore him. Go ahead with it."

"For chrissakes, he's a federal judge," Marky countered. "We can't just ignore him." The truth was, no one knew exactly what jurisdiction Tuttle had. There had never been a case precisely like this. The glow in Marky's gut turned to a dark, hot hole. Seven years of work, for what? For this? Seven years of grinding toward the finish line, and now some retired liberal judge comes in and stops the race a stride from the tape? "Aw, God, George," Marky said. They were stymied, weren't they?

Marky collected his things and went home, but he couldn't sleep. After an hour in bed he was still wound so tight he could hardly lie still; his engine was still revving past the red line. He'd been over and over and over the papers . . . over and over and over the cases . . . over and over the transcripts . . . over and over his pleadings . . . the air blue with cigarette smoke, his stomach boiling with coffee acid. It was final exams to the tenth power, all his biggest cases rolled into one. He was so close to winning. You don't just stop—boom!—game's over. Momentum kept his mind racing, churning, straining.

It wasn't fair. Marky stared into the darkness. Maybe someone could reach Tuttle, talk some sense into him, explain the law, clear up the facts. But who? Certainly not him. He remembered a plane trip he'd taken to Atlanta many years earlier. He had been a young prosecutor, headed to a hearing on a lawsuit brought by the dean of Florida's civil rights bar, an attorney named Tobias Simon. Simon was a firebrand, an idealist, a cage rattler; he cranked out lawsuits by the ream.

He was always in court somewhere, sticking up for the underdog (or, as Marky preferred to call them, "the bad guys"), and he won with surprising frequency. Simon was a formidable opponent, and young Ray Marky was even more jittery than usual about facing him. So when the plane thumped to the runway and rolled to the gate, Marky sprang from his seat and snapped open the overhead bin. It dropped—*thunk!*—and Marky's briefcase lurched out and fell on the head of an elderly gentleman in the next row. Popped him a good one.

The old man was stunned, but only for a second. Then, as Marky remembered it, he turned in his seat and started yelling: You stupid this. You ignorant that. As if Marky had done it on purpose. Ray tried apologizing, but it didn't do any good. Eventually, the guy ranted himself out. What an asshole, Marky thought, but he held his tongue.

Next morning, Marky went to court, ready to represent the People of Florida against the liberal demon Toby Simon. His hair was greased and his horn-rims polished; he was ready. "All rise!" said the bailiff, and the door swung open, and striding onto the bench came the old guy from the airplane. The Honorable Elbert P. Tuttle.

Marky was not the one to reason with Tuttle. He flopped disconsolately in the bed. If only he could sleep, just get a little rest before he started running again down the road with no end. Maybe that was the nature of this whole insane business: The State pressed toward an execution; the defense rallied for a last-minute stay; the State bowed graciously; and the warrant expired. Then they all began again. As relentless as it was futile. The thought deepened Marky's exhaustion.

But goddamn! It wasn't right. In his heart, in his roaring, racing brain, Ray Marky could not find one iota of justice in Tuttle's decision. It was nothing but pure, capricious power: a federal judge blocking a state execution simply because he felt like it. Where's the justice in that? Where's the justice? Marky thought—and he himself stopped in mid-thought. He was sounding like Toby Simon. "Where's the justice?" That's just the way liberals talk. Something clicked, and another story, another courtroom, came into his head.

The details were vague, but he could see Toby Simon standing before the bench, arguing another of his high-flown appeals. During a recess, Marky asked him, "Man, don't you ever get tired of slinging this bullshit?" He'd asked in a friendly way, with a little laugh—but really wondering. And Marky saw Simon laughing too, and he remembered the answer: "No, Ray, and I'll tell you why. I don't think it's bullshit, for one thing. Besides, you can't get relief if you don't ask for it."

Relief was the legal term for the glorious moment when a judge takes action to heal what's hurting you. Relief: just the thing Marky wanted desperately right now. You can't get relief if you don't ask for it.

Marky sat up in bed. If he wanted justice he was going to have to ask. He threw off the covers and began dressing quickly. Where was it written that he had to concede graciously? There were two days left on Spenkelink's death warrant—two days to demand relief. Two days left to win this thing, and Marky resolved to fight down to the last tick of the clock. Under his breath he said, "I'm gonna file me some shit!"

He had no time for his customary research. Marky simply returned to his office, sat down, and started writing. He knew the case cold, but the brief that flowed out of him had little to do with the specifics of John Spenkelink's crime. "It was a battle for something bigger," he recalled years later. "It was a battle for the law."

As he wrote, he recalled an old college textbook, one of the tomes he had read and reread and read yet again. The title, as he remembered it, was *The Sense of Injustice,* and it argued that people are not moved by a passion for fairness so much as by the sting of unfairness. That was what now moved Marky: a sense of injustice. This feeling was odd, perhaps, because Marky fully realized that Spenkelink was far from the worst killer on death row. Marky had great respect for David Kendall; every appeal Kendall filed was, in Marky's judgment, worthy and well grounded. But Marky was an assistant attorney general, and his client was the State of Florida. He perceived injustice through the lens of the prosecution.

The words poured out of him and onto the page—not much law, but a lot of angry philosophy. Normally, Marky prided himself on briefs that came from the head, but this one was visceral. He worked all night, and the writing heightened his outrage. When he completed the last page, he stood at the window, watching the sun rise, and swore silently: "They aren't going to pull this off. If they do, it's gonna be over my dead body."

As soon as Jim Smith, the new attorney general, arrived that morning, Marky walked the brief into his office and watched nervously as Smith read it. Maybe it was too strong, Marky worried; maybe he had "gone a little looney-toons." Smith did not exactly share Marky's ferocity. He was a young millionaire landowner, and neither his background nor his inclinations had prepared him to pursue criminal cases. Smith had never really given capital punishment much thought, but he hoped to be governor one day, and he knew that for Florida's top law-enforcement official the death penalty was where the rubber met the road. Smith, too, was inclined to fight. "I like it," the attorney general said. "We're gonna do it."

Marky's plan was two-pronged. Using a rule created after Justice William O. Douglas had unilaterally blocked the execution of Julius and Ethel Rosenberg, Marky would ask the U.S. Supreme Court to vacate Marshall's stay, and also to overrule Tuttle. That was the first prong. The second was trickier: At the same time as they petitioned the high court, the prosecutors would ask the Fifth Circuit Court of Appeals to undo Tuttle's action. Though retired, Tuttle was still considered a judge of the appellate court, and as such, there were time-consuming procedures and protocols that had to be gone through before he could be overruled by his peers. But Marky had dreamed up a shortcut. His contention was that Tuttle, by taking direct action in the Spenkelink case, had acted in the role of a lesser district judge, which therefore gave the court of appeals jurisdiction to reverse his stay immediately. It was a slender technicality, but if the court wanted to help the State of Florida, this would give it a leg to stand on.

Smith quickly assembled a "strike force" to polish Marky's work, flesh it out with legal citations, and type it up. The two sets of papers were ready by late afternoon. By then, no commercial airline could get them from Tallahassee to the appeals court in New Orleans and then on to the Supreme Court in Washington. The governor's official jet was made ready. As Smith prepared to board the plane, along with Marky and two other lawyers, he told the Associated Press, "This is grim business at best."

They raced into the New Orleans courthouse at ten minutes past closing time, but the clerk was waiting for their papers. They didn't reach the U.S. Supreme Court until almost midnight, so they had to be content to leave their pleadings with a guard. On the flight home, Marky got half sloshed on the governor's liquor, and wondered why it took the attorney general and an entourage of three to hand a sheaf of papers to a Supreme Court guard. But Smith had already suggested the answer when he was interviewed by the AP. "For the State of Florida," the attorney general had said, "the death penalty is a very, very important issue."

While Marky was working furiously, Spenkelink's team spent Tuesday night celebrating, giddy with relief. None of them knew what to expect next. Some confidently predicted that the State would give Judge Tuttle time to hold a proper hearing. The death warrant would expire, calm would be restored, and everyone would realize what a dreadful mistake this all was. Others doubted it would be so easy. One thing was certain, there would be no execution in the morning, and that was reason enough to feel good.

Kendall caught an early flight to Atlanta Wednesday morning, where he joined Farmer's team, already at work building a legal foundation under the protective cover they had raised. Reinforcements arrived throughout the day, summoned on short notice from far-flung points. For example, Farmer telephoned an assistant public defender in Miami, Karen Gottlieb, and, though he barely knew her, said simply, "Listen, we've got this stay from Judge Tuttle. I don't know what's going to happen next, but I need your help. Get on a plane and get up here." A few hours later, she was hard at work in Atlanta, and slept Wednesday night on the office floor.

They had to give Tuttle some firm ground to stand on, so they typed and photocopied and put their brains together on a brief that was meant to show that Spenkelink's attorneys had failed him. Kendall was bone-tired; he had averaged three hours of sleep for the past five days. But there was no time to rest; only he, among the lawyers gathered, knew the Spenkelink case inside and out. He was the historical brains of the operation, even though the ineffective counsel claim included an attack on his own work. Nor were his own feelings the only ones hurt. Kendall was given the emotionally draining job of calling Spenkelink's trial lawyers and breaking the news that the new appeal would charge them with incompetent representation. "It is obviously not something a lawyer likes to hear," he said later.

As the day wore on, intelligence drifted in from Tallahassee, and it became clear that the pessimists at the previous night's celebration had been correct. The State of Florida was fighting back. Farmer's team went to work on papers for the Supreme Court. More time passed, and they realized that the State was going to ask the Fifth Circuit to over-turn Tuttle. Attorney General Smith had declined Tuttle's offer to meet with the prosecution and defense that afternoon and schedule a hear-ing; the State intended to defeat the judge, not meet with him. This news caused the defense team to shift gears again and begin work on a brief arguing that the appeals court had no jurisdiction to reverse the stay of its own former chief. It was a day of flying paper and spent typewriter ribbons, a frenzy.

On Thursday morning in Washington, the nine justices of the U.S. Supreme Court met in conference and once again weighed the question of ending John Spenkelink's life. Three times the Court had denied his appeals, the most recent just two days earlier. This morning, two justices were particularly inclined to dissolve Thurgood Marshall's stay of execution—because they had been approached by the defense attorneys before Marshall had been and had denied the same request. The first was the archconservative William Rehnquist, who fielded Spenkelink's petition because the justice who ordinarily handled emer-gency matters in the Fifth Circuit was unavailable. In denying the plea, Rehnquist had written, "He has had not only one day in court, he has had many, many days in court." Justice John Paul Stevens had also considered, and denied, the petition for a stay. The Inc. Fund defense team had gone through the court roster until they found a justice who would help them, eventually reaching Marshall.

Rehnquist and Stevens had no trouble gathering a majority to lift

Marshall's stay. But the high court declined to act on the Tuttle question. Instead, the justices (with Rehnquist dissenting) advised the Fifth Circuit to handle the matter. But they reserved the authority to reconsider after the lower court reached a decision.

Even under the best of circumstances, trying to understand the Supreme Court involves a lot of reading tea leaves and scrying for portents in seemingly innocuous sentences. But this decision was so hedged that even the most experienced court watchers were divided as to its meaning. The Spenkelink team was heartened, figuring that if the high court refused to overturn Tuttle, then the Fifth Circuit Court of Appeals surely wouldn't either. Ray Marky interpreted the decision differently, though, and he too was heartened. Marky figured that by instructing the appeals court to weigh Tuttle's action (and threatening to review the court's work), the justices were saying, in effect, Clean up your house, or we'll do it for you.

Late that afternoon, the Fifth Circuit assigned the issue to a three-judge panel: Judges James P. Coleman, Peter T. Fay, and Alvin B. Rubin. They were all highly regarded jurists, but the emergency procedure they adopted was hasty and unorthodox. Given less than a day before the death warrant expired, faced with unprecedented complexities of jurisdiction and judicial authority, weighing a state's sovereignty on the one hand against Judge Tuttle's authority on the other—with a man's life in the balance—the esteemed judges decided to hear the case via a telephone conference call.

The conference call took everyone by surprise. At his office over a pool hall in New York's Greenwich Village, Ramsey Clark didn't even have time to reach for a few law books. At the Team Defense office in Atlanta, Farmer, Kendall, and Margery Pitts Hames crowded around Farmer's speakerphone. In Tallahassee, the key players on the government's side—Robin Gibson, Jim Smith, Betty Steffens—were hastily summoned to Deputy Attorney General Ken Tucker's office. Ray Marky was out of the building, so George Georgieff took a seat on the corner of Tucker's desk, beside the speakerphone. As always, Georgieff was confident and spoiling for a fight. All the participants were ordered, according to Clark, not to record the proceedings.

About 7 P.M., James Coleman and Alvin Rubin came on the line from New Orleans. (The third judge, Peter Fay, was "unavailable," reportedly out to dinner.) The conference, which lasted about an hour, was bitter and bizarre. In all the confusion, the judges had not seen the defense team's papers, and the defense team had not seen the State's papers, nor had the State seen anything from the defense. As several participants remember it, Ramsey Clark took the lead, suggesting an order for the arguments.

Georgieff would have none of that. "Hell," he growled into the speaker. "That's the judge's job."

This rough start was partly a matter of principle on Georgieff's part—he believed a lawyer should never give an inch to an opponent—and partly a deep-seated disdain for Ramsey Clark. Georgieff was as unreconstructed in his conservatism as Clark was unrelenting in his liberalism, and Georgieff, being Georgieff, naturally personalized this difference. He liked to call Clark "a pissant," and often asserted that the man would never have amounted to anything if he hadn't been the son of Tom Clark, who had served Harry Truman as attorney general before being appointed to the U.S. Supreme Court. During the conference, when Clark began a sentence with "I'm sure Mr. Georgieff will say . . . ," Georgieff shouted at the phone, "Stop telling them what the hell I'll say. If I have something to say, I'll say it!"

Georgieff charged that the defense team was sandbagging, that they had planned all along to claim ineffective counsel and had saved the issue until the last minute to derail the execution. Clark and Farmer heatedly denied the charge. And even if the judges believed it, Clark added, they should punish the lawyers and not John Spenkelink.

Maybe Georgieff was coming on a bit too strong. Ken Tucker—the number-two man in the attorney general's office—tried interposing himself. In his cool commercial lawyer's tone, he said the State of Florida would suffer "irreparable damage" if Tuttle's stay remained in force. By now, Marky had arrived; he chimed in with an attack on Tuttle's jurisdiction, laying out his contention that the three-judge panel had the authority to dissolve the stay.

Through it all, David Kendall remained "uncharacteristically quiet," though he had the best understanding of the case from the perspective of the defense. He knew that if he spoke he would undermine the claim that his own work had failed Spenkelink. That left the burden on Clark and Farmer, who had no more than two days' experience on the case and no expertise in Florida's rules and procedures. The lack of preparation showed. As soon as Clark cited an earlier court decision to bolster his argument, Georgieff was on him again, angrily insisting that Clark was misconstruing the earlier decision. Georgieff had been reading precisely that decision just the day before, and now, from memory and with unfiltered bravado, he was able to refer the judges to the precise page, column, and paragraph that would prove his point. "It was an absolutely masterful performance, like something from an old Spencer Tracy movie," Betty Steffens recalled.

Things were clearly going against Spenkelink. Clark complained that the conference call, with unprepared lawyers arguing to unbriefed judges, was "worse than meaningless. It's dangerous." He pleaded for time to present evidence on the ineffective counsel claim. Judge Coleman replied that the court was not legally obligated to hear even these hasty arguments; the judges could simply rule. "Well," Clark said, "I've been practicing law for thirty years, and I've never been involved in an emergency telephone hearing on any case, let alone a capital case." And he added that, if the judges were going to reverse Judge Tuttle, they should at least give the defense a few extra hours to lodge an appeal of the unorthodox procedure with the U.S. Supreme Court.

Judge Coleman promised enough time for the appeal. Then he asked each of the parties for direct phone numbers where they could be notified when the panel reached a decision. At 8 P.M., an hour after it began, the call was over.

A moment later, the phone rang on Jim Smith's private number—the one the Florida lawyers had just given to Judge Coleman. It was Ramsey Clark. The conference call, he said, had been totally unsatisfactory, a disservice to justice. In the name of God, he pleaded, give us time for a proper hearing.

"We're ready to take our chances," Smith answered.

"Well, God have mercy on your soul," Clark said furiously. Smith cradled the receiver, and for the rest of the night his private line rang with callers who shouted "Murderer!" and "You fucker!" into the phone. Forever afterward, Smith would blame Ramsey Clark for this.

∴

Over the next three and a half hours, Judge Alvin Rubin tried to persuade Judge James Coleman to stand by Tuttle's stay. Meanwhile, the defense team in Atlanta—minus Kendall, who left to return to the prison—prepared a petition for the U.S. Supreme Court. If Tuttle's stay was lifted, this petition would be flown to Washington, where Clark would meet it and deliver it to the high court. The evening slipped by. In New York, Clark began to worry that he would miss the last flight to Washington, so he called Judge Coleman for news. Coleman said the panel was having trouble agreeing.

About ten minutes before midnight, long after the last flight had departed, Clark received a call from the clerk of the circuit court in New Orleans. "We are convinced, for reasons which will hereafter be stated in a formal opinion, that the aforesaid stay should be vacated," the clerk read from the panel's order. The order would take effect at nine-thirty the following morning, at which time the State of Florida was free to electrocute John Spenkelink. Coleman was joined in the majority decision by Judge Fay—who had neither heard the conference call nor, apparently, read the defense brief. Judge Rubin dissented, and reserved the right to spell out his reasons at a later date. As it would turn out, none of the three judges would ever file a formal opinion in the matter.

In New York, rain was falling in sheets, and the last train for Washington had left Penn Station. Ramsey Clark called Jack Boger of the Inc. Fund, and at 2 A.M. they set out in Boger's car on a five-hour drive to the U.S. Supreme Court.

Farmer found a friend with a private plane who agreed to fly the petition to Baltimore from Atlanta, where a car would pick up the document and carry it to meet Clark.

In Tallahassee, an anti–death penalty activist named Scharlette Holdman frantically worked the phones. She talked a local lawyer, Howell Ferguson, into preparing some sort of argument—anything—to support a stay from the Florida Supreme Court. She also drafted Steve Goldstein, a law professor at Florida State University, to help. Ferguson called the state's chief justice, Arthur England, rousting him from bed to alert him that something was in the works. The groggy jurist in turn dialed his court clerk and told him to summon the other justices to a 7 A.M. session at England's home.

At the prison, John Spenkelink repeated the grim ordeal of saying farewell to his loved ones. He hugged and kissed his mother, hugged and kissed Carla Key. When the visits were over, and Spenkelink was led back to the death-watch cell, Key's daughter began sobbing in the waiting room. "Please!" she shrieked. "Don't let them kill my daddy!"

Reverend Tom Feamster spent the night outside Spenkelink's cell. "I was with him from about 8 P.M. to 8 A.M. Once again, we were sitting, John on the mattress, me on this chair outside the bars. It was a dark and stinking little cell downstairs at the prison. I was scared to death. I felt terrible. God, what do you say to a man who is about to be executed?

"For a time, I felt nothing but anger at Brierton, at the governor, at the guy who pulled the switch—but finally I realized, hey, I'm a part of this, too. I sat outside the cell with the guards. I was a part of the system. I can't wash my hands of it. It comes down to what I said to the press after it was all over: 'People who are of a persuasion to pray, don't pray for John. Pray for us.'

"I spent all night with John. He was smoking constantly. He would get up, walk around the cell, then sit back down on the mattress. He vacillated between anger and trying to understand. The anger was classic convict stuff: 'These bastards can't do nothing to me.' It was obvious he was scared. But John never felt he had the right to be afraid. We had talked about that for two years—that he didn't have to be as tough as he acted. I could say that to him, because I'm six-foot-eight and I played pro football. I can look at some prison tough guy and say 'You're not so tough' and get away with it. You know, it was John's tough act that did him in. He hung himself when he got on the witness stand. His lawyer should never have let him.

"There was a lot of quiet time. Every now and then, John would look at me and blow out some smoke and shake his head and say, 'In America, they just don't kill people like this.' I don't think he ever came to grips with it. I mean, given the things Syzmankiewicz did to him, John felt the guy deserved it. When he was shooting him and beating the corpse, he felt the guy deserved every bit of it. I asked him during the night—so it wouldn't come down to the last minute—if he would like to have Communion before I left. And he said 'Yeah.' I don't know if he was ever baptized. I never asked."

Feamster served Communion as sun rose over Starke, a wafer and a sip of wine from the reserve he had consecrated for visits to hospitals and nursing homes. He performed the liturgy from a flustered memory. But if the priest flubbed the service, Spenkelink didn't know. It was his first Communion.

Florida State Prison.
Execution Day.
The schedule:

4:30 A.M. The Food Service Director will personally prepare and serve last meal. Eating utensils will be a plate and spoon.

Spenkelink ordered nothing. A meal of steak and eggs was brought to his cell, in case he changed his mind. The steak was cut into bite-sized pieces because Spenkelink was not allowed to have a knife. But the chef, so that the prisoner wouldn't feel like a child, painstakingly reassembled the pieces into the shape of a steak.

5:00 A.M. The Administrative Assistant or designate will pick up executioner, proceed to the institution, enter through Sally Port and leave the executioner in the Waiting Room of the Death Chamber at 5:00 A.M. A security staff member will be posted in the chamber area.

The executioner, whose job was to trip the circuit breakers, had been chosen from several hundred applicants who had answered a classified ad. His identity was painstakingly concealed: He was picked up on a lonely road and driven to the prison by a circuitous back route; his

$150-dollar fee was paid in cash so no record would appear on any checking account.

5:50 A.M. Authorized Media Witnesses will be picked up at the media onlooker area by two designated Department of Corrections staff escorts. . . .

6:00 A.M. The Assistant Superintendent for Operations will supervise the shaving of the inmate's head and right leg. [The crown and the calf are the contact points for the electrodes; these points are shaved to reduce burning.]

The Assistant Superintendent for Operations will supervise the showering of the condemned inmate. Immediately thereafter he will be returned to his cell and given a pair of shorts, a pair of trousers, a dress shirt, and socks. The Correctional Officer Chief IV will be responsible for the delivery of the clothes.

Switchboard operator will be instructed by Superintendent to wire all calls to Execution Chamber from governor's Office through switchboard.

The Administrative Assistant, or designate, three designated electricians, physician, and a physician's asst. will report to the execution chamber for preparation. . . .

This schedule assumed a 7 A.M. execution. But the circuit court of appeals had delayed its order lifting Tuttle's stay until 9:30 A.M., so the execution was running three hours late. Times were adjusted accordingly.

Ramsey Clark, after his wild ride through the storm, met the defense papers at the U.S. Supreme Court clerk's office, read them through, and filed them shortly before 7 A.M. Then he settled in to wait. The execution was now three hours away. Periodically, Clark asked whether the papers had been delivered to any of the justices, but for more than an hour, no one would say whether any member of the Court was even in the building.

At the same time, in Tallahassee, the newly drafted defense team of Howell Ferguson and Steve Goldstein arrived at the home of Arthur England, chief justice of the Florida Supreme Court. Marky was there with his boss, Jim Smith, and most of the court's justices had gathered. There were so many cars outside the England home that neighbors wondered if there had been a tragedy. Inside, England was ready with rolls and orange juice, pencils and legal pads. He wore shirtsleeves, no tie, like a man welcoming guests to a weekend brunch. Ferguson and Goldstein kept their suit jackets on and declined the food. They wanted to impress the solemn nature of their mission on the justices.

This strange tribunal settled into England's sofas and chairs. Goldstein did most of the talking. The defense attorney's argument offered little that was new—just an overwhelming sense that events had gone badly wrong to put Spenkelink in this spot. Goldstein argued fervently, and the justices listened intently. But they were skeptical. "What about finality?" one justice asked. "When does it end?" Another justice, his mind apparently made up already, asked repeatedly whether Spenkelink was spelled with one *l* or two.

And the clock ticked down. At last, Marky interjected, "Look," he said, "I don't mind listening, but this man is being shaved and prepped as we speak. If the court is going to enter a stay, you better go ahead and do it now, out of consideration for him." That caught everyone's attention. Goldstein hastened to a close. Marky offered a brief rebuttal. England asked the lawyers to leave the room while the justices deliberated.

A few minutes later, Goldstein and Ferguson were summoned back inside and told that someone had called from Orlando claiming that the execution was covered by an obscure law requiring that all acts of government be published in advance through legal notices. The defense attorneys knew nothing about this claim, but what did they have to lose? They asked England to incorporate it into their brief.

The waiting resumed. "I remember talking to Ray Marky," Goldstein recalled, "and him saying that he didn't want us to think he was a bad guy, that he was just doing his job."

∴

Scores of protesters had spent the night outside the governor's mansion, chanting and singing and banging pipes against the iron fence. Bob Graham passed the noisy night alone, except for his bodyguards. His wife and four daughters had been secretly moved to the home of a family friend. The strain was enormous: The younger girls were frightened by the clanging and shouting, and the older ones were angry at the things being said about their father. "My daddy's not a killer," one of them wailed. There were fears for the family's safety. Jim Smith's wife and children were in hiding, too, after a series of death threats.

That morning, the protesters from the mansion joined the protesters at Graham's office, and together they numbered over a hundred. When the doors to the governor's suite were opened, the crowd surged into the reception area, where they began stomping on the floor and pounding on the walls and pressing against the locked double doors leading to the inner office. It happened so quickly that one receptionist was trapped and wound up cowering inside a closet. The protesters commandeered her telephone console and began shouting "Murderer's office!" into the receiver each time a call came in. A television cameraman clambered onto the desk for a better angle. Another stepped up onto a newly upholstered chair. Soon people were swarming over all the furniture; when it was over, all the fabrics and finishes had to be redone.

Behind the locked doors, sheriff's deputies in riot helmets formed a human barricade, and everyone who could be moved upstairs was swiftly evacuated. The rest of the staff watched nervously as the doors heaved inward and the pictures rattled on the walls. Outside, police snipers watched from the rooftops of the capitol and the nearby supreme court building. An escape route from the governor's office had been plotted on old blueprints, and a helicopter sat on the lawn, ready to whisk Bob Graham away if the protest turned to an attack.

At the center of it all, Graham sat at his desk, flanked by his personal secretary and his chief of scheduling . . . going through the morning's mail. If folks thought it weird, so be it: This was his way of coping with stress, to bury his emotions under a blanket of mundane detail. Graham had always done this. On the day of his wedding, he had irritated his bride by chattering vacuously about dairy cows. He was comforted by specifics, soothed by data; he wrote down every little thing that happened to him—each person he met, the price of every meal—in color-coded notebooks, a different color for each season of the year. Few people ever glimpsed beyond the wall of cool meticulousness that fronted Graham's personality.

Not that he was immune to the pressure that was squeezing him from every direction. The newspapers were almost unanimously opposed to the execution, and even some of his aides hoped he would reconsider. On the other hand, nearly everyone in the legislature was urging him on, and his phone rang constantly with unsolicited advice. The young governor of Arkansas, Bill Clinton, called with several picayune legal questions, concerned that Graham might make a mistake that would hamper the return of the death penalty in other states. Graham wrestled with the moral implications in conversations with George Bedell, a close friend and ordained minister. At one point, according to an ally, Graham had even considered reversing himself and commuting Spenkelink's sentence—an action his advisers believed would surely be political suicide. But if he had wavered, it was for only an instant, and by that Friday morning his resolve was granite.

Robin Gibson stood behind Graham, keeping the phone line to the execution chamber open. Betty Steffens was on another phone, waiting for word from Arthur England's house. A third aide kept a line open to the attorney general's office, where lawyers were monitoring the federal courts. Everyone had to speak loudly so they could be heard over the din of the protest; Gibson, especially, grew more and more exasperated as the protest continued. Suddenly, he strode from the office toward the locked double doors. "Of course, we had direct lines to the courts and the prison, but the protesters didn't know that," Gibson recalled. "I figured I would go out and tell them that we were waiting for a call and that those phones they were disrupting were the only way to save John Spenkelink. So I opened the double doors.

"It was crazy. There were people up on top of the desk. Everyone was shouting and stomping. I tried to tell them that the best thing they could do for John Spenkelink was to quiet down and stop disrupting the office. Well, that didn't do any good. As soon as I said it, they immediately began chanting again like before."

Gibson's friends saw this as a display of incredible naïveté. "He had read somewhere that if you could just find the leaders of a protest and reason with them, the rest of the crowd will disperse," Steffens said. But to the crowd in the reception area, Gibson's gambit was grossly cynical. Bob Graham had the power to save Spenkelink, and if he wanted to he could. They began chanting "Bloodsucker! Bloodsucker! Bloodsucker!" The renewed clamor further infuriated Gibson, and when he slammed the doors and turned to the armed deputies, he was trembling. "Nobody," he shouted, "gets past this line!"

Graham kept plodding through his mail. He looked up from one letter and asked his secretary to call upstairs for a speechwriter named Bill Shade. When Shade answered his phone and heard that the governor needed him immediately, he thought, Oh, shit. He's gonna cancel it and he needs an instant speech. Shade hustled into Graham's office, where he found Gibson pacing, Steffens on a divan, and the governor plainly struggling with his nerves.

"You wanted to see me?" Shade asked.

Graham nodded, and handed him a letter from the stack. It was from a voter, complaining that her son was going to have to pay a fee to play in the school band. "Bill," the governor said above the racket from outside, "could you draft a response on this?"

Incongruous as it might seem, Dave Brierton wanted to make John Spenkelink as comfortable as possible before killing him. He thought about a tranquilizer but knew he'd catch hell if the press learned that the prisoner was drugged. Somewhere in his wide-ranging reading, though, Brierton had come across the fact that Anne Boleyn—just before she was beheaded on orders of her husband, Henry VIII—had been given a stiff drink to bolster her. If it was good enough for royalty, Brierton decided, it was good enough for Spenkelink.

He poured two generous shots from a Jack Daniel's bottle into a flask and gave the flask to his assistant, Richard Dugger. Dugger was headed down to the death-watch cell to supervise the shaving and showering.

"Would you like a drink?" Dugger asked when he reached the cell.

Spenkelink looked skeptically at the flask. "You first," he answered.

Dugger hadn't expected that—but he poured a mouthful into a paper cup and knocked it back. It burned, but the burn was welcome. Dugger was getting awfully nervous about strapping a man into a chair and watching him die.

"I'd like some of that," Spenkelink said, with a tight grin. He had himself one long bourbon, then another.

Arthur England called the lawyers back into his living room and announced that the request for a stay of execution had been denied. There was an awkward silence—no one knew what to do next. Then Justice Joe Boyd brightened. "Let's watch it on TV," he said.

Someone tuned the set to the local ABC affiliate, which was broadcasting live reports from outside the prison. Everyone huddled around. Ray Marky thought the whole scene was repulsive. Grown men glued to the set like they were watching the Super Bowl. He wandered into another room.

Justice Alan Sundberg followed him. The two men stood a moment, realizing they had nothing to say. So they, too, snapped on a television set, but they tuned it to cartoons, and tried to lose themselves in the cheerful noise.

Zero hour, 10 A.M., was approaching. At the U.S. Supreme Court, Ramsey Clark was handed a piece of paper. "The application for stay of execution, presented to Mr. Justice Powell and by him referred to the Court, is denied," he read. "Mr. Justice Brennan and Mr. Justice Marshall would grant the stay. Mr. Justice Blackmun took no part. . . ." At the bottom of the page were the initials "W.E.B.," hand-written by Chief Justice Warren E. Burger. Now every court had been heard from.

∴

"The Lord is my shepherd, I shall not want," David Kendall intoned. He was standing next to Tom Feamster in the back of a windowless waiting room. Soon, a van would take them two hundred yards to the death house, to witness the execution. "What comes next?" he asked. Feamster said nothing.

"The Lord is my shepherd, I shall not want," Kendall repeated. "He leadeth me beside the still waters. He anointeth my head with oil, my cup runneth over. No, wait— He maketh me to lie down in green pastures. He, uh, He leadeth me beside still waters. Is that right?"

"Man, I don't know," Feamster answered.

"You're the preacher."

Kendall started again. "The Lord is my shepherd, I shall not want. He maketh me to lie down in green pastures. He leadeth me beside still waters. Something, something. He restoreth my soul. He—Thou?— anointeth my head with oil, my cup runneth over. Help me out with this."

"I told you I don't know."

"You should know this. The Twenty-third Psalm. Pretty famous stuff. Don't you learn these things at seminary?"

Pause.

"You probably don't even know the word 'selah.' "

Feamster looked at him blankly.

" 'Selah.' It's Hebrew. They put it at the end of the psalms. It means 'right on!' Preachers should know that. C'mon," Kendall continued. "The Lord is my shepherd, I shall not want. He maketh me to lie down in green pastures. He leadeth me beside the still waters. What comes next?"

Feamster wanted to say, "Shut your mouth! What's your problem?" Yammering on at a time like this. For a priest, Tom Feamster—as he sometimes admitted—was not terribly religious, in the Bible-quoting sense. At a time of trouble, Scripture was not the first thing that sprang to his mind. He would get more solace, at this moment, from putting a big fist through the wall. Kendall, however, was at it again, "The Lord is my shepherd . . ." Feamster tried to remember the psalm, if only to satisfy the lawyer. All he could think about, though, was that somewhere close by, John Spenkelink was being readied for death. Feamster felt stupid, he felt angry, and most of all, he felt helpless. But he held his tongue; apparently this was Kendall's way of dealing with it.

"The Lord is my shepherd . . ." The room went dark.

Somewhere in the bowels of the prison, workers had switched off the feed from the local power company. About thirty seconds later, the prison's own generator kicked in, and the lights came back on. Utility executives had insisted on this; they were worried about bad public relations, or even sabotage, if their electricity was used to power the chair.

"Yea, though I walk through the valley of the shadow of death, I will fear no evil, for Thou art with me," Kendall intoned.

"Thy rod and Thy staff, they comfort me. Thou preparest a table before me in the presence of mine enemies. Something, something, something.

"Surely goodness and mercy shall follow me all the days of my life. And I will dwell in the House of the Lord forever."

He looked at Feamster. "Selah!"

Then the van came.

Joe Ingle had taken Lois Spenkelink to a room at the ratty old Dixie Motel in Starke, where he hoped no reporters could find her. He pulled the drapes, asked the manager to hold any calls, and sat down beside the tired woman.

This ordeal had been a unique and devilish torture for Lois Spenkelink. It's a hard thing for a mother to lose a child, bitterly hard, unnatural and out of time. But to have a child—so healthy looking in his tight T-shirts, so seemingly harmless in his letters dotted with smiley faces—separated out from all God's children as one unfit to live . . . To think of that child being shaved, showered, and exterminated . . . It was almost impossible to bear. She had tried her best, loved him and honored her every duty to him, and no doubt she once had dreamed that her investment would pay a dividend of pride. Instead, there was this insuperable shame, this shocking indictment that said her child was unlovable, irredeemable, incorrigible, and must die.

Perhaps a woman of a philosophical bent could find some meaning to it all, but Lois Spenkelink was not a philosopher. She was a simple schoolteacher, modest in her aspirations, noteworthy only in her sorrows. She was not a worldly woman, and was mystified by much of the frenzy around her. One night, earlier in the week, she had sat in a room full of lawyers and activists while they discussed their prospects in the U.S. Supreme Court. Ingle had recited the names of the justices, and the group had estimated their chances with each one. Lois had looked up and said, "I'll tell you one of them we don't need to worry about. One of them will do the right thing."

And Ingle asked, "Who's that, Lois?"

"Judge Wapner," she had said.

She had tried everything the Spenkelink team could think of to save her son. She had spoken at rallies and given television interviews and placed calls to anyone who might be in a position to help—Jerry Brown, the progressive governor of her home state of California; Ted Kennedy, the keeper of the liberal flame; even President Jimmy Carter. The president was not categorically opposed to capital punishment, but he was very public about his religious devotion. Lois Spenkelink hoped a "Christian appeal" to Carter would persuade him to call for mercy. Now, less than an hour from the scheduled execution, she sat on a worn bedspread and wondered what more she might have done. The ringing of the telephone startled her. Lois answered, listened a moment, then passed the phone to Ingle. The White House was calling.

"Please tell Mrs. Spenkelink the president sympathizes with her deeply," a presidential aide said. "But as you probably know, this is a matter of state law, and he doesn't think it would be proper for him to intervene."

Ingle erupted; his voice was desperate. Didn't they understand? This wasn't about the law. "We called him for help because he claims to be a Christian," Ingle said. "We are pleading with him"—Ingle put his whole heart into the word pleading—"in the name of Jesus Christ, to call Governor Graham and stop this execution. Would you please give him that message?" The man at the White House promised he would.

What happened next would later strike Ingle as "the strangest, most wonderful thing, a miracle." At the hour of her greatest pain and fear, Lois Spenkelink, utterly drained, drifted off to sleep. Joe Ingle quietly turned on the television, leaving the volume off, and waited for a news bulletin.

A good-sized crowd was jammed into the Q-wing corridor when Dave Brierton reached Spenkelink's cell. Every prison staffer, it seemed, wanted to witness history being made. A list had been prepared of people who were allowed to be there, but a number of others had schemed or scammed their way in. A technician, for example, chose just that moment to replace an oxygen bottle at the first-aid station. He was turned away at the grille, but a staff psychologist took the bottle and the gambit worked for him. The prison chaplain arrived, a man whom Spenkelink deeply loathed as an unholy cog in the death machine. "Get him out of here," Spenkelink seethed, and when the chaplain did not immediately leave, he shouted: "Goddammit, get that piece of shit out of here!" Afterward, the whole crowd would have stories to tell; a good number of those present would personally take credit for having said, "John, it's time to go."

Brierton recalled it this way: "The execution was scheduled for ten A.M., and I waited until five past ten before I went in there to get him. I was obsessed with the idea that we would get some last-minute calls after he was in the chair. I didn't want that. So I waited. Originally, I wanted to wait until ten-fifteen, but Richard Dugger convinced me that it would look too much like I was running my own show.

"I went back there figuring John would probably be at the acceptance stage. He'd spent the night with his priest, after all, and I kind of figured he would have worked it all through. But I got down there and, man, he was *angry*. And it hit me. You know, I don't think John ever really believed it was going to happen. There he was with his head shaved, and I don't think he believed it would happen until I walked up. I said, 'John, it's time.' And he stood up and he was really obviously angry. He shouted, 'You motherfuckers really think you're tough, don't you!' John had a temper on him."

Others remember Spenkelink also said: "You can't do this, this is America! This is murder!"

Brierton: "And I said, 'John, I really don't think this is the time for this.' And after a minute, he came out. For a minute there, I wasn't sure what he was going to do, whether he was going to make us drag him out. But he got up and came out of the cell. There was no fighting at all."

Spenkelink was handcuffed, and a thick white paste, called Electro-creme, was smeared on his head to enhance the flow of juice. It made him look comical, like a bald man having a shampoo. The strap squad walked him briskly down the corridor, through a heavy door and into the execution chamber. The prisoner saw the electric chair for the first time. It was a massive piece of furniture, scaled more like a throne than a chair. It was dark, shiny oak, heavy, angular, functional, with wide arms, a ladder back, two wooden pinions for a headrest, two stout legs in the rear and two more narrowly spaced legs in front. The brown chair completely dominated the tiny room, which had white walls, a white ceiling, and a white floor, like a piece of art dominating a bare gallery wall.

In one swift motion Spenkelink was thrust into the chair and the practiced hands began moving over him, cinching the leather straps tight. "We came in and we strapped him into the chair and I remember John was looking all around the room, almost like he was curious," Brierton recalled. "He turned his head and looked back at the executioner standing there in his black hood. He just stared at the guy. And then, I believe, his nerves started to go." The last strap was a wide band that went over Spenkelink's mouth and chin and anchored his head firmly against the pinions.

While this was going on, venetian blinds remained closed over the window that separated the execution chamber from the witness room. During rehearsals, Brierton had concluded that the strapping-in was a spectacle potentially demeaning both to the prisoner and to the squad. "Why do they have to see him coming in?" he asked Dugger. "Let's put in some blinds."

"I don't think that would be a good idea," Dugger answered— and it turned out he was right. In the months that followed, people would charge that Spenkelink had been dragged to the chair, that he had been gagged under the head strap, even that he had been beaten to death or strangled before he ever got into the room. Investigations would be launched. Newspaper columnists would fulminate. A flaky Jacksonville evangelist would paper the state with letters claiming that Spenkelink had been murdered to prevent him from revealing, at the last moment, knowledge of a drug conspiracy reaching to the highest levels of Florida government. Eventually, Spenkelink's corpse would be exhumed by a big-name Los Angeles coroner in a gruesome publicity stunt.

All of this because of those venetian blinds. The execution would become the circus Brierton had dreaded.

There were twenty-four white wooden chairs with heart-shaped backs crowded into the little witness room. They looked like overgrown pieces of a child's tea-party set. These were filled by twelve designated observers and twelve reporters. As many people from the prison staff as could fit crammed into the standing room.

Kendall carried in his coat pocket a copy of a 1947 U.S. Supreme Court decision, *Francis v. Resweber,* in which the court had agreed to consider whether it was cruel and unusual punishment to electrocute a man a second time if the chair malfunctioned and merely jolted him the first time. The case had not gone well for the man in question, because the justices concluded that what's acceptable punishment once should be acceptable twice. But to Kendall the question itself was grounds for an appeal, and he was ready to jump up and wave the opinion if the equipment malfunctioned this time.

There was nothing else he could do, so he put on a brave face. "We're still trying to get a Supreme Court justice to stop it," he informed a reporter in the witness room. "I can't tell you which one." Then he leaned toward Feamster and whispered, "Tom, he can see us from here."

"We sat there at least ten minutes, staring at the closed blinds," Feamster remembered. "I was thinking that I should do some kind of civil disobedience. I thought about throwing my chair through the window. Just standing up and slinging it through. It wouldn't stop the thing, but it would disrupt it. But then I realized that surely the window would be shatterproof, and the chair would bounce off, and they would take me out of there and I wouldn't be there for John.

"It seemed like years," Feamster said. "Then, *snap!* The blinds came up and John's eyes were staring right at me. There was a strap across his face pulling his head back and pressing his jaw down. His eyes were staring right at me. Then they rolled, they rolled around the room and . . . shut."

Inside the chamber, Brierton was stunned by how close the witnesses were. If not for the glass, he could reach over and touch the legislators in the front row. They hadn't rehearsed with witnesses, and the audience flustered the warden. Brierton caught sight of Kendall flashing a thumbs-up sign, and his heart raced faster. Did the lawyer know something was up?

There were three telephones on the rear wall, one beige, one green, one black. A squad member listened a moment at the first phone, which was connected to the attorney general's office, then announced quietly, "No stays."

Brierton turned to Spenkelink. "Do you have any last words?" he said hurriedly.

"I can't talk," Spenkelink gasped.

The man's nerve had failed. That was obvious to Brierton. Others present, including Richard Dugger, came to a different conclusion: The strap across his mouth was too tight. Spenkelink wanted to speak, but physically could not. There was no time to resolve the question, though, because Brierton had already stepped across the room to the black phone, and the electrician had begun fastening the electrodes.

Robin Gibson was on the other end of the line in the governor's office. "I was standing there with the phone, and I heard them enter the chamber. I could hear it over the phone. The feet shuffling. I heard a few syllables of what they were saying, Brierton asking Spenkelink if he had any last words. I don't know if he said anything. If he did, it was very short.

"Brierton came on the line, and I handed the phone to Bob. He was obviously very tense. He took the phone and said, 'This is Louis Pasteur.' The code. But he was supposed to just say, 'Louis Pasteur,' not 'This is Louis Pasteur.' He was nervous."

A press aide, who knew nothing of the password, was standing near Graham's desk, and when she heard the governor say "This is Louis Pasteur," she let out a burst of involuntary laughter. Had the man cracked? Graham ignored her. "There are no stays at this time," he said solemnly. "May God be with us." A nice touch, Gibson thought. "May God be with us." Clearly, his friend had been thinking about just the right words for the history books. It was a phrase to remember.

But actually, as it turned out, what Gibson himself would recall most vividly was "the feet shuffling. That's the strongest memory. I can still hear those shuffling feet."

Brierton gave the signal. There was a dull slap of sound, then another slap, with a harder edge to it, as the executioner opened the power to the control panel. Then, back to back, two loud metallic snaps, like gunshots, as the hooded man threw the switch.

Spenkelink stiffened in the chair. His right hand tightened slowly into a fist, like a wad of newspaper balling up in a fire. His left hand also made a fist, but then the thumb shot up and the forefinger distended grotesquely, pointing backward toward his stomach. The knuckles stood out like an arthritic's. The surge lasted perhaps a minute.

"Then the executioner turned off the power, and the doctor went over and opened one button of John's shirt and put the stethoscope to his chest. He listened, then he shook his head," Feamster recounted.

"Brierton signaled again, and the switch was thrown again. Now there was a little smoke curling up from John's leg. After a little while, the doctor listened at his chest, then shook his head. For the third time, they threw the switch," Feamster continued. "This time, his leg was burning. No flames, but a lot of smoke." The flesh under the electrode split open and turned black. Again, the power was cut off. "Then the doctor went to John and listened, and this time, he nodded his head, real slow," Feamster remembered. "Then, *slap!* Down came the blinds."

It was 10:18 A.M., Friday, May 25, 1979. The death penalty had returned to America.

∴

Richard Dugger: "At that time, remember, there was nobody who knew how to operate the electric chair. The old-timers were all gone. We were told the electric chair runs at a full two-minute cycle, but that it is never allowed to run the full time. But no one could tell us, well, how you decide when there has been enough?"

Feamster broke the silence in the witness room. "Gentlemen," he boomed. "I hope that you pray that this is a just and merciful punishment in the name of God—for our soul's sake." No one answered him.

Behind the closed blinds, the strap squad began undoing the restraints. Brierton was working on the chest strap. "Uh, maybe you oughta leave that one on," said one of his assistants. Brierton gave him a quizzical look.

"So he don't fall out," the man said.

At the Dixie Motel, a rerun of *All in the Family* was playing silently when the bulletin scrolled slowly across the screen. Ingle moved over to the bed and gently put a hand on Lois Spenkelink's shoulder. She didn't wake. He shook her lightly, and when she stirred said, "I'm afraid I have some bad news."

"They've killed my Johnny," she answered flatly.

The gathering at Chief Justice Arthur England's house took the news quietly. The justices and lawyers milled about the living room. Nobody felt much like going to work. "It was so totally dispiriting," England remembered. "Just an awful day." England wandered outside into the bright, breezy morning. There, in the driveway, he found Ray Marky.

Exhaustion had finally caught up to him—Marky had nothing but shreds left inside. Shreds, and the release of knowing the ordeal was finally over. And something more: When the news came, in a flash Marky realized he would pay a long time for this victory. He abruptly comprehended that, for the rest of his life, he would be remembered for relentlessly pursuing a killing. "I had to face the fact that somehow I'd come to epitomize the bloodthirsty prosecutor," he recalled. "And I knew that wasn't me. I'd almost killed myself for the State of Florida. And I felt like, here I'm the goddamn black hat and all these people screwing with our system, they're gonna be the white hats."

Marky leaned against a car, his glasses in one hand, his face in the other, and began to sob.

The execution of John Spenkelink was expected to be America's top story, the biggest news in the most powerful nation on the face of the earth. A hundred-foot television tower was erected near the prison to beam the reports that would lead the network newscasts. *Newsweek* magazine planned a big spread, and arranged for a motorcycle courier to rush their photographer's film to the nearest airport, so it would reach New York in time for Monday's edition. But on that same morning, a DC-10 lost an engine and crashed in Chicago, killing hundreds. Spenkelink's death was pushed down the front pages of America's newspapers and shoved back in the lineups of the major broadcasts. *Newsweek*'s big spread was reduced to a single column of type with a tiny mug shot of the dead man.

Coverage stuck pretty close to the conventional wisdom: The execution of John Spenkelink had broken the logjam, opened the floodgates, set the stage—choose your favorite cliché—for much swifter justice. Florida officials were quoted as saying that this would all soon be routine. Supporters of the death penalty believed the process was, at last, under way. In Jacksonville, a police softball team quickly raised thousands of dollars by selling T-shirts emblazoned with the slogan "One down, 133 to go."

The Spenkelink case was hugely significant, but in their haste to decode its meaning, the commentators and experts misread what was signified: enormous resources required to execute a single man. Judges differed intensely over the requirements of rationality and fact finding in the new death penalty law. And compared to the more complicated nature of most death penalty appeals, the Spenkelink case was relatively simple—a defendant who confessed, no allegations of suppressed evidence or prosecutorial misconduct, no claims of illegal searches, no disputes over sanity, no recanting eyewitnesses or late-blooming alibis. Spenkelink's death actually portended just how contentious and crazy and tortured the whole process was going to be. One man's execution illuminated the oceans of money and brains and energy the death penalty could consume. The Spenkelink legacy was not certainty, but rather a great big mess, a legal jumble, an emotional tempest. That's what proved to be significant. But everyone missed the story.

John Arthur Spenkelink was eulogized in a crowded service at Tallahassee's historic First Presbyterian Church, a picturesque white steepled building situated roughly midway between Bob Graham's home and his office. The survivors on death row sent a huge spray of flowers. He was buried in a California cemetery under a stone carved with his chosen epitaph.

His place on death row was almost immediately filled; again there were 134 to go. Then 135, 136, 137 . . . By the end of the year Florida's death row had grown by nearly two dozen. Theodore Robert Bundy, America's most notorious serial killer, was dispatched to death row in July 1979 for the murders of two women at a Tallahassee sorority house. Days after that, half brothers William Riley Jent and Earnest Lee Miller were arrested near Tampa and charged with the murder of an unidentified woman found burned in a forest. Soon they, too, were on death row. And scores more would arrive before the next execution, which—for all those unseen reasons—would be a long way off.

PART II

DANCING ON THE HEAD OF A PIN

The breakfast carts rattle through the concrete prison at about half past five, and as they approach death row the first sounds of morning repeat the last sounds of night—remote-controlled locks clanking open and clunking closed, electric gates whirring, heavy metal doors crashing shut, voices wailing, Klaxons blaring. A maximum-security prison has no soft sounds.

At the end of each corridor of death-house cells, a guard opens a heavy door of steel bars, and a prison trusty pushes a breakfast cart inside. The door closes behind him, and when it locks, a second door opens and the trusty is on the tier. He steers his cart along the corridor, stopping at each cell to pass a tray of powdered eggs and lukewarm grits through a small slot in the bars. Inside the cell, on a thin mattress perhaps thirty inches wide, an inmate wakes, blinks his eyes. He is, perhaps, confused for a moment: Is he facing the dull concrete wall to his right, or the identical dull wall a single body length away to his left, or the identical dull ceiling of his featureless box? In any case, he orients himself in a moment, then stands, takes one step to the bars, and hauls in his tray. He sits on the bunk and eats with his tray on his knees. When he is finished, he returns the tray to the slot and, typically, goes back to sleep. Sleep—"downy sleep, Death's counterfeit," as Shakespeare put it—is the best way to pass time on death row.

Toward nine o'clock, the day resumes as the men of death row come reluctantly awake again. Perhaps a man now runs his eyes around the place he calls his "house." There are three concrete walls to it, a concrete floor, and a concrete ceiling. The fourth wall is made of bars, which open onto the corridor, which is about eight feet wide. On the other side of the corridor, beyond another grille of steel, are grimy little windows, and beyond the windows are empty prison grounds bounded by coils of razor wire. From side to side, his house is about two paces wide; from back to front, about three paces deep. It is one pace from the steel bunk to the steel sink-and-toilet combination. The toilet has no seat, just a molded rim of steel. Concrete and steel, steel and concrete.

Under the bunk or next to it is a small steel locker for the prisoner's belongings. Tightly fixed to one wall is a small bar for hanging a towel. High up the rear of the cell is a ventilation grate about a foot square, and from this grate the prisoner has probably run a clothesline to the bars at the front of the cell. Dangling from the line are his damp white socks, white boxer shorts, blue dungarees, and orange T-shirts— the men of death row wear orange to distinguish them from the rest of the prison population. The prisoner does his laundry in the sink or in the toilet and hangs it overhead to dry. Laundry is a good way to pass time. Once a man learns the slowest, most meticulous way of washing socks, he can stretch that task out over several hours.

The man's walls may be bare, or decorated with his own artwork, or with pictures of family, or pictures of far-off places, pictures of Jesus, or of Muhammad, or of nude women, or of nude men. A condemned prisoner can survey his whole house with one quick sweep of his eyes: It is essentially a bathroom with a bunk where the tub would ordinarily be. He spends an average of twenty-three hours a day inside, knows every hairline crack and rusty paint chip. If this is a winter morning, it is very cold on death row; if this is summer, it is very hot. It stinks the same regardless of the season, the air thick with the odor of smoking, sweating, dirty, defecating men.

Morning is typically the time for calisthenics, if a man still cares about keeping fit. He lies down on the floor between his bunk and the wall and does sit-ups, then flips over for push-ups, then stands for some knee bends or a little shadowboxing. Perhaps he chins himself on the bars like a monkey, or jogs in place, pumping a book in each hand to tone his biceps. Then he turns himself to the staggering task that is every man's burden on death row: filling the hours until he can sleep again.

The options are few. There is talk—endless, disembodied, cacophonous, mostly inane talk. The prisoner steps to the front of his cell and begins declaiming loudly, and his voice echoes along the corridor. No one can see him because all the cells face the same way, with thick walls between them. But everyone can hear him. Talking this way is called "getting on the bars," and some men will get on the bars for hours at a stretch, yammering about motorcycles or politics or blood or fishing. They will tell their life stories for the hundredth time. They'll debate the relative merits of Ferraris versus Lamborghinis, of Ted Nugent versus Marvin Gaye, of the Lakers versus the Celtics, of white women versus black women, of AK-47s versus MAC-10s. They'll describe the engineering specifications of a Harley-Davidson motorcycle from stem to stern. They'll make bets on whether it will rain before sundown. Some men are insane, and get on the bars to rave about astral projection or screaming vaginas or men coming through the ventilation shafts at night. Sixteen men live on each tier, so the conversation soon gets stale, yet it continues, month after month, year after year.

It is possible to shout messages through the air ducts to prisoners on the floors above and below, but "getting on the vents," as this is called, is no way to hold a discourse. It suffices for brief communication only, like smoke signals or semaphore. Real talk is limited to the tired palaver on the bars, and ways must be found to escape its loud monotony. So a man on death row soon learns to cut earplugs from the spongy soles of his prison-issue shower slides, and to sew dental floss to them in case a plug gets stuck in his ear canal. Most men also own a boom box with a set of headphones, which they slip on to slip away. If the music moves a man, perhaps he dances in place. Perhaps he sings along, and his flat, toneless voice joins the rest of the noise on the tier.

Some men keep their houses very tidy, which passes some time and keeps the roaches at bay. Reading passes more time, at least among the men who are literate. Books, newspapers, and magazines make their way from cell to cell, and it's an unwritten but absolute rule that no one steals the reading material. There is no clear logic to the list of publications permitted by Florida's prison officials. Gun magazines are understandably forbidden, but so are many travelogues of such distant places as France and Italy—these are banned under the no-maps policy, as if a map of Tuscany could help a man escape from Starke. *Playboy* and *Playgirl, Penthouse,* and *Hustler* are allowed, apparently on the theory that masturbation has a pacifying effect. A pathological pederast got parts of the Montgomery Ward catalogue through the mail so he could savor the pictures of boys in their underwear. But an inmate who wanted to have a Mozart score sent to him was turned down. Prisoners are allowed to receive up to four books in the mail four times a year, which means that voracious readers have to ration their pleasure. They savor maybe twenty-five or fifty pages before putting the book down for a day or two, lest their allotment go too fast. And while it is possible to request books from the prison library, this service is unreliable: One man sent in a request for Dickens and got back Louis L'Amour. This reflects the taste of the average prisoner. The day L'Amour died was a sad day on Florida's death row.

At about 11 A.M., the trusties rattle up once more with their carts and pass lunch trays through the slots in the cell bars. A typical lunch might be a thin sandwich on enriched white bread, a carton of milk, a starchy vegetable, and a square of cake. After lunch, perhaps another hour can be killed with a nap. Then, a literate inmate has writing to do. Long letters to friends, family, lawyers; bad poems and bad novels; journal entries spun from empty days; convoluted claims of innocence, to be shipped off to journalists; legal briefs challenging prison conditions—a few of which are quite ingenious. One inmate came across an Eastern religion that required its adherents to eat only vegetarian meals and to pray each day while kneeling on a special rug. Declaring himself to be among the faithful of that sect, he filed suit demanding his religious freedom. Eventually he won, and soon his religion became the hottest one on death row, as men discovered the joys of special meals and a patch of carpet on their concrete floors. The sect lost some of its popularity, though, when prisoners saw that their vegetarian meals came on trays labeled with their names. This made it too easy for an enemy somewhere in the prison to mix a little spit or urine or ground glass into their food.

Some men's writing is devoted to elaborate cons. They comb personal ads in magazines and newspapers, looking for likely marks. A popular diversion is to strike up pen-pal relationships with lonely homosexuals, then get on the bars and scornfully read the letters they receive. One guy came across the address of an elderly woman in Georgia, and sent her a moving letter. He said he was a pilot, he had been badly injured in a crash, and he needed a few thousand dollars for an operation. The woman's tender heart was touched, and she sent a check for the full amount. The scam would have worked had the warden not called the woman's bank. Other ploys have worked even better. One day, a man arrived at the prison administration building and announced he was there to pick up Frances. The warden was summoned. "What on earth are you talking about?" he asked.

"Frances," said the man. "She is in your prison and today is her release date. I'm here to pick her up, and we're going to be married." Solemnly, the man acknowledged that Frances had done some bad things in the past, but he knew from her letters that she had mended her ways. And he produced the letters, each one lovingly cherished in its original envelope. On each envelope, in compliance with prison regulations, was the author's cell number, which was on death row. "Look," the warden said. "There's no Frances getting out today or any day. Your pen pal is never walking out of here. Go on home."

When an inmate gets tired of writing, he can draw. On sketch pads purchased from the prison canteen, he can engineer airplanes. He can map the battles of great wars, real and imagined. He can design vast mansions, down to the last inch of the floor plan, every stick of furniture, each swatch of upholstery, each doorknob and light fixture. He can draw Christ on the cross, or a muscular biker with evil tattoos. He can sketch an electric chair draped with the American flag, or scenes of hideous gore. (In recent years, a small but lucrative market has sprung up for inmate art. John Wayne Gacy, a serial killer executed in Illinois in 1994, sold drawings of clowns and cartoon characters for as much as two thousand dollars.)

And still all of these activities don't begin to fill the time—not when there are 365 identical days of the year and the years pile up one on the next. Time is the thing these men have in crushing abundance; they struggle to consume it in profligate portions. A condemned man learns to make picture frames from aluminum foil. He plays poker with the man in the next cell, each of them crouched close to the bars on either side of their common wall, dealing the cards onto a towel in the corridor. He plays chess with the guy three cells down, getting on the bars to shout his moves. Anything to make the time slide: Crocheting is popular. The killers of death row hook yarn into hats, slippers, shawls, oven mitts. Knitting is banned, because you can kill a man with a knitting needle.

Caged in a room two paces wide and three paces deep, even the most creative man, bent on self-distraction, needs something more powerful than his own wits to get him through. That something is television. God, it drives the hard-liners in the legislature and the fire-brands of talk radio crazy to think that prisoners on death row have TV sets in their cells. Coddling the criminals! Indulging them with luxuries! It would be hard to find a prison guard, though, who opposed the sets. Television is the only thing that makes death row manageable. The prison staff has a special nickname for those TV sets, thirteen inches diagonal, black-and-white screen, one in every cell. "Electronic tranquilizers," they call them. Once, when a Florida lawmaker told a prison official he should strip those sets from the cells of those vermin, the prison man said, "Fine. You go in there and take them out." The place could not exist without the tube.

Some dim bulbs on death row watch cartoons all day long. (One man heard about his last-minute stay of execution while watching *The Flintstones*.) Some men are devoted to soap operas. Whole tiers get on the bars every night and race one another for the right answers during *Jeopardy!* Some watch the cop shows and cheer for the bad guys. At noon, and again at six in the evening, most prisoners watch the news—and they all watch the same station so they can have something in common to talk about. Sensational murder trials are followed with acute interest, and if the defendant gets something less than the death penalty, the men on the row get on the bars to decry the sentence. "Man, that bastard should be sitting here with me!" someone shouts. "What the fuck? I killed one guy and I'm here, he kills two and gets rewarded?"

Television fuels the gambling. The men of death row bet the ball games, bet the boxing matches, bet the dog race results. A couple of death row prisoners once discovered that by listening to the finishes at the dog track live on an obscure AM radio band, they could learn the winners a full hour before the information turned up on TV. They cleaned up on bets, losing just enough to cover their scam.

And television nourishes the last tendrils of identity by which the inmates distinguish themselves from the gray heap of waste souls around them. A World War II documentary comes on the tube, and the white supremacists cheer Hitler. A Malcolm X documentary comes on, and now the Muslim brotherhood is cheering. A man falls in love with the lady who does the weather. Another man fantasizes about the blond boy on a particular sitcom. Yet another man measures his week by the approach of the Saturday afternoon bass-fishing shows. When the human mind runs out of ideas—as it does very quickly on death row, where the men are mostly stupid and the time is very long—television fills the void. And so the tube glows and natters almost ceaselessly as life crawls by in the death house.

Dinner arrives about 4 P.M.: a pork chop, or a piece of liver, maybe chicken, or "mystery meat," and more starchy vegetables. Prison cooks know about a million ways to fix potatoes. As the prisoners sit on their bunks, facing their toilets with their trays on their knees, they shout complaints about the food. Someone finds a hair in his tray. "Musta been a black guy fixed my food," he calls out. "I got wool in my mystery meat." Someone calls back, "Mine musta been a blond."

The other luxury that makes the time barely endurable is the canteen cart. For each man on death row, the prison maintains a sort of bank account, where the inmate collects the money he gets from family, lawyers, friends, and the suckers he can con without being caught. He is allowed to spend up to $25 a week from this account at the prison canteen. Since he can't get out of his cell to go to the canteen, the canteen comes to him. On Thursdays, runners take orders for "dry goods"—chips, pastries, coffee, tea, hot chocolate, tobacco, paper, pens, and so forth. The limit is four of each item (with the exception of candy bars; ten of those are permitted), but the limits can be evaded. Death row is a thriving barter economy. Say a man wants more than four pastries—he bargains. Maybe he doesn't smoke, so he orders extra cigarettes for the man next door while the man next door orders pastries for him. The bargaining is endless, and another way to pass time. More expensive items are also peddled by the canteen: radios, sneakers, art supplies.

Dry goods ordered on Thursday are delivered the following Monday. On Tuesday, runners take orders from the canteen for sandwiches, dry soups, and sodas. These are delivered on Wednesday. On Friday the ice cream cart comes around, stocked with bread, lunch meat, and Howard Johnson's ice cream. The canteen also sells orange juice, of course—it wouldn't be Florida without orange juice. On the row, juice is the essential ingredient in "buck," which is home-brewed prison booze. Take orange juice, add a little sugar and a few bread scraps for yeast, and—in the heat of a cell in summer—fermentation begins. Most buck doesn't taste very good, but, hey: If a man plans properly, he can brew enough during the week to get buzzed while watching a ball game on Sunday. Just like home. And if a man has no juice he can get some buck going using the syrup from the fruit cup at lunch. Resourcefulness is all.

A man learns to shift. Even on death row, he is part of that same human race that figured out how to budge boulders with a stick, how to chip flint into arrows, how to coax fire from a spark. He has technology in his genes. So he learns to use a handheld mirror—a "spook"—to see what's going on along the corridor. He holds the mirror through the bars, at a forty-five degree angle to his face; he can see everything. He learns to make a fan from a piece of cardboard, a length of yarn, and a pen. He learns to make a "waterbug," a crude wire heating element that can boil water for coffee or soup. And then he learns other uses for his waterbug, like heating baby oil into a sort of napalm.

At one point, the men on death row learned to make zip guns: A section of radio antenna formed the barrel, the heads of matches worked for gunpowder, and the bullets were balled-up pieces of toothpaste tube. The zip gun problem got so bad that the warden proposed banning matches, which the guards promptly told him was nuts. A prison without matches? What are they gonna light their cigarettes with? The zip gun problem persisted.

Finally, the desperate warden took a couple of disposable butane lighters into the cellblocks and handed them to a lifer with a gift for fashioning explosives. "Make a bomb," the warden said. You have to take risks to run a prison. A week later, the lifer pronounced the task impossible; there was no way to detonate a butane lighter, he said. So matches were banned, and that was the end of the zip-gun era. But something more lethal may yet come along; the men of death row can be devilishly clever. "Hell," one boasted once, "if they'd give us a little education in physics, I bet we could come up with cold fusion."

Twice a week, the sixteen men on each tier are taken outside for two hours of exercise in a narrow yard, reserved for them. There is just space enough for half a basketball court, a volleyball court with a string for a net, and a bench with a rusty set of weights. In the early days of the modern death penalty, there was a patch of dirt for playing football, dusty in summer, muddy in winter, but that was soon paved over. More blacks than whites play basketball; more whites than blacks play volleyball. Some men do not exercise at all, preferring to loll by the fence in the sunshine, trying to get some color on their prison pallors.

A chain-link fence separates the death row yard from the main prison yard; now and then, a man from the general prison population might sidle up to the other side of the fence and slip a marijuana joint or a few pills through the mesh. Some men do not come outside at all, for reasons of sloth or safety. Older, weaker men might come out only once every few months, and then only in pairs, to talk and walk in slow circles around the fence. They travel in pairs for safety. Snitches and child molesters almost never take exercise; someone might try to kill them. Still, there isn't a lot of fighting on the yard because each infraction means losing your exercise privilege for a year.

Twice a week, usually after dinner, there is shower time. A man strips to his shorts, slips his feet into his shower slides, and shuffles alongside a guard to a steel cage the size of a shower stall. He's locked in, and the water comes on. He hopes it is warm. Five minutes later, the water stops, and he's led back to his house.

Lights out comes at 11 P.M., but only the ceiling fixtures in the cells are dimmed; the corridor lights burn eternally. Televisions flicker with talk shows and old movies into the wee hours. Men lie on their bunks and stare. Sex on death row is primarily a solo affair, consummated in these dark hours with fantasy lovers conjured from imagination and porn. It is not unheard of, though, that an enterprising trusty might, for a fee, arrive at the bars of a man's cell to perform fellatio. Or on visiting day, a guard might—again, for a fee—look the other way as a man and his guest duck into the bathroom together.

The prison is never completely quiet. Gates are always clanging, there's the tread of guards, the nightmare ravings of the insane, the muffled sobs of despair. Night noise segues into the din of a new morning. The clock creeps round to 5:30 A.M., and another, identical, day comes to death row.

In this dull hell there are those men who, like John Spenkelink, use the time and discipline and solitude of death row to make something more of themselves than they ever managed on the outside. Vernon Ray Cooper, for example, had been a high school dropout and sometime cab driver. He and a friend named Steve Ellis held up a grocery store in Pensacola in January 1974. They made their getaway in Cooper's black Camaro. As they sped onto Interstate 10 heading west, deputy sheriff Charles Wilkerson spotted their car and switched on his flashing lights. The Camaro stopped on a dark stretch of road. Someone —either Ellis or Cooper—got out of the car, walked quickly to the cruiser, and fired two shots into Wilkerson's head. The killer raced back to the Camaro and the car roared away.

Two more deputies, in separate cars, quickly caught up to the robbers and, after a wild chase, forced them to a stop just across the Alabama line. Ellis jumped from the driver's side and put his hands over his head. One of the deputies, gun drawn, began patting him down. Just then, Cooper, still inside the car, fired a shotgun blast into the floorboard. The lawman flinched—and in that momentary diversion Ellis pulled a .38 from under his coat. He raised it toward the deputy, but the deputy was quicker. The lawman fired, and Ellis was dead.

Cooper squeezed off another round from the shotgun, shattering the rear window of his car, and slipped the Camaro into gear. Hunched low, he steered the car more than a mile as the deputies fired round after round after him. When he crashed into an embankment, Cooper slipped out of the passenger door and started running. Some five hundred people joined the search. It was like something from a movie, flashlight beams streaking wildly through the trees, dogs baying, men shouting. After several hours, Cooper was discovered lying in a ditch, the sawed-off shotgun pressed beneath him. Charged with Wilkerson's murder, he steadfastly maintained that his dead partner had been the triggerman. The prosecution offered a life sentence if Cooper would plead guilty, but he declined. He drew the death penalty.

On death row, Cooper began educating himself, reading widely and deeply, choosing his books carefully, everything from the Greek classics to modern poetry. Over time, he transformed himself from an ignorant cracker into the sort of man who would quote the forlorn poetry of a lesser English writer named Thomas Hood. "But now 'tis little joy," Hood wrote in a favorite poem of Cooper's, "to know I'm farther off from heaven than when I was a boy." If you asked Vernon Cooper to describe his prison life, he would politely direct you to Oscar Wilde:

> I know not whether Laws be right,
>   Or whether Laws be wrong:
> All that we know who lie in gaol
>   Is that the walls are strong;
> And that every day is like a year,
>   A year whose days are long.
>
> . . . .
>
> The vilest deeds like prison weeds,
>   Bloom well in prison-air;
> It is only what is good in Man
>   That wastes and withers there:
> Pale Anguish keeps the heavy gate,
>   And the Warder is Despair.
>
> . . . .
>
> Each narrow cell in which we dwell
>   Is a sad and dark latrine,
> And the fetid breath of living Death
>   Chokes up each grated screen,
> And all, but Lust, is turned to dust
>   In Humanity's machine.

There are such men on death row, seemingly redeemable souls, men who could live out their lives behind bars with a little dignity and some grace. There are also men so vile as to beggar imagination.

Johnny Paul Witt was one of these. On an October morning in 1973, Witt set out from his home near Tampa with a friend named Gary Tillman. They were going hunting—for a human being. They had gone hunting together like this before, without success.

This time, they spotted a boy on a bicycle leaving the parking lot of a 7-Eleven store, where he had gone to buy some candy. Witt and Tillman stalked the boy as he rode through a woods toward home. Witt sprang, battered the boy's head with a drill, and then, with Tillman's help, gagged the boy tightly and stuffed him into the trunk of their car. They drove about ten miles to an orange grove, stopped, and pulled the boy from the trunk. He had died of suffocation.

They raped the body, first Tillman, then (impotently) Witt. They cut off the boy's penis and put it in a jar, like a trophy. They buried the child in a shallow grave, buried the jar in another forest. Tillman got a life sentence for testifying against Witt; Johnny Paul Witt was condemned to death. On death row, he never left his six-by-nine cell, because he knew what would happen if he stepped outside.

Mere boys have gone to death row. George Vasil was just fifteen years old when he was sentenced to die, the youngest American in a death house at the time. He wanted what boys want at fifteen, wanted it desperately—but he was never able to get any because he was pimply with a mess of greasy black hair and wore thick glasses and had no charm. His first attempt at seduction was also his last; he fumbled and groped and when she resisted it turned to rape. Vasil was so agitated that he couldn't manage an erection, and that frustrated him so much that he picked up a rock and hit the poor girl over the head. She began screaming so he stuffed her panties into her mouth. She died, battered and choking. Vasil was death row's wretched youth.

Jacob John Dougan Jr., on the other hand, was an impressive and magnetic man, proprietor of the Black Karate Association at Jacksonville's Afro American Cultural Development Center. Dougan was suave with the ladies, and much admired by young men, who flocked to his martial arts classes. Dougan's teachings were an idiosyncratic blend of the physical and the philosophical, karate mixed with militant black nationalism. Dougan formed a coterie of his admirers into a brigade which he called either the Black Revolutionary Army or the Black Liberation Army—he waffled back and forth on the name.

On June 17, 1974, Dougan and four members of his army set out in their car in search of a white "devil" to kill. In a nearby beach town, they found an unlucky hitchhiker named Stephen Orlando, offered him a ride, then drove to a garbage dump and ordered Orlando out of the car. Elwood Barclay stabbed Orlando twice. As the victim struggled, Dougan fired shot after shot into his head until the gun jammed. Cheap American-made gun, Dougan later complained. He had wanted to fire more.

After killing the hitchhiker, Dougan took a note which he had prepared in advance and stuck it to the corpse with a knife. "Warning," said the note, "to the oppressive state. No longer will your atrocities and brutalizing of black people be unpunished. The black man is no longer asleep. The revolution has begun and the oppressed will be victorious. . . . All power to the people." Over the next several days, Dougan and Barclay recorded a number of rambling screeds about white devils and black oppression and the comparative size of brains among the races. Then they sent the tapes to local radio and television stations. Jacksonville was terrorized, and for two months, there were no clues.

The case broke on a fluke. A detective happened across a letter of resignation from an antipoverty program, and something about the handwriting struck him as familiar. He retrieved the note that had been stuck to Orlando's body. The writing was the same; the signature on the resignation letter was Jacob Dougan's. Later, the voice and fingerprints on the tapes were also matched to Dougan. Ever the ladies' man, Dougan was arrested by police in the bedroom of a girlfriend—a white devil, as it happened.

There were old men, too, on death row. Anthony Antone, an eccentric inventor, occasional jewel thief, and middleman in a murder-for-hire, was sixty-one years old when John Spenkelink was executed. During an earlier stint in prison, Antone's head had been smashed by an inmate in a case of mistaken identity. After that, things were never quite right between the ears of the amiable Antone. "They removed part of my brain due to an infection of cockroaches crawling around in my head," he explained. The spindly old man wandered the exercise yard sweetly giving his neighbors the creeps. He would buttonhole them to explain that he had discovered the secret to escaping gravity. Just push an invisible button and off you go. Flying!

David Washington was death row's beautiful athlete, quick, lithe, and graceful. When he wasn't in the exercise yard, he could often be heard weeping in his cell. True remorse is rare on the row—most of the men there have nothing but empty space where their conscience should be. But even hardened observers tended to agree that Washington's remorse was real and gut-wrenching. He had a wife and a baby in a Miami slum when, in September 1976, he lost his job and fell completely, violently, to pieces. Washington was in a laundromat one day, worried about being evicted, when a man approached and identified himself as a minister. The minister suggested they might get together for a date, suggested there might be a little money in it for handsome David Washington. So Washington went to the man's house. The minister proposed that Washington strip and straddle his face.

"I just stabbed him with a knife," Washington later told an interviewer. "I stabbed him about five times. The only thing going through my mind, I said, 'Here I am out here trying to get some money to feed my family, and here go a minister, supposed to be a minister in the church, running around doing stuff like this.'"

Tragically, once he snapped he stayed broken. In the span of a week, David Washington killed three times. He barged into the home of some old ladies in the neighborhood—he believed they ran a fencing operation, though newspapers reported only that the old women "ran frequent yard sales." Washington brandished a gun and began tying them up. One of the women rose from her chair, and Washington started firing wildly. Blood everywhere, one woman dead. Next, Washington kidnapped a student from the University of Miami, robbed him of eighty dollars, and considered holding him for ransom. Instead—as the young man recited the Lord's Prayer—Washington stabbed him to death.

He waived a jury trial, confessed everything to the judge, and received a death sentence. Until they paved the dirt football field in the death row exercise yard, Washington juked and glided through the defense like a gazelle. He spent most of his time admitting and apologizing for what he'd done, which made many of the other men on the row uneasy.

Contrition was not the route that Bob Sullivan chose to pass his time. Indeed, when Sullivan's death sentence was imposed, the judge noted that the defendant displayed not "one scintilla of remorse." Sullivan's explanation was simple—he insisted he was innocent—but the evidence was very strong that Sullivan did rob a Howard Johnson's restaurant and murder the night manager. Many of the men on death row steadfastly protested their innocence; Sullivan was just the most energetic. Joseph Green Brown was unusual because when he said he was innocent, he actually appeared to be telling the truth.

Brown was convicted of raping and murdering a clothing store clerk in 1973, largely on the testimony of a man who claimed to be an accomplice. Within eight months of the trial, the alleged accomplice admitted that he had fabricated his story because he had a grudge against Brown. No other evidence linked Brown to the crime. His gun had been produced in court as the likely murder weapon; unfortunately for Brown, his attorney neglected to subpoena the FBI ballistics expert who could prove that Brown's gun had not killed the clerk. Brown waited sullenly as his appeals ground slowly through the courts, hoping for a sympathetic judge.

No man was better liked on the row than "Crazy Joe" Spaziano, a motorcycle gang member who was sentenced to death for the rape-murder of a teenaged girl. Spaziano was tough, crude, and funny—all traits admired by his fellow inmates. No man was more despised than Arthur Frederick Goode III, who raped and murdered two boys and gloated about it afterward. Goode spent all day on the bars, delivering running commentary on the "sexy" child actors on television, and he whimpered through the night. When prisoners passed along the corridor outside his cell, they often tossed a cup of urine or a ball of feces or a flaming page of newspaper at him. The guards generally ignored this —they hated Goode as much as the inmates did; he was always asking them if they had young sons at home. Eventually, after the inmates signed a petition demanding that Goode be moved off the row, he was relocated to the isolation cells of Q-wing, where he wrote rambling letters about the joys of pedophilia.

Even the lawyers and chaplains and activists who routinely visited death row inmates dreaded spending time with Goode. On the rare occasions when someone did take pity and paid him a visit, the only way to endure the hour was to ignore his paranoid and perverted rants. One day a lawyer named Joe Nursey traveled to death row to visit a client, the newly incarcerated serial killer Ted Bundy. As a favor to a softhearted friend, Nursey also agreed to see the despicable Freddy Goode. He met first with Goode, and for an hour the prisoner blabbered senselessly about a "bad one" who had somehow stolen into his cell and devoured his supply of cookies. Nursey nodded and smiled and let his mind drift. Christ, he thought, this guy is bizarre. At last the hour was over and Goode was led from the visiting room and Bundy was brought in.

At the time, Bundy was also living, temporarily, in an isolation cell on Q-wing. "Joe," Bundy said after he settled into a chair, "I have a confession to make." Nursey braced himself. When Ted Bundy says he wants to confess something, God knows what's coming next.

"I'm in the cell next to Goode," Bundy said. "And last night I talked him into giving me a cookie, and when he did—I feel really bad about this, see—well, I ate the whole box." It was true: A bad one had stolen Goode's cookies. A very bad one, indeed.

So many stories, each unique in its sordid details. Benny Demps had been one of ninety-seven prisoners on Florida's death row in 1972 when the news came that the U.S. Supreme Court had struck down the death penalty. He had known the relief of having his sentence reduced from death to life. But then he had stabbed an inmate to death, and now he was the only one of the ninety-seven who was back on the row. Daniel Coler was the only one facing death for a crime other than murder. He had raped his daughter, and though the U.S. Supreme Court had eliminated the death penalty for rape, Coler was still waiting for the Florida courts to comply with that order. Steve Beattie was the only man on death row who could say he had been Ann-Margret's bodyguard. After his star-guarding days, he had opened a health club in Miami; he had then murdered his business partner as part of an insurance fraud. Beattie passed long hours in his cell planning the best way to commit suicide. There were more than 130 death row stories by the late spring of 1979, and what was unique began to fade as they intertwined in a hideous tapestry. This was the death house: a mixed bag of misfits, failures, and predators; half-wits and a few semisavants; figures of tragedy and figures of horror; crazy men and sane ones. It's scary, and deeply depressing, how many ways there are for human lives to go wrong, how many faces evil wears, how many modes can be found to flout even the simplest of the Ten Commandments: Thou shalt not kill.

Two days after John Spenkelink went to the chair, *The Miami Herald* ran a postage-stamp-sized mug shot and a sentence or two describing every man on the row. This project required two entire broadsheet pages. They were as densely packed as freshman photos in the yearbook of a huge state university. In the governor's office, the *Herald* package was like a tennis racquet in the face. No one had really stopped to think just how many men were waiting to die. How could anyone keep them all straight, let alone get them all executed?

The shock of all those faces peering out of the pages of the *Herald* was also felt among the people who worked to thwart the death penalty. Before May 25, 1979, they were a pretty confident group. They had believed that the ambiguous facts of John Spenkelink's case would stymie the State, that his execution would be blocked, and months, or even years, would pass before prosecutors could push another, stronger, case to its end. Spenkelink had everything going for him, they thought: His crime was not unmitigated, he had shown himself fit for rehabilitation, and he had a terrific group of lawyers. (David Kendall would later become the personal attorney to President Bill Clinton.) They had not counted on the willingness of so many judges to let Florida get on with its grim business.

But now Spenkelink was dead, and the thought dawned that everyone on death row was vulnerable. Moreover, there was no great public outcry against the execution; any hopes of turning political pressure against the death penalty faded rapidly. The battle was going to have to be waged primarily in the courts.

It was a dizzying prospect: If every man was vulnerable, and if the battle had to be fought in the courts, then every man in the *Herald*'s death row census would potentially require the superhuman efforts marshaled on Spenkelink's behalf. Someone gifted with foresight might have looked at all those mug shots and realized that the drama of the modern death penalty was not going to be the gruesome story of inmates and their crimes—it was going to be a chaos of lawyers and litigation.

But where would all the lawyers come from? Under state law, a death-sentenced inmate in Florida was entitled to free legal counsel only through the first appeal to the state supreme court. After that, he was on his own. The small community of death-penalty opponents quickly realized that neither the Inc. Fund nor Millard Farmer's Team Defense had anything approaching the resources necessary to defend upwards of 130 condemned clients in Florida.

Over the next ten months, Governor Bob Graham signed six more death warrants; volunteer lawyers were found to block each execution with an appeal. Victories were still possible. In the same period, however, death row grew by more than twenty new inmates. Local trial judges around Florida were handing out death sentences like highballs at Caesar's Palace: The rate of new sentences soon approached one per week. The central problem—the problem of finding sufficient resources to fight the Spenkelink fight a hundred and fifty times over—only deepened.

Finding the lawyers to represent the flood of condemned men was like bailing out the *Titanic* with a teaspoon. The teaspoon had a name: Scharlette Holdman. Scharlette Holdman had a title: director of the Florida Clearinghouse on Criminal Justice.

It was a rather grand title, but anyone who has spent much time around the lobbies of government knows that, as a rough rule of thumb, the grander an organization's name, the smaller its actual resources. Exxon, the Tobacco Institute, the Rand Corporation—simple names, huge clout. By contrast, the Florida Clearinghouse on Criminal Justice was basically Holdman and a secretary and a few occasionally compensated volunteers. The Clearinghouse had a one-room office in a drab two-story office block known around Tallahassee as the FOG Building, short for Forces of Good. Low rents for the FOG Building's shabby little offices attracted a broad array of underfunded, over-matched public interest organizations. Holdman, with an annual budget rarely exceeding $25,000, operated on one of the shortest shoestrings of them all.

Scharlette Holdman had brains, passion, charm; she had a foul mouth, a dark sense of humor, and a bottomless well of energy; she hated authority, scorned convention; she saw the world in starkly simple terms: The haves screw the have-nots. Crime, in her eyes, was the inevitable fruit of an unjust, racist system. If this view was too spare, too easy, it was nonetheless one she had come by honestly, and it was essential to her work. There were times when she stood virtually alone against the will of the public and the force of the State, and such stands are impossible without certainty.

She was the daughter of a hardheaded businessman from White Haven, Tennessee, a man who had started with nothing and hauled himself into the upper middle class as a landlord of the Memphis slums. Holdman's childhood coincided with a terrible time for the South, when racial segregation was laid bare. The body politic was shown to be diseased . . . and yet the institutions and authorities claimed that this system was a healthy and vital organ. Because Scharlette Holdman was an intelligent, spunky child—editor of the yearbook, captain of the cheerleaders, "president of everything" at her high school—she saw that power was being abused in defense of bigotry. And this turned her against authority, as it turned so many of her generation.

Her view of authority was also corroded at home. Holdman's father tolerated no back talk, brooked no dissent, even from Scharlette, who was arguably his favorite child. The father perceived great promise in his clever, energetic daughter, and looked to the day when he might turn his business over to her. Toward that end, he often took Scharlette along when he went to collect rents and evict clients at his slum properties. He called this "going niggering." His racism only deepened Holdman's sense of an unjust social order and her contempt for power.

She saved her rebellion until she was out of the house, and at first it was mild—joining registration drives for black voters, that sort of thing. Her father disapproved, of course, so Holdman left Memphis State and moved to Washington to get some distance from him. She joined the antiwar protests there, but she still had a lot of the well-behaved yearbook editor in her. Holdman met and married the first man she dated in Washington, a third-generation college professor and Republican from Pennsylvania. She was twenty-one years old and worried about becoming an old maid. Her husband offered the prospect of a quiet and orderly life. "He didn't drink or beat up women," she later told an interviewer. "I said . . . 'I'll marry him.' "

Holdman was, apparently, more changed than she realized. Domestic life was too conventional for her, and at twenty-five she packed up her two small children, daughter Summer and son Tad, and moved to Boston, where she went to work in an organic bakery. Her split from the middle class was complete. She threw herself into liberal causes, eventually landing a job as director of the American Civil Liberties Union in Hawaii. From there, she moved with the ACLU to New Orleans, to Mississippi, and eventually to Miami. To Holdman, Florida in the late 1970s was the center of the action, the fulcrum of a great national change. Outsiders, many of them Yankees, were pouring into the state. When Holdman arrived, Reubin Askew was the governor, perhaps the best of the New South progressives. Battles were being fought over gay rights, abortion, the Equal Rights Amendment, and the death penalty, and Holdman could picture winning some of these battles. She threw herself eagerly into fundraising, cajoling potential donors with her view of Florida as "the bellwether state."

Money for the Miami ACLU chapter soon dried up, however, through circumstances outside Holdman's control. The national ACLU was defending the right of Nazis to march through the mostly Jewish city of Skokie, Illinois, and the liberal Jews who formed the spine of Holdman's support in Miami closed their checkbooks. She took a job that paid $600 a month, heading the Clearinghouse on Criminal Justice in Tallahassee. She had been on the job just a few months when John Spenkelink was executed.

Holdman, perhaps more than anyone else, perceived the legal vacuum on death row, perceived it in the most personal way possible. "I said, Wait a minute. You mean, if I don't find lawyers for these guys, the State's gonna kill them all?" she recalled. And she concluded that the answer was yes. Holdman took on the job despite being imperfectly suited to it. Along her vagabond activist's path, she had managed to earn a master's degree in anthropology, but she knew almost nothing about the law. The Latinate language of legal writ writers—*mandamus, habeas corpus, certiorari*—was all Greek to her. Someone told her that a maximum of ten appellate steps stood between a death sentence and the electric chair. Holdman found an old ledger and divided the pages into ten columns, one for each step. Then she took the ledger to Deborah Fins of the Inc. Fund and asked Fins to mark the steps where an inmate was most vulnerable to a death warrant. Next, Holdman created a line for every condemned prisoner in Florida, and began marking which steps each man had completed. This was painstaking work, and the men on death row were little help; most of them had even less understanding of the legal process than Holdman did. They had no idea whether they were on step two or step eight; some of them couldn't even read. Even the smart ones could be flummoxed by legal procedure. (Doug McCray, a former honor student, once received a sheaf of routine legal papers in the mail, along with a note from a secretary saying the papers were "for your execution"—meaning that they required his signature. McCray saw the word "execution" and went into a panic.) Holdman had to scrounge through legal files and hunt down lawyers across the state, trying to figure out precisely who stood where on the road to Old Sparky.

Eventually, though, after months of effort, she compiled a crude, but fairly complete, log of the legal status of Florida's death row. Whenever a new inmate was sentenced to death, Holdman added another line in the ledger, and as the months went by and cases crawled through the courts, she updated her ledger using pencil and correction fluid. She was like a medic performing triage at a train wreck: The first job was to determine who was closest to dying.

Yet that task was easy compared to the second: finding attorneys willing to represent her clients. On the surface, this might not have seemed so difficult; Florida was crawling with lawyers, some thirty thousand of them licensed to practice. The state was a burgeoning mecca of millionaires and entrepreneurs, real estate developers and boiler-room scam artists, drug dealers and grifters and tax-dodging financiers, and lawyers flourished amid all that money. Neither Scharlette Holdman nor the men on death row had any money to offer, though. Moreover, public-spirited lawyers had hundreds of needy and decent causes clamoring for their pro bono efforts. Churches and charities and destitute widows all needed free legal help, and all made more appealing clients than some murderer in the death house. Public opinion polls showed that upwards of 80 percent of Floridians favored the death penalty, and many of them might balk at the idea of taking their business to a defender of condemned thugs. For that matter, most lawyers in Florida felt the same way about capital punishment.

Even the few attorneys who believed in Holdman's cause could be intimidated by a death case. All they had to do was look at David Kendall's long fight for John Spenkelink. A proper appellate defense could drain thousands of dollars for private investigators and legal researchers, thousands more to prepare and copy and file briefs, and still more thousands traveling to far-flung courthouses. The cases could drag on for years and—worst of all, in the minds of some lawyers—the cost of failure was nearly unbearable. It was one thing to lose a landlord-tenant dispute done free through the Legal Aid Society. Your client would probably find another apartment. Take a capital case and lose, though, and you have a dead man on your conscience.

All day, every day, Holdman sat at her telephone in her shabby office at the FOG Building, chain-smoking Benson & Hedges cigarettes with one hand and dialing with the other. Quite a sight she was: hair frizzed, feet bare, body rocking in a cheap swivel chair, face lost in a cloud of smoke. She called the heads of local bar associations and asked for recommendations. She called managing partners at big law firms and inquired about their pro bono programs. She got rosters of various liberal organizations and cross-indexed them with the state legal directory, targeting potentially friendly lawyers for calls. She haunted law conferences, scouting for likely prospects. Holdman spent so much time on the telephone in search of lawyers that one Christmas her secretary gave her a cushion for the receiver to prevent cauliflower ear.

Luckily for Holdman—and, more to the point, for her clients—

she had a glorious gift of gab. From the moment a lawyer answered the phone, Holdman kept up a steady line of pleading, cajoling, flattering, and noodging, all spiced with a dark but hilarious wit. Scharlette Holdman talking was a natural force, like a hurricane or a rockslide; she was unstoppable. If she was in the mood to tell the truth, she would ask the lawyer for "three years of your life and ten grand out of your pocket," which was her estimate of what a decent capital appeal might take. But Holdman was rarely so candid. Instead, she'd say that so-and-so on death row was in danger of dying unless a simple appeal was filed, and couldn't the lawyer just give her a week . . . just three days, maybe . . . a weekend . . . to draw up the brief? The lawyer on the other end of the line might start stammering for an excuse, but it had not taken Holdman long before she had heard every imaginable excuse and had learned how to cut in quickly and quash each one. She'd promise to gather all the files. She'd arrange all the typing. If the lawyer protested that he knew next to nothing about criminal appeals, Holdman would answer, in her sweetest former cheerleader's drawl: Don't worry, we'll get somebody to help you.

At the end of each call, she made a notation on an index card and added it to the pile she kept beside her ledger. "A street fighter," she wrote on the card of one eager prospect. "Will help us but only in a crunch," she noted on the card of a less enthusiastic possibility. "Only into $$$$$," she scribbled under the name of one unpromising target. Most of the time she had nothing to note but an outright rejection. But Holdman kept going, fueling herself with Kentucky Fried Chicken and coffee in the daytime, cheap whiskey or jug wine at night. Sometimes, during a frantic day of phone calls, she'd look up and it was 8 P.M. and she'd realize she had nothing in the refrigerator for the kids to eat. On such days, Holdman would make a mad dash to McDonald's and then hurry back to work. More than once, her electricity was cut off because she had been too busy to pay the bill.

It was an impossible job, countering the full power of Florida's government with nothing but a telephone, a pencil, and a motorized mouth. But her work allowed her to upset authority, and there was nothing Holdman loved more. Now and then she would take time away from the phone to organize a Yippie-style protest. One time, for example, she and about a dozen volunteers, including the radical priest Daniel Berrigan, interrupted a meeting of the state cabinet with a mock execution. Another time, after discovering that Florida Attorney General Jim Smith's birthday fell on the anniversary of the Spenkelink execution, Holdman baked a cake and decorated it with black licorice crosses, one for each of the death warrants signed to that point. She rounded up a group of kids to deliver the cake to Smith. When the attorney general emerged from his office to receive what he thought would be birthday greetings, he was met by a chorus of "Happy Deathday to You." (Holdman later heard that a bomb squad had been called in to examine the cake. "If I'd known he wasn't going to eat it, I wouldn't have used real cake mix," she joked.)

After about a year of her impossible work, Holdman had identified perhaps a hundred lawyers willing to help to some degree, ranging from the barest cooperation—a grudging agreement to sponsor the work of an out-of-state lawyer—to a few full-fledged commitments to shoulder one case after another. The population on death row was pushing 160 by then. She kept dialing.

Scharlette Holdman was the heart of the campaign to save the doomed of Florida's death row. Craig Barnard was the brains. Holdman found the lawyers, Barnard advised and educated them. Law schools don't teach you how to craft death penalty appeals; this was an arcane and complicated world unto itself, a world just beginning to be made. Craig Barnard, the chief assistant public defender in West Palm Beach, knew everything there was to know about this world.

His title hardly matched his status. Barnard's official job was to run a single public defender's office in one medium-sized district of the state. But death penalty opponents were in no position to worry about the authority granted by official titles. Craig Barnard had talent, vision, and dedication; he knew how to organize and how to lead people. They quickly made him their teacher, guide, rabbi, counselor, and chief strategist in the effort to save Florida's condemned.

Holdman and Barnard were yin and yang—Holdman a brash, hard-drinking, sixties throwback; Barnard the quiet, pipe-smoking, sober son of Midwest Republican stock. What they shared was a fervent belief that the government could not be trusted to decide who would live and who would die. Holdman recruited lawyers and Barnard mapped tactics; together they devoted themselves to preventing quick and easy executions. In the first months after Spenkelink, they succeeded case by case. Governor Graham signed four more warrants in 1979, and six in 1980. In all ten cases, defense lawyers were found, appeals were filed, executions were stayed.

Craig Barnard could count, however, and the math was flowing against him. Death row was growing like mold, and a small army of inmates was advancing steadily through the boxes in Holdman's ledger. As long as they had the lawyers, they could fight case by case—but they didn't have enough lawyers. Barnard's task, the job of the guru, was to develop legal issues that would cut across many cases; if he could find the perfect issue, it would wrap up every case on death row.

Picture the distinction: Say John Doe is on death row. John Doe's lawyer could file an appeal claiming that the key witness at Doe's trial had an undisclosed grudge against Doe. Police knew about the grudge, and by law they should have disclosed it to the defense. They didn't. The appeals lawyer had to dig it out. Therefore, Doe's death sentence is illegal. Such an appeal might take months of investigation to develop, hundreds of hours of a lawyer's time. And even if it was successful, it wouldn't help anyone besides John Doe.

What if the lawyer could show, instead, that a certain provision of the Florida death penalty law, or a common practice of the Florida courts, was unconstitutional? An appeal like that would reverberate from case to case. If the law, or the common practice, was unconstitutional for one inmate, it would be for them all. Even if the law was eventually determined to be sound, the courts might take years to settle the matter. And everyone would be safe while the question was pending.

If Barnard could find and develop good, expansive, legal issues, and get them to the attention of key courts, then they might become constitutional roadblocks to every death warrant the governor signed. Given the shortage of lawyers, if he failed to come up with large-scale legal issues an army of inmates would soon begin marching to the electric chair.

Of course, Craig Barnard didn't invent the idea. Essentially, he was hoping to regain some of the momentum of the 1960s and early 1970s, when a few great lawyers with a few broad issues blocked hundreds of executions at a stroke. That was the Golden Age for anti–death penalty lawyers, and Barnard looked to it for guidance.

For most of American history, capital punishment was a state or even a local issue. Criminals were judged, convicted, and sentenced according to local rules and customs, and their executions were generally carried out by town sheriffs in courthouse squares. Federal judges took almost no interest in the death penalty, and even state appeals courts tended to give the matter little consideration. In frontier states like Florida, the death penalty was often a matter of expedience: Small towns in the wilderness simply couldn't maintain secure jails for long-term prisoners, and the job of transporting an outlaw hundreds of miles to the state prison was more than the sheriff cared to do. Criminals were hanged in part because there was no place to lock them up. Thousands of people were executed in America under entirely local jurisdiction, with only cursory appeals at best.

Not surprisingly, a disproportionate number of the people executed under these customs were black, and the execution rate was most dramatically skewed for the crime of rape. Intercourse between black men and white women, if discovered, was widely prosecuted as rape regardless of the actual facts of the case, and few defendants got the sort of spirited defense that Atticus Finch provided in *To Kill a Mockingbird*. Black men were executed for raping white women so frequently that, in Florida and elsewhere, newspaper accounts simply reported that the defendant had committed "the usual crime." Everyone knew what that meant. One such Florida prisoner was electrocuted just seven days after his sentence was imposed in 1937.

As sensibilities became more refined, however, decent folks began to object to the spectacle of local executions. In Florida in the 1920s, a coalition of women's clubs lobbied the legislature to ban the practice, arguing that the sight of bodies swinging in town squares had a brutalizing effect on their communities. Similar efforts around the country led to the centralizing of executions at state prisons, where they took place outside the public view, often at midnight or dawn. Still, the death penalty remained a state matter, with the federal government extremely reluctant to exert its own authority. Washington kept its nose out of the death chambers, just as it steered clear of the schools, courtrooms, prisons, and voting booths.

All that changed, and changed dramatically, in the 1950s and 1960s, when the U.S. Supreme Court, in the era of Chief Justice Earl Warren, asserted more vigorously than ever that the protections of the U.S. Constitution applied to actions in the states. For the first time, federal standards of equality were used to strike down such state and local practices as school segregation, segregation of buses and trains, poll taxes, and voter tests. The lengthened arm of the federal government reached into police stations: For example, in *Miranda v. Arizona,* the U.S. Supreme Court required that suspects be advised of their constitutional rights when arrested. The long arm reached into the courtrooms: In *Gideon v. Wainwright,* the high court declared that the federal guarantee of due process required that felony defendants in state trials be provided with lawyers.

Opponents of capital punishment urged the courts to reach into death rows as well. Anthony Amsterdam, at the time a Stanford University law professor, crafted arguments to persuade the federal courts that the death penalty violated the Eighth Amendment (which bars "cruel and unusual punishments") and the Fourteenth Amendment (which guarantees "equal protection of the laws"). Amsterdam's arguments won serious consideration in the newly aggressive federal courts. In Florida in 1967, the zealous civil rights lawyer Tobias Simon filed a class action lawsuit based on Amsterdam's theories. His suit blocked every Florida death sentence while the issues were considered. Then came *Furman v. Georgia,* the greatest of Amsterdam's lawsuits, which overturned more than six hundred death sentences nationwide.

Furman v. Georgia was the ultimate "big issue" case, striking down all existing death penalty laws in the United States. For several years leading up to it, at Amsterdam's urging, the U.S. Supreme Court had wrestled over capital punishment; in 1968 the justices seemed within a hair's breadth of abolishing it. But the Court lost two liberal justices, Earl Warren and Abe Fortas, during the same tempestuous months in which Lyndon Johnson's presidency ended and Richard Nixon's began. In his election campaign, Nixon had strongly supported the death penalty as part of his "war on crime." He appointed two justices, Warren Burger and Harry Blackmun, who believed strongly that executions were constitutional. The arrival of Burger and Blackmun shifted the balance; nevertheless, a number of the justices remained disturbed by the practice, if not the theory, of capital punishment. Their concerns came to a head on January 17, 1972, when the Supreme Court heard oral arguments in *Furman*.

Amsterdam delivered a brilliant four-pronged attack on capital punishment. He began by presenting statistical proof that the death penalty in America was overwhelmingly used against the poor and minorities. More than half of the people legally executed in America since 1930 had been black, though blacks had committed far less than half of all crimes. Moreover, 90 percent of the people executed for the crime of rape had been black. These disparities were so great as to defy any claim that the executioner was color-blind.

Next, Amsterdam argued that the death penalty was imposed arbitrarily, almost randomly. Judges and juries meted out the sentence without clear standards to guide them, and as a result some men were on death row for armed robbery, while nearby, murderers served life or less. The only difference between them might be that the robber was tried by a "hanging judge," or that his jury didn't like the smirk on his face. Discretion in death sentencing was virtually unfettered.

Amsterdam's third point was his most audacious, but it turned out to be crucial: The death penalty was so rarely carried out in contemporary America that it could no longer be justified as a deterrent to crime. This point, too, was well documented. In the years leading up to Amsterdam's argument, use of the death penalty had steeply declined. There were forty-seven executions in America during 1962. The number dropped to twenty-one in 1963. Fifteen in 1964. Seven in 1965. Just one in 1966. Two in 1967. And none thereafter. (By comparison, 199 people were executed in America in 1935—the busiest year for the nation's executioners—and no year passed in the 1930s or 1940s with fewer than a hundred executions.) What made this argument so daring was that the sharp drop in executions was partly a result of Amsterdam's own legal campaign to abolish the death penalty. He was, in effect, challenging a state of affairs he had helped to create.

In closing, Amsterdam argued that the death penalty had become "unacceptable in contemporary society," that the "evolving standards" of decent behavior had moved beyond the point of legal killing. This was the weakest of his arguments because nearly forty states still had death penalty laws on the books, and the justices tended to view state legislatures as barometers of social standards. But previous U.S. Supreme Court decisions suggested that the shortest route to abolishing the death penalty would be to persuade a majority of the justices that "standards of decency" had changed. Amsterdam had to try.

Behind closed doors, the nine justices of the Court revealed a wide range of reactions to Amsterdam's case, according to *The Brethren,* a detailed history of the Supreme Court in the early 1970s. Justices William Brennan and Thurgood Marshall, the Court's liberal stalwarts, accepted every point of the argument and voted to abolish capital punishment outright. Justice William Rehnquist, the new conservative beacon, came down on the opposite extreme. He rejected all of Amsterdam's case. These justices marked the frontiers, Left and Right.

Justice William O. Douglas, a cantankerous libertarian, agreed that the death penalty was arbitrary and should be struck down, but he was unpersuaded by the notion that standards of decency had evolved to the point that capital punishment was cruel and unusual punishment. He lined up closest to Brennan and Marshall. Chief Justice Burger and Justice Blackmun both expressed personal opposition to capital punishment—if they were legislators, they would vote against it—but they believed that the language of the Constitution clearly left the matter to the states. The Court had no business preempting the debate, they said, and sided near Rehnquist. That made three votes to strike down the death penalty and three to sustain it.

Justice Lewis Powell also strongly objected to the Court taking the question of the death penalty out of the hands of elected legislatures. This would be an egregious example of the sort of judicial activism he had always opposed. Though moved by Amsterdam's showing of racial discrimination, Powell believed this was a vestige of the past and could be dealt with case by case, without a sweeping decision in *Furman.* With Rehnquist, Burger, and Blackmun, Powell's vote made four to sustain the death penalty; one more and executions of the more than six hundred people on America's death rows could resume. Justice Potter Stewart, painfully aware of these 600-some lives dangling on his vote, moved toward Douglas's view that the death penalty in practice had become unconstitutionally arbitrary. With Brennan, Marshall, and Douglas, Stewart's vote made four to strike the death penalty as it existed.

That left Justice Byron White, known to all observers of the Court as a strict law-and-order man. In his brusque opinions, White backed prosecutors and police at almost every turn; no one would normally expect him to reach a decision that would reduce the punishment of some of the coarsest criminals in the country. But he was deeply impressed by Amsterdam's presentation; he told his law clerks that it was "possibly the best" oral argument he had ever heard. The point that had won White was Amsterdam's boldest: that the death penalty was applied too infrequently to serve any purpose. White cast the deciding vote to strike down the death penalty, not because he wanted to see an end to capital punishment, but because he wanted to see more of it.

Some awfully tortured thinking went into yoking together such disparate views as Marshall's blanket condemnation of capital punishment and White's gung-ho call for more executions. Yet somehow they wound up on the same side. The product of these deliberations was one of the most difficult decisions in the long history of the U.S. Supreme Court, published on June 29, 1972. The broad impact of *Furman v. Georgia,* which struck down hundreds of separate laws in nearly forty separate jurisdictions, was unprecedented. In its rambling, inchoate length—nine separate opinions totaling some fifty thousand words—it was easily the longest decision ever published by the Court. But for all its wordy impact, *Furman* was almost useless as a precedent for future cases. It set out no clear legal standards. As Powell noted in his stinging dissent:

Mr. Justice Douglas concludes that capital punishment is incompatible with notions of "equal protection" that he finds "implicit" in the Eighth Amendment. . . . Mr. Justice Brennan bases his judgment primarily on the thesis that the penalty "does not comport with human dignity." . . . Mr. Justice Stewart concludes that the penalty is applied in a "wanton" and "freakish" manner. . . . For Mr. Justice White it is the "infrequency" with which the penalty is imposed that renders its use unconstitutional. . . . Mr. Justice Marshall finds that capital punishment is an impermissible form of punishment because it is "morally unacceptable" and "excessive." . . .

I [will not] attempt to predict what forms of capital statutes, if any, may avoid condemnation in the future under the variety of views expressed by the collective majority today.

In other words, totally missing from the longest U.S. Supreme Court decision in history was any clear notion of how the death penalty might be fixed. Chief Justice Burger, in his own dissent, acknowledged this confusion, noting that the effect of *Furman* was to demand "an undetermined measure of change" in the nation's death penalty laws. He nonetheless invited the legislatures of the country to "make a thorough reevaluation of the entire subject."

That painfully splintered 5-to-4 vote turned out to be a high-water mark of the U.S. Supreme Court's willingness to intervene in the business of the states. In *Furman,* the Supreme Court justices were willing to abolish the death penalty as it existed. But the justices were not willing to forbid executions forever. They kicked the question of whether the death penalty was "cruel and unusual" back to the state legislatures. For nearly twenty years, the states—especially the southern states—had felt pounded by the Supreme Court. Rarely had they gotten the chance to answer. The Court had not asked what they thought about school desegregation, or voting rights, or the right to counsel. But *Furman v. Georgia* invited the states to answer a hostile Supreme Court decision.

Within days of the *Furman* decision, key members of the Florida legislature petitioned Governor Reubin Askew to call an immediate special session to write a new death penalty law. Askew resisted moving so hastily; given the sheer size of the *Furman* ruling, it was unlikely that more than a handful of people had even finished reading it yet. But the public backlash was so intense that the issue could not possibly wait for the legislature to resume its normal business the following January. Askew promised to call a special session to deal with the death penalty after the November elections, and in the meantime he appointed a blue-ribbon panel (chaired by Ray Marky's uncle, Harris Drew) to study the matter. Leaders of the state house of representatives, perhaps suspicious of Askew's liberal tendencies, appointed a study commission of their own. These commissions collected a hodgepodge of conflicting advice, reflecting the jumble of the *Furman* ruling.

Legal advisers to the governor's commission, drawn from the faculty of Florida's five law schools, unanimously predicted that no capital punishment law would ever satisfy the high court. The panel rejected that professional advice, however, and turned instead to a nugget from Justice Douglas's opinion. Douglas wrote that the problem with the pre-*Furman* laws was that they left "to the uncontrolled discretion of judges or juries the determination whether defendants committing these crimes should die or be imprisoned. Under these laws no standards govern the selection of the penalty." Douglas seemed to be saying that judges and juries needed rules to guide their sentencing. But how?

The governor's panel suggested a new law spelling out "aggravating" circumstances—such as a defendant's criminal record and the degree of violence involved in the crime—which, if proven, would make a guilty man eligible for the death penalty. The law should also spell out "mitigating" circumstances, such as a defendant's age or mental state, that might suggest a life sentence instead. The panel called for a team of three judges to weigh the "aggravating" circumstances against the "mitigating" circumstances and decide what sentence to impose. The jury would have no role in sentencing, under this proposal.

The House of Representatives Select Committee reached a different conclusion, simply by fastening on a different snippet from the

Furman ruling. Figuring that Byron White was the most likely justice to change his position, they combed his opinion for clues. White had complained that "The legislature authorizes [but] does not mandate the penalty in any particular class or kind of case. . . ." That phrase seemed crucial: "authorizes [but] does not mandate." Apparently, White would prefer to see death made mandatory for certain crimes. In hopes of winning his approval, the house panel proposed a bill that would automatically impose the death penalty for a specific set of crimes—including premeditated murder, sex with a person under thirteen, and setting off a bomb that kills someone.

Furman was as cryptic as the Gnostic gospels. The law professors read it and concluded that no law could pass muster. The governor's commission read it and concluded that a complicated weighing mechanism was called for. The house panel read it and concluded that a flat set of mandatory penalties was the answer. Robert Shevin, the state's attorney general at the time, was just as confused. He summoned George Georgieff and Ray Marky to explain *Furman*.

"I've been reading it since it came out," Marky told his boss, "and I still have no idea what it means."

None of the prosecutors liked the idea of mandatory death sentences—not even Georgieff, the ultimate hard-liner. "I mean, it's just terrible," Georgieff said long afterward. "Not everyone should be killed." But as they pondered Byron White's opinion, they reluctantly came to believe that this might be the only route available. Apparently, Chief Justice Burger had reached the same conclusion; in his dissenting opinion he lamented that *Furman* would lead to mandatory sentencing. And so the prosecutors began to lean in that direction. "I knew if we went to a mandatory death penalty we would fill the gallows in a year and a half," Marky remembered. "But at that point, public opinion was really driving things. It was absolutely clear we were going to get a death penalty of some kind—the public demanded it. I figured if it was a piece of garbage, the U.S. Supreme Court would be to blame."

But Governor Askew considered mandatory death sentences barbaric, and he vowed to make a stand against them. In his opening address to the special session of the legislature, on November 28, 1972, Askew insisted that Florida law make room for the quality of mercy.

Senate president Louis Dellaparte sided with the governor: There was no way he would allow the house bill, with its mandatory sentences, to pass his chamber. "I would rather pass a good bill and have it declared unconstitutional than pass a bad bill just to be sustained," the senator declared.

Mandatory sentences were going nowhere, but what would take their place? While the rank-and-file lawmakers made interminable tough-on-crime speeches in the house and senate chambers, Florida's power brokers hashed out a deal behind closed doors. Edgar Dunn, Askew's general counsel, represented the governor. He quickly discovered that Askew's proposal for three-judge panels to weigh death sentences was not going to get through the senate. It was too costly, too cumbersome. But *Furman* seemed to say that the power of life and death could not be placed in the hands of a single judge.

Dellaparte, the senate president, proposed a modification: After a defendant was found guilty of a capital offense, the jury would hear evidence of aggravating and mitigating factors. Then, by majority vote, the jurors would recommend either life in prison or the death penalty. If they recommended life, it was final. If they recommended death, the judge would be required to reweigh the aggravating and mitigating factors. That plan, however, smacked too much of the old system to satisfy the house leadership. The jury would still have complete discretion to decide whether or not to set the machinery in motion toward a death sentence. "Hell," said Georgieff, who was present as an expert adviser, "if juries couldn't have discretion before *Furman,* they obviously can't have it now."

Edgar Dunn broke the logjam. What if the jury's recommendation was "advisory," and the judge imposed the final sentence? And what if the judge's decision was then automatically reviewed by the state supreme court? In this scheme, everyone would have a role: The legislature would guide the sentencing by defining aggravating and mitigating circumstances; the jury would consider these factors and advise the judge; the judge would impose the sentence, justifying it in writing; and then the sentence would be reviewed by the state's highest court. In this way, perhaps, they could thread the *Furman* needle: setting standards, limiting discretion, erasing caprice—all while avoiding mandatory sentences.

They were a few men in a back room, trading power and guessing about an incoherent U.S. Supreme Court document. It was not a particularly promising start. Nevertheless, their compromise passed overwhelmingly, giving America its first legislative answer to *Furman*. Immediately, officials from states across the country began calling Florida for advice and guidance. And very soon, lawyers and judges began to discover that the law drafted in confusion and passed in haste was going to be hell to administer.

Anthony Amsterdam recognized it immediately, and when Craig Barnard began his death penalty work a few years later, he saw it, too: Underneath the tidy, legalistic, polysyllabic, etched-in-marble tone of the new law was a lot of slippery mishmash. They believed the new law was flawed at its heart, in the weighing process, where the lists of aggravating and mitigating factors were toted up to determine whether death was the appropriate sentence. "Aggravating circumstances shall be limited to the following," the law declared:

(a) The capital felony was committed by a person under sentence of imprisonment;

(b) The defendant was previously convicted of another capital felony involving the use or threat of violence to the person;

(c) The defendant knowingly created a great risk of death to many persons;

(d) The capital felony was committed while the defendant was engaged or was an accomplice in the commission of, or an attempt to commit, or flight after committing or attempting to commit any robbery, rape, arson, burglary, kidnapping, aircraft piracy, or the unlawful throwing, placing or discharging of a destructive device or bomb;

(e) The capital felony was committed for the purpose of avoiding or preventing a lawful arrest or effecting an escape from custody;

(f) The capital felony was committed for pecuniary gain;

(g) The capital felony was committed to disrupt or hinder the lawful exercise of any governmental function or the enforcement of laws;

(h) The capital felony was especially heinous, atrocious or cruel.

Some of the circumstances were simple matters of fact. For instance, if the defendant was in prison for armed robbery and murdered another inmate, the first aggravating circumstance plainly applied. In the case of a murder-for-hire, the sixth aggravator—"for pecuniary gain"—was obvious. Others on the list were awfully vague, however. "A great risk of death to many persons," for example. One judge might feel that described a drive-by killer who sprays a whole street with gunfire; another might apply it to a burglar who stabs a man to death while the victim's wife slumbers nearby. How much risk makes a "great" risk, and what number of persons constitutes "many"?

The last circumstance on the list was even harder to interpret—"especially heinous, atrocious or cruel." The idea was to identify only the worst of the hundreds of murders each year in Florida. But wasn't the act of murder itself "heinous, atrocious or cruel"? Again, this aggravating circumstance was very much in the eye of the beholder: To one judge, stabbing might seem more cruel than shooting, because it involved such close contact between the killer and the victim. Another judge, however, might think it crueler to place a cold gun barrel to a victim's head before squeezing the trigger. One jury might find it especially heinous for a victim to be killed by a stranger, while the next set of jurors might find it more atrocious for a victim to die at the hands of a trusted friend. And so forth. It was an attempt to define the undefinable.

The imprecision was even more obvious on the side of mitigation. "Mitigating circumstances shall be the following," the law read:

(a) The defendant has no significant history of prior criminal activity;

(b) The capital felony was committed while the defendant was

under the influence of extreme mental or emotional disturbance;

(c) The victim was a participant in the defendant's conduct or
consented in the act;

(d) The defendant was an accomplice in the capital felony committed by another person and his participation was relatively
minor;

(e) The defendant acted under extreme emotional duress or under
the substantial domination of another person;

(f) The capacity of the defendant to appreciate the criminality of
his conduct or to conform his conduct to the requirements of
law was substantially impaired;

(g) The age of the defendant at the time of the crime.

How much past criminal behavior was required to reach the level
of "significant history"? What constituted "extreme mental or emotional disturbance"—given that any defendant who reached the sentencing phase had already been deemed sane to stand trial? What was
"relatively minor" participation in a fatal crime? Driving the getaway
car could be "minor" to one judge, while another could think it was
major. Acting as a lookout—major or minor? And how could you
measure "substantial domination" by another person? The law gave no
guidance regarding "the age of the defendant." One judge might think
fifteen was old enough to face to the death penalty, while another
might have qualms about executing a man who was "only" twenty.
What about elderly criminals? Was there an age beyond which a man
should qualify for mercy—and if so, what was it?

Clearly, a lot of discretion was left to the judge and jury. But
remember: Too much discretion was banned by *Furman*. And the lists
of aggravating and mitigating factors were not the only slippery spots.
There was the matter of how these factors were supposed to be
weighed.

According to the new law, the death penalty was appropriate if
"sufficient aggravating circumstances" existed alongside "insufficient
mitigating circumstances . . . to outweigh" them. Did that mean the
judge and jury should simply count them up—for example, three ag-

gravating circumstances versus two mitigating circumstances equals death? Or could a single really strong mitigating factor outweigh two rather weak aggravating circumstances?

And what were the rules for counting? Imagine that a criminal walks into a convenience store, cleans out the register, and kills the clerk. A classic candidate for the death penalty. But how would the court count the aggravating factors? The murder of the store clerk was a capital felony committed in the course of a robbery. That's aggravating circumstance (d). A prosecutor could also argue that the murder was committed "for pecuniary gain." That's aggravating circumstance (f). Could one fact, stealing the money, be counted as two aggravating circumstances?

Or another case: A man driving a stolen car is pulled over by a police officer. Fearing jail, the thief shoots and kills the cop. That would be a capital felony committed to avoid a lawful arrest, aggravating circumstance (e). But the prosecutor could also argue that it hindered the enforcement of laws, aggravating circumstance (g). Should both aggravators apply? The law gave no guidance.

The same sort of thing could happen on the other side of the scales. If, for example, a man lost his job, went on a drinking binge, had a nervous breakdown, and shot his former boss, a good defense lawyer no doubt would argue that the defendant had suffered an "extreme emotional disturbance": mitigating circumstance (b). The same lawyer might also argue that his client's ability to conform his behavior to the law had been "substantially impaired": mitigating circumstance (f). Could the same fact, the man's nervous breakdown, count twice in his favor? And if it could count twice, would it be "sufficient" to outweigh one aggravating circumstance (for example, if the man shot his boss in the middle of a crowded office, thus endangering many persons)?

A step further: If the judge decided that shooting the boss was especially cruel, there would be two aggravating circumstances. If the nervous breakdown could count twice in the defendant's favor, there would be two mitigating circumstances. Two in favor, two against— what then?

It was enough to make even the best lawyer's head spin. But Amsterdam, and later Craig Barnard, saw still more riddles, and every riddle was another way to attack the new law on appeal. Could a prosecutor present evidence of aggravating circumstances that weren't listed in the law? Could a defense attorney present evidence in favor of a lighter sentence that didn't fit the list of mitigating factors?

What, exactly, was the jury's role in sentencing? The new law said that after the jury found a defendant guilty of a capital crime, it must hear evidence for and against a death sentence. Then, by majority vote, the jurors would render an "advisory sentence," after which the judge would impose the actual sentence. The law never said how much weight the judge should give to the jury's advice. How strong a reason did the judge need to overrule the jury? Did a 7-to-5 vote in favor of a death sentence carry less weight than a unanimous vote?

Under the new law, the state supreme court was to "review" each sentence. Did that mean the justices were supposed to reweigh the aggravating and mitigating factors? Or were they merely referees, making sure the proper steps were followed? Was the court supposed to compare death cases to similar cases where life sentences had been imposed—to be sure that equal crimes got equal justice? Or was the review restricted to the confines of each individual case?

These questions might have seemed tendentious and picayune, but for the fact that as soon as Governor Askew signed the new death penalty law, Florida's prosecutors and judges got busy using it. Dozens, then scores, of capital cases made their way to the Florida Supreme Court, and these seemingly trivial questions became the crux of life-and-death litigation—much of it, in those first years after *Furman,* masterminded by Anthony Amsterdam and coordinated by the Inc. Fund. The law, shot through with question marks, became a lawyer's playground. After all, their clients were going to be killed for breaking the law. It seemed only fair that they should ask what the law actually meant.

Amsterdam and the Inc. Fund had their eyes set on the inevitable return of the death penalty issue to the U.S. Supreme Court. The new state laws would have to pass muster with the high court before prisoners could be executed. In the meantime, there were battles to fight in the state supreme courts. These were critical tests, because what was true in Florida was true everywhere: The legislatures had created a legal labyrinth with their new laws. Trying to find a clear path through the maze would be the job of the state high courts. Laws were supposed to be clear and fixed; they were supposed to mean the same thing from day to day, courtroom to courtroom, town to town. As the first death sentences moved to the Florida Supreme Court, lawyers on both sides watched, wondering if the slippery points could be pinned.

On their first official look at the new law, in 1973, most of Florida's supreme court justices swooned. The case was called *State v. Dixon*. A man facing murder charges under the new law was challenging its constitutionality. While Dixon's trial was delayed, the justices vaulted the case to the top of their docket and rendered an opinion scarcely four months after the law was signed.

"No longer will one man die and another live on the basis of race, or a woman live and a man die on the basis of sex," the majority opinion enthused. Under the new law, death sentences would apply only in "the most aggravated and unmitigated of crimes." The justices, except for two dissenters, were confident in their own ability to promise consistent results. "Review by this Court guarantees that the reasons present in one case will reach a similar result to that reached under similar circumstances in another case. . . . If a defendant is sentenced to die, this Court can review that case in light of the other decisions and determine whether or not the punishment is too great."

The majority was certain, too, that the language of the new law was clear. "We feel the meaning of such terms is a matter of common knowledge, so that an ordinary man would not have to guess at what is intended," they wrote. Still, the justices took their first stab at nailing down a few of the more elusive aspects of the law. For example, they explained that "heinous" means "extremely wicked and shockingly evil," while "atrocious" means "outrageously wicked and vile." Such crimes were "conscienceless . . . pitiless . . . unnecessarily tortuous."

In retrospect, it was a bad omen that the court's first step toward clarifying this difficult law was simply to substitute one set of vague terms with another. The law was spongy at its core—and merely piling on the adjectives was not going to give it precision.

State v. Dixon was an entirely theoretical case; it did not involve an actual death sentence. When death sentences under the new law began arriving at the court, the grand promises expressed in *Dixon* immediately came up against harder realities. One of the earliest reviews was the case of Anthony Sawyer, argued during the 1974 term. Sawyer held up a liquor store. During a struggle with the owner, Sawyer's gun went off and the son of the store owner was killed. Despite the jury's recommendation of a life sentence, the judge imposed the death penalty.

This case gave the Florida Supreme Court some real problems to sink its teeth into. First was the question of whether the judge had given proper weight to the jury's recommendation. Further, Sawyer's case did not clearly satisfy the *Dixon* standard of singling out "only the most aggravated and unmitigated of crimes." The firing of the gun might have been accidental. Beyond that, three of the four aggravating circumstances applied by the trial judge were not even listed in the new law. The three—Sawyer's prior arrests, his drug abuse, and his violent temper—might seem sensible to many people, but the lawmakers had not included them. In this single case the justices found vagaries of procedure, of definitions, even of philosophy. And this was just one of what would soon be hundreds of cases stumbling over this same legal ground. In any event, the justices flinched. Instead of the meticulous review they had so recently promised in *Dixon,* they delivered only a brusque affirmation of Sawyer's death sentence, scarcely touching on the broad issues raised.

Anthony Amsterdam and his colleagues were hopeful as they watched these struggles. Surely the U.S. Supreme Court would look at cases like Sawyer's and see that the new laws were no more reliable than the old ones. Further cases only increased their confidence.

For example, in the 1975 case of Mack Reed Tedder, the Florida Supreme Court took on the question of judges overruling the advice of juries. Tedder shot and killed his mother-in-law. His jury recommended a life sentence, but the judge sentenced him to death. Tedder's case was part of a trend that surprised and disturbed the justices. In *Dixon,* they had envisioned calm, experienced trial judges putting the brakes on emotionally inflamed juries. Instead, many judges—who had to face the voters every four years—were using their authority to increase, rather than restrain, the use of the death penalty. Judge after judge was upping the ante from a life sentence to a death sentence. So the Florida Supreme Court reinstated the jury's recommended sentence for Tedder, and set a rule for overruling juries in the future. "In order to sustain a sentence of death following a jury recommendation of life, the facts . . . should be so clear and convincing that virtually no reasonable person could differ," the justices declared.

Here was a straightforward attempt to clear up one of the vague points of the law. Courts frequently use the "reasonable person" standard in a wide variety of legal situations. Any competent judge has some idea how to apply this standard. But it didn't work. The trial judges of Florida continued to override jury recommendations with abandon: One-fourth of all death sentences in Florida were imposed despite jury recommendations of life. The trial judges were ignoring the state supreme court, but only because the justices themselves failed to stick to their own standard. For example, the year after the Tedder decision, the Florida Supreme Court upheld the death sentence of Howard Douglas, despite the jury's unanimous recommendation for life. To convict Douglas, the jury had to conclude he was guilty "beyond and to the exclusion of any reasonable doubt." The justices affirmed that reasonable decision. In the next breath, however, they upheld the judge's death sentence, implying that none of the jurors met the test of a "reasonable person" able to see the "clear and convincing" need for the death penalty.

Amsterdam and his colleagues believed that confusion like this—there were many similar examples—would surely kill the law when it reached the U.S. Supreme Court.

By the time the U.S. Supreme Court returned to the question of capital punishment, in March 1976, some thirty-five states had passed new death penalty laws. In the wake of *Furman,* several justices had privately predicted that America would never see another execution. The rush of the state legislatures to restore the death penalty shocked them with its vehemence and delivered a loud, clear message: America loved its death penalty. The U.S. Supreme Court scrutinized five state laws—from Florida, Georgia, Texas, Louisiana, and North Carolina—covering the range of approaches throughout the country.

Of the nine justices, only the two most liberal—William Brennan and Thurgood Marshall—were willing to say, in spite of the public outpouring, that capital punishment was flatly unconstitutional. Four of the justices—Warren Burger, Byron White, William Rehnquist, and Harry Blackmun—believed all of the laws before the Court passed constitutional muster. (The furious efforts in Florida and elsewhere to figure out what White would approve of turned out to be wasted; he voted for every law proposed.) Once again, the issue would come down to the justices in the middle: Lewis Powell, who had voted against *Furman;* Potter Stewart, who had voted for *Furman;* and John Paul Stevens, who had replaced William O. Douglas on the Court. This troika of justices, led by Stewart, seized control of the cases and would define the contemporary parameters of capital punishment.

Unfortunately for the armies of lower-court judges who would have to apply the high court's decision, the troika used more gut than reason. Quite simply, the three swing justices were appalled by the idea of mandatory death sentences, in which everyone found guilty of a capital crime is automatically sent to death row. This seemed to them a throwback to less enlightened times. And this feeling was only deepened by the facts in *Woodson v. North Carolina,* which tested a mandatory-death law.

The justices heard the appeal of James Woodson, one of a gang of men involved in a convenience store holdup. Anthony Amsterdam argued for Woodson; U.S. Solicitor General Robert Bork was among those arguing for the State. During the robbery, Woodson waited behind the wheel of a car as two accomplices went inside, rifled the cash register, killed the clerk, and wounded a customer. When police arrested the gang, one of the two accomplices inside the store—possibly the one who pulled the trigger—offered to testify in exchange for a reduced sentence. Woodson received no such deal. Convicted of felony murder for participating in a crime that led to a killing, he was automatically sentenced to die. The man who copped the plea got twenty years, even though he clearly had more to do with the murder than Woodson did. This obvious disparity seemed eloquent proof that mandatory death sentences would not eliminate the caprice condemned in *Furman*.

But one flawed case scarcely justified finding all mandatory death sentences unconstitutional. What grounds could the troika apply? The clearest route would be to declare that mandatory sentences violated the "evolving standards" of decent society. It was a tough claim to make—the Court strongly believed that state legislatures should serve as the key measure of society's standards. But now various legislatures across the country had passed brand-new mandatory death sentences. The Court could hardly say these states were missing out on the evolution of standards.

Yet that was the foundation on which the troika built. Deftly, the three swing justices theorized that the legislatures would never have passed such barbaric laws if the *Furman* case had not pushed them to it. They were thinking, apparently, of those few words from Justice White's opinion in *Furman*—"authorizes [but] does not mandate"— which Ray Marky and George Georgieff found so troublingly persuasive. The three swing justices decided that laws passed under the influence of this phrase were not a fair measure of the nation's moral standards.

This argument was so obviously shaky that Justice Stewart went a step further to shore up the troika's position. He said the problem with the pre-*Furman* laws was that they had allowed similar cases to be treated differently—that is, one criminal could get a life sentence while a similar man got executed. The problem with mandatory laws, Stewart said, was precisely the opposite: They took different cases and treated them the same. James Woodson, a passive accomplice to murder, got the same death sentence as a serial killer. Whether similar cases were treated differently or differing cases the same, it was capricious—and therefore violated the spirit of the *Furman* decision. On these grounds, the troika voted, along with the two liberals, to strike down mandatory death sentences by a 5-to-4 majority.

This raised the stakes. In striking down mandatory sentences, the swing justices had apparently made constitutional doctrine out of the idea that death penalty laws must treat "same" cases the same and "different" cases differently. But the thousands of capital crimes committed each year in America raised a mountain of peculiarities—each criminal and crime was subtly unique. Somehow the law must penetrate this mountain to discern some conceptual key that would consistently identify cases that were the "same" and cull out ones that were "different."

Furthermore, in dealing with the mandatory death sentences, the swing justices declared that the Constitution required extraordinary reliability and consistency from capital punishment laws. "The penalty of death is qualitatively different from a sentence of imprisonment, however long," Stewart wrote for the troika. "Because of that qualitative difference, there is a corresponding difference in the need for reliability."

Each year, some twenty thousand homicides are committed in America, and the swing justices expected the death penalty laws to steer precisely and consistently through this carnage to find the relatively few criminals deserving execution. Somehow, using the black-and-white of the criminal code, the system must determine the very nature of evil. King Solomon himself might demur. It was like demanding a precise count from those medieval philosophers who asked how many angels can dance on the head of a pin.

This was the task the Court was setting, however, as the justices turned to the laws, like Florida's, that guided sentencing through the use of aggravating (and, in most cases, mitigating) circumstances. The case before the Court from Florida was a weak one. Ray Marky and George Georgieff had hoped for a torture-slayer or multiple murderer, but the order in which cases reach the high court is often a matter of chance. The case at hand, *Proffitt v. Florida,* cut a little too close to the slippery heart of the new law for the prosecutors' taste.

One night in July 1973, Charles Proffitt got drunk and decided to burglarize a house. As he gazed on the sleeping homeowners, an overwhelming urge came over him to commit murder, something he had never done before. He got a butcher knife from the kitchen and plunged it into the chest of Joel Medgebow, a high school wrestling coach. The victim's moan awakened his wife. Proffitt slugged her and ran from the house.

In pronouncing the death sentence, Proffitt's trial judge had found four aggravating circumstances: The crime occurred during a burglary; Proffitt had a propensity to commit murder; the murder was especially heinous, atrocious, or cruel; and Proffitt had created a great risk to many persons. Here was an example of a trial judge relying on an aggravating circumstance outside the law. ("Propensity to commit murder" was not a part of the statute.) Here, too, was an example of mushy definitions. Was a single stab wound to a sleeping man "especially" heinous, atrocious, or cruel, compared to other murders? And since only one other person was in the room during the crime, was this really an example of "great risk to many persons"?

But the U.S. Supreme Court troika gave almost no attention to the facts of Proffitt's case. Instead, they looked to the Florida Supreme Court's enthusiastic promises in *State v. Dixon*. The Florida law would "guarantee" similar results in similar cases, *Dixon* had pledged. Each Florida death sentence would be compared alongside the others, to "determine whether or not the punishment is too great." The state supreme court would assure that same was treated same and different was treated different.

Even as Justice Stewart quoted these passages, he knew that the Florida Supreme Court was not always so rigorous and reliable. He made reference in a footnote to the slapdash *Sawyer* decision and admitted that he wasn't sure whether the state court would permit death sentences to be justified by aggravating circumstances outside the law. But he breezed by this question, saying merely, "It seems unlikely it would do so." The troika was not interested in problems. For example, the Florida Supreme Court had decided that stabbing a man in his sleep met the same standard of "conscienceless . . . pitiless . . . unnecessarily torturous" murder as beating a man, slitting his throat, and suffocating him. Was this an example of treating different things differently? Stewart let this go in another footnote.

The swing justices were not concerned with specifics. They fixated on the Florida Supreme Court's promise to turn out life-and-death decisions with the precision of diamond cutters. Proffitt's case was fine with them; the troika cast its votes to uphold Florida's death penalty, along with similar laws in Georgia and Texas.

Anthony Amsterdam and his colleagues had counted on victory. Now, despite the slippery quality of the new laws guiding discretion in death sentencing, the death penalty had been restored. But the U.S. Supreme Court, by speaking of "guaranteed" standards and the "need for reliability," had given the anti–death penalty lawyers plenty of room to continue fighting. Precision and consistency in death sentences had become a matter of constitutional dimension. "The main legal battle is over," declared *The New York Times*. But in fact the battles were only beginning.

Some battles were fought over questions affecting a single inmate, like the appeal of Jasper Mines, who murdered a woman on Florida's eastern coast in 1975. Mines's lawyer successfully argued to the Florida Supreme Court that his client's mental state at the time of the murder had not been properly weighed. At the same time, defense strategists searched for big issues. The Inc. Fund, through David Kendall, had raised two potential blockbusters in John Spenkelink's first round of appeals. Kendall had tried to prove racial bias in death sentences by showing that people who killed white victims got the death penalty more often than killers of black victims. If the courts had accepted that argument, Florida's new law might have fallen for one of the same reasons that the pre-*Furman* laws had been struck down. Kendall's second claim—that Florida's modern death penalty violated the Constitution by limiting the chance to present evidence in favor of mercy—might have sent every man on death row back for a new sentencing procedure. That would have meant years of delay.

Florida officials had poured everything into those issues, and they had succeeded. Future courts might change their minds—the Inc. Fund urged defense attorneys to keep raising the issues. But Craig Barnard knew in the meantime he had to look elsewhere for the next big issue. He found it in an issue Kendall had chosen not to raise.

On Monday, May 20, 1979, as the fight for Spenkelink's life was raging, two lawyers on the Inc. Fund team, Andrew Graham and Joel

Berger, were plotting strategy in the restaurant of the Tallahassee Holiday Inn. Into the restaurant walked a pair of attorneys from the local public defender's office, Margaret Good and Louis Carres. Excitedly, they told the Spenkelink lawyers an intriguing story that had been brewing at their office for a year and a half. On an August day in 1977, Ted Mack—a colleague of Good and Carres at the public defender's office—had received a call from a client on death row. The prisoner, Bobby Lewis, was angry. Prison officials had just told Lewis that the Florida Supreme Court had ordered a psychiatric evaluation of him. Lewis wanted to know what the hell was going on.

Mack had no idea what the prisoner was talking about. Lewis repeated his story, but it was just as mystifying the second time. In death penalty cases, the state supreme court's job was to review the work of the judge, jury, and lawyers at the trial and sentencing. Any information beyond the trial and sentencing could be brought to the court's attention only by a particular kind of appeal—and there had been no such appeal in Lewis's case. The court had no business considering psychological reports years after the trial. Right or wrong, this was the law. So what was going on?

Baffled, Mack instructed his client to refuse the evaluation. Then he began trying to solve the mystery. A series of phone calls led him to the agency in charge of the state prisons, and there, in Lewis's inmate file, Mack found a letter. "This is to request a copy of the latest psychiatric evaluation made on the above named defendant, who is on Death Row," the letter said. Signed by the deputy clerk of the Florida Supreme Court, the letter was proof that the prisoner's story was true. Mack kept searching, and over the next several days he found similar letters in the files of other condemned men. Apparently, there was a systematic process under way at the state supreme court to collect information outside the scope of the trial.

This discovery was tantalizing but incomplete. Mack had no way of knowing who was behind the orders, or where the reports were going, or whether any of the justices ever saw them. Something strange was going on, but Mack couldn't be sure what it was. He filed the material away and waited for a time when it might be useful.

About eight months later, Margaret Good was arguing an appeal before the state supreme court on behalf of Paul Magill, another death row inmate. Magill had been a good student, a dedicated member of his high school band, but he'd gone inexplicably off the rails, robbed a convenience store, and raped and murdered the store clerk. Magill insisted he had no memory of his horrible deed. A good kid gone bad, the claimed loss of memory—naturally, those charged with deciding his fate were perplexed by the flawed mechanics of his mind. At the state supreme court hearing, Justice Ben Overton began questioning the prosecutor about Paul Magill's psyche.

"We have a copy of the psychological screening report," Overton said, "and that screening report says, in part, that he shows very limited control in stressful situations, and then also shows that he will become possibly suicidal."

Margaret Good knew every page of Magill's trial record, but she had no idea what Overton was talking about. Psychological screening report? When her turn came to speak, she said: "First of all, Your Honor, I'd like to request—Justice Overton—what you mean when you refer to a psychological screening report. I don't know that I have had access to such a thing."

Justice James Adkins spoke up helpfully. "Psychological screening report filed with us on June 6, 1978, a screening report from the Department of Offender Rehabilitation . . ."

"I have not received a copy of that, nor did I know it was in the record of this case," Good answered.

And Justice Overton began backpedaling—because he knew what any good law student would know: The report was outside the record of the case, and it was wrong to include it in his deliberations. "Well, let me say this just so it's clear," Overton began. "We do not ask for this particular information. We ask for the information that the trial judge used in the sentencing process. . . . We have not asked for this type of information, and I did not—I just saw 'psychological screening report,' and I . . ."

Margaret Good got the picture. The justices had been looking at material that had nothing to do with the trial. Moreover, they were looking at it without her knowledge, even though she was the lawyer for the condemned inmate. She wanted to ask more, but Overton quickly steered his questions to another tack.

Not long after that exchange, Chief Justice Arthur England's law clerk began the tedious job of sorting through the files of every death penalty case before the court, weeding out the offending reports. The clerk collected the inappropriate documents, and when she had culled them all, she disposed of the whole pile. She wasn't sure, the clerk later said, but she believed she fed them through a paper shredder. She said she couldn't remember who told her to do this.

To Spenkelink's lawyers, sitting in the hotel restaurant, the implications of the story were immediately clear. A recent case, apparently similar, had mucked up a number of Florida death sentences. In early 1977, before the events Good and Carres had just described, the U.S. Supreme Court had reversed the death sentence of a Florida inmate named Daniel Gardner. Gardner had been convicted of beating his wife to death, and the jury had recommended a life sentence. The trial judge had overruled the jury and imposed the death penalty. Unbeknown to Gardner's lawyers, the trial judge had studied a psychological report on Gardner before deciding on the harsher sentence. When the defense discovered this, they appealed to the U.S. Supreme Court, arguing that a defendant has the right to confront all witnesses and all evidence against him, including reports from shrinks. Since the defense lawyers had had no chance to rebut the secret report, Gardner's sentence was unconstitutional, they argued. The high court agreed.

The Gardner case had sent at least one U.S. Supreme Court justice through the roof. Potter Stewart was a key vote in holding Florida's new death penalty constitutional, but he angrily declared that Gardner's experience was almost enough to change his mind. "This court upheld that statute on the representations of the state of Florida . . . that this was an open and above-board proceeding," Stewart intoned from the bench. "This case gets here and it's apparent that it isn't." The Gardner case shook the Florida death penalty down to its foundations.

Wouldn't the state supreme court's practice of reading undisclosed reports fall by the same reasoning? The question for the lawyers at the Holiday Inn was this: Had the state high court ordered a psychological evaluation of Spenkelink? If so, it might be the legal flaw that could save his life. Graham and Berger, the Spenkelink team lawyers, relayed the idea to David Kendall. He knew every page of the Spenkelink court file cold, and there wasn't a hint of any secret psychological evaluation. He saw no grounds on which to raise the issue. (At the time, no one knew that the offending reports had been removed from the files and destroyed.) The matter was dropped, left to dangle from the fabric of the Spenkelink case. A loose thread, waiting to be pulled.

Soon after the Spenkelink execution, Craig Barnard learned of the secret reports in the files of the Florida Supreme Court. He called a meeting in Jacksonville of his most trusted anti–death penalty colleagues, followed by another in West Palm Beach a few months later and a third in Tallahassee early in 1980. The lawyers pondered the ramifications, and the more they contemplated the matter, the more excited Barnard became. He had consulted with Daniel Gardner's attorneys in their attack on the use of secret reports by a trial judge. Their victory had swamped the Florida courts with death row inmates claiming that the same thing that had happened to Gardner had happened to them. Many of these inmates were winning new sentencing hearings, with the hope of life sentences rather than death.

If exposing the mistake of a single trial judge could cause that much damage to the death penalty machine, imagine the fallout that might come from showing that the state's high court had committed the same error. And if Justice Potter Stewart, a swing vote in favor of capital punishment, could be moved to anger by the Gardner case, what effect might this larger case have? Barnard savored the possibilities. According to the U.S. Supreme Court, Florida's death penalty law was constitutional in part because every death sentence had to be reviewed by the state's highest court. No one could be executed without the state supreme court's okay. This automatic review was a pillar of the entire enterprise; it had been copied into the laws of every state where the death penalty was legal.

Barnard could picture a row of dominoes waiting to fall. First, he and his colleagues, using the Gardner case as the precedent, would attack the state supreme court's use of psychological reports without the knowledge of the defense. Next domino: The revelation of these reports would shake the confidence of the U.S. Supreme Court in the reliability of automatic appellate review. Florida's death penalty law would be invalidated—and because Florida was the pioneer state in these matters, its failure would shift the momentum toward abolishing capital punishment outright.

That was the most they could hope for. More realistically, the issue might be a roadblock to further executions while the courts worked to resolve it—a process that could take years. Buying time is the next best thing to total victory for opponents of the death penalty. Following the apparent breakthrough of the Spenkelink execution, Barnard wanted desperately to buy some time.

Barnard and his colleagues worked quietly to build their case. They gathered prison files and court records to show that the Florida Supreme Court was, in fact, using inappropriate information. As the work continued through the summer of 1980, special care was taken not to tip off George Georgieff and Ray Marky at the attorney general's office. When, in the late summer of 1980, the *St. Petersburg Times* published a story documenting the secret psychological reports, Barnard moved into his endgame.

Bob Graham had signed death warrants on two prisoners, Carl Ray Songer and Lenson Hargrave. (Hargrave was known as "Minnesota" because—like the billiards legend—he was fat.) They were a couple of classic death-house cons: Songer killed a state trooper in the line of duty; Hargrave murdered a convenience store clerk during a botched robbery. Their deaths were scheduled for October 8, 1980. But instead of coming into court with straightforward appeals based on the facts of their trials, lawyers for the two men joined more than eighty other defense attorneys—including Anthony Amsterdam, David Kendall, Margaret Good, and Craig Barnard—in filing the class action petition Barnard had been masterminding. The suit listed as plaintiffs 123 of the men on death row, and it laid out the case against the secret reports.

According to procedure, they went first to the Florida Supreme Court, claiming that the court had violated the Fifth Amendment right to confront evidence, as expressed in the U.S. Supreme Court's *Gardner* decision. "The capital sentencing process in Florida has been distorted from the form in which it was approved by the Supreme Court of the United States and has become tainted at its highest and most important level," Barnard's group argued. The suit was a direct attack on the state supreme court's integrity. The group demanded that all records relating to death penalty cases be maintained—a pointed reference to the apparent shredding of documents. The suit further asked that a special magistrate be appointed to comb each case for possible taint by undisclosed psychological reports (implying that the state's loftiest judges could not be trusted to handle the task themselves). "When the court's decision is one involving the ultimate penalty of death, the Constitution cannot tolerate anything short of full notice and disclosure of any and all facts being fed into the life and death equation," the lawsuit declared.

The Florida Supreme Court, without comment, stayed the executions of Songer and Hargrave until it could consider this attack. A jubilant lawyer for one of the men on death row had a copy of the suit hand-delivered to the governor's office, along with the suggestion that Bob Graham "should be aware of this proceeding in considering whether any death warrants should be signed." Graham's death penalty aide, Betty Steffens, told the press that the governor would not be deterred by the pending lawsuit. "That is something that is between them and the supreme court," she said. Scharlette Holdman was more effusive. "Essentially," she said happily, "we've caught the state supreme court cheating."

The class action suit, which came to be known as *Brown v. Wainwright*—Joseph Green Brown was the first of the 123 plaintiffs in alphabetical order, and Louie Lee Wainwright was the head of the Florida prison system—struck at the integrity and honor of the seven Florida Supreme Court justices. Newspaper accounts of the suit focused on the secrecy, the shredding, the "cheating," as Holdman put it. No one seemed to understand the burden that the death penalty was placing on the justices—not just as human beings charged with life-and-death decisions, but as an institution operating at the fulcrum of a politically and emotionally potent issue.

Challenging the Florida Supreme Court's integrity was picking at a scab. Several years before *Brown v. Wainwright* was filed, the court had been devastated by a shameful string of scandals, and the memory was still fresh in Tallahassee. Three of the seven justices of the state's high court had been threatened with impeachment for varying offenses. Two resigned. (One of them was later arrested for dope smuggling. He skipped bail and died a federal fugitive.) The third—a man who liked to brag that his judicial qualifications consisted of serving as a judge in the Miss Hialeah beauty pageant—held his seat only after he agreed to a psychiatric evaluation. This yearlong debacle had left a backlog of nearly a thousand cases at the court, of which an ever-increasing number had been death penalty reviews.

Demoralized and overburdened, the Florida court struggled to catch up. Aided by law clerks, the justices pored over thousands of pages in each death penalty file. Each case was a new twist on the old confusions. Together, the cases pushed up a mountain of peculiarities. The justices debated and anguished in search of decisions. They drafted and redrafted opinions. When they approved the new death penalty in the 1973 *Dixon* case, the justices had spoken of the modern process as if it were a subtle, carefully constructed marvel of legal checks and balances. By the time *Brown v. Wainwright* was filed, seven years of experience had begun to teach them that it was, in many ways, a slapdash machine designed in confusion, built of spare parts and baling wire. They found themselves, again and again, devising bubblegum patches to hold it together. The Florida Supreme Court was devoting roughly 40 percent of its time and resources to the death penalty—40 percent, while the rest of the state's legal business languished. And yet, for all that work, the justices could see little progress. One man had been executed, but Spenkelink's death had not put an end to the flood of legal questions raised by the new death penalty.

New cases were constantly pouring into their chambers, and they were not getting any simpler to decide. The justices knew something scarcely imagined by the public—that despite the Spenkelink execution, the death penalty in Florida was teetering on the brink of chaos. By the end of 1980, Florida courts had handed out close to three hundred death sentences, and roughly half of the sentences had been reversed because judges or lawyers had misapplied the complex law.

The rest of the condemned men, minus Spenkelink, were still on death row; some were entering their eighth year.

Arthur England was a blue-chip lawyer from Miami, appointed to replace one of the disgraced justices. Scholarly, creative, impartial, England restored some respect to the court, but the challenge of the new death penalty defeated him utterly. "The workload imposed by the new capital statute was very heavy," he later explained. "Each case brought a very, very large record. The cases raised more points on appeal than any other class of cases. Nevertheless, we found ourselves faced with this new statute and a mandate from the U.S. Supreme Court that it was constitutional, so we felt an obligation to make it work.

"To me, this meant that the aggravating and mitigating circumstances should be given context and content, to find those cases in which death was truly the appropriate penalty," England said. "For example, 'heinous' must mean something more than just anything that is offensive. It must be something that truly goes beyond the pale. Of course, there was not always agreement on these definitions. But say we reached agreement in a particular case. The next case comes along and there is some small variation in the facts. What if a person shoots a man to death in the presence of his wife? Is that heinous? What if he shoots the person with some advance warning? What if he shoots a police officer but the victim never sees it coming?

"What I found was that it was impossible to draw lines that were consistent. People do not all have the same sense of what constitutes a heinous or atrocious crime," England explained.

Was it any wonder that the justices in Tallahassee came to feel like Sisyphus, who spent eternity pushing a boulder up a mountain only to have the stone fall back each time he neared the summit? Or like Hercules, shoveling an endless supply of shit from the Augean stable? Nor was it any wonder that they might grasp at any shred that could help them in their task—even if it meant peeking at psychological evaluations that they were not, through some dainty point of law, supposed to see.

So they felt awfully damn insulted when Craig Barnard and the rest of Florida's death row defense lawyers attacked the court's integrity and its diligence, in the megasuit known as *Brown v. Wainwright.*

At the secret strategy sessions where the lawsuit was hatched, a key question was who should present the arguments in court. Everyone turned to Craig Barnard. It only made sense: He was the guru, the mastermind; he had earned the right to deliver this potentially paralyzing blow to the death penalty. But Barnard declined. From the start, he realized that *Brown v. Wainwright* was going to be a prickly suit, challenging the very integrity of the Florida Supreme Court. Barnard had someone else in mind—Marvin Frankel, an esteemed New York lawyer. Frankel practiced in a faraway state, so he would not have to worry about crippling future cases by offending the justices. Moreover, Frankel was a former federal court judge. He had been on the bench, he knew the difficulties of a judge's life. Barnard believed it could only help to have this assault on a panel of judges argued by a peer.

Barnard passed up the glory of a highly publicized case in pursuit of a wisp of strategic advantage. This was altogether typical of him. Lawyers aren't the world's most self-effacing bunch, but Barnard was an exception. Even as a boy growing up in Michigan, he had never mentioned to his parents the academic honors and awards he collected at school. Whatever drove him toward excellence, it was entirely within. He didn't need applause.

Craig Barnard was raised in a comfortable middle-class home on the shore of a lake in Portage, Michigan. His father was a conservative Republican accountant, his uncle a Republican state senator. Barnard's youth was a suburban idyll of ice skating in the winter, Detroit Lions games in the autumn, fishing and the Tigers in summer. Barnard was quiet—he preferred walking to school alone rather than taking the boisterous bus—but popular, playing on the high school football team until a shoulder injury left him on the sidelines. Unlike many of his colleagues in the crusade against the death penalty, he did not dream from boyhood of being a lawyer. His first steps toward a career, in fact, were taken with the McDonald's hamburger empire. Even before he could get a driver's license, Barnard finagled a job at the local McDonald's, and worked his way up to assistant manager. That experience helped him earn a scholarship to study hotel and restaurant management at Michigan State. But he soon tired of cooking and bed making, and decided to become a computer programmer.

Then the sixties caught up with Craig Barnard. The dutiful young Republican grew his hair long, fell in love with Bob Dylan's music, and began protesting the war. (On his birthday in 1970, four antiwar protesters were killed at Kent State; Barnard never celebrated his birthday again.) He wanted to do something to change the system, so he switched majors again, this time to prelaw. By then, Barnard's father had moved to southwestern Florida, where he built a retirement village. Craig followed him south, enrolling at the University of Florida law school. When he graduated in 1974, Barnard joined the public defender's office in Palm Beach County. The man who hired him was the county's elected public defender, Richard Jorandby.

In every judicial district of Florida, an elected prosecutor, called the state attorney, supervises the government lawyers trying to put people into jail. And an elected public defender supervises the government lawyers trying to keep these same people out of jail. Typically, the state attorneys are the conservatives and the public defenders are the liberals, but this was not so in Palm Beach County. Dick Jorandby was a true-blue conservative, a rock-bottom Republican who quoted Barry Goldwater as a prophet and solemnly assured his young employees that someday Richard Nixon would be vindicated. All Jorandby's stands—anti-Communist, pro–free enterprise, low tax, small government—derived from his faith in individual freedom under a government of laws. Where he parted company with most of his fellow conservatives, however, was when the tenets of his faith were pushed into the field of criminal law.

To Jorandby, the most ominous danger of government incursion on personal freedom was not in the area of taxes or business regulation. It was in the government's authority to strip a man of his rights as a citizen and lock him up in prison. This awesome prerogative of the state had to be checked and balanced with vigor, so that it would never be abused. And when the penalty went beyond prison to death . . . well, the need to keep a rein on the government's actions was even more acute. There is no government power greater than the power of life and death; no government intrusion is more invasive. And so, more than any other public defender in Florida—in fact, more than any of his peers across in the country—Dick Jorandby fought the death penalty. Craig Barnard was, very quickly, Jorandby's star assistant; naturally, Jorandby gave him authority over the region's death row cases. Barnard, with his studious bent and modest personality, was drawn to the detail-oriented, conceptual world of appeals. He never missed the hurly-burly of criminal trials.

Barnard was also a fine manager, and soon Jorandby entrusted him with the day-to-day operations of the entire office. In this role, Barnard recruited a cadre of death penalty specialists to work with him. Over time, the Palm Beach public defender's office became one of the most important centers of capital appeals in the nation. Running the office was no simple task. Dick Jorandby was great when it came to vision and philosophy—he was a pioneer in such areas as alternative sentencing, for example. And he was good at squeezing money from even the most reluctant sources. But he was less effective with internal operations. Fact was, most of his employees found their boss a little strange: Jorandby replaced the sturdy armchairs in his office with rocking chairs, and whenever someone came in with a problem or a complaint, he required them to sit and rock awhile. At the beginning and end of each day, Jorandby cleared his schedule, told his secretary to hold all calls, closed his office door, and meditated. He was not an organization man.

Craig Barnard did the work of at least three men. As the leader of the death penalty team in Palm Beach, he was chief strategist and often lead litigator on more than a dozen capital cases in his own jurisdiction. Beyond his jurisdiction, he consulted frequently with lawyers for other death row inmates. If there was any coordinated strategy for fighting executions in Florida, Barnard was the strategist. And as Jorandby's chief assistant, he supervised the daily office drudgery, from drafting budgets to purchasing supplies, from hiring new lawyers to counseling old ones, from the lowliest prostitution case to the most complicated murder trial.

As a result, Barnard worked constantly. At his desk by 6:30 or 7 A.M., he labored steadily until eight or nine at night—then lugged a pile of papers home with him. He was the first one into the office and the last one out. A lawyer, under pressure from a big case, might show up bright and early on a Saturday morning, fully expecting to be alone. But the aroma of Barnard's pipe would be wafting down the corridor. On Sundays, Barnard worked to the sound of the Miami Dolphins games on the radio.

His abiding loves were cars—he owned a succession of nifty sportscars—and work. He worked a lot and slept just a little. He ate (plenty, judging from his build, a round face on a round body), but he cared not a whit about food. His glove compartment was always jammed with fast-food coupons, and the freezer compartment of his refrigerator was packed with frozen dinners. He took his lunch at his desk; only once a year, on Secretaries Day, did he eat lunch at a restaurant.

And most years, he took just one brief vacation, always the same: a week at The Island House on Mackinac Island, at the northern tip of Michigan. Barnard loved the white-columned, historic hotel for the happy memories it evoked of boyhood holidays, and for the peace and quiet of a place with no cars and few telephones. Even there, however, he felt the urge to read law review articles, and to call the office several times a day. By week's end he was jumpy from lack of work.

But for all his intensity, Barnard was never brusque, much less arrogant. The greenest young attorneys, handling the smallest misdemeanors, felt welcome to poke their heads into his office for advice. Barnard would calmly stop his work, puff his pipe as he listened intently to the question, then patiently offer an answer. Or perhaps a lawyer across the state would call in a panic over an arcane death penalty issue. Barnard would quietly soothe the caller and steer through the problem—and if the question required some legal research, Barnard would drop what he was doing and pore over law books until he found the answer. Or a colleague would call from the public defender's office in another county, frantic at the prospect of preparing an annual budget. Barnard would take fifteen, twenty minutes, maybe half an hour—whatever time it took—to commiserate and offer advice.

Frequently, the emergencies came from Tallahassee, where friends of Scharlette Holdman kept Barnard apprised of her troubles. Her electricity had been shut off again. She was late with her rent. Life was always a crisis with Scharlette. Every time, Barnard would put his own work aside long enough to get Holdman straightened out. Often this involved sending a check drawn on his personal account. Barnard spent hours soothing, counseling, talking people through their problems, but he remained a very private man. He gave help, never asked for it; he was opaque as obsidian. No one really knew him. His parents were sure he was a Republican; his colleagues were just as sure he was a Democrat. Even some of his closest friends had no idea if he had any romantic life. On the rare occasions that Barnard could be roped into attending a party, he spent his time in the corner and left as early as possible. Quite by accident, one associate discovered that Barnard had a passion for kitschy souvenirs, the sort of junk sold in shops at the exit ramps along Florida's interstate highways. Word spread, and soon Barnard boasted perhaps the state's finest collection of cheap plastic flamingos, all tokens of esteem and affection.

He kept the more substantive facts of his personal life almost entirely to himself. His epilepsy, for instance. The disease had revealed itself only after Barnard was grown. One night, during a convention in Texas, he woke with a searing pain and a mouth full of blood. He had apparently bitten his tongue half off in his sleep. Barnard went to see a doctor, but the doctor was dismissive: Probably just a little too much to drink, he diagnosed. Not long afterward, Barnard was standing at his bathroom mirror, razor in hand, when suddenly—nothingness. He came to in the bathtub, writhing with pain from a dislocated shoulder.

This time the doctors took him more seriously. They ran CAT scans, searching for a brain tumor. The tests came up clean. More tests were run, and eventually the doctors concluded that Barnard was suffering dangerous epileptic seizures. With medication, the seizures were brought under control. (Barnard never had to surrender his precious driver's license.) Still, he lived with the knowledge that the day might come when he would black out and never awaken. Grand mal seizures can be fatal. So it was that Craig Barnard shared something very personal with his death row clients. Like them, he knew the sense of something powerful waiting to snuff you out.

The Florida Supreme Court set oral arguments in the case of

Brown v. Wainwright for October 27, 1980, less than a month after the case was filed. Barnard worked even harder than usual, though such a thing seemed scarcely possible, to assure that Marvin Frankel's crucial oral argument would go well.

It is best for a death row defense attorney when the world mostly forgets about your clients. The prisoners of death row have done hideous things, and when the bloody details are fresh the public cries out for punishment, the harsher the better. A Craig Barnard, an Anthony Amsterdam, a Millard Farmer, typically works best when the crimes have faded and passions are cool. The fight becomes legal or philosophical rather than emotional. For the defense attorneys, the weeks leading up to oral arguments in *Brown v. Wainwright* would have been a good time for anonymous quiet on death row. Instead, there came a shocking reminder of the sort of man the lawsuit was designed to save.

The danger of death row could easily be forgotten in the mind-numbing routine of the place. As a rule, the inmates understood the value of docile anonymity; their lives hung on favorable treatment from the courts or the governor. Furthermore, the design of death row—with each inmate locked in a solitary confinement cell and few occasions when prisoners were gathered in groups—increased the relative safety. Many guards found work among the prison's general population far more threatening than work on death row. General population at the state prison was the end of the line for Florida's bad guys. To get there, inmates had to prove themselves too mean, too crafty, too crazy for lesser prisons. They slashed and killed one another with near impunity. Compared to that, death row was an oasis.

Or so it might have seemed to Richard Burke, a retired naval petty officer, father of two adopted kids, newly hired as a death row guard at Florida State Prison. He always seemed relaxed and jovial. He enjoyed bantering with the prisoners, calling out "It's time for your douche!" in a singsong voice whenever he led a man to the shower room. He tried to be pleasant even with Thomas Knight, one of the meanest men on the row.

On a July morning in 1974, Knight had kidnapped a Miami businessman, Sydney Gans, as Gans arrived at work. Knight forced Gans to drive home, where he took Gans's wife, Lillian, as a second hostage. They proceeded to a local bank. While Knight held Mrs. Gans at gunpoint in the car, Mr. Gans went into the bank and withdrew $50,000 from his account. During the transaction, Gans told the bank president what was happening. But rather than wait for police to arrive, Gans bravely returned to the car, hopeful that handing over the money would save his wife. It didn't. Police and FBI agents soon found the car abandoned in a field; inside were the bodies of Stanley and Lillian Gans, each shot to death through the throat. Knight was found hiding in some weeds about a quarter of a mile away, his rifle and the money buried beneath him.

On death row, Knight was a surly and uncooperative prisoner. He spent many hours under his headphones, dancing and singing to soul music; his remaining time was largely devoted to confrontations with the prison authorities. When Knight announced that his name was now Askari Abdullah Muhammad, that he had joined the Ansaru Allah Community of Islam, and that his religion required him to wear a beard, the warden and the guards concluded that he was pulling another scheme to piss them off. They had a hard-and-fast rule requiring all inmates to shave, and when Knight, or Askari, refused, an order came down that he should be locked up and stripped of visiting and canteen privileges until he complied.

One morning in October 1980, Knight got word that his mother had arrived at the prison for a visit. This was big news, because she hadn't been to see him since he got to death row. Knight called to the guard on the wing, Richard Burke, the new man with three months under his belt guarding the prisoners of R-wing. And Burke said, Sorry, man, but you can't have visitors because you won't shave.

Look, Knight answered. We pass by the barbershop on the way to the visitor's park. We'll stop in there and I'll get a shave.

Can't do it, Burke answered.

My mom visits me once in five years. You're gonna stop me from seeing her? Knight asked. And Burke said, Those are my orders. Someone on the row heard Knight say: "Man, when I get angry I go to stickin'." And Burke's reply: "Do what you gotta do."

That seemed to be the end of it. About 4:30 P.M. on Sunday, October 12, Burke walked confidently down the corridor toward Knight's cell. "C'mon, Knight," he called. "Time for your douche!" To the guard in the control room, Burke shouted: "Pop number nine!" Knight's cell door opened. The prisoner charged out, brandishing a soup ladle, its handle filed down to a point. He thrust the shank into Burke's chest.

The guard did not resist. As the other inmates rushed to the bars of their cells, holding out mirrors to see what was happening, Burke threw up his hands and cried, "What have I done? Let's talk it out." Knight jabbed again.

"My god, he's killing him!" a prisoner shouted. "What do you think?" someone answered. Knight slipped to the floor, grabbed Burke's shirt, and pulled the guard down with him. He straddled his victim, kneeling on Burke's arms, and stabbed repeatedly, clutching the shank in both hands. "Please, please, please," Burke gasped. "Don't hurt me."

By now the officer at the end of the corridor had called a "Signal 24"—the code for trouble on death row. The supervising officer, Sergeant Harry Owen, rushed into the corridor, followed by several other guards. "Knight, that's enough!" he shouted. "You've done what you wanted to do. You've hurt him. Let me have the knife. Let me see if I can help him."

Dripping blood, Knight staggered to his feet and charged Owen, raising the knife for another attack. But the force of his assault on Burke had wrapped the blade around his hand, like brass knuckles. He flung the weapon away, and it clattered into a nearby cell. Inmate Ronald Straight kicked the knife back into the corridor. "Not in my house, man!" Straight shouted.

Owen picked up the mangled knife as the other guards tackled Knight and shackled him swiftly. Burke lay on the bloody floor, moaning and gasping as the life drained out of him. Medics arrived from the prison hospital, and as they lifted Burke on a stretcher, Ronald Straight and another prisoner—his partner in crime, Timothy Palmes—began singing: "Another one bites the dust." For the first time in Florida's history, a guard had been murdered on death row.

Dave Brierton had by this time been promoted to the post of inspector general for the state prison system, and his assistant Richard Dugger was now warden. Dugger ordered an immediate crackdown. The cell of every death row prisoner was raided for illegal weapons. Every item of "contraband"—including Doug McCray's library of about eighty books—was seized, along with Bob Sullivan's legal papers, a pile of homemade fans and waterbugs, even stashes of candy bars. Dugger further ordered that death row prisoners not be allowed out of their cells without handcuffs.

The orders sparked an uprising on the row. Inmate Gary Trawick somehow got his hands on a piece of welding rod, which he sharpened and strapped to a broom handle. Two days after the Burke murder, Trawick thrust the weapon at a passing guard, wounding the man in his side. Stephen Booker got the makings of a new waterbug, heated a cup of water, and flung the boiling liquid into a passing guard's face. Warden Dugger responded with tear gas, and an uneasy calm was restored.

Thomas Knight got his shave—in handcuffs, leg irons, and a headlock. He also got a second death sentence. And no death row guard was ever again quite so jovial as poor Richard Burke.

Two weeks later, Marvin Frankel rose to face the seven black-robed justices of the Florida Supreme Court, and began one of the toughest arguments any lawyer could make. He asked the justices to admit that their actions had tainted justice. He wanted the judges to judge themselves. Frankel, who had worn the black robe himself, stepped gingerly on the feelings of his fellow jurists, but he might as well have been wearing hobnailed boots.

"Our best understanding of how the situation arose is that it was probably because of a commendable desire by a court saddled with a grim responsibility to leave no stone unturned," Frankel ventured. Nevertheless, "along comes this revelation that the Supreme Court of Florida, in administering this statute, has been led to this very fundamental kind of what we respectfully call 'misbehavior.' "

In even the smallest civil cases, defendants had a right to confront any material that might be used against them, Frankel reminded the justices. The U.S. Supreme Court's decision in *Gardner v. Florida* had underlined this right for condemned inmates. Frankel continued: Now that the secret psychological reports had been expunged from the Florida high court's files, there was no solution to the lawsuit except to have a special magistrate examine every case—even if that meant putting the justices themselves under oath and cross-examining them. The death penalty had been compromised, Frankel said. "The practice of which these petitioners complain, however it evolved, discloses defects so pervasive and so fatal in the capital sentencing system of this state as to invalidate that system and to invalidate the statute under which these sentences were imposed."

Arguing the case for the State of Florida was George Georgieff. As always, he was blunt, and spoke off the monogrammed cuff. Some individual inmates might have a bona fide beef, Georgieff allowed. But that didn't justify a blanket ruling in favor of 123 prisoners. "You don't burn the barn to get rid of the rats," he said. As for the defense's claim that it couldn't prove misconduct in every case because the court files had been purged—that was just an excuse for laziness. "Are you telling me they can't discover more than what they have in that lousy petition?" he asked rhetorically. "I don't believe that!" Georgieff was joined at the podium by his boss, Jim Smith, who put the case more formally. No prisoner had proven that his case was tainted by the reports, Smith argued. The problem should be handled on a case-by-case basis. "Violations which might have occurred against a few cannot be said to have permeated every petitioner's case. There are no allegations of fact by any particular petitioner to show his constitutional rights were violated."

The justices tried to listen impartially to each side, but it wasn't easy. Frankel's argument for the prisoners was like a kick to their kidneys. Justice Arthur England, for one, reminded himself again and again that Frankel was just doing his job. Still, it hurt like hell to listen to it. The pain was compounded by extensive reports in the press, some of which strongly implied chicanery on the part of the justices—a powerful charge, given the state supreme court's recent record of scandal. "It seemed that everything we were trying so hard to do was being questioned, over a simple error," England later recalled.

In chambers, the justices quickly found that they were unanimous in rejecting the lawsuit. Several maintained they had never seen the reports in question; others insisted that, though they had read the reports, they had not been swayed by them. Even Joseph Boyd, the court's lone wolf, agreed that it was impossible to believe that the court had been biased by a few psychological reports. There was no debate. However, none of the justices wanted to write the decision; they all preferred to remain, as much as possible, removed from this attack on their integrity. At last, England agreed to take on the job. Professorial, perhaps even imperious at times, England prided himself on his command of the law and his mastery of logic over emotion. But even he could not keep the anger and defensiveness out of his writing in this case.

"We cannot pass this opportunity to put this case in a more rational perspective that it has been accorded by counsel and the media," he wrote, acid welling up in his pen. "This case emerges from society's continuing wrangling over the moral and social justification for capital punishment. Regrettably, the thunderous emanations of this great debate . . . [have] cast a pall on the integrity of the painful process by which this court attempts to deal with the responsibility it has been assigned." England was wounded, and it showed. "It seems to us both unwarranted and unseemly to vilify those who endeavor to follow the Constitution; we are, after all, the messengers and not the message," he wrote.

Clearly, Craig Barnard's choice of a former judge to argue the prickly case had done no good. To England, Marvin Frankel's gentle approach was "unseemly" vilification. And so England lashed back. He branded the case "singularly unpersuasive." He promised that any more class action appeals "will be rejected summarily."

None of this went to the legal issue at stake, however. England had to find some distinction between a trial judge weighing a secret report—which the U.S. Supreme Court had declared unconstitutional—and the reading of undisclosed reports by the state supreme court. England executed a dainty dance along some fine conceptual lines. First of all, he wrote, there is a difference between imposing a sentence and reviewing a sentence. Trial judges imposed; the supreme court re-

viewed. This was true, he postulated, even though sometimes the supreme court's "review" resulted directly in a lesser sentence. England
did not explain these slippery terms so much as simply assert them: "It
is evident," he wrote, "once our dual roles in the capital punishment
scheme are fully appreciated, that nonrecord information we may have
seen, even though never presented to or considered by the judge, the
jury, or counsel, plays no role in capital sentence 'review.' "

It was not one of England's finest efforts. The supporting cases he
cited did not really support his conclusions and his hurt was poorly
masked. He was inconsistent, first claiming that the court had the right
to consider the secret reports, then doubling back to announce that the
reports had never been considered. England proposed that his opinion
be published anonymously, as the voice of all seven justices. In the face
of such a direct attack, the court should answer as one.

But the loner, Joe Boyd, refused to go along with England's
strong rhetoric. On January 15, 1981, *Brown v. Wainwright* was dismissed by the Florida Supreme Court with England's ringing denunciation signed by six justices and a terse note from Boyd: "I am
convinced that no member of this court was influenced by any extraneous material. Although I don't agree with all the language in the majority opinion, I concur in the result."

The lawyers for the inmates immediately announced that they
would appeal to the U.S. Supreme Court.

Bob Graham was a pioneer, blazing a trail for contemporary
American governors into a realm of power unpracticed for most of a
generation. Dealing with the environment, with education, with immi-
gration and social services, Graham was a forward-looking man, one of
the promising new faces of the Democratic Party. Dealing with the
death penalty, however, he led the way back, not forward—back to a
time before the social upheaval of the 1960s and 1970s, back to the days
when governors had to spend long hours weighing questions of mercy,
of justice, of life, and of death. For the generation of governors before
his, the death penalty was little more than something to talk about. It

wasn't real. Bob Graham was the first American governor in many years for whom the death penalty became a matter of routine business.

It consumed many hours of his time. Though *Brown v. Wainwright* had turned the courts into a roadblock, Graham regularly held clemency hearings, signed death warrants, and—every now and then—exercised his sovereign authority to extend mercy to a condemned man. This power of mercy was not entirely the power of a Roman emperor; Graham couldn't save a man with a simple thumbs-up. Technically, he needed the approval of half the state's elected cabinet to commute a sentence from death to life. But in practice, his power was nearly Caesarean. Whenever he recommended life, he always got the votes.

The governor's grant of mercy was a time-honored tradition in Florida. All Graham's predecessors, at least back to 1925, had used it, with varying frequency. Some had been more merciful than others, but they had all spared the lives of between 10 and 40 percent of the prisoners who beseeched them.

Soon after his election, Graham got his hands on a law review article tracing a governor's right to commute death sentences back to the divine right of kings. He pored over the article, discussed it with friends, took it to heart. Clemency was an act of sublime grace—in ways it outshone any other authority of the office, this power over life and death. Graham hired a savvy lawyer, Betty Steffens, to advise him on clemency, and encouraged her always to make the strongest possible case in favor of mercy. At their frequent meetings, he quizzed Steffens intently on the details of each case, and after Steffens resigned to pursue private practice, Graham kept up the quizzing with her replacement, Art Weidinger.

He believed in the power of clemency, and for a time he exercised it as his predecessors had. His first grant of mercy was a leftover from the Askew years (just as his first death warrant was inherited from Askew).

Clifford Hallman was an ex-con with a record of accosting young women in parking lots and threatening to cut their throats. He threatened, but he never cut. One night in April 1973, Hallman was drinking, as he often did, at the North Town Tavern in Tampa, and he said something to the barmaid, Eleanor Jean Groves. Whatever he said, she didn't like it.

Groves slapped Hallman and knocked his drink to the floor. Hallman snatched up a shard of the broken glass and slashed at her throat. Panicked, Hallman then rifled the cash register to make it look like a robbery had taken place. He fled, and the barmaid managed to get herself to the hospital. After about an hour of wandering, Hallman turned himself in to police.

Four days later, Eleanor Groves died, and Hallman was charged with first-degree murder. On October 12, 1973, he became the first man in Florida sentenced to death under the state's new law. After the trial, however, an employee of Tampa General Hospital charged that Groves's death had resulted not from her wounds, but instead from hospital malpractice. Groves was sent home from the emergency room despite internal bleeding, and she was suffocated by the blood. The hospital hired a doctor to investigate the case, and—to the hospital's chagrin—the expert concluded that the wound Hallman inflicted shouldn't have been fatal. The hospital paid a substantial settlement to Groves's survivors.

Askew had considered Hallman's case for clemency but left the matter to Graham. On June 26, 1979—a month and a day after John Spenkelink was executed—Graham quietly commuted Hallman's sentence to life in prison. The same day, Graham recommended clemency in another case. Learie Leo Alford had been sentenced to death row four days after Hallman. On January 7, 1973, a thirteen-year-old girl was kidnapped in West Palm Beach on her way to the ocean. Her body was later found on a trash heap, raped, blindfolded, and shot four times. Alford was sentenced to death on the recommendation of an all-white jury. After the trial, though, defense attorneys discovered witnesses who said that a car spotted at the crime scene belonged to another man, not Alford. This hint of mistaken identity unsettled Graham, and he decided to reduce Alford's sentence to life in prison.

Graham offset any suggestion that he was going soft on criminals by signing eight death warrants before his next grant of clemency. (All eight were stayed.) The next lucky man was Richard Henry Gibson, a thug from the Jacksonville seaport. Gibson and a friend, Tom Calvin, were at a bar one night when they noticed two sailors on shore leave from a Brazilian freighter. The sailors, with their fat pay packets, looked like easy marks. Gibson and Calvin recruited their girlfriends to seduce the sailors, but instead of sex, the sailors got a ride to a nearby alley. There, Gibson and Calvin pulled guns and demanded their money; when the sailors resisted, they were shot. One of them died. Gibson got the death penalty; Calvin was sentenced to life in prison.

Gibson's appellate attorney, Baya Harrison, was a big man around Tallahassee, a former deputy attorney general. He dug into the court transcripts and discovered conflicting theories of the crime. In the trial of Tom Calvin, the prosecutor had claimed Calvin did the shooting. At Gibson's trial, the same prosecutor had said Gibson was the triggerman. Harrison took the two conflicting transcripts to his friend Betty Steffens, the governor's clemency aide. Wasn't it unfair, he asked, to let one of these guys live while the other died, given that the state was uncertain who did the killing? Steffens made the case to Graham, and apparently the governor agreed.

"Apparently" Graham agreed: The governor made a point of never saying publicly why he chose to commute a man's sentence. This was in keeping with his tight-lipped approach to all death penalty matters; Graham worried that if he spelled out his reasons for granting mercy, clemency would become just another quasi-judicial proceeding. He preferred the idea of ineffable grace. But by spring 1980, Graham's silence on matters of mercy was beginning to cause him political trouble. Learie Leo Alford's case had infuriated many citizens in Palm Beach County. Petitions were circulated, angry letters dispatched— some charged that Alford had gotten mercy as a political favor, because Alford's father was a minister with sway in the local Democratic Party. James Watt, a Republican legislator from West Palm Beach, introduced a bill that would require the governor to list his reasons whenever he commuted a death sentence. Graham's aides had to lobby furiously to block the bill.

The experience taught a lesson: Clemency could have a political price. And when Graham reduced the sentence of Darrell Edwin Hoy, in June 1980, the backlash was even fiercer. Hoy was big, burly, and "dumb as a box of rocks," in the words of his attorney; he passed his time in the company of Jesse Lamar Hall, who was smaller, smarter, and meaner. On an August day in 1975, Hall and Hoy were hanging out at Dunedin Beach, where they spied an attractive teenage couple, David Sawyer and Susan Routt. They approached the couple. Hall brandished a gun and announced that Hoy would like to have sex with Routt. They went to a secluded stretch of beach; once there, Hoy grabbed Routt and forced her to the sand. David Sawyer broke free from Hall and tried, heroically, to help his girlfriend—but Jesse Hall shot him dead. After Hoy finished, Hall raped Routt savagely, then shot her in the head. Hoy raped her again as she died.

This evil tragedy gripped and sickened the people of Tampa Bay like few other cases of its time. The trials of Hall and Hoy took place in a blaze of publicity, and their death sentences were widely welcomed. But the Florida Supreme Court, reviewing Hall's sentence, ruled that his attorney had been denied the chance to cross-examine Hoy. Faced with a second trial, prosecutors allowed Hall to plead guilty in exchange for a life sentence. This twist meant that Hall, the instigator and shooter, would avoid the death penalty while Hoy would face execution. Graham reduced Hoy's sentence to match Jesse Hall's.

No doubt the governor saw Hoy's case as a matter of equity, but people around Tampa tended to see only the end result. Instead of two executions to avenge the ghastly crime on Dunedin Beach, there would be none. And so the angry citizens signed petitions, even more than had been signed in West Palm Beach after the Alford clemency. They flooded Graham's office with mail. They held meetings and staged protests and poured out their fury on the evening news. Suddenly, Graham—the only governor in America who had dispatched an unwilling man to death—was catching heat for being too merciful. Because of this heat, or maybe for some other reason, the governor became more sparing in his exercise of clemency and signed another eight death warrants before he reduced another sentence.

Again, this one was apparently for reasons of disparate sentencing. There had been a falling-out among thieves in Miami; three of the crooks conspired to murder the fourth. One thief got a ten-year sentence, another got life . . . and the third, Michael Salvatore, was sent to the death house. When Graham reduced Salvatore's sentence, no one protested, because in this case there were no good guys. That was the last time Bob Graham pushed for mercy in a capital case, though he did agree to one more clemency—for Jesse Ray Rutledge, nearly a year, and nine death warrants, after Salvatore. Mercy for Rutledge came at the instigation of the state insurance commissioner, a member of the elected cabinet. The commissioner was not sure Rutledge was guilty.

Jesse Rutledge had been sent to death row for a murderous attack on a neighbor and her three children. Two children survived, and one of them testified against Rutledge. But defense attorneys later discovered another suspect—a man who had had a violent affair with the murdered woman. This man had been overheard threatening to kill her and her children. And the lawyers found a police report in which one surviving child described the attacker as having a mustache and missing a front tooth. This description fit the second suspect, not Rutledge. Graham was persuaded to spare Jesse Rutledge. Then, for reasons known only to Graham, official mercy dried up in Florida. Though he continued to hold formal meetings of the clemency board, though he listened patiently to the pleadings of defense attorneys, though he met routinely with his clemency aides—and though there were men on death row with cases at least as strong as Darrell Hoy's and Jesse Rutledge's—Graham never again exercised his power of grace. During the first three years of his term, Graham balanced death warrants with clemency in a ratio consistent with his predecessors'. By the time he left office, he had shown less mercy than any Florida governor for whom records were available.

Graham later explained that he had come to count on the courts to weed out injustices. And it's true that the extensive appellate review of modern death cases did much culling that used to fall to the governors. But Graham's critics couldn't help noticing the governor stopped granting mercy at about the same time he began running for reelection.

Clearly, experience had taught Graham that mercy could be politically volatile. And the truth is that Graham did not actually stop sparing lives on death row—he merely developed a low-profile, private way of doing it. Graham continued to take great interest in the details of troubling cases, and when he was sufficiently troubled, he simply declined to sign the necessary death warrants. If it was too politically risky to save men by action, Graham nevertheless did so by inaction. In some twenty cases through the rest of his tenure, Graham prevented executions by quietly declining to sign death warrants. These men went into limbo: they were not permanently assured of living (another governor could someday sign a death warrant), but neither were they dead. It was a political masterstroke, the ultimate pocket veto.

Graham was Florida's ablest politician—opponents of the death penalty couldn't lay a glove on him. Everything they did seemed to play into his hands. Their protests seemed only to improve his standing. As Graham traveled around the state and across the country, hecklers often met him with banners denouncing "Bloody Bob!" or "Gov. Death!" Yet all along, Florida's murder rate was soaring, carrying support for the death penalty into the ionosphere. Linking Graham to executions did nothing to hurt him.

But death penalty opponents continued to attack him. Protesting was morally invigorating, and it was fun. When death penalty opponents learned that Graham was scheduled to deliver the nominating speech for President Jimmy Carter at the 1980 Democratic National Convention, they decided to dog him to New York. They wanted to disrupt the young governor's national political debut, poison his moment before the network television cameras. "Operation Besmirchment" was hatched in Scharlette Holdman's smoky office in the FOG Building in Tallahassee; the idea of getting in Graham's face appealed to Holdman's barefoot Yippie soul. But though she blessed the project, she kept her distance—Holdman realized that it could hurt her standing with mainstream Florida lawyers if she was seen as harassing the governor. Instead, Jimmy Lohman, Holdman's assistant (and sometime boyfriend), was dispatched to Manhattan to ruin Bob Graham's big day.

Lohman and a handful of conspirators worked quietly amid the madness of convention week. It was no easy thing to get protestors onto the floor of a convention, but Lohman had one thing going for him: 1980 was an unhappy year for the Democrats. As the Carter presidency foundered, Senator Edward Kennedy of Massachusetts had tried to claim the nomination for the party's liberal wing. And though Kennedy had failed, his delegates remained disaffected. Lohman began picking at this wound. He worked the phones in search of disgruntled Kennedy delegates who might donate their floor passes to outside demonstrators. He appealed to leaders of the black caucus, asking for volunteers to join the protest. He pitched his scheme to gay delegates, antinuke delegates—anyone who might have a beef with the party. Whenever he found a friendly reception, Lohman dispatched a packet of protest materials: photos of John Spenkelink, anti–death penalty editorials, even black executioner's hoods to be worn during Graham's speech.

When his idea began to catch on, Lohman moved his plot out of the shadows. He began buttonholing journalists, from the piddliest Florida newspaper reporter to the biggest newsman of them all, Walter Cronkite. At first, Lohman was met mostly by yawns. A hundred or so protesters in a field of more than three thousand delegates? Big deal. But the yawns turned to interest when Lohman mentioned his coup de grace: Lois Spenkelink—mother of the man Bob Graham had ordered executed—would be on the convention floor for Graham's speech. What journalist could resist? It would be an overwhelming image, a sorrowful, white-haired woman facing the man who had killed her boy. When the moment of Graham's speech arrived, Walter Cronkite introduced CBS viewers to Florida's little-known governor with a lengthy account of Graham's death penalty activities. Then cameras from all three networks fastened on the broad, sad face of Lois Spenkelink. Lohman had begged a seat for her among the New York delegation, front and center. She sat beneath a banner bearing a photograph of her Johnny, a sketch of an electric chair, and the hand-lettered message: BOB GRAHAM KILLED MY SON.

As protests go, Operation Besmirchment was a huge success; the morning after Graham's disappointing speech, the face on the front pages of many Florida newspapers was not the governor's. It was Lois Spenkelink's. As political action, though, it was another failure. Americans everywhere supported the death penalty and admired politicians willing to carry it out.

∴

Nationwide, support for capital punishment ran above 70 percent in most polls. In Florida, the number approached 90 percent. Americans rarely showed that level of agreement on anything. Judges and juries were dispatching criminals to death row in greater numbers than at any other time in American history. On the political battleground, the issue was a rout. And yet the death penalty was stymied. Virtually no one was being executed. More important than the political battleground was the legal battleground—and there the defense was still ahead. The only men being executed in America were those who gave up on their appeals and demanded death. On October 22, 1979, in Nevada, Jesse Bishop went willingly to the executioner. No one was executed in 1980. In Indiana, Steven Judy was voluntarily executed on March 9, 1981. Then there was another hiatus of seventeen months before the next volunteer came along—Frank Brooks in Virginia.

The Spenkelink execution had turned out to be a fluke. Across the country, state and federal courts were finding that their new laws, with the promise of almost scientific reliability, were in fact riddled with glitches. The death row population in America was greater than it had ever been, bumping up toward a thousand. Of all those cases, not one could be steered through the confusions and inconsistencies and legal conundrums of the modern death penalty. Florida was the national leader, ready to execute dozens—but *Brown v. Wainwright* still stood in the way. As promised, Craig Barnard and his colleagues had appealed the Florida Supreme Court's angry denunciation of their megasuit to the U.S. Supreme Court. Most of 1981 went by without an answer. At last, in early November of that year, by a vote of 7 to 2, the high court declined to hear the case.

Finally, the logjam might be broken. In Tallahassee, Attorney General Jim Smith said he would advise Governor Graham to start cranking out death warrants at a swifter pace. Turn up the heat. Within forty-eight hours of the U.S. Supreme Court's vote, Graham ordered the executions of two men. They were apparently strong candidates for the electric chair—Alvin Ford had killed a police officer in Fort Lauderdale; Amos Lee King had raped and murdered an elderly woman while on work release from prison.

But Craig Barnard was not finished with the secret psychological reports. When reporters called for his reaction to the Supreme Court setback, he puffed his pipe and said calmly that the fight would go on. True, his class action suit—lumping the claims of 123 condemned men together—was dead, but each man could still raise the appeal individually. Even the prosecution had acknowledged that some prisoners might have valid claims; Barnard planned to let the courts sort them out one by one. "The case is still as viable as the first day we filed it," he said.

Barnard and his assistants handled Alvin Ford's case, and they rushed to challenge the secret psychological reports in federal court. Seventeen hours before Ford was scheduled to die, the circuit court of appeals in Atlanta agreed to hear the case, and his execution was stayed. Amos King also got a reprieve. The logjam remained.

This is the way a good death penalty defense lawyer works: Run all the traps, fight every issue, hit every court. Go to the state supreme court, to the federal district court, the federal appeals court, the Supreme Court of the United States. Fight an issue on broad terms, and if you lose, fight it again on narrow terms. Turn every stone, poke into every mushy spot in the law. Read every opinion rendered by every court, and when some other death row inmate wins his case, shoehorn his issue into your own client's appeal. Make the law do what it promises. Make it be perfect.

Unfortunately for Craig Barnard, the Alvin Ford case was a weak one for testing the issue of the undisclosed psychological reports. His case had been considered by the Florida Supreme Court while the reports were being collected, but there was no clear evidence that any inappropriate documents had ever been part of his file. Barnard's team could only maintain that, since the files had been purged, there was no way to be certain that offending papers had not been plucked from Ford's file and shredded.

In this respect, the Ford appeal raised the touchiest aspect of the whole debacle, because the only way to find out if any of the justices had ever seen a secret report on Ford would be to put the justices on the witness stand. This would involve subpoenas, swearing oaths, and cross-examination: The highest officials of the Florida judicial system would be treated like common riffraff. It was an ugly prospect to any judge with a sense of legal decorum, and it would strike at the dignity of Florida justice. Florida justice was a powerful concept for the judges of the newly created Eleventh Circuit Court of Appeals, because Florida was the biggest state in the circuit, and thus a number of them were Floridians. One, in fact, was a former member of the Florida Supreme Court: Judge Joseph Hatchett. If Craig Barnard was allowed to subpoena Florida justices, some of those documents would have Hatchett's name on them.

This is not to say that the case was an obvious lost cause. Some of the appeals court judges were shocked that the reports had been collected and then shredded. Among them was John Minor Wisdom of Louisiana, perhaps the court's most distinguished jurist; Wisdom found it "incredible" that the Florida Supreme Court claimed it had not been influenced by the documents. Judge Phyllis A. Kravitch of Atlanta bristled at the suggestion that no harm had been done by collecting the reports, calling this notion "illogical."

Ford's case was assigned to a panel of three judges, in accordance with customary practice. (There were twelve judges on the court of appeals.) One was a Floridian, Judge Paul Roney of Saint Petersburg; Phyllis Kravitch was the second; and the third was Virgil Pittman, a federal district judge from Alabama doing substitute duty on the court. Roney, the Floridian, sided with the Florida Supreme Court and wrote a blistering opinion against Ford's appeal.

There was "not an iota of evidence," Roney wrote, to suggest that the Florida Supreme Court had mishandled Ford's case. Moreover, defense attorneys should not be allowed to go on "a fishing expedition" for evidence of misbehavior. And in a ringing defense of his home state's sovereignty, Roney concluded that if the Florida court said it was right, then it was right. "As the highest court in the state, the Florida Supreme Court's interpretation of its procedural role is the law of the state, and we do not question it," he wrote. Judge Pittman joined Roney, and Ford's appeal was denied by a vote of 2 to 1. Judge Kravitch, dissenting, said she found the decision "disturbing."

That was not the end of the controversial reports, however. Other inmates had been raising the same issue when Bob Graham signed their death warrants, and their cases were scheduled to be heard by other three-judge panels. Those panels might rule differently. To avoid such a circus, the court of appeals decided to reconsider Ford's case with the entire membership participating. They would settle this question once and for all. (Judge Hatchett declined to participate, citing his service on the Florida Supreme Court as a conflict of interest.)

While the question remained unresolved, the appeals court instructed federal judges in Florida to block all death warrants. Their decision in the Ford case could affect almost everyone on death row.

The Eleventh Circuit Court of Appeals, minus Judge Hatchett, heard the case of *Ford v. Strickland* on June 15, 1982. The stakes were enormous. On his way into the hearing, a prosecutor paused to tell reporters: "If they rule against us, it could just destroy Florida's death penalty statute."

Marvin Frankel, the former federal judge from New York, once again handled the oral presentation. Again, Frankel tried to step lightly on the dignity of the judges he was attacking. "I don't think the Supreme Court of Florida did anything purposefully evil or consciously wrong," he offered gently. "It just made a grave mistake." But, Frankel continued, the fact remained that the justices of the Florida Supreme Court had material in their files that defense attorneys did not know about. This violated the right to confront evidence—and for men facing the ultimate penalty, such rights are especially precious.

Frankel asked for a full-blown proceeding where he could call witnesses, subpoena documents, and cross-examine anyone who might know if tainted material had reached Alvin Ford's file. By implication, he was also asking for similar proceedings on behalf of more than a hundred death row inmates. That raised the question of decorum. "Isn't the ultimate thrust of your argument that justices of the [Florida]

Supreme Court must testify under oath and specify what they did?" demanded Chief Judge John Godbold.

Frankel demurred. "We'd use that as a last resort, not a first resort," he said. "But it might come to that." Judge Gerald Tjoflat was not satisfied. Since the files had been purged, what other way was there to get to the truth? "How could you make your case without asking them to testify?" he demanded. This time Frankel tried to minimize the significance of such a request. "If the court needs to testify through its justices, well, it won't be the first time a judge has testified," he said.

Arguing for the State of Florida was Assistant Attorney General Charles Corces, who began by acknowledging that "non-record" material had indeed gotten into the files of an unknown number of death row inmates. However, he insisted that the material had not been "secret"; the fact that defense attorneys had not been "notified" was simply "a bureaucratic mess." Some court clerk had misunderstood what, exactly, was supposed to go into the files. Besides, Corces said, echoing Arthur England's passionate opinion on behalf of the Florida Supreme Court, even if some of the justices had "read" or "reviewed" the offending material, they certainly had not "considered" it in reaching their decisions.

Judge Robert Vance was obviously unsatisfied by these verbal distinctions. "I'm trying desperately to understand you," he interjected. "I just want one plausible explanation." Judge Tjoflat hammered away repeatedly at Corces, demanding to know why the records had been purged. "How can [an inmate] be expected to prove what the information was when it is no longer in existence?"

Under attack, Corces fell back on his gut-level argument—the dignity of the state supreme court. "We are not dealing with a lawsuit with private citizens. We are talking about judges. Judges who have almost absolute immunity," he said. Corces appealed to the court's sense of itself, of the station and integrity of their office as judges. An institution as lofty as the Florida Supreme Court must be given the benefit of the doubt, he insisted. "When they say they did not consider it, we have to accept it."

The hearing went about as well as it could have for the anti–death penalty lawyers. They had always known the problem with their case: A victory for them would mean havoc for the Florida Supreme Court. Federal judges were inevitably wary of that. Still, the judges had put some very tough questions to the prosecution, which suggested that the court had an open mind. A victory seemed possible—but even a protracted debate among the judges would be nice. Delay is the next-best thing to victory for a death penalty defense lawyer.

Weeks turned to months without a decision from the appeals court. The population on Florida's death row rose toward two hundred—still the largest in the nation. Bob Graham knew there would be no executions until the *Ford* case was decided; federal judges were complying with their appellate court's instruction and entering automatic stays of execution. Still, Graham churned out death warrants at an unprecedented rate. In the first three years of his term, he had signed a total of nineteen death orders. Now, in his fourth year alone, he signed twenty-six. That was the year he ran for reelection.

What was going on? Scharlette Holdman and her circle believed that Graham was plainly playing politics, and some federal judges seemed to share that view. U.S. District Judge Lynn Higby, of Panama City, took the unusual step of scolding Graham publicly. In light of the *Ford* case, Higby said, the signing of death warrants "ranges between legally unsound and futile." But Attorney General Jim Smith made no apologies for the governor's prolific pen. The problem, he said, was that the Eleventh Circuit Court of Appeals lacked the "intestinal fortitude" to deal with the death penalty. Smith was the government's public pit bull on the death penalty. He traveled widely, making speeches in which he said the lack of executions could be blamed on a few weak and meddlesome judges. To Smith, the problem wasn't confusion about the law, or undisclosed documents: It was a simple matter of us versus them. "If we show any sign that they're whipping us down," he said, "we're giving in."

Graham said little as he cranked out warrants he knew would be blocked. Whatever his reasons, the public approved. One newspaper poll shortly before the 1982 election found that Graham got higher marks for his handling of the death penalty than for any other issue. In conservative Florida, the death penalty shielded Graham against attacks from the Right—as his Republican opponent quickly discovered. "If there's anything that Graham has going for him with people who ordinarily would vote for a conservative Republican like me, it's that he's signed so many death warrants," said former Congressman Skip Bafalis. "I hear that over and over and over."

Graham clearly understood this himself. "This is an issue on which deeds speak louder than words," was all that he said. He was reelected in a landslide.

Scharlette Holdman was having nightmares—or rather, the same nightmare, over and over. She was in a room, surrounded by her death row clients. Suddenly, the concrete walls began to crumble. So she hustled her clients into the next room . . . but those walls, too, began to give way. Panicked, she rushed her flock through another door—hurry up, hurry up! From room to room they ran, as rubble rained down around them. Now she could see her way to safety—hurry up, follow me! But looming in her path was a huge prison warden. "You're not taking those guys past me!" the warden thundered. "If you try . . ."

And then the nightmare took one of those freaky turns that nightmares take. The warden raised his giant hand and brandished . . . a mouse. "If you try, I'll bite this mouse's head off!" Holdman would awaken in a sweat and wonder: Who's the mouse?

For Holdman, Graham's accelerated schedule of death warrants was crushing. It ruined her life and played havoc on her mind. More death warrants meant more hours on the telephone; more urgent pleadings with more reluctant lawyers; more cigarettes chain-smoked as she paced nervously, barefoot, at the end of her phone-cord leash; more cups of coffee; more buckets of greasy fast-food chicken; more bursts of profanity and wild, angry laughter. More warrants meant even less time with her children; she began to fret that her work might be damaging them. Tad, her son, sketched electric chairs in his idle time. Maybe she wasn't cut out to be a parent, Holdman nervously confided to friends. She went ballistic over the smallest things, like the time Summer, her daughter, asked for a pretty dress and some lipstick. Was this rebellion? Holdman's friends began to worry that she was drinking too much.

And daily her flock worked their desperate paths through the ten steps toward death in her handwritten ledger. Every one of them needed a lawyer. It was true that stays were coming easily—but that might end any day. Anyway, to get a stay someone had to file an appeal, and if the lawyers didn't get every available issue, large and small, into the first appeal, they might not get a second chance. Each death warrant required a full-scale legal response. So many cases, so few lawyers.

When Amos Lee King's death warrant was signed, Holdman scanned her ledger and discovered that King had no lawyer. The execution date was five days away. Holdman picked up the phone and began dialing. How many ways can people find to say no? Holdman had heard them all. Eventually, she tracked Baya Harrison to a hospital where his wife was giving birth to a daughter. Harrison had come through for Holdman once before, winning clemency for Richard Henry Gibson. Now she was pleading with him to take King's appeal.

Baya Harrison III was not typical of the lawyers in Holdman's index card file. He wasn't a rabble-rousing criminal defense attorney or a liberal law professor or even a blue-chip corporate lawyer with a conscience and a pro bono budget. Harrison was the idiosyncratic scion of one of Florida's most influential legal families, the son of a bold figure on the Florida stage, Baya Harrison Jr.: A full colonel and war hero at the age of twenty-nine (Van Johnson played him in a World War II movie called *Go for Broke*), chairman of the state Board of Regents, president of the Florida Bar, reigning partner at one of the Tampa Bay area's most important law firms.

The younger Baya Harrison eschewed the family firm for a small private practice, but he never went so far as to embrace the subversive activism of Scharlette Holdman and her set. Harrison would represent bad guys, but he would not love them; he would force the system to work precisely by the rules, but he wouldn't reject the system as irretrievably flawed. He gave his time to Scharlette Holdman, but he also hosted political fundraisers for her enemy, the attorney general, Jim Smith.

Harrison had sworn after the Gibson case that he was finished with death row. The work was too exhausting; the stakes were too high. But now Holdman was on the phone, pleading with him to represent Amos King. Harrison protested that he was sick. "I just threw up," he said. Holdman kept at him. "My wife just had a baby," Harrison attempted. Holdman wouldn't give up. She gave him the full Scharlette treatment—a mile a minute in her profane drawl. "She was a con artist in the best sense of the word," Harrison later recalled. "She knew how to deal with a lawyer's ego, and she'd talk you—against your better judgment—into taking these cases. She told me what a marvelous lawyer I was, how eloquent I was, how wonderful I was. She told me no one else could save this guy. He'd die if I didn't take his case. She was just brilliant, convincing me that I had to take it, that there was no other answer. She tricked me into doing it."

At last Harrison relented. Holdman arranged to send him a copy of King's trial transcript. He skimmed the record and was immediately struck by the poor job King's trial attorney had done in defending him. Even the best lawyer in the world might not have been able to save King, who had escaped from a prison work-release program, broken into a woman's home, raped her, stabbed her forty times, and burned down the house. Nevertheless, Harrison concluded that his strongest argument would be ineffectiveness of counsel.

This claim—that an inmate's lawyer had failed to represent him competently—had become a mainstay of the anti–death penalty attorneys. (Millard Farmer had used it, with brief success, in the last hours of Spenkelink's life.) Sometimes the argument was pretty strong. On death row there were men whose court-appointed lawyers had never handled a capital case, and men whose lawyers made no effort to find evidence in their favor, and men whose lawyers were later disbarred. One man's defense attorney was such a notorious drunk that the judge asked the prosecutor to smell the guy's breath each morning before trial.

Other times, the case for incompetence was far weaker, based on little more than the notion that any lawyer whose client is sent to death row must have screwed up somewhere. King's case was somewhere in between; his lawyer had perhaps been too soft on some cross-examinations, and had appeared ill prepared for the sentencing phase of the trial. At one point, in the jury's presence, he said something along the lines of: "I'm an assistant public defender, I have to defend this guy." That couldn't have helped matters any.

On two days' preparation, Harrison went into federal court for Amos Lee King. The hearing was a shambles. He called Pat Doherty, another stalwart from Holdman's card file, as his expert witness. "I didn't know anything about this case," Harrison later recalled. "I put Pat on the stand and started asking him questions. The prosecutor objected, and cited some case I'd never read. It turned out to be the controlling case on the question of competent counsel. That's how unprepared I was."

This sort of thing was almost routine for Holdman's lawyers— defending a man's life on a couple of days' notice, arguing a cause without time to master the case law, rushing into some of the nation's loftiest courts armed with little more than strut, passion, quick wits, and audacity. Maybe they had gotten a crash course from Craig Barnard or Millard Farmer. "This was the crazy way we handled those cases," Baya Harrison said later. "We were like barnstorming pilots in the old days. We weren't sure how to fly the plane, but we were just dumb enough to get up there and try."

The story repeated itself over and over. In March 1982, Graham signed the death warrant of Doug McCray, who had been represented at his clemency hearing by a state-appointed lawyer who candidly admitted that he had never read the trial record. Shortly afterward, the lawyer's license was suspended on grounds of mental instability and theft from clients' trust accounts, and the lawyer had disappeared, a fugitive from federal authorities. "Can you imagine what it is like to be told that your death warrant has been signed and you don't have a lawyer and no means to contact one?" McCray asked a reporter.

Scharlette Holdman made nearly fifty calls to lawyers, begging someone to take McCray's case. At last she found a young man in Saint Petersburg, Bob Dillinger, who had just left the public defender's office to start a private practice. Dillinger protested. This was no time for him to be taking on pro bono projects. But Holdman pushed. She was "frantic, almost desperate," Dillinger recalled. And he relented.

McCray's trial record ran to more than fifteen hundred pages.

Dillinger had less than two weeks to digest the material and prepare an appeal. With six days left before McCray's execution, the Florida Supreme Court—despite having affirmed McCray's death sentence in its first review—agreed to consider a request for a new trial, and issued a stay.

Baya Harrison was preparing for a hearing in the Amos Lee King case when, in June 1982, Holdman begged him to save Timothy Palmes, a Jacksonville murderer whose scheduled execution was just two weeks away. Twenty-five lawyers had already turned the case down. "They are running us ragged," Harrison complained to a reporter. "They are beating us to meat." It was nuts. Laurin Wollan, a Tallahassee lawyer and professor, estimated he had lost twenty pounds while trying to win a single stay. Ray Makowski was hospitalized for exhaustion after winning a last-minute stay for Ronald Straight. Lawyers June Rice and Steve Stitt, a husband-and-wife team from Key West, said their defense of Ray Meeks had cost them "thousands of hours and thousands of dollars and we've never been paid anything at all." Holdman found Bob Gerber at a prestigious law firm in New York City and cajoled him into taking the case of Eligaah Jacobs. Gerber prepared for Jacobs's clemency hearing the way he might prepare for a multi-million-dollar corporate lawsuit. When it was over, he said the same work would've cost a corporate client a hundred and fifty thousand dollars.

There simply weren't enough people willing to take on such burdens. We're gonna start losing people, Holdman warned the Inc. Fund and the ACLU, and these titans put the arm on wealthy firms in New York, Boston, and Washington. Several firms agreed to take on some cases. Still, Holdman's boat was leaking. The nightmares kept coming. Who was the mouse?

On the other side of the battlefield, prosecutors saw none of the panic; only the unbroken string of stays. Jim Smith refused even to speak Scharlette Holdman's name after she ruined his birthday with a cake decorated with black crosses, but he spoke often of her enterprise. To him, Holdman's lawyers were a well-oiled machine, light-years ahead of the state, fiendishly clever, richly endowed. "Governor Graham and I have been in office forty-four months and he's signed forty-three warrants, and we've had one execution," Smith told an interviewer in the autumn of 1982. "I think that speaks for itself. I think the defense lawyers, frankly, have been a step ahead of the State. They're certainly winning the delay battle going away."

Holdman found such remarks darkly comical, as she dialed her telephone and lit up another Benson & Hedges. She was sending volunteers to the library at Florida State University to root through wastebaskets for usable typing paper. Her budget wouldn't even cover the cost of the paper an appeal was printed on. This was her well-oiled machine? Sometimes, in frustration, she'd call Pat Doherty, one of her stalwart attorneys, a man who shared her mordant sense of humor, and she'd confess her fears in a patter of joking profanity. All this time working with murderers was skewing her sense of the world, she once told Doherty. "I've given up hoping that the kids grow up to be doctors," she said. "I just hope they don't kill the fucking neighbors."

And in return Doherty regaled her with stories from his colorful practice and his bottomless supply of jokes. One day, he told Holdman about a recent death threat—he received them frequently, because he defended some of the Tampa Bay area's most notorious killers. "Some nut calls and says he's gonna kill me," Doherty told her. "A few minutes later, I hear shots outside. I figure he's come for me."

One of Doherty's clients had been ordered to surrender his gun collection, so Doherty happened to have a small arsenal sitting in the office. Doherty grabbed one of the guns and began trying to load it. "Shells were flying everywhere," he said. "Clips were jamming. Hell, I don't know anything about guns. Finally, I take the gun, creep over to the window and look out. Some guy's standing on the street with his pants around his ankles and a Clearwater cop is shooting at him! No flashing in Clearwater, man!"

Doherty shared Holdman's view that Jim Smith was being ridiculous. There he was, the top law enforcement officer of one of the biggest states in the country, head of a battalion of lawyers with all the resources of government behind them . . . complaining about the advantages enjoyed by Scharlette Holdman and her little band of volunteers. "Reminds me of a joke," Doherty said one day.

"There's an Arab army encamped in the desert, a whole huge

army. They're sitting there, and this Israeli comes right up to the camp. Challenges the whole army to a fight.

" 'All right,' says the Arab general, and his army gets its gear ready—guns, grenades, mortars, tanks. They go marching toward the Israeli. Suddenly, the general yells: 'Retreat—it's a fucking trap! There's two of them!' "

On January 7, 1983, the Eleventh Circuit Court of Appeals—by a single-vote margin of 6 to 5—closed the book on the question of the Florida Supreme Court's collection of psychological reports. Ultimately, the judges took the word of the Florida justices that their deliberations had not been affected by the reports. In a barrage of conditional language, the majority declared: "Even if the members of the court solicited the material with the thought that it should, would, or might be used, the decision of the Florida court that it should not be so used, the statement that it was not used and the rejection of the notion that it affected the judgment of the reviewing judges . . . ends the matter." A shift of a single vote and Craig Barnard might have had his big issue. The death penalty in Florida could have been knocked off the rails for perhaps a decade.

As it was, Barnard's lawsuit had stalled executions for nearly two and a half years, and that alone was a victory for him. In death penalty defense work, a lawyer had won as long as his client was still breathing. Anything short of death was a success. The challenge to the secret reports had kept more than a hundred men alive at precisely the point when the Spenkelink execution had seemed to put them in danger.

But now the issue was gone; there was no serious hope that the U.S. Supreme Court would overrule the appellate court. The high court was becoming a very cold place for death row inmates, and 1983 turned out to be the worst year for them since the new death penalty had been affirmed in 1976. The U.S. Supreme Court decided four major capital appeals in 1983, from Florida, California, Texas, and Georgia. The appeals raised various issues—in *Barclay v. Florida,* for example, the justices considered a question that had troubled Florida for a decade: If a trial judge, while sentencing a man to death, used aggravating circumstances that weren't spelled out in the law, was the sentence automatically invalid?

On July 6, 1983, the U.S. Supreme Court upheld Elwood Barclay's sentence—one of a flurry of opinions striking down impediments to executions. Four big cases, four victories for the prosecution. Four years after the Spenkelink execution, the Court's message seemed clear: Time to get on with it. In Florida, the message was heard. The ground had shifted away from the endless stall tactics. Prosecutors and defense attorneys alike agreed that someone was likely to die by year's end. The smart money was betting on Bob Sullivan.

Most people support capital punishment. They give a lot of reasons, but ultimately, these boil down to three basic positions:

The deterrence argument says that an effective death penalty will deter crime. Common sense seems to support this argument. Criminals will see the horrible fate awaiting them and they will decide not to commit aggravated murder. George Georgieff, the cocky prosecutor at the Florida attorney general's office, was big on deterrence. He often regaled his pals with a story about a time he had been deterred from murdering his wife. Georgieff even told the story to reporters: "I was having a fight with one of my ex-wives, and I found myself choking her, and I saw her eyes start to pop out, and suddenly off to the left or the right I saw the electric chair. It deterred me."

The problem with deterrence is that there is no way to prove it exists. Even Georgieff's crude anecdote doesn't prove anything. After all, he of all people—a death penalty professional—knew that men are almost never executed for killing their wives in a fit of anger. Purely domestic murders rarely end in the death penalty. If Georgieff's story was true, if he'd actually considered killing his wife, the thing that had stopped him was surely a moral barrier, not a legal barrier. Some shred of decency prevented him, not the electric chair. He certainly knew he wouldn't get anywhere near Old Sparky.

It makes sense that the death penalty should stop people from killing. It also makes sense that a boulder should fall to the ground faster than a wad of paper. But in both cases, common sense is wrong.

Some states with no death penalty have very low murder rates; others with vigorous death penalties have astronomical murder rates (Florida, for example). There are cases of sons who watched their fathers hang— a pretty stern deterrent message—who went on to commit capital offenses themselves. There are even cases of hangmen who were later hanged.

Experts have been studying the question of deterrence for decades, with little success. In 1975, a University of Chicago economist claimed to have proven, by a statistical method known as regression analysis, that the death penalty deters murders. A war of the eggheads ensued. Ever more complicated mathematical models were devised; computers spewed out enough dense math to navigate the space shuttle. Eventually, the prestigious National Academy of Sciences announced that the economist's "proof" was flawed. Some scientists claim, in fact, to have found evidence that executions actually provoke more violence.

In a sense, the whole exercise is fundamentally ridiculous, because it rests on the notion that the hyperrational tools of mathematics can measure the irrational brain of a murderer. The problem with deterrence, as applied to aggravated murder, is that it assumes killers calculate risk and reward. The reality, with few exceptions, is that murderers are not clear-thinking people. They are impulsive, self-centered, often warped; overwhelmingly they are products of violent homes; frequently they are addled by booze or drugs; and most of them are deeply antisocial. The values and sanctions of society don't concern them. They kill out of mental illness, or sexual perversion, for instant gratification or sheer bloody-mindedness. Some murderers actually seem drawn toward the death house. Hubert Goddard, who raped and killed a teenager in Miami, had but one request after his confession: "Now I want the electric chair." On January 29, 1940, he got it.

Another broad justification for the death penalty is retribution. Vengeance. Eye for eye, tooth for tooth, life for life. This way of thinking has a plain, if harsh, beauty to it, a symmetry, balance. And yet, most people shy away from the idea of retribution. It seems uncivilized, atavistic, base. Qualities that ennoble society—mercy, restraint, judgment—are lost; society merely reacts spasmodically to the murderer's action. A man does something bad, so the society does the same bad thing to him. Retribution is tainted by dragging the community down to mirror the criminal.

The third basic argument for the death penalty rests neither on the fallacy that murderers are rational, nor on the debasing spirit of retribution. This view holds that any society worth living in must cherish goodness and exalt the human capacity to restrain evil. Crimes in such a society are more than offenses by one person against another; they are attacks on the society itself. Society has a right—indeed, a duty—to condemn these attacks, and the graver the attack, the graver the condemnation ought to be. The most egregiously evil acts demand utter condemnation.

As the philosopher Walter Berns put it in his book *For Capital Punishment:* "Capital punishment . . . serves to remind us of the majesty of the moral order that is embodied in our law and of the terrible consequences of its breach. . . . The criminal law must possess a dignity far beyond that possessed by mere statutory enactment or utilitarian or self-interested calculations; the most powerful means we have to give it that dignity is to authorize it to impose the ultimate penalty. The criminal law must be made awful, by which I mean awe-inspiring, or commanding 'profound respect or reverential fear.' It must remind us of the moral order by which alone we can live as human beings."

In other words, some crimes are so evil that the criminals who commit them cannot be permitted to remain a part of society—not even on the very margin of society, locked away in a maximum-security prison. To continue to make a place for such criminals erodes the moral order of the community. In long-ago times, banishment might have served the same purpose, but banishment is no longer a possibility. The whole world is inhabited, and who would accept our killers? There must be a way for society to say: This person is beyond our tolerance.

However, what the Supreme Court of Florida—and courts around the country—were learning by 1983 was that this grand philosophical construct is difficult to apply. Who, precisely, is beyond the pale? Walter Berns mentions Lee Harvey Oswald and James Earl Ray, the assassins of John F. Kennedy and Martin Luther King Jr. But these are easy cases, when you think about them. Their offenses against society were immense, and, thank God, unusual. What about the more ordinary murderer, given that the U.S. Supreme Court had outlawed the mandatory death sentences that would simply kill them all? The modern death penalty demands that distinctions be drawn among murderers. Who is irrevocably cut off from society?

Robert Austin Sullivan, the adopted son of a Harvard-educated doctor, posed such questions by his very existence. He wasn't John Spenkelink, whose execution was so plainly a fluke—the man who failed to plead guilty to second-degree murder and wound up in a riptide of history flooding toward death. Sullivan's crime was dastardly: In April 1973, the body of Donald Schmidt, assistant manager of the Howard Johnson's in Homestead, was found facedown in the Everglades muck. Schmidt's restaurant had been robbed shortly after closing time; he had been driven into the wilderness west of Miami. His hands bound behind him with adhesive tape, Schmidt was ordered out of the car. He stumbled, and his abductor beat him over the head with a tire iron. Then the killer fired four shotgun blasts into Schmidt's skull.

About a week later, Sullivan and a boyfriend, Reid McLaughlin, were arrested in New Hampshire. Sullivan knew all about the Homestead HoJo's; he had been fired from his job there after he was caught embezzling. And detectives had established an even more damning link: Sullivan had been using Schmidt's credit cards—his handwriting matched the signatures on the card receipts. In the motel room where the fugitives were arrested, police found twelve hundred dollars—in HoJo's ice cream containers. In the trunk of Sullivan's Cadillac was a shotgun, a tire iron, and a roll of adhesive tape. Under interrogation, Sullivan gave a detailed confession. Reid McLaughlin testified that he had been with Sullivan during the crime and that the details of the confession were correct. McLaughlin remembered Sullivan's words after the murder: "I don't feel any different." In the words of the trial judge, Sullivan showed not "one scintilla of remorse."

And yet, Bob Sullivan was not cut off from, or cast away by, society. Sullivan was a singular man, perhaps the most resourceful inmate in the history of Florida's death row. He was a fat man who stammered under pressure, a college dropout with a C average, a liar, a thief, and a killer. In the death house, though, Sullivan blossomed as a leader, an entrepreneur, and a first-rate jailhouse lawyer. From his little cell on S-wing of a remote prison in the middle of the Florida nowhere, Sullivan presided over a thriving network of decent people, global in scope, diversified in its enterprises, whose business was to save his neck.

He grandly called it the Robert A. Sullivan Legal Defense Fund, but—possessed of a bureaucratic turn of mind—he generally referred to the operation as RASLDF. His enterprise included hundreds of supporters across the country and around the world, and he kept these backers energized by writing at least a dozen letters a day in his looping, feminine script. Sullivan generated hundreds of memos scrutinizing the fine points of his defense, and numbered them for easy filing: "R.A.S. Memorandum 130-A," for example. RASLDF produced multipage newsletters and dispersed them in mass mailings; he once complained that 750 mailing labels would not be enough for his latest newsletter. Society had not, entirely, rejected him.

The director of RASLDF was a man named Ralph Jacobs, an engineer from Boston with a wife and two children he worked hard to support. He knew Bob Sullivan as a boy; they grew up around the corner from one another in the prosperous Boston suburb of Belmont. They played football on the playground: Sully threw the passes and Jacobs caught them. Sully went to the Catholic church in Belmont's town center; Jacobs attended the Congregationalist church nearby. They lived and died with the Red Sox—'67 was heaven, when Yaz won the Triple Crown—and they shot pool in Jacobs's basement. As much as possible, Jacobs steered clear of Sully's bitter, oppressive mom.

Jacobs lost touch with his friend when Sullivan went to Miami for college. Then, in 1976, he got a letter with Sullivan's death row address in the corner of the envelope. "I looked at those numbers after his name, and I just couldn't figure it out. I thought maybe he was in the service," Jacobs remembered. "Well, in this letter he said that he was in some kind of situation down in Florida, and would I like to correspond with him. I wrote back and said sure, and the next letter that came he explained what had happened."

"Explained" is perhaps not the best word. Sullivan's letters to his network of supporters were masterpieces of omission and deceit. He spun out a captivating case for his innocence, scarcely mentioning the evidence against him—let alone his own confessions. Sullivan talked about the weather, volunteered his predictions for the coming baseball season, speculated on trades the New England Patriots might make, praised the Bruins, handicapped presidential primaries. He regularly inquired after the health of Jacobs's mother. "Greetings once again," he wrote in a typical letter to Jacobs,

> A few things have come up so I thought I'd write you today. I remain generally well, however, I am a bit tenser than I like to be wondering when and how my 11th Circuit panel will rule on my appeal. I am trying hard to keep busy in the hope of worrying less. As I had felt, the pro football strike has not been resolved swiftly. . . . In contrast, I am enjoying college football and the baseball playoffs more than other years. . . .

In short, Sullivan's demeanor, in his letters and in person, was calm, literate, mundane, and occasionally banal. He spiced his correspondence with factoids from his diligent reading. (His magazine subscription list included *Time, Business Week,* and the journal of Cornell's hotel and restaurant management school.) He was meticulous in his instructions regarding gift packages from friends. (Two-pound bags of M&Ms were a favorite gift—plain, never peanut.) Sullivan's writings were so palpably letters from a respectable, middle-class man, a man of normalcy. A man within society. For the hundreds of people on his mailing list, it was almost impossible to think of Sullivan as a menace to the moral order. This was especially true of his friends in Massachusetts, who remembered the gentle Bob Sullivan, ever solicitous of the feelings of younger kids; the polite Bob Sullivan, shyly stammering his y-y-yes ma'ams and n-n-no sirs; the diligent Bob Sullivan, who kept the lawns cut and the snow shoveled on Belmont's Richmond Street.

Through Sullivan's letters, Jacobs became intimately familiar with the alibi defense the prisoner insisted would prove his innocence. A rising star of the Miami defense bar, Roy Black, was handling the appeal, arguing that Sullivan's trial lawyers had failed to develop an adequate defense. With the help of Virginia Snyder, a private investigator, Black had shown what a better lawyer might have been able to accomplish. Snyder located several witnesses who said they remembered Sullivan being with them at a gay bar at the very moment that Donald Schmidt was murdered. When, in 1980, Black won a hearing in federal court, Ralph Jacobs paid his own way to Fort Lauderdale, eager to see his friend exonerated.

But the two-day hearing was not what Jacobs had hoped for. When Sullivan's trial lawyers saw their competence being attacked, they fought back. The first lawyer, Ray Windsor, had quit Sullivan's case, explaining simply that there had been a "communications breakdown" with his client. Now, in federal court, Windsor explained what the "breakdown" had been: Sullivan had confessed the crime to him in writing—Windsor produced the letter—but despite the confession, Sullivan had demanded that an alibi be manufactured. Windsor had refused to do it. Attorney Dennis Dean replaced Windsor. Dean told the federal court that he had sent Sullivan to take a lie detector test. As Ralph Jacobs sat shaken in the federal courtroom, the lie detector operator took the stand to say that Sullivan had confessed to him, too. Anyone who knew the record of Warren Holmes, the lie detector operator, knew this testimony was overwhelming. Holmes was regarded as one of the best in his business, but, more important, he was known in Florida legal circles for going to heroic lengths to free innocent people from prison. Four people falsely convicted of murder were free in large part because of the efforts of Warren Holmes. It was unthinkable that he would invent a story that might lead to the execution of an innocent man. Added to a confession at the police station, and the written confession to Windsor, this made three times that Sullivan had admitted he had killed Donald Schmidt.

Ralph Jacobs was even more troubled by the fact that when Sullivan took the stand, he repeatedly invoked the Fifth Amendment to avoid answering tough questions. Still, he couldn't square the Sully he knew with the cold-blooded killer of Donald Schmidt. Anguished, Jacobs questioned Sullivan himself, and Sullivan tried to console him with an explanation for every alleged confession. The police threatened him. Windsor tricked him. Holmes was lying. Sullivan had an answer for everything, and what the answers lacked in plausibility he made up for with sheer volume. He reminded Jacobs of the alibi witnesses. He alluded to a grand conspiracy in which he had been framed to cover up the crimes of a Boston-based gay mafia. "Dear Ralph," he wrote from prison a few weeks after the hearing,

> I am eager to see your reaction to the answers to your questions. I am deeply concerned by your being upset by parts of the hearing. In retrospect, the strategy of taking the 5th may not have been the wisest move. I wasn't 100% in favor of it, but I bowed to Roy's opinion. Since we had explained everything once, we felt there was too [much] risk to rehash the same territory over and over again. Only time will tell if we were right or wrong.

Jacobs swallowed his doubts. Everything he knew about his friend made it impossible to believe that Bob Sullivan was a killer. He knew that Sullivan was a model prisoner, taking college courses by mail, dutifully preparing his homework while sitting on the cold concrete floor, using his bunk for a desk. Sullivan spent hours teaching a retarded inmate in the next cell how to read and write. He patiently explained the court system to the guys on his tier. Once, he even talked a man out of committing suicide. Sullivan was a patriot, too, a conservative supporter of Ronald Reagan, and he decorated his cell with a home-made American flag in support of the invasion of Grenada. "No one could say 100 percent certain that Bob was innocent—only Bob knew that—but it was clear to me that the State had not been fair to him," Jacobs later explained.

He redoubled his efforts to save Bob Sullivan. He organized RASLDF raffles each year to raise money; first prize was a donated TV, second prize was a mess of lobsters Jacobs had trapped himself. Along with other Sully supporters, he sold the raffle tickets from a card table in front of the First National grocery store in Belmont's town center. One year, he even organized a fundraising dance, an enormous endeavor, hiring a hall and a band and an off-duty cop, enduring the hassle of securing a liquor permit. Eventually, Jacobs was spending his entire lunch hour, a couple of days a week, endorsing checks and filling out deposit slips and standing in line at the bank in Waltham. The money went right back out to Roy Black and Virginia Snyder, who continued to build the unlikely case for Sullivan's innocence. Soon there were three alibi witnesses, then four, then (after Snyder tracked a man all the way to Hawaii) five. And the new leads required more newsletters, which in turn generated more contributions, which sent Jacobs trudging back to the bank. The checks came from Canada, England, Australia, and states across the country. Ralph Jacobs was the chief drone on the project. Bob Sullivan was the mastermind. "Dear Ralph," he wrote in a typical letter,

> I have proofread a second draft of the RASLDF Report and yesterday returned the corrected copy to Ralph Walker. I have written all the necessary letters to respond to letters sent to you, that you forwarded to me (copies of two of these letters enclosed). Lastly, I have written and mailed to Richard Carr the next RASLDF Newsletter for typing. I should get it back within 7–10 days at which time I'll mail it to you for printing (copy included here for your reference). In addition to getting the newsletter printed, as a reminder, let me list a few matters that will need YOUR attention.
> 1) get raffle tickets printed.
> 2) get labels made for second mailing—if you want me to write them please send me 750 blank labels ASAP, plus a list of all returned mailings, a Xerox of that last mailing, and all letters giving names of people who may assist us.
> 3) advise me if you've spoken to Linda and the results thereof.

Sullivan was a field marshal, an executive vice president, not a pariah—not in the eyes of Jacobs; nor in the eyes of Father Robert Boyle, his boyhood priest; nor to the seven Roman Catholic bishops of Florida, who pleaded with Bob Graham for mercy.

∴

By autumn 1983, experts on both sides of the death penalty issue believed they were hearing the squeak and grind of floodgates opening. On December 7, 1982, Texas had carried out its first involuntary execution under its modern law, a killer named Charlie Brooks. Brooks was the first black man executed since *Furman*. Four months later, on April 22, 1983, Alabama electrocuted John Evans against his will—although it took three tries to do it. They kept zapping him and zapping him and he wouldn't die. Another four months passed, during which the U.S. Supreme Court decided those four key appeals against death row inmates. On September 2, 1983, Mississippi got started, executing Jimmy Lee Gray.

Bob Sullivan by then had been on death row longer than any man in the United States. (He was the third to arrive on Florida's death row, and the two before him had both received clemency.) He was the obvious choice for Bob Graham's next death warrant, and on November 8, 1983, it came. The execution was scheduled for November 29. Sullivan was moved to his death-watch cell, where he sat on the bunk and cried. On Sunday, November 13, he asked the sergeant outside his cell to tune the television to NBC. Sullivan's beloved New England Patriots were playing the Miami Dolphins—Miami, the hometown of Bob Graham; Miami, the city where Sullivan had ruined his life and the lives of Donald Schmidt and his family. Sullivan was in a desperate, mystical mood, and prayed to God for a sign that he would be saved. Please, God, please. Let the Patriots represent me. Let the Dolphins represent Graham and all the powers bent on my death. As he settled down to watch the game, Sullivan noticed that the name of the Patriots' stadium had been changed that year to Sullivan Stadium. A happy omen! So he prayed again, this time offering God a point spread. If the Patriots won by ten or more, it would be like lamb's blood splashed on the lintels of the Israelites: Bob Sullivan would be spared. Sullivan cheered and groaned; he sweated in spite of the prison cold. The game ended as twilight faded from the North Florida sky . . . and New England had won by eleven. He prayed again: God, let this truly be a sign!

But the Almighty does not gamble on point spreads. By Monday, November 28, one day before his scheduled execution, no force had intervened to save him. He devoted that morning to an attempt to do good, giving a sworn statement on behalf of James Hill. Hill was a more typical death row inmate. Where Sullivan was middle-class and college-educated, Hill was poor, illiterate, and retarded. His attorneys were preparing an appeal based on the proposition that their client lacked the capacity to assist his defense—or, for that matter, even to understand completely the charges against him. "James's whole thought process," Sullivan testified, "which I think is very important, is very child-like. . . . He had no idea about the death penalty or death row until he arrived here."

"Do you—" Hill's lawyer interjected.

"If I may add one more thing," Sullivan continued, "something I have learned from direct experience with James. James, you can explain something to him, but many times he will acknowledge that he under-stands it, but when you try to probe into it, he has zero understanding of it. . . . Basic simple things that I have tried to explain to him, one has to go over them time after time after time before he even gets a basic understanding of it. Therefore, based upon that experience, I just find it incomprehensible that he could possibly have understood what was going on because nobody ever explained it to him."

It was one last example of the mystery at Bob Sullivan's heart: Preparing to die for the pitiless murder he had committed, Sullivan made a kindly gesture on behalf of a less fortunate friend. It wasn't easy—Sullivan broke down crying near the end of the session—but this gesture added one more person to the ranks of Sullivan's supporters; one more citizen concluded that he didn't need to be killed. As the doomed man sobbed, the stenographer who was transcribing the state-ment tore a narrow slip of paper from her machine and jotted a quick note.

Robert
Good luck
I'll be sending
lots of prayers
Your way!
Tess

It had been four and a half years since the execution of John Spenkelink. After so long, Sullivan became a new milestone. There were protests at the governor's mansion, vigils at the prison, a candle-light prayer service at the Catholic church in Starke. In Boston, Ralph Jacobs marched alongside several dozen Sullivan supporters at the Massachusetts statehouse. Pope John Paul II issued a plea to Graham to rescind the death warrant.

The frantic, desperate maneuverings of exhausted lawyers were the same as they had been for Spenkelink. The lawyers won a brief, last-minute reprieve—two days, just like Spenkelink's. But as it had been for Spenkelink, the reprieve was lifted, and Bob Sullivan's huge, flabby body was strapped into Old Sparky at 10 A.M. on November 30, 1983. Warden Richard Dugger had learned the lesson of earlier experience: The venetian blinds in the execution chamber were kept open throughout the process; the chin strap was not fastened until Sullivan had read his final statement. Sullivan recited the Sixty-second Psalm. Then Sullivan was banished from human society via electricity. Many years and many executions later, Warden Dugger summed up the experience by saying, "It was hard to despise Bob Sullivan."

Two weeks after Sullivan's death, America saw executions on consecutive days, for the first time in decades: Robert Wayne Williams in Louisiana on December 14, and John Eldon Smith in Georgia on December 15. Thus, by the end of 1983, every state in the Death Belt had weighed in. (The "Death Belt" runs across the South from Florida to Texas, embracing Georgia, Alabama, Mississippi, and Louisiana. In the modern era, these states have invariably been the headquarters of the capital punishment business.) The wheels appeared to be turning at last: Within a year, six executions had been carried out, and none of them had been volunteers. Bob Sullivan's death devastated Scharlette Holdman's anti–death penalty crusaders. They had, naïvely, expected to save him, especially after the Pope had asked for mercy. (Holdman laughingly called this her "habeas Popeus" appeal.) In the month following the Sullivan execution, Bob Graham signed no death warrants—he never signed warrants around Christmastime—and Holdman's circle spent December mourning for Sullivan and for themselves. They were caught a little flat-footed when, fresh from the New Year's holiday, the governor signed the death warrant of Anthony Antone.

If the idea was to choose only the most irredeemable, unmitigated, bloodthirsty killers for the electric chair, Florida was still having a hard time. Anthony Antone was a crook, no doubt about it, but there were plenty worse on death row. For one thing, Antone had never killed anyone.

On October 23, 1975, a swashbuckling Tampa cop named Dick Cloud had climbed out of bed to answer the doorbell. "Can you tell me where R. V. Turner lives?" asked the man at the door. "R. V. Turner? No, I don't think so," Cloud had answered. The man at the door had opened fire. Police believed it was a Mafia hit; Detective Cloud had been planning to give damaging testimony to a grand jury. After a four-month investigation, police concluded that a mobster named Victor Acosta had ordered the murder, and that Anthony Antone, as Acosta's lackey, had hired the two gunmen. Acosta and the man who pulled the trigger both wound up dead in their cells, apparently suicides. The second hitman turned state's evidence. That left Antone—who had neither planned the murder nor pulled the trigger—as the odd man out, the last bad guy vulnerable to prosecution. Cutting deals with the prosecution is like musical chairs: The slowest man loses. Antone went to death row.

Other facts added to the sense that Antone was a strange choice for the electric chair. He was crazy as a loon, wandering the prison yard talking about astral projection and UFOs and roaches eating his brain. And he was an elderly man, sixty-six years old, sickly, frail, certain to die in prison long before any possible parole date. To Governor Graham, however, Antone represented "the most calculated and premeditated form of murder, a contract for the deliberate assassination of a law-enforcement officer." The courts apparently agreed. One of Scharlette Holdman's loyal troupers, Tom McCoun, had spent two years trying to convince judges that Anthony Antone was on death row only because of poor legal representation. The trial attorney, McCoun maintained, should have done more to show the jury that Antone was brain-damaged and delusional.

Now, racing a death warrant, McCoun had little choice but to try again. He imported a Harvard psychiatrist named Ward Casscells to buttress his case. Casscells examined the prisoner a week after the warrant was signed. It was an interesting conversation. "His thoughts were generally well connected," Casscells reported, "but as the interview went on he expressed more and more unusual beliefs." Antone warned the doctor that their conversation was being recorded by cosmic beings; they were interested in him because of his detailed knowledge of UFO bases. He also explained how he learned to escape the pull of gravity by contemplating the flight of bumblebees. Antone told Casscells the story of a fascinating journey he had recently taken in the company of a Tibetan astral guide: Antone had left his body in his death row cell and floated across the continent to the Pacific Ocean. He and his astral guide had plunged into the salty water, down, down to the ocean floor. In those dark depths Antone discovered that California was about to fall into the sea. When he got back to his body, he dashed off a letter to his sister, warning her to move away from Florida, which would be inundated by a tidal wave when California sank.

Clearly he was nuts, but was that grounds for an appeal? The U.S. Supreme Court had never considered the question of whether a state could lawfully execute a crazy person, much less how a state should determine whether a condemned man was sane. "Just don't confront him," Dr. Casscells advised Scharlette Holdman. "Be there for him. That's all you can do."

But no one could tell Holdman "that's all you can do." She didn't have a single passive fiber in her body. She cursed, she shouted, she cried. She racked her brain. A few hours before the scheduled execution, she came up with an idea. What about the Mafia? After all, they had gotten Antone into this mess; why couldn't they get him out of it? She decided to call the godfather. She would ask him to contact the governor and explain that Antone was just a pathetic pawn.

Maybe Antone's delusions were contagious, or maybe Holdman was just being Holdman, never giving up, turning every stone, fighting to the end. Anyway, she asked Pat Doherty to tell her the name of the man who ran Florida's mob. It seemed the sort of thing Doherty would know, and he did not disappoint: Santo Trafficante, he said. Holdman asked if he could get Trafficante on the phone, and Doherty, always game, offered to try.

Some people believe that Santo Trafficante had a part in the crime of the century, the assassination of John F. Kennedy. In any case, it was certainly true that the don had racked up the better part of a century's worth of crimes. He was an old and powerful criminal, a man other thugs killed for and died for—not a man to trifle with. But Holdman had moxie to burn, and when Doherty pulled a few shady strings, found Trafficante's number, and rang him up, Holdman took the phone.

"Uh, Mr. Antone is going to be killed," she said, in a quavering drawl. "I understand he used to, uh, work for you. And I was wondering, is there anything you can say or do to help him?"

There was a pause, and then Holdman heard a raspy whisper exactly like Marlon Brando's in *The Godfather*. "Tony was a good boy," Trafficante gasped. "Give him my regards."

After a thirty-six-hour stay of execution, during which the U.S. Supreme Court decided not to hear an appeal, Anthony Antone was executed on January 26, 1984.

Three hundred people had jammed into the governor's office to protest the Spenkelink execution. About seventy-five attended a vigil in the capitol to protest Sullivan's death. For Anthony Antone, the number dwindled to fewer than fifty. United Press International asked: "Are executions now so frequent that they have become routine?" Not quite, but that's the way things appeared to be headed.

On the other hand, nothing involving Scharlette Holdman would ever be routine. She lived in a house of mirrors where bad guys were the heroes and the law was the enemy, and strange and funny things were always happening to her. For example: Two days after the Antone execution, Holdman's secretary, Gail Rowland, went to the front door of the FOG Building to pick up the mail. A long white limousine pulled up to the curb. Who would show up at their cruddy little office in a limousine with tinted windows? "My God!" Rowland screamed. "The Mafia's here!" Trafficante was after them.

But the man who got out of the long white car was not the godfather, nor one of the don's muscle-bound thugs. He was a swinging dude in a polyester suit, collar open, gold chain dangling in his chest hair. "Hey, baby!" he called out. "Lookin' for the Clearinghouse." Rowland led him inside to Scharlette's office.

The dude introduced himself as Glen. He said he was a Hollywood producer and he was making a movie of a novel called *Deathwork*. Published in 1977, *Deathwork* was the story of a fictional Florida governor named Morgan J. Kingsly, who fueled his political ambitions by ordering the executions of four murderers on a single day. (Bob Graham had a copy on his bookshelf.) Glen the producer had a lot of questions about death row. Hey, what's it like? Tell me about some of the inmates. How do they fry 'em? Holdman regaled him with stories, and Glen was ecstatic. "That's gold, baby!" he cried after each anecdote. "Baby, that's gold!"

The limo driver was a huge, hulking man, and he, too, was fascinated by the stories. Most of the time, he stood quietly, but occasionally he interjected a question, then nodded solemnly at the answer. At last he said: "You know, I like you girls. I blew my stepfather's head off when I was twelve. So I really like you girls."

"I'm gonna give you girls the thrill of a lifetime," Glen announced, after several hours of discussion. "Huh? Huh? Glen's gonna give you a ride home in the limo. How do you like that?" Holdman and Rowland had never been in a limousine. They bounded outside and into the long white car, where they found a well-stocked bar and helped themselves. There was a phone, too. Rowland snatched it up and dialed her husband. "I'm coming home in a limo!" she said gleefully. And when the awesome vehicle rolled up to the apartment complex where Rowland lived, a crowd of neighbors awaited her arrival. It was glorious.

The big car pulled away, and that was the last they ever saw of Glen. He never made the movie.

Because Antone's mental problems had not been the focus of his appeals, his death had not settled the question of whether an insane man can be executed. This was a good example of an increasingly apparent problem across the Death Belt: Though executions were beginning to come at a steady rate, they were not bringing much definition to the law. Each execution seemed to mean little more than the bad luck of a particular inmate. The larger questions lived on.

As it happened, the sanity issue resurfaced almost immediately. Two months after Antone, Graham signed a death order for Arthur Frederick Goode III.

Freddy Goode was as miserable a character as ever walked—homely, stupid, weak, and warped. Almost from the day he was born, in a working-class neighborhood outside Washington, D.C., his parents knew they had a defective model on their hands, and they shuttled among school counselors and child psychiatrists in search of repairs. But things only got worse, and when Freddy entered adolescence, he began molesting boys.

Bud Goode, Freddy's father, tried beating the boy, but Freddy just looked back at him, hurt and uncomprehending, like a dog. "He had no understanding," Bud said. Later, Bud encouraged Freddy to sleep with a mildly retarded girl who lived nearby, suggesting he take her to a motel room, thinking his son might forget boys if he had sex with a woman. That didn't work, either. Admittedly, these are not textbook treatments for pedophilia; they aren't discussed during seminars of the American Psychiatric Association. Bud and Mildred Goode were ordinary people faced with an extraordinary curse; they tried everything they could think of. Mildred prayed, and Bud urged his son to start drinking, on the theory that a sluggish alcoholic is at least harmless. But Freddy didn't like the taste of booze. He liked ice cream.

Finally, by 1976, Freddy had tormented enough boys that Bud and Mildred Goode were able to get him admitted to a Maryland psychiatric hospital. There, Freddy was treated with Depo-Provera, a drug that quenches the sex drive. The doctors considered recommending that Goode be committed to a hospital for the criminally insane, a step that would have been a blessing to Bud and Mildred, to Freddy himself, and to countless third- and fourth-graders. But before that step could be taken, Freddy left the facility and took the bus to Cape Coral, Florida, where his parents had recently retired.

It has been suggested that some vast force must pick up the United States every now and then, giving the country a hard shake that sends all the loose bits and garbage drifting down to Florida. Freddy Goode was one of the loosest bits imaginable; untethered from the hospital, he rattled south. Soon after he got to Cape Coral, a nine-year-old boy was found raped and strangled to death. Goode climbed back on the bus.

He returned to the Maryland hospital and tried to check himself in, but the receptionist was busy and asked him to take a seat. Instead, Goode left again, kidnapped another boy, and—in the company of that child—raped and strangled an eleven-year-old in Virginia. Now he commuted back to Florida, where he was promptly arrested. In an appalling spectacle, he was permitted to conduct most of his own defense; he was, of course, convicted. Goode begged the judge for the death penalty and got it.

He was a monster in the guise of an overgrown child. His brown hair hung straight on his head in a sad echo of a Prince Valiant cut; his face was pasty and pocked with acne; his flesh hung on his bones like sacks of gelatin; his dark eyes darted when he talked. And lord, could he talk! Endlessly, horribly—a breathless stream of filth and paranoia and childish blather. Goode talked nonstop about his fear of prison, his passion for ice cream and television, his hunger for little boys. Sometimes he delivered separate monologues on each of these topics. Sometimes he jumbled them together. For example, when people told him sex with children was wrong, Freddy Goode would say, "It's like ice cream. You don't know if you like it until you try."

Goode churned out letters, too, endless stacks of hysterical, often revolting letters, written in an unmistakable scrawl of block letters, chicken-scratch, exclamation points, and multicolored inks. He wrote letters to grade school principals, asking if they let their male students wrestle naked. He mailed perverted notes to kids who advertised for pen pals in children's magazines. Worst of all, Goode sent obscene letters to the parents of his victims, in which he savored each moment of his crimes. It was a curse to have your address fall into the hands of Freddy Goode, and the curse befell everyone from the president to the governor to the attorney general to lawyers and journalists from coast to coast. Goode might write you a letter at noon, and then write you again at five o'clock, angrily demanding to know why you hadn't answered yet. His letters were raving, paranoid, and grossly obsessed with the perversion that had landed him on death row—a lethal desire for prepubescent boys.

Just one from the thousands of letters he generated is enough to get the idea. This one was addressed to a lawyer in New York:

> I <u>hope</u> you have received my two letters by now! I want to meet you as <u>soon</u> as possible here! My parents gave me your address and I understand you are on my case too! "URGENT"! → → Im in a bad situation here again! As I told you in my last two letters, they keep "MOVING" the inmates around here! Right now they got a guy beside me who looks like a "MAD-MAN"! And im all "UPSET" and "WORRIED" that he will try "KILL-ING" me or ect.!!!! . . .
>
> I am just so "WORRIED" and "MISERABLE" <u>all</u> the time, that I "CAN'T" ever think about working on my death sentence!, and I "DON'T" even sleep well at night either! You "CAN'T" imagine <u>how</u> "UPSET" and AFRAID I really am here! <u>Everybody</u> "HATES" me due to their atrocious feelings they have "AGAINST" the horrible crimes I committed on all them little "BOYS" and ect.!!!! I am <u>trying</u> to "COOPERATE" here, but im just so "UPSET" and in extreme "FEAR" <u>most</u> of the time!
>
> I talk to my <u>only friend Jesus</u> our "LORD"! I know "JESUS" <u>understands</u> my terrible desires and ect. I have tords little boys! And I have "GOOD-REASON" for every bit of it! And the main reason I <u>murdered</u> them little "BOY'S", is because our society is so "AGAINST" the fact of "CHILDREN-DOING-SEX" together or with anybody! I believe <u>children should</u> be "ABLE" to <u>do sex</u>! And I can "ARGUE" that all the way to the U.S. Supreme Court! "SEX" is a great "GIFT" that <u>Jesus</u> gave us all!!!! I'll be happy to explain this in <u>great detail</u> to you when you come "VISIT" me!

He would do anything for attention. As a boy, Goode took snapshots of family vacations and organized them into slide shows, which he insisted on showing to the whole neighborhood. The neighbors suffered through his long-winded narrations, and Goode was in his glory. When his parents bought him a telescope, it wasn't enough simply to gaze at the stars. Goode had to deliver pedantic lectures on astronomy. He bordered on being mentally retarded, could barely read and write, but he was dogged. When he latched onto a hobby, he could master enough jargon and gibberish to speak about it relentlessly. Goode idolized TV weathermen—they were the luckiest people on Earth, the way they got to lecture the masses night after night with their maps and pointers. "Any attention was good attention," his father summed up.

This devouring need for attention had terrible consequences. In prison, Goode discovered that television crews and newspaper reporters would travel miles, sit rapt for hours, to hear him discourse on his crimes. And he would say anything to keep them coming, to keep the cameras rolling. He would complain because he couldn't have a little boy live with him in his cell. He would proclaim that if he ever got out of prison he'd head straight for the nearest child. He would describe the feel of a child's mouth on his body, discuss the death throes of a strangled boy. These were not proud moments for the Florida press, turning over ink and airtime to a lunatic. But Goode's interviews virtually guaranteed that he would one day sit in Old Sparky. They were like bloody shirts waved before a mob.

People with a clearer view of Goode found him less menacing than pathetic. He was sick. Betty Steffens, clemency aide to the governor, knew more about the men on death row than virtually anyone. "He didn't have the capacity to form criminal intent," Steffens said years later. "He was a captured butterfly, and we should've preserved him and studied him." She tried to make this case to Bob Graham, without success, because any politician could see that commuting Goode's sentence was out of the question. On the southern Gulf Coast, where Goode had committed the first of his two murders, thousands of citizens had signed petitions demanding his prompt execution. In the headlines, he was simply "Child-Killer Goode." And when it was discovered that he had sent obscene letters to the parents of his victim— well, that was the last straw.

He was a pariah; he sickened even the most understanding people.

Scharlette Holdman searched the state for a lawyer to handle Goode's appeal. At last she persuaded Sandy Bohrer, an attorney at a distinguished Miami firm. Immediately, Bohrer learned what a disastrous case he'd taken. First came a long note from one of his partners, which, boiled down, declared: I can't believe you're squandering the firm's good name and resources on that animal. Then the wife of a prominent local newspaper editor—Bohrer had represented the paper in libel cases —announced that she wasn't sure she could ever speak to him again. An awful lot of people wanted Freddy Goode dead. Bohrer, however, believed that "the thing that distinguishes our system of justice is its tremendous emphasis on procedural fairness. If the system works for a despicable person, it will also work for me." He threw himself into a whirlwind effort to save his despicable client.

He decided to argue that it is unconstitutional to execute someone who is insane. Bohrer learned that Florida had a policy for determining sanity before an execution, but when he examined the policy, he concluded that it was a farce. In cases where a prisoner's sanity was questioned, the governor was to appoint a panel of three psychiatrists. They would consider two questions: Did the prisoner understand what an execution was, and did he understand why it was happening to him? There was no provision for the defense to present its own evidence. In Goode's case, the examination had lasted about thirty minutes. Bohrer argued that this proceeding violated the constitutional promise of due process. Three doctors, appointed and paid by the governor, examining a man for thirty minutes—that was a sham, the lawyer maintained. Justice required a proper hearing, fair to the defense as well as the state.

Like most Florida lawyers handling death penalty appeals, Bohrer consulted with Craig Barnard in West Palm Beach. At the time, Barnard and a colleague named Dick Burr were working on a similar appeal for a client of theirs—Alvin Ford, the same man whose case had tested the secret psychological reports. Having lost with that issue, they were expecting a new death warrant, and when it came they planned to argue that Ford was insane.

By death row standards, Alvin Ford was a fairly bright guy—he could read and discuss books—and he was unusually honest. Ford admitted that he had killed a policeman in Fort Lauderdale, a crime he blamed on cocaine. To be smart and honest is not necessarily a blessing in the death house, though. When Ford came within hours of being executed in 1981, he thought so long and so clearly about his predicament that it drove him mad. Or so it appeared to Gail Rowland, Scharlette Holdman's secretary. She visited Ford regularly on death row, and she watched him fall apart. "The first sign," she recalled, "was just a complete obsession with the Klan, which I thought was pretty reasonable coming from a black man in the South. The papers had run some stories about Klan activity around Jacksonville. But then Alvin began writing letters to people all over the place, claiming to explain various 'codes' he had discovered in the dictionary. Then he started complaining that certain radio disc jockeys were playing songs aimed directly at him. Eventually, it got to the point where he thought he was the Pope."

Ford had always been rather vain, considering himself quite a ladies' man; he always spruced himself up for Rowland's visits. But as his decline accelerated, he stopped eating or showering, and as his flesh starved away his face came to resemble a death's-head. Ford became convinced that Rowland—and Margaret Vandiver, another frequent visitor to death row—were prowling the ventilation ducts behind his cell. "He wrote tons of letters to Ronald Reagan and Edwin Meese complaining about the fact that I was hiding in the pipe alley singing and playing the piano all night," Rowland said. "He told them that I was causing all sorts of natural disasters, a bad flood somewhere in America, a big earthquake over in China. One time Margaret and I were visiting him, and he suddenly started yelling, 'I can't hear you! Your vaginas are shouting too loud!' " For a time, prison authorities thought Ford was faking it. They suggested that Rowland and Vandiver were coaching him. But the "act" continued for years, and even some skeptics began to believe that Ford had in fact lost his mind.

Barnard and Burr shared some ideas with Bohrer over the telephone, but they were careful not to get their case too closely linked to Goode's; he was such a liability. Sandy Bohrer plunged ahead with the appeal, and in little more than two weeks produced a masterpiece of constitutional law. He reasoned well, he wrote clearly, he drew on sources ranging from antique British common law to the latest U.S.

Supreme Court opinions, from academic treatises to the grand dissents of Felix Frankfurter. The richest corporation could not have asked for a better piece of legal work.

The men who ran the prison agreed that Goode was mad. "I saw Arthur every month," warden Dave Brierton said. "He would come in for a talk, and it was always the same: He couldn't understand why society didn't allow him to have sex with boys. I tried explaining the historical development of sexual taboos, but it never sank in. He would start crying and asking why he couldn't have a boy in his cell. He was one of a kind, impossible. 'So-and-so didn't go to sleep last night,' he'd say. Or, 'Your officer only checked the cell block four times, not five.' Or, 'I couldn't get Channel Six last night. I got snow on my TV set.' One time he comes in and says, 'I don't want to live here anymore.' "

He didn't want to live there anymore. Goode didn't get the picture, he missed the point of punishment—as his father put it, "He had no understanding." That was the State's own test of sufficient sanity to be executed. A prisoner had to understand what was happening to him and why. "I don't think Arthur ever understood that when you're executed, we can't come back the next day and talk about it," said Richard Dugger, Brierton's successor as warden. "It was like dealing with a child. He could make a rational appearance. He could answer your questions and appear to carry on a conversation. But he just didn't understand what you were saying."

Only one person ever got through to Freddy Goode. She was Margaret Vandiver, an ineffably sweet, shockingly smart graduate student from Florida State University. Like many of her friends in the anti–death penalty camp, Vandiver saw capital punishment as essentially a civil rights issue. It was the strong killing the weak, and from girlhood Vandiver's heart had always been on the side of the weak. She was an angel of death row, spending thousands of hours visiting inmates and assisting their lawyers; a saint among the vilest sinners. But even she found Goode repulsive. "If there was ever an execution that I would not care about, that was going to be it," she said much later.

He was already under a death warrant when Vandiver first met him. As always, Goode sat with his back wedged in the corner of the visiting room—he feared enemies coming through the walls. He looked "awful in every way," Vandiver recalled. When she went to shake his hand, Goode pulled away, reached into his pocket, and produced a newspaper photo of Ricky Schroder, the cherubic boy actor. Goode was in love with Ricky.

Then he started his loathsome talking. Vandiver trembled as he spoke. At first, she tried interrupting him, patiently explaining all the reasons why it is wrong to sodomize children. But she soon saw it was hopeless. Midway through the excruciating meeting, Vandiver excused herself, rushed to the bathroom, and ran cold water on her wrists to calm herself. You're out of your mind! she scolded herself as the water flowed over her burning skin. Arguing morals with a plainly deranged man. But she returned and finished the ordeal, and the next day she saw Goode again, and ultimately Vandiver met with him every day for the next two weeks. She discovered a trick: When Goode began ranting, she fastened him eyeball to eyeball, gazed intently, and said, "No, Arthur," in a strong, calm voice. "We are not going to talk about little boys." Like a nanny talking to a three-year-old. Goode's reaction surprised her. He seemed relieved. Finally he had met someone who was not interested in a freak show. "Arthur desperately needed attention," Vandiver said later, "so desperately that it was better for him to have center stage as a murderous pedophile than to be ignored."

Vandiver was the first person who could make Freddy Goode shut up, if only for a moment. Gazing steadily, she would latch onto his restless eyes, and when she had them she could feel the change come over him. He would relax, his shoulders would drop slightly, and a sense of calm would take hold. But the calm lasted only as long as she held his gaze. "I felt like a water pitcher. Everything inside of me, all the peace and strength, was just pouring into him. His gaze was like a newborn baby's: totally unwavering, unfiltered, direct, and unbelievably intense," Vandiver explained.

Then he would go back to chattering. Goode loved to send Vandiver to the canteen for food. She jotted his orders in a quivering hand. "Two ice cream sandwiches / two milks—one chocolate, one white / steak & cheese sandwich / V–8," she wrote one afternoon. When Vandiver returned with the food, Goode would become apoplectic: "If I eat the ice cream first the milk will get warm so maybe I should drink my milk first but if I drink the milk then the ice cream will melt and what about the sandwich? Maybe I should eat the sandwich with the milk and save the ice cream except the ice cream will melt if I try to save it. . . ." Until at last Vandiver fastened his gaze and said, "Arthur, eat your food!"

Goode was frightened of the electric chair, but the way a child is frightened of the dentist. "Will it hurt?" he demanded over and over. His only solace was the fact that Richard Dugger, the warden, would shepherd him. "Will Mister Dugger be there?" he asked, pathetically missing the point. Yes, Dugger would be there. Dugger would strap him in. Dugger would signal the executioner.

Margaret Vandiver slumped into Dugger's office one day shortly before the execution. "He wants you to go down there and stay with him," she said gently. "All night and all day. He says he wants you to take a sleeping bag down there and stay with him."

Dugger stared, then said quietly, "I don't think that's something I can do."

Perhaps his death would bring some solace to the families of the boys he murdered. His mother, Mildred, prayed nightly for those poor families, even as she neared the day she would join them in that grief-stricken wasteland where parents mourn children violently dead. She wrote poetry, contemplated suicide, clung to God. She felt guilt and failure. When she went to Starke to visit her son, she always told the desk clerk at the Dixie Motel that she was there to see a nephew. The shame. The horror. One of her poems:

My son is on Death Row;
dear God, how can it be!

He was always a troubled child,
always a bit behind.

I go to bed at night and toss 'til 3,
or I wake up at 5, and roll the years back;
roll the years back like reflections in a mirror.

He always was a troubled child;
always looking for a friend who was not there.
He loved animals, he had a black dog.
And a Siamese cat, he wouldn't hurt a fly.

Dear God, he's on Death Row;
How can this be!

It's 10 years now, it seems like forever.
When I see him, he's 28, but he looks 15;
you see, he was always a little behind.
Mothers always know.

Dear God, how could this have happened?
I loved children, I tried to be a good mother.
My heart almost bursts with grief of what he did,
with what happened.
I pray every night for those left behind.

Dear God, I love my son;
it's in your hands now
Dear God, how can this be!

Goode called a press conference the day before his scheduled execution. "I'm proud of the fact that I murdered those children, because society is prejudiced against me because I'm a child molester," he announced. "My execution is the only thing I want because I'll never have sex with young boys again unless I escape, which is impossible." Between answers, Goode asked the reporters which stations they represented. The interview was a tawdry affair, and ludicrous: grave reporters questioning Goode as if he was some expert on deviant psychology from Columbia or Johns Hopkins. "Pay your penny and see the freak," Margaret Vandiver said bitterly.

Judge after judge rejected Bohrer's appeal. As the end neared, Vandiver and Dugger each pleaded with Goode to show some shred of decency before he died. "I told him he should say something about how he appreciated his parents sticking by him," the warden later recalled. Vandiver remembered saying, "This will be the last chance you will have to say something nice, Arthur," and suggesting that he should say he was sorry.

"Will it hurt?" Goode asked Vandiver.

"You'll feel an impact, and then nothing," she answered, unsure.

"Mister Dugger will be there?"

"Yes."

"Who'll scratch my nose if it itches?"

He went to Old Sparky the morning of April 5, 1984. Freddy Goode could scarcely walk the short distance from his cell to the death chamber; guards supported him under each arm. His spindly biceps were like mush in their hands, thin bags of aspic wrapped around flaccid bones. The appalling mop of hair was gone; his soft, bald head was gooey with Electro-creme. As he had hoped, Mr. Dugger was there.

The warden's small jaw was tight as he cinched the wide leather straps. The trousers of Goode's death suit flapped at his scarecrow ankles. He hadn't taken a single hour of exercise in nine years. His funeral shirt hung from his pasty form.

The executioner was behind him, in the corner. It was just as Goode had always feared. Death was coming from behind him, from the corner.

Goode's eyes darted over the beefy hands swarming around his body, as the execution squad tightened the straps on his wrists and arms and chest and legs. They laced the cuff tightly around his calf and he flinched. Normally, he would have complained about a thing like that. The BAD ONES are HURTING! my LEGS!!! But something about this proceeding—something about the shaved head and the leather straps and the hooded man in the corner—some shard of reality grabbed his attention.

Dugger's voice echoed in the little room: "Arthur Goode, do you have any last words before sentence is carried out?"

"I'm very upset," he rasped into the microphone held in the

warden's outstretched hand. Goode's dark eyes searched the room. "I don't know what to say, really." He gulped for air. "How much time do we have?"

As he said it, Goode fastened his infant gaze on the man with the microphone. It was the same constant, needy stare that had leeched the strength from Margaret Vandiver. Now it settled on the man he naïvely hoped would keep him safe. Dugger stared back blankly.

"How much time do I have?" the prisoner asked again.

The warden simply dipped his head, almost imperceptibly, and Goode remembered what Mr. Dugger wanted him to do. "I want to apologize to my parents," Goode blurted.

Dugger was relieved. His fears of an obscene outburst dissolved with this welcome declaration, and when Goode then paused, the warden began to stow the microphone for the final act. Goode's eyes began jumping around the room again. Would it hurt? How long would it hurt? How long? Would it hurt?

He fought off the confusion and the rising panic. There was something else he was supposed to say. Something for Margaret. "I have remorse," he croaked. The words were almost inaudible as Dugger tugged the microphone back toward the prisoner. "I have remorse," Goode said again, "for the two boys I murdered. But it's hard"—and here his voice broke—"for me to show it."

That was more than all he had within him. Freddy Goode sagged against the chest strap and sobbed. As Dugger put the microphone away, strong hands drew the chin strap tight against Goode's fuzzy cheeks. The electrician affixed the death helmet with a hard twist. The thick smell of leather closed in on Goode as the hood fell over his face.

Then the circuit breaker clapped, and the switches were turned, *pop! pop!* Freddy Goode's pale, weak fingers turned baby-pink, then darkened. Behind the hood, his brown eyes froze forever in the familiar empty stare.

"Arthur Goode was the hardest," Richard Dugger later said. "I had some real reservations about that one. Let's face it—he was a nut. Geez, he didn't trust anybody but me. And I was the one who was gonna make sure he was gonna die. He was sure I would take care of him."

∴

Three weeks later, Governor Graham signed a death warrant on Alvin Ford. Craig Barnard's colleague, Dick Burr, filed an appeal virtually identical to the one Sandy Bohrer had filed for Freddy Goode. The courts had found no merit in the arguments when Bohrer had raised them, but now a federal judge decided they were important enough to order a stay of execution. The next year, the U.S. Supreme Court agreed to consider Ford's case.

Another year passed before oral arguments were scheduled. On June 26, 1986, the high court published its decision. Two questions were decided. The first was a broad constitutional question: Could an insane prisoner be lawfully executed? By a vote of 5 to 4, the Court ruled that the Constitution prohibited killing the insane. The second question was narrower: Did Florida's procedure for determining the sanity of a condemned prisoner violate the right to due process? On this, a larger majority of 7 to 2 voted in favor of Ford. Dick Burr and Craig Barnard had won on both counts. Reading the opinion, Sandy Bohrer felt like Julius Caesar: a laurel on his brow and a knife in his chest. The U.S. Supreme Court's opinion read like a synopsis of his work for Freddy Goode.

Bohrer, arguing for Goode, had set out a history of court opinions to support his appeal, including *Solem v. Helm, Furman v. Georgia, Gregg v. Georgia,* and Felix Frankfurter's dissent in *Solesbee v. Balkcom.* The Supreme Court, finding in favor of Ford, cited the same four cases.

Bohrer, for Goode, had traced a long tradition of legal theory against executing the insane, drawing on such erudite sources as *Hawles's Remarks on the Trial of Mr. Charles Bateman, Blackstone's Commentaries,* and J. Chitty's book on criminal law. The Supreme Court cited the same tradition, using the same sources.

Bohrer had mentioned a footnote in an article in the *Stanford Law Review.* The Supreme Court mentioned the same article, same footnote. Bohrer had cited a case called *Greenholtz v. Morrissey* to support the right to due process before the governor. The Court agreed, based on the same case.

"Petitioner had no notice [of his sanity examination], no opportunity to be heard," Bohrer had written, summing up his case. The Supreme Court now agreed: "If there is one 'fundamental requisite' of due process, it is that an individual is entitled to an 'opportunity to be heard.' "

Justice is represented by a lady in a blindfold, but in Goode's case a lottery ticket might have been more apt. Bohrer remembered being scolded for his appeal when he appeared before U.S. District Judge Terrell Hodges. The appeal, Hodges had declared, was "frivolous and . . . an abuse" of the law. Two years later, Bohrer's appeal *was* the law.

Goode was dead, Ford was alive. Either the law varied from one person to the next—a blatantly unconstitutional, un-American concept —or the courts still weren't sure what they were doing with regard to the death penalty. There was some truth to both explanations. Plainly, the law had varied: Florida's procedures regarding insanity were legal one day and illegal the next. Bohrer's theories were frivolous one day and in the law libraries the next. But this was not entirely the fault of the courts; the modern death penalty was a labyrinthine legal edifice, pages and pages of arcane language, constructed by lawmakers working too quickly under intense political pressures. And it was built on sand; its theoretical foundation was the notion that degrees of evil and de-pravity and menace can be reliably distinguished and fixed into print by legislative draftsmen and consistently applied by judges of a thousand worldviews and temperaments.

In reality, the nature of the criminal soul is the terrain of a Dosto-evsky, a Dante, a Camus. It defies the grasp of legal definition as a blob of mercury defies a tweezers. Modern death penalty laws try to get their arms around a cloud—a dark cloud, but nonetheless evanescent— and as a result, the laws are complicated and ornate but ultimately hollow; hollow in the sense that their language is utterly open to new and shifting interpretation. What judges might not see in the law as applied to Freddy Goode, for example, they suddenly saw when they looked again for Alvin Ford.

Like most lawyers on both sides of the death penalty battles, Craig

Barnard was maddened by this failure of the law to hold still. He had seen Daniel Gardner and many others win new sentencing hearings because their judges had considered undisclosed reports. And he had seen a different result when secret records were found in the files of the Florida Supreme Court. When he won a stay of execution for Alvin Ford while the insanity questions were decided—so soon after Goode had lost on the same issues—Barnard rightly believed that another judicial flip-flop was coming. But this inconsistency could also be a consolation to Barnard, especially in 1984, when the machinery seemed to be moving toward frequent executions. He needed another roadblock, a new logjammer, and because the law was a changeling, he could search among arguments rejected one day for issues that might save a client the next.

As he puffed pensively on his pipe, or waited for another frozen dinner to heat, Barnard focused his hopes that year on two arguments in particular. The first was national in scope, potentially the biggest of the big issues. Scientists were finding more and more data to suggest that death sentences in America were being skewed by racial bias. In study after study, killers of white victims were more likely to be sentenced to death than killers of black victims. Did the death penalty somehow abet a racist remnant of the American psyche, holding that the loss of a white life was a greater outrage than the loss of a black life? This question was enticing to Barnard and to the rest of the nation's anti–death penalty strategists. Anthony Amsterdam had won *Furman v. Georgia* in part by showing racial bias: Blacks in the old days were more often executed than whites. Now Amsterdam was working on this new evidence of bias, which was more subtle but perhaps just as powerful from a legal standpoint. Barnard talked often with the master.

Barnard's second hope was more limited because it applied only to Florida. But it, too, had powerful implications, because if he won on this issue, dozens of inmates would likely get new sentencing hearings. It would be the biggest Florida case since the secret psychological reports. It was a terribly arcane point, having to do with one of those bubblegum patches devised by the state supreme court. Florida's capital punishment law contained lists of "aggravating" and "mitigating" factors to be weighed in deciding whether to impose the death penalty.

Racing against the political clock, harried bill writers in the Florida legislature had written that aggravating circumstances "shall be limited to" the list in the law. Mitigating circumstances, they had written, "shall be" the ones listed. Trial lawyers, juries, and judges drew on these words as they performed the weighing process.

But what, exactly, did they mean? We have already seen that some judges applied aggravating factors not listed in the law. These were always struck down on review, for the law plainly said, "Shall be limited to." In 1976, the Florida Supreme Court had turned to the question of mitigating factors outside the legal list. The case was that of Vernon Cooper—the poetry-quoting cracker of Florida's death row. From the start, Cooper maintained that his dead accomplice, Steve Ellis, fired the shot that killed a sheriff's deputy on a darkened road outside Pensacola. Nevertheless, he was found guilty of murder.

Hoping to mitigate the sentence in favor of life, Cooper's trial lawyer had produced evidence that Ellis had a reputation for violence but Cooper did not. The lawyer presented evidence that Cooper had often tried to avoid Ellis, and that Cooper had a decent employment record, suggesting he was not irredeemable. But the trial judge would not to allow this evidence into consideration because it did not fit any of the mitigating factors listed in the law. Mitigating factors "shall be" the ones listed, the judge noted. And in 1976 the state supreme court agreed with the trial judge. "The Legislature chose to list the mitigating circumstances . . . and we are not free to expand the list," the justices declared.

But two years later, the U.S. Supreme Court ruled that states could not limit the evidence introduced in favor of mercy. Anything that might weigh against a sentence of death should be considered— whether or not it was listed in the law. This ruling directly refuted the *Cooper* opinion, and Craig Barnard exulted when he heard the news. "This could be the end of the death penalty in Florida!" he gushed. David Kendall had rushed to add the issue to his appeal for John Spenkelink. But the Florida Supreme Court instead patched over the problem. The justices simply looked at the law again, in the case of an inmate named Carl Songer, and announced a verdict precisely the opposite of the decision they had reached in Cooper's case. Clearly, the court pronounced, "shall be" is different from "shall be limited to." Florida's law did not limit mitigating factors, the justices wrote, and they denied that they had ever said it did. People must have misunderstood the *Cooper* ruling.

It was an audacious step. "We are not free to expand the list," the justices had written in their *Cooper* decision. Legal language doesn't get much straighter than that. What was to misunderstand? If one law says "The name of your dog shall be Rex, Spot, or Fido," and another law says "The name of your dog shall be limited to Rex, Spot, or Fido," it would be clear that both laws limited the choice of pet names. Of course, the law limited favorable evidence. Few jurors who were instructed by the judge that mitigating factors "shall be" the ones listed by the law would think they could consider other ones. And a judge who knew that the law said mitigating circumstances "shall be" the ones listed would be unlikely to permit lawyers to present evidence of other factors. It would be a waste of time. The same with defense attorneys. They would be unlikely to take the trouble to present evidence beyond the list in the law.

But the justices of the Florida Supreme Court had a very slippery law on their hands and scores of capital cases piling up for review, and every few years they had to face the voters. Their job was to make the thing work, not toss it out. So, abracadabra! They stuffed the problem up their own sleeve. Despite the clear language to the contrary, they denied that their *Cooper* opinion had had anything to do with the list of mitigating factors itself. They had merely meant to say that Cooper's lawyer had not provided adequate proof of any factors beyond the list. Florida courts were welcome to consider any relevant information in favor of mercy, the justices said in their *Songer* ruling, and always had been.

An increasing number of federal judges believed that the death penalty should be the province of state courts—this attitude had carried John Spenkelink to Old Sparky, and it had carried the day in the matter of the secret reports. In the matter of mitigating factors, this attitude had led the federal courts to defer to the Florida Supreme Court's sleight of hand. The law in Florida meant whatever the state supreme court said it did, even if those pronouncements were wildly inconsistent.

Both issues—racial disparities and limitations on mitigating evidence—had been raised and rejected in the Spenkelink appeals. But Craig Barnard could not believe that they would not eventually be winners. Throughout 1984, as the tide shifted against the death row inmates and one after another they marched to the executioner, Barnard urged defense attorneys to keep raising these issues wherever they could. The racial issue had been renewed and rejected in Bob Sullivan's case. The question of mitigation had been thrown out in Anthony Antone's appeal. Barnard kept trying. It wasn't pleasant—judges saw these failed arguments appearing over and over, and many of them grew hostile. They blasted the appeals as "frivolous," "abusive," "without merit." Barnard was not cowed. That was what they had said about the Goode insanity appeal, and if Barnard had paid attention then, Alvin Ford would be dead. In the chaos of the death penalty, he knew today's loser can be tomorrow's victor.

But while he continued to raise these large questions, Barnard knew that he and his colleagues had to start doing a better job with the small issues unique to each case. What looked to him like a bloodbath was under way: Across the country, seven men had been executed in the first four months of 1984, which was as many as in the previous sixteen years combined. Florida was leading the way. The defenders needed every tool, large and small, to save their clients; they needed to exploit every possible advantage, from the tiniest detail to the loftiest constitutional principle. On the client roster at his own West Palm Beach public defender's office, Barnard had a case that he hoped would set a new standard for comprehensive capital appeals: the case of James Adams, whose death warrant had been signed a week after the execution of Freddy Goode.

On November 12, 1973, a prominent rancher in St. Lucie County named Edgar Brown had come home to find a burglar in his house. Moments later, Brown was dying, his head caved in by a fireplace poker. James Adams's car, an old Rambler, was seen careering from the crime scene, and later some items stolen from the rancher's house were discovered in the trunk of a car belonging to Adams's wife.

Police had no difficulty believing that Adams was the killer. He was a fugitive from the Tennessee prisons, having escaped while serving a ninety-nine-year sentence for rape, and he had convictions on his record for assault and larceny. On this strong circumstantial evidence, Adams was convicted and sentenced to die.

Even before Adams's death warrant was signed, Barnard and his associates had recognized how little they had to go on in the bare facts of the case. An escaped violent criminal had been closely tied to the aggravated murder of a leading citizen. They decided that to win they would have to dig deeper than the trial record, deeper than even the best death penalty defense lawyers had gone before—into the costly and tedious tasks of reinvestigating the case from the ground up, attacking every shred of evidence, discrediting each witnesses, unearthing police files, profiling their client's life from the womb to the present.

This approach—going back to square one with every death case, unearthing a man's childhood demons, crawling inside his head—consumed enormous resources, but Barnard got everything he needed. His boss, Dick Jorandby, saw to that. Somehow, Jorandby always found the money to send an investigator across the country to dig up an ancient file or long-lost relative. More important, perhaps, Jorandby found the money to hire more lawyers. By spring of 1984, Barnard had three skilled attorneys working full time on the death penalty. No other public defender in America was doing as much in defense of death row clients as Dick Jorandby, the staunch Reagan Republican.

Many colleagues have said that Craig Barnard got more work done than any lawyer they ever knew. Part of it was certainly his own tireless labor; but another part of it was his knack for hiring complimentary talents and delegating projects efficiently. The lawyers he hired were not like him and they were not like each other. Their strengths were unique. Richard Burr was the poet on Barnard's team, a soft-spoken man who wore his heart on his sleeve and a beard to mask his baby face. Burr's brief career had been focused entirely on the death penalty. When he graduated from the University of Kentucky's law school in 1979, he immediately joined the Southern Prisoners Defense Committee to represent death row inmates. Work for the SPDC required constant travel across the South; by 1982, Burr was ready to settle down, preferably back home in Florida. He knew Scharlette Holdman—she knew every lawyer on the continent willing to defend a condemned prisoner—and she fixed him up with Barnard. Where Barnard was circumspect, Burr was emotional; where Barnard was monkish in his devotion to work, Burr insisted on a good family life. He rushed home every evening for dinner with his family. Many a night, after the kids were in bed, Burr went back to work and pulled an all-nighter.

Richard Greene had a head for politics. As a law student at the University of Texas, Greene organized campus activities against the death penalty, and he always saw capital punishment as more of a political issue than a legal one. It was natural, then, that he would end up working with Millard Farmer. Greene spent a summer at Team Defense, marveling as Farmer transformed the Dawson Five cop-killing case into an autopsy of racism in rural Georgia. And again, it was Holdman who eventually matched him up with Barnard; she loved Greene's sardonic sense of humor.

The youngest of the team was Michael Mello, a smart kid from a top law school—the University of Virginia—who sometimes struck the others as just a little uppity. Mello knew he wanted to be a lawyer from the day he discovered Clarence Darrow in high school. After law school, he won the considerable honor of clerking for Judge Robert Vance on the Eleventh Circuit Court of Appeals. The court covered cases in Florida, Georgia, and Alabama; as a result, it was swamped with death penalty appeals. To keep up with the glut, each judge assigned a "death clerk" to work exclusively on capital cases. Mello was Vance's death clerk. His job was to summarize each appeal in two or three pages, but when Mello started plowing into the pile he was appalled by the shoddiness of the legal work he found. His case summaries grew longer and longer as he tried to repair the work of second-rate defense attorneys. By the time his term was up, Mello's "briefs" were running twenty-five pages, and he was convinced he was needed as a fighter in the trenches. Craig Barnard's shop, he knew, was "the center of the universe" in death penalty matters. He begged for a job, pestered and badgered, and eventually Barnard relented.

They made an excellent team, and Barnard assigned work depending on the talents required. If he needed to tug heartstrings, he called on Burr. If he needed to strike political chords, Greene. If he needed a legal egghead, he had Mello. Barnard was the chief, the coach, and the star of the team.

Barnard and company figured that James Adams had gotten the death penalty in large part because of his past—the criminal record and the prison escape. Perhaps they could knock a few holes in the prosecution's picture of their client; to find out, they dissected his past all the way back to the cradle.

Adams was one of fourteen children of a dirt-poor sharecropper in rural Tennessee, born in the depths of the Depression. He had grown up with nothing, not even an education, in times that were hard for everyone but especially for blacks. By the time the Barnard team went looking for old jail records, many had been lost forever, but they discovered that the larceny charge that stained his record was for the theft of a pig to feed Adams's hungry family. And they learned that in both his larceny and assault cases, Adams had faced trial without benefit of a lawyer. Barnard's team could thus argue that both convictions were rendered unconstitutional by the Supreme Court's landmark 1963 decision in *Gideon v. Wainwright*.

They turned to the 1962 rape conviction. Again, the files had disappeared. The lawyers searched courts and office buildings all over Tennessee. Nothing. Finally, almost by chance, Dick Burr unearthed the documents in a long-forgotten archive in Atlanta. The trial transcript told a strange story. Adams was convicted of raping a white woman whom he had asked for work. Her testimony was harrowing and racially charged: A "nigger male" had violently attacked her, beating her so ferociously that she lost consciousness several times. Oddly, though, the doctor who examined the woman testified that he found no bruises, nor any semen or other signs of a violent sexual assault. The case came down to a question of a white woman's word against the word of the "nigger male." The jury believed the woman.

Barnard's team next excavated the sociology of juries in Dyer County, Tennessee, circa 1962. They pored over old statute books and found that all citizens over the age of twenty-one "of good character and judgment" had been eligible for jury service. They dug up the master list of Dyer County jurors for 1962, and went painstakingly through the 500 names, trying to ascertain the race of each. Of the 490 they could identify, every one was white. Then the lawyers went one step further, scrutinizing old census records to find the racial breakdown of the county. Fourteen percent of residents twenty-one and older were black; the jury rolls told them that, at most, only 2 percent of prospective jurors had been black. Obviously it was no accident that Adams's jury was all white—blacks had been excluded from the pool. The Barnard team now could argue that the rape conviction was unconstitutional, too, because a defendant has a right to be tried by juries free of racial discrimination.

They dug still deeper. What about the prison escape? From musty files at the Tennessee parole board, Barnard's team learned that Adams had compiled a sterling record during a decade in prison. In fact, the board had recommended parole. "Mr. Adams' institutional record has been exemplary," the board had advised the Tennessee governor. "Due to the circumstances surrounding the crime and his conviction . . . he has served an adequate number of years." Adams had done so well in prison that he was assigned to work as a trusty at a low-security jail in Nashville. (It was a facility for teenage girls; apparently his jailers did not consider Adams a dangerous rapist.) He had been on the brink of freedom, but the custom in Tennessee was to defer to a prosecutor's wishes in such matters, and the prosecutor objected to Adams's release. Something along the lines of "over my dead body." Adams concluded he would never get out of prison as long as the district attorney was alive.

As a trusty, Adams was allowed to drive prison vehicles on errands; one day he climbed into a truck and simply drove away. That was the predator's great escape.

Uncovering all this information was costly and time-consuming work, but when it came together it seemed to put James Adams into a different light. The three-time felon portrayed at trial was now a man who, Barnard could argue, had never been constitutionally convicted of a crime. The brutal rapist had quite possibly never raped anyone.

The treacherous fugitive was, in fact, an exemplary inmate who had quietly driven away from jail when he learned that good behavior might never earn him his freedom. In this new light, Adams looked less like a perfect candidate for the electric chair.

Barnard did not stop there. He assigned an investigator to redo all the police work in the Adams case. Leon Wright took the job with no great enthusiasm. As a veteran detective from the Philadelphia police force, Wright had plenty of street-level experience with bad guys. He supported the death penalty and figured Adams was as guilty as sin. But when he plunged into the murder of Edgar Brown, he began to have doubts. The murder had occurred about 10:30 A.M. When police had interrogated Adams, he had said that he arrived at the home of a woman named Vivian Nickerson before ten-thirty on the morning in question and remained there all day, playing cards. He recalled that Nickerson borrowed his car shortly after he arrived and, along with a man named Kenneth Crowell, went off to buy a deck of cards.

Nickerson's testimony regarding this alibi was crucial—and at trial she blew the defense apart by swearing that Adams did not arrive at her home until after 11 A.M. After the crime, in other words. But as Leon Wright worked through his investigation, he noted that in an earlier sworn statement Nickerson said that Adams arrived before ten-thirty, and that she had his car during the time when the murder was taking place.

That car was seen by an employee of Edgar Brown's in the driveway of the rancher's home. The same employee, a man named Foy Hortman, saw someone rush from the house immediately after the murder, climb into the car, and speed away. Hortman testified at trial that the person he saw could have been James Adams. Wright retraced the work of the sheriff's detectives who interviewed Hortman the day after the murder and came across a handwritten note describing Hortman's examination of a photo lineup. A picture of Adams had been included in the lineup, but the detective noting Hortman's response had written: "No I/D of any man in lineup . . . positive no of these men involved." Hortman told police he saw a man with a thin, clean-shaven face and very black skin. Adams had broad cheekbones, a mustache, and medium-dark skin. When events were freshest in his mind, Hortman "positive" Adams was not the person he saw.

Leon Wright next tracked down a witness who testified that he saw Adams driving wildly from the scene of the crime. Willie Orange gave the only positive identification of Adams at trial, and his testimony was vivid: He said he had been driving a huge truck loaded with fertilizer up the road toward Edgar Brown's ranch. A brown Rambler came roaring toward him, forcing him to swerve onto the shoulder. He said the man behind the wheel of the Rambler was James Adams. Wright poked into this damning testimony—and he learned that Willie Orange nursed a powerful grudge against Adams. Orange believed Adams was sleeping with his estranged wife, Cleo.

Cleo Orange told Wright this story: "He came over to my house and told me he had heard that I was messing around with James Adams. He asked me if I was messing around with James Adams, and I said no. My husband said, 'Well, he'll get what he deserves anyway.'" Wright combed St. Lucie County for others to confirm what Cleo had told him. He found a coworker who recalled Orange talking about the alleged affair between Adams and Cleo Orange. More significant, Wright located another witness in the Adams trial, a man named Ward Lesine, who swore he heard Willie Orange threaten Adams. "Willie Orange said to me, 'I'm going to send him because he's been going with my wife. . . . He'll never walk on land again.'"

Wright went back to Willie Orange and talked him into taking a lie detector test. Such tests are not flawless, but Orange flunked badly. Thus Barnard's investigator chipped away at the case, raising doubts about the witnesses who put Adams at the crime scene. He chipped away also at the physical evidence: Wright noted, for example, that the items stolen from the Brown ranch—later found in the trunk of a car at Adams's house—were never tested for fingerprints. If, as Wright was coming to believe, Adams had been set up, fingerprints on these items might have pointed to another suspect. And then there was the strange matter of a strand of hair that a deputy claimed to have recovered from Edgar Brown's grasp. The hair belonged to an African-American person, presumably to Brown's assailant. Several days after the trial was over, the state crime lab released the results of its analysis: The hair was not Adams's.

Lawyers for the State of Florida argued that the deputy had fabricated the hair evidence. That did nothing to placate Leon Wright. If the hair was faked, how could any of the evidence against Adams be trusted?

None of this was clear-cut proof that Adams was innocent, of course. The facts remained: Brown was dead, and a lot of circumstances tied James Adams to the murder. But by the time Bob Graham signed Adams's death warrant, Wright had put some serious dents in the case. Police had conducted "a lousy, incompetent investigation," he said. In fact, the tough Philly detective held his thumb and forefinger about a half inch apart, and told his friends he was "this close" to proving James Adams was framed.

Barnard poured still more resources into the appeal, arranging for a psychiatric evaluation of his client. Quite by chance, he had come across the theories of Dr. Dorothy Otnow Lewis, a professor at New York University and Yale, who had found intriguing correlations between head injuries and later violent behavior. Lewis had also documented the fact that violent adults were very often the product of violent childhoods. One morning, as Barnard was dressing for work, he happened to hear Lewis being interviewed on the CBS morning show. Riveted by her brief appearance, he rushed to the office and began tracking her down. Soon Lewis was part of Barnard's growing arsenal of expert consultants.

After several hours with James Adams in an office at the Florida State Prison, Lewis concluded that the prisoner likely suffered from a "psychomotor seizure disorder" that caused rages, dizziness, blackouts, and amnesia. She theorized that the disorder was the result of a beating Adams endured at the age of seventeen, when a guard in a Tennessee jail bashed his head with a baseball bat. Dr. Lewis noted a dent in Adams's skull, still there after some thirty years.

When James Adams had been convicted of murder and was facing death, his lawyer had come up with precious little to say on his client's behalf. He presented no favorable evidence, instead offering only a brief speech. "Ladies and gentlemen, you have all heard the evidence and you have found James Adams to be guilty of first-degree murder," he said. "I understand how Mrs. Brown felt during her testimony . . . in which she saw her husband lying there in the condition he was. I understand Mr. Brown's reputation in the community. I think you understand the situation. . . . Yet I find it necessary to ask for you to consider that you save his life in spite of all this and let this man live, for no other reason than that he is a man. Thank you."

Now, some ten years later, after thousands of hours of strenuous and costly effort, Craig Barnard's team had reams of material to present on Adams's behalf, material that cast new light on the man's past, on his mental condition, even the very question of his guilt. Unsatisfied with the trial record, they had rebuilt the case from the ground up. For good measure, they renewed Barnard's favorite constitutional issues. They had found fresh statistics, from a study by two Stanford researchers, indicating racial disparities in Florida's death penalty. The study found that between 1976 and 1980, killers of white victims in Florida were eight times more likely to get the death penalty than killers of black victims. Blacks who killed whites were the most likely of all to go to death row. They also raised the problem of mitigating evidence. Maybe if Adams's trial lawyer had realized that there were no limits on favorable evidence, he would have made a better case for mercy than simply that Adams "is a man."

Their appeal did set a new standard for thoroughness, just as Barnard had intended, attacking the death sentence on constitutional grounds, on grounds of new evidence, on grounds of justice, on scientific grounds, on grounds excavated from old census records and dusty archives. Though people frequently complained of appeals based on "technicalities" and "loopholes," this was no mere technicality. The heart of the death penalty was in the belief that courts could take the full measure of a man, his past and his future, down to the center of his soul. Barnard was arguing that the courts had no idea who James Adams was.

Beneath the surface, there was something ominous about the extent of this appeal: If it became, as Barnard hoped it would, the state of the art, the result would be huge additional demands on the lawyers and judges already swamped by the volume of death penalty reviews. How many cases of that intensity and scope could the system handle? One a month? A new man was being sentenced to death row nearly every week in Florida. The last thing the system seemed ready to handle was a quantum leap in the complexity and depth of each appeal. But that was where Barnard was headed, because he believed that was what the law had promised. Death sentences would take into consideration the individual circumstances of each criminal and crime.

For James Adams, though, this breakthrough came too late. His appeals had already been up the entire ladder of state and federal courts before Barnard's team completed its exhaustive work. Judges from Fort Lauderdale to Tallahassee to Atlanta to Washington ruled that the new appeal was either repetitive of the earlier appeals, or—where the courts acknowledged new facts—that the material should have been discovered the first time up the ladder.

Adams's last hope was the racial bias issue. A researcher named David Baldus had been studying the question of racial disparities in Georgia's death penalty, and his work had taken the effort to a new plane. The Baldus project was more rigorous, more thorough, more scientific than any previous undertaking, including the study of Florida done by the Stanford researchers. Like the earlier researchers, Baldus had found marked differences in sentencing depending upon the race of the victim. But the quality of his work gave it special authority. In the months leading up to the scheduled execution of James Adams, the Eleventh Circuit Court of Appeals in Atlanta had blocked two Georgia death warrants because of the bias issue and had scheduled an in-depth hearing on Baldus's statistics.

Surely, Barnard thought, the same court would see the similar data from the Stanford researchers that he had included in the James Adams appeal, and the judges would give him a similar stay of execution. On May 8, 1984, the eve of the Adams execution, it happened.

At the Florida attorney general's office, the stay of execution for Adams hit like a thunderbolt. Everyone knew the implications. This question of racial fairness cut to the heart of the death penalty, and if it was enough to block the Adams execution, it might block every execution in the pipeline. It would likely take at least two years before the matter could be resolved. Capital punishment had been moving in Florida, after so much effort by the prosecutors and lawmakers and many judges—but this would stop it cold again. Prosecutors flew immediately to Washington and asked the U.S. Supreme Court to reverse the appellate panel's ruling. This was a long shot. The high court had already agreed to block executions in Georgia while the racial fairness issue was resolved.

But the lawyers from Tallahassee had a lever on the high court. Florida had executed four men, and in all four cases the racial bias issue had been raised (it had been especially prominent in the appeals of John Spenkelink and Bob Sullivan). The high court had not seen the merit of the issue in those challenges. Were the justices now going to change their minds?

Justice Byron White made the decision. He had cast the deciding vote to block the Georgia executions; now he shifted and voted to remove the roadblock in Florida. White never explained why Florida was different from Georgia. His vote was mysterious, but powerful: All the work of Craig Barnard and his team of lawyers and detectives, their state-of-the-art appeal . . . all of it went down the drain, along with the life of James Adams, who died on May 10, 1984, on the first jolt from Old Sparky, the first black man executed in Florida in twenty years.

"It's beyond logic and rational analysis," Scharlette Holdman fumed to Neil Skene, the death penalty expert at the *St. Petersburg Times*. "That court's going to allow race discrimination in Florida and prohibit race discrimination in Georgia."

That was a bald way of putting it, and probably unfair. Justice White was always tight-lipped; that didn't necessarily make him capricious. Maybe there were good reasons to distinguish between the two states. But Scharlette Holdman was always putting things baldly, and often unfairly, because her job was to advocate, not to referee. Her broader point was correct: Executions were coming along every six weeks now in Florida, but no clear selection process was emerging.

The law, and the way courts interpreted the law, were jumping around like a live cable on a storm-slicked street. Every now and then, the cable whipped through a crowd of people and zapped somebody dead. More than twelve hundred people were on America's death rows in the spring of 1984—over two hundred of them in Starke. The zapping of Bob Sullivan, Anthony Antone, Freddy Goode, and James Adams defied rational analysis. Why them and not four others? Perhaps more executions would bring more logic. Maybe a cathedral of law would be built stone by stone, where each stone was another decision by the courts that a particular inmate met the test to die. Maybe as that cable hopped and jerked along the street, a pattern would emerge among the onlookers being zapped.

Perhaps. You could not find a prosecutor or judge in Florida who could discern a rational pattern. It drove them crazy trying. But . . .

Perhaps.

Carl Shriner was a career criminal whose career began when he was just eight years old. He was violent, incorrigible—just the sort of man the death penalty was designed for. On parole from a sentence for armed robbery, he robbed a convenience store in Gainesville. Shriner forced the clerk, a hardworking, good-natured mother of four, into a storeroom and shot her five times.

Shriner came from a family of ten children that would now be called "dysfunctional." In those days, such fancy terms were unknown. Police in Cleveland, Ohio, simply referred, disgustedly, to "those damn Shriner kids." Carl's father regularly beat him and the other kids, a brother and sister later testified; Carl was raped by an older relative. His life became even more violent when he was removed from his home to a series of juvenile reformatories. Beatings and rapes were so commonplace that Shriner actually welcomed his periodic stints in the "strip cell," where the boy would sit, naked and alone, for as long as three weeks. The strip cell was cold and humiliating, but it was safe. Maybe some children are scared straight by such brutal confinements. Shriner was not. He fit perfectly into psychiatrist Dorothy O. Lewis's findings that death row inmates come, overwhelmingly, from violent back-grounds.

For all intents and purposes, he spent his entire life in the custody of the state. When he was thirty, Shriner reflected all the way back to his tenth birthday and could recall only three Christmases that he had not spent in jail. Any decent theory of personal responsibility would lay the onus of his wasted life on his own broad shoulders. But any fair accounting would also have to acknowledge that the well-meaning agencies of society had failed utterly in his case.

Even Shriner's strongest supporters believed that he belonged in prison. "Carl was a dangerous man, very dangerous," said the Reverend Fred Lawrence, a Methodist minister from Gainesville who counseled death row inmates. "If they had ever tried to let him out, I would have opposed it." But these same supporters thought that Shriner's brutal childhood, and the failure of the State of Ohio to help this troubled boy, were facts that should have been weighed in deciding whether to give him a life sentence.

As the man awaited execution, his lawyer argued that the trial judge and jury should have considered, at least, the proposition that the garbage heap of Carl Shriner's life was not entirely of his own making. No such evidence had been presented at trial. His appellate attorney maintained that this had been because of Florida's law regarding mitigating factors—the same argument Craig Barnard had urged in nearly every appeal since Spenkelink's. Now, for the first time, the Eleventh Circuit Court of Appeals polled its members to see if they wanted to reopen this question. Shriner's execution was delayed for a day while the vote was taken. (These delays of a day or two were becoming so common that defense attorneys now had a name for them: "baby stays.")

The court voted not to hear the matter, and on June 20, 1984, Shriner was executed—the fifth Florida execution in seven months.

David Washington, the sinewy athlete who had stabbed and shot three people during a twelve-day rampage in Dade County, died in the electric chair three weeks later.

He was ashamed and remorseful to the very end; he had that small credit. As his twelve-year-old daughter sobbed through their final visit, he cupped her trembling chin in his hand and said: "I want you to look at me, and I want you to see where I am . . . and I want you to do better." Hours later, strapped into the electric chair, he said of the survivors of his victims: "I'm sorry for all the grief and heartache I have brought to them. If my death brings them any satisfaction, so be it."

Washington also left his name on an important U.S. Supreme Court decision. For years, appellate attorneys had been attacking death sentences by charging that trial lawyers were incompetent. It was the appeal of last resort—when all else failed, attack the lawyer. After all, few of the men on death row had money to hire the best available attorneys. By 1984 literally hundreds of appeals were bouncing around the American court system based on the claim of ineffective counsel. But the courts had no clear, nationwide standard for deciding what constituted ineffectiveness in the era of the new death penalty.

Dick Burr, Craig Barnard's assistant, crafted one of these appeals for David Washington. Burr argued that by failing to present psychiatrists and character witnesses to argue for a life sentence, Washington's trial attorney had shortchanged his client. In January 1984, the U.S. Supreme Court heard Washington's plea and used the case to lay down some guidelines.

By a vote of 8 to 1, the justices set out a two-step test. First, the work of the trial attorney had to be so deficient that it plainly fell below "prevailing professional norms." Appellate courts were instructed to give trial attorneys the benefit of the doubt. Even if the work was proven to be shoddy, another hurdle had to be crossed. The inmate had to show a "reasonable probability" that a better lawyer would have gotten a better result.

In other words, if the circumstances of the crime were awful enough, it didn't matter if the lawyer was ineffective. In the case of David Washington, lower courts had been split on the question of whether his lawyer was inadequate, but given the nature of his crimes —three murders in twelve days, including the stabbing of a college student as the young man recited the Lord's Prayer—no one could say with any confidence that a better lawyer could have saved Washington's life. The U.S. Supreme Court therefore affirmed Washington's death sentence. The opinion was unusual in one respect: Even Justice William Brennan, one of the staunchest opponents of capital punishment on the high court, joined the majority in approving the tough test for effective counsel. He dissented, though, when it came to upholding the death sentence; Brennan never approved of a death sentence. Even as he helped to clarify this one muddy corner, Brennan insisted that the larger field of the death penalty was still a morass. "The Court's judgment," he wrote in a stinging footnote to the Washington case,

> leaves standing another in an increasing number of capital sentences purportedly imposed in compliance with the procedural standards developed in cases beginning with *Gregg v. Georgia*. Earlier this Term, I reiterated my view that these procedural requirements have proven unequal to the task of eliminating the irrationality that necessarily attends decisions by juries, trial judges, and appellate courts whether to take or spare human life. The inherent difficulty in imposing the ultimate sanction consistent with the rule of law is confirmed by the extraordinary pressure put on our own deliberations in recent months by the growing number of applications to stay executions.

In this dissent, Brennan proved his point by quoting earlier opinions by his fellow justices. Even though the execution machinery was picking up steam, neither liberals nor conservatives, it seemed, were remotely satisfied with the death penalty. Justice Thurgood Marshall, a liberal, had complained of "haste and confusion" that was "degrading to our role as judges." Justice Lewis Powell, a death penalty conservative, had chided the court for "dramatically expediting its normal deliberative processes to clear the way for an impending execution." Chief Justice Warren Burger, a conservative hard-liner, had bemoaned the fact that death penalty battles were undermining "public confidence in the courts and in the laws we are required to follow." And so forth. If the death penalty was causing that much confusion at the high court in Washington, surely it was gumming up the works in state and local courts, Brennan ventured. And he was right.

∴

Scharlette Holdman had tried to prepare herself for this: Some of her clients were going to die. She gave speeches all over the country— *Newsweek* and *People* magazines made her famous as "The Mistress of Delay"—and everywhere she went she would say it simply. People are going to die.

And then she'd launch into a string of darkly funny riffs on death. People would ask her about the men on the row, expecting some heartbreaking tales of broken lives, and she'd say, "What really gets me is that none of them has a sense of humor!" And her eyes would widen comically. "I go up there, give 'em joke after joke, and they look at me like stunned dachshunds. Is it my timing? My delivery? I finally figured out that half of 'em are retarded and the other half are seriously crazy, so I try not to take it personally." She would talk about executive clemency, about Bob Graham's grants of mercy to half a dozen men, about the mysterious end of official mercy. "There must be some way to get to Graham," she'd say, "but we just can't figure it out. We've become superstitious—one person chants while I toss chicken bones." Maybe she'd tell the story about the Florida prison inmate who was denied parole because he masturbated too much. Maybe she'd tell the story of her desperate phone call to Santo Trafficante, the Mafia godfather, and break everyone up with her imitation of the Brando rasp: "Tony was a good boy."

The old saw: laughing on the outside, crying on the inside. Deep down, Holdman never really expected to lose her clients, and it was tearing her apart. "You're going to have a tough time with this," an inmate had told her, "because you white folks aren't used to losing." Damn right—Holdman was not used to losing. With her lousy ledger and beige telephone, her coarse charm and chutzpah, she had faced down the governor, the attorney general, and overwhelming public opinion for four and a half years. "It can't last forever," she would say, putting up that brave front—but deep down she wondered why the hell not? Jim Smith, the attorney general, had a team of lawyers with good government salaries; he had investigators and legal secretaries and computers and high-speed photocopiers and government airplanes.

Scharlette Holdman had passion. Why couldn't she prevail? "I grew up with Martin Luther King on the television every night," she said, as if that explained everything.

Holdman's life in 1984 was a roaring sea of despair, one wave of panic crashing on the next, a frenzy of barren labor, a chasm of loss. Each new death warrant was a potential catastrophe for her, and the warrants were coming two or three per month. All over the state, lawyers had learned her drill and now refused even to take her calls. Holdman was reduced to working the Yellow Pages. She'd take the book for Orlando, or Jacksonville or Miami, and simply run down the list of attorneys from A to Z, cold-calling—the hardest kind of sell there is. She gave up cajoling, gave up moral blandishment, and went straight to whining. "Hellooohhuuh? This is Scharrrrlette Holdmannnnnnn. The governor signed this man's warraaannnt, and he'll die if he doesn't get a lawwwwyerrr." When she finally found a grudging volunteer—after twenty or thirty or fifty calls—she and her assistant, Gail Rowland, would do all the legwork, tracking down files, interviewing inmates, calling relatives.

A warrant meant that sixteen-hour workdays became twenty-hour workdays, and as the execution neared, the days turned to round-the-clock marathons. Holdman and Rowland took sleeping bags to the office, slept on the floor amid the heaping cardboard boxes of inmate files and trial transcripts. They took turns at the typewriter (they couldn't afford a word processor), and sometimes Rowland banged the keyboard until she couldn't see and she literally collapsed over the keyboard. She'd go home and sleep for two hours before returning. They copied briefs on a crude desktop copier that took forever to copy a single page. For a year, Rowland felt as though she did nothing but type and copy, copy and type. They lived on fried chicken, cigarettes, and cheap wine.

Volunteer lawyers would arrive at Holdman's office expecting to find a tidy, well-stocked operation—after all, this woman was battling the State of Florida—and instead they walked into a dingy room that looked like it had been hit by a meteor. Crates of papers were stacked on the floor, on the tables, on the desks. Files were strewn like a schoolboy's notebooks flung sky-high on the first day of summer. Ashtrays heaped with butts, stale coffee simmering in a grimy pot, photos of inmates taped to the cheap vinyl paneling. Holdman kept all her notes on scraps of wastepaper. "And we would hand the new hot-shot lawyer a file stuffed with Scharlette's scraps of paper, and he would just about have a stroke," Rowland recalled. "These lawyers would talk about it like they'd been stranded in the African bush. It was crazy. This vital life-and-death litigation in the highest courts of the land was being run by a couple of cranks in a little smoke-filled room in Tallahassee."

By spring 1984, Holdman was spending an hour a day just keeping her ledger up to date. And the work continued to expand. Every few weeks another family would arrive in North Florida to face the possible extinction of a son, a brother, a father. Scharlette Holdman raised their bus fares, found them someplace to stay. Some of those sons and brothers and fathers did die; Holdman arranged the funerals. Gail Rowland became an overnight expert in the laws governing interstate transportation of corpses. Holdman, as always, worked the phone: "I need three hundred dollars for a funeral; can your church group handle it?" Or "You've got six acres out there; can we bury somebody on your land?" Holdman's son Tad came home one day and found a station wagon in the carport with a big box in the back. "Is that what I think it is?" he asked. It was. The dead followed her home.

She worked constantly—her first day off that year came in November—but she confided that she cried as much as she worked. She cried though she hated to be seen crying. (When a photographer snapped a picture of her sobbing at a vigil for Anthony Antone, Holdman announced that she would no longer attend such protests.) Death became her life, and it subsumed the lives of those around her. "I got to the point where all I did was buy black clothes," Gail Rowland said. "I learned so many damn funeral songs. I hope I never sing 'Amazing Grace' or 'Will the Circle Be Unbroken' again."

There were moments when the tension broke, moments of bitter laughter. Gail Rowland's puppet, for example. At the U.S. Supreme Court, one justice was assigned to each region of the country to handle emergency appeals. Florida's justice was Lewis Powell; naturally, he became a particular target of Holdman's scorn. Rowland made a hand puppet that she called "Mr. Justice Powell," and the puppet offered running commentary on events in the office. If, for instance, Holdman and Craig Barnard were talking about an inmate's deprived background, Mr. Justice Powell would pop up and shout, "Oh, shut up! Not another bed-wetting darkie!" Or Jimmy Lohman would strum a folk tune on his guitar, and Mr. Justice Powell would chime in with some grossly racist, sexist lyrics. Holdman either laughed or cried; it was a time of emotional extremes; her nerves glowed like incandescent filaments.

The people who worked at the Clearinghouse learned every way in the world to be murdered—every depravity imaginable and depravity beyond imagining. They lived in the medium of blood. Gail Rowland reached a point where she refused to enter a convenience store unless she saw the clerk, safe, through the window. She began to lock her car doors even when she was driving. She never felt a cool breeze as she slept, because the windows were always down and locked. Tragedy was the nearest thing to her mind. One day, Rowland arranged to pick up her daughter up at noon because the grade school was giving the children a half day off. When she arrived and her daughter wasn't there, she "absolutely freaked out. I was sure we would find her dead in the laundry room," Rowland later recalled. "It was the first thing that popped into my mind." Holdman phoned home one afternoon to check on her son, and when he didn't answer, she got hysterical. "Tad's been murdered!" she screamed over and over. "My God, Tad's been murdered!"

Holdman had given herself completely to her cause, and it drained and warped her. She never saw movies. She didn't take walks or ride a bike or curl up with a lighthearted book. She never went to the beach or the shopping mall. "I wish I had a car that always ran, and I wish I had tuition for my son to go to college, and money for me to go to the dentist," she mused one night over a whiskey bottle with writer David Finkel. "And in the bathroom, I'd like faucets that turned all the way off and screens that fit." But that would be life. Scharlette Holdman—like Tiresias in T. S. Eliot's great poem *The Waste Land*—walked among the lowest of the dead. The warped and half-witted killers of death row made up her future; more and more, her past was filled with bad, burnt men.

If she had an hour or two late at night to call her own, Holdman spent it listening to protest music and drinking from a tall glass. Wine was fine, Scotch was better, Grand Marnier was paradise. Now and then friends would sidle up to Gail Rowland and say in low voices, "Gail, you've got to talk to her about her drinking." And Rowland would say, "To hell with that, you tell her."

To hell with that. When death overtakes your life, maybe you feel like dying a little yourself. A lot of booze was washing down the gullets of a lot of beat-up people that year, people struggling to save the men on death row and people ground down by the work of getting them killed. In West Palm Beach, Michael Mello's girlfriend was on the verge of leaving him. In Tallahassee, George Georgieff and Ray Marky were grinding along toward a couple of heart attacks. At least Scharlette Holdman wasn't having her nightmare anymore. She wasn't waking sweaty in the darkness wondering "Who's the mouse?" Her life was her nightmare.

The insanity of Scharlette Holdman's enterprise did not escape the attention of the media. There were the articles in *Newsweek* and *People*. *Esquire* magazine profiled her, as did *The Boston Globe*. *The New York Times* and *The Wall Street Journal* ran front-page articles on the shortage of lawyers willing to volunteer hundreds of hours, thousands of dollars, and the respect of friends and colleagues to defend death row inmates.

Best of all, Phil Donahue called. Holdman loved Donahue; she kept a beat-up portable TV at the office so she could watch him. In one sense, her appearance on Donahue was a fiasco: Holdman was matched with the families of several murder victims and a man in a wheelchair, paralyzed by gunshot wounds. The audience was not with her. But Donahue gave her a chance to talk to her biggest audience ever.

All this publicity was making the legal lions of Florida uncomfortable. Millions of people were meeting Scharlette Holdman in print and over the airwaves, and the message she carried was distinctly unflattering: Florida was willing to execute men who had no lawyer, and lawyers didn't seem to care. Scharlette Holdman was a big black eye on the Florida Bar.

Judges hated her operation, too. She was ruining the decorum of their courts by sending in her panicky volunteers with their hasty briefs typed on paper scrounged from trash cans. Too many of her lawyers were ill prepared, the judges said, and too many were zealots. The law was supposed to be a temple; Holdman's ragtag operation was making it into a sideshow. The judges turned to Florida Bar president William O E. Henry and said, in effect, Do something.

In June 1984, Henry announced that he was commissioning former Bar president James Rinaman to develop a plan for drawing the state's major law firms into death penalty cases. Henry was not interested in blocking executions. Of Holdman's volunteers he said: "A lot of them are more interested in thwarting the death penalty than in representing their clients. Our objective is to make sure each inmate's constitutional rights are protected and, at the same time, to make sure the system isn't being abused." He was interested in saving decorum and shoring up the reputation of his profession.

James Rinaman paid a visit to Holdman's crummy little office. Rinaman was a courtly man; his goal, he often told reporters, was to see the death penalty handled "in a more lawyer-like fashion." Holdman, though she was the opposite of courtly, found her visitor unfailingly polite, "the consummate southern gentleman." In return, she was at her most charming. "He wanted to tell me they intended to take over, and he hoped there wouldn't be a turf battle," Holdman later recalled. Rinaman gingerly sounded her out, this strange dynamo, this sharp-spoken hippie. What would she think if the Bar got involved in recruiting volunteers? "I'd love it!" Holdman declared, perhaps surprising him. "I'm desperate to get the Bar involved." And Rinaman asked, Well, what would she do if the Bar came in? "I'd close my doors," Holdman answered.

Rinaman seemed relieved—Holdman got the clear impression that he wanted to tell her she wasn't welcome, but was too polite to say it. "Hell," she remembered later, "I knew I wouldn't fit in. It was like

Sesame Street: Look at me, look at Rinaman. One of these things just doesn't belong."

They turned to the matter of money. Holdman told Rinaman she ran the Clearinghouse on ten or twenty thousand dollars a year. In a good year the grants were $25,000. "But you aren't going to find anyone to do what I'm doing on that money," she said bluntly. Rinaman asked, What do you think it would cost? Holdman paused for a moment, trying to think of the biggest number she was brave enough to utter. "Two hundred and fifty thousand," she said at last. Rinaman looked a little shocked—ten times as much as Holdman had? Surely she wasn't ten times better than the professionals. He did not say this, though, merely thanked Holdman cordially and went on his way.

But Scharlette Holdman was ten times better. After several months of study, Rinaman reported to the Florida Bar's Board of Governors that it would cost $235,000 a year to recruit and advise volunteer lawyers for death row inmates. The cost of the actual legal work would have to be borne by the state's major firms.

What were the legal lions getting themselves into? Rinaman described a recent experiment. An attorney named Sarah Blakely had volunteered to file an appeal for an inmate named Jimmy Lee Smith. Blakely's little firm did not have the resources for such effort—perhaps ten thousand dollars just for out-of-pocket expenses. Rinaman had matched her up with Holland & Knight, Florida's biggest law firm. Holland & Knight had given Blakely use of its libraries, secretaries, and two associates. "It totally wiped out three lawyers for two weeks," Rinaman reported to the Bar's Board of Governors. "They were working twenty hours a day. . . . But they were successful in getting a stay."

That last point was not necessarily popular with all of the board members. Personally, they weren't all sure they wanted death row inmates to win stays. Obstruction was not the point of their project. But Rinaman had mastered some statistics during his study, which he now shared. "Even with the last-minute nature of appeals," he said, "the reversal rate—in which the death penalty is completely expunged—has been 50 percent." That figure astounded the assembled blue suits. Half of all death sentences were turning out to be seriously flawed. "There will be people executed who should not have been" unless they get good lawyers, Rinaman said. The board approved the money.

The immediate effect of the Bar's action on Holdman's life was precisely zero, however. Great institutions of the establishment do not move swiftly. James Rinaman was not going to run out to an office supply store, buy himself a ledger and a stack of index cards, and start dialing. His project would take months to get rolling. And in the meantime, Bob Graham was signing death warrants.

On August 8, 1984, Graham ordered the execution of Earnest John Dobbert Jr. Holdman fielded the case; her pal Pat Doherty was the lead attorney, aided by two other Holdman stalwarts, Bill White and Steve Malone.

The Dobbert case was a tangle of horrible violence and strange jurisprudence. First, the violence: John Dobbert was raised by a brutally abusive father, and, like many abused children, grew up to abuse his own kids. John and Virginia Dobbert had four children, none of whom John wanted, and the parents often vented their rages on the kids. Husband and wife were both abusive, but John was the worst. He hit the kids, kicked them, beat them with belts and sticks. Once he held his eldest son's hand over a gas flame until the skin blistered. When Virginia went to jail in 1971 for kiting checks, Dobbert pleaded with her to let him send the kids to live with her parents—he couldn't handle the responsibility. But Virginia insisted that she would divorce him if he gave up on the family. Bitter, overwhelmed, and vicious, Dobbert responded with even worse outrages. He broke bones, gouged eyes, kicked stomachs, held heads under water until the children were nearly drowned. The trailer where the Dobberts lived soon looked like a hospital ward: John III, who was eleven, had suppurating wounds on his back; the eldest daughter, Kelly, who was nine, had internal injuries so severe she couldn't eat; Ryder, seven, could scarcely walk; Honore, five, cowered in fear.

Neighbors informed authorities that the Dobbert children were being abused, but the resulting investigations—there were at least three —produced no action. Once a nurse and a policeman filed reports that commended Dobbert's handling of "a bad situation." (John III and Honore eventually won a million-dollar settlement from the City of

Jacksonville.) The horror of the Dobbert home was not discovered until John III ran away. He was found in a city park, limping, infected, and blind in one eye.

The boy told police a ghastly story. His sister Kelly had choked to death on her own vomit the previous December, and Ryder had died in February. Both were buried in a field somewhere, the boy said: He had been forced to hold the flashlight as his father dug the graves. A few days after police found John III, little Honore turned up on the doorstep of a Fort Lauderdale hospital. She was clutching a teddy bear, two dollars, and her grandmother's name and phone number.

The FBI found Dobbert seven months later in Houston, reunited with his wife. At trial, the surviving son, John III, told a story that differed slightly, but crucially, from the one he had first told police. His father had strangled his sister to death, he said. She had not choked on vomit; it was murder. Solely on the strength of this testimony (the bodies were never found), Dobbert was convicted of first-degree murder in the death of his daughter Kelly. He was also convicted of second-degree murder in Ryder's death (second-degree because the State could not prove Dobbert intended to kill the boy) and of child abuse and torture.

Dobbert's case tested a trial judge's power to override a jury's recommended sentence. His jury voted 10 to 2 in favor of life in prison. Why, when faced with such facts, had so many jurors opted for mercy? They might have felt Dobbert's own abuse as a child had partly fueled his later offenses. Or perhaps they believed that city authorities shared some piece of the blame for failing to take the children from this wretched man. Maybe some believed Dobbert's own statement that Kelly had choked on her own vomit, and that he was trying to resuscitate her when she died.

But was that last theory possible? The jurors had convicted Dobbert of first-degree murder, which requires an intent to kill. But the trial judge, for some inexplicable reason, had given the jury an outdated, unconstitutional instruction. If Kelly had died during "an abominable and detestable crime against nature," the judge told the jury, it was first-degree murder, "even though there is no premeditated design or intent to kill." This instruction had been stricken from the books;

nevertheless, the judge gave it no fewer than six times during his charge to the jury.

This glitch might have explained why the jurors could vote for first-degree murder while still believing that Kelly had not been strangled. But then the judge had overruled their recommendation of mercy. Pat Doherty attacked the judge's decision, based on the Florida Supreme Court's 1975 ruling that a jury's recommendation must be followed unless the facts supporting a death sentence were "so clear and convincing that virtually no reasonable person could differ." Surely, he reasoned, at least one of the ten jurors who had voted in favor of mercy for John Dobbert qualified as a "reasonable person."

As Doherty learned more about the trial, he liked this issue even more. After all, the reason for allowing judges to override jurors was that Florida's lawmakers thought calm, experienced judges might be called on to check inflamed emotions. But Dobbert's trial judge was not a calm man. Hudson Olliff wielded a gavel of doom; by 1984, Olliff had ignored more jury recommendations than any judge in America. He sent men to death with an eccentric flair, salting his orders with harrowing memories of his experiences as a combat soldier in World War II. Clerks in appellate courts from Tallahassee to Washington grew so accustomed to Olliff's rhetoric that some took to parodies: "I've seen war! I've seen concentration camps! But never have I seen anything as awful as this!" Pat Doherty found it hard to imagine that appellate courts would think Hudson Olliff was more reasonable than ten Dobbert jurors.

But Doherty had something more on his side as he fought to block Dobbert's second death warrant. When the first warrant had been signed in 1982, Doherty had received a telephone call from Dobbert's son, John III, whose testimony had been the key to the death sentence. Now a young man, John III told Doherty that he had lied in court. His first statement to police, that Kelly had choked on her own vomit, was the truth. Doherty was in the middle of a trial when he received this phone call. He contacted Millard Farmer, the tireless warrior, explained the situation, and asked Farmer to go to Wisconsin to get a sworn statement. "I'm packing a bag," Farmer drawled.

"I did not testify truthfully about the cause of my sister Kelly's death at the trial," John III said in the notarized document. The boy told Farmer that he had feared his father might get out of jail; he "wanted to be sure he'd be locked up where I'd be safe from him." John III also said he had heightened his testimony in hopes of pleasing his social worker, a woman who'd shown him more kindness than he had ever known. And he said he had been under the influence of Thorazine and hypnosis when he had testified.

The boy's statement had won Dobbert a stay of execution. In keeping with procedure, the matter had been sent back to Judge Olliff, who dismissed the new evidence with a wave of his hand. Characteristically, Olliff began his ruling with a combat-related anecdote. "This case has been pending for a longer period of time than this nation was involved in World War II and the Korean War combined." Then he brusquely pronounced that there was "no evidence or proof" that the testimony was untrue. Olliff's judgment was affirmed by the state supreme court, which opened the door for the second death warrant.

Now Doherty went back to the state supreme court, attacking the override, the flawed jury instructions, and Olliff's cursory look at John III's new testimony. For good measure, he attacked the fact that John III's testimony had been enhanced by hypnosis. The justices in Tallahassee rejected every issue. (Later that year, in another case, the same court ruled that testimony "enhanced" by hypnosis was inadmissible in Florida trials. The slippery law just wouldn't hold still.)

The federal courts deferred to the courts in Florida, clearing the way for Dobbert's execution. U.S. Supreme Court Justices William Brennan and Thurgood Marshall, the embattled foes of the death penalty, wrote especially strong dissents on behalf of Dobbert, however. Brennan called Olliff's treatment of John III's recantation "absurd on its face." He charged that Olliff's mind had been made up even before he saw the son's affidavit.

Marshall latched onto the unconstitutional jury instruction. Granted, he wrote, the jury instruction did not change the fact that "Dobbert abused and tortured his children," nor did it alter the truth that Dobbert's attacks on his dead daughter had been "callous and reckless." But if the child's death was not premeditated, it was not a capital offense in Florida. Had that been clear to Dobbert's jury? No appellate court had ever tried seriously to find out. "Dobbert is certainly no innocent man," Marshall wrote, "but he may well be a guilty one to whom Florida's legislators have not chosen to apply the death penalty."

On September 7, 1984—after a tearful reconciliation with his daughter Honore—Earnest John Dobbert Jr. was electrocuted, a few minutes after 10 A.M.

To Laurence Tribe, the liberal professor of constitutional law at Harvard Law School, the Dobbert case stood out above all others as a sign that the U.S. Supreme Court cared less about the strictures of law than about keeping "the grim line of the condemned moving briskly." Even the appellate prosecutor on the case, Carolyn Snurkowski of the attorney general's office, was a little surprised that she won. "It was certainly a case with a lot of issues," she said.

If the Dobbert case raised so many issues, why did he get a pass to Old Sparky? Judges are not immune to abominations such as drenched the Dobbert case. Reporters called Dobbert "the most hated man on death row"; perhaps some of the judges who considered his appeals had seen that in print. Actually, Dobbert was well liked in prison. Warden Richard Dugger, who gave the order for the executioner to trip the switch, was particularly troubled by killing Dobbert. "I got to know him at the very end," Dugger later explained, "and somehow, despite what he had done, I didn't think he was an evil man. I think he just couldn't cope with all the demands on him. Sitting down to talk to him was like sitting down to talk to an uncle. You can never see to the heart of a bad person, but after a number of years around killers, you begin to think you can tell a few things."

Pat Doherty once asked his client how he had come to be known as the worst man in that vile place. "Beats me," Dobbert answered. "No one's ever said an unkind word to me here. These have been the happiest days of my life. I couldn't hack it outside."

Two weeks later, James Dupree Henry, another client of Dick Burr and Craig Barnard and the West Palm Beach public defender's office, was executed for the felony murder of Z. L. Riley, an Orlando civil rights leader. Henry had bound and gagged Riley during a robbery; the old man had suffocated on the gag. For his last meal, Henry asked for a dozen raw oysters because he had never tasted them and wondered what the fuss was about. He liked them fine.

Speaking on behalf of the victim's family, William Riley, the son of the murdered man, issued a plea to Governor Graham to spare Henry's life: "If my father taught me anything about life, it is that God gives life and only He has the right to take it away. We suffered as a family when my father died, and we ask you not to add to our suffering by killing James Dupree Henry."

Graham's response had an odd tinge of poor taste—odd because it came from a man who was widely admired for his graciousness and sensitivity. Not only did Graham ignore the family's plea for mercy; in his postexecution statement released to the press the governor expressed "special sympathy to the family of Mr. Henry's victim," and said he hoped the execution would affirm "our respect for such a life." It was one thing to disregard the family's wishes; government policy can't be dictated by individuals. Graham would never order an execution just because a victim's family begged him for it, and neither would he prevent one. But after the deed was finished, it was a gaffe to suggest that he had somehow honored the family.

A gaffe, even a small one, was surprising coming from Graham, for his handling of the death penalty had been nothing short of masterful. He took office in 1979 with a reputation as a doe-eyed liberal, a pushover for the tougher titans of the state legislature. During his first legislative session, the bosses ran roughshod over him; he had little to boast of beyond a repeal of the auto inspection law. Graham's handling of the legislature was so weak that the *St. Petersburg Times* eventually dubbed him "Governor Jello."

But ever since he had captivated the Florida voters with his "Workdays"—those media-friendly campaign events in which he had sweated and strained and dirtied his hands—Graham's strength had become his tie to common people. And none of them saw a weakling in the governor's office. They saw a man willing to make life-and-death decisions, to stand up in the face of intense criticism and do the will of the people. Tallahassee insiders may have believed Graham lacked the tenacity to carry out an execution. Looking back on the first, Tom Fiedler, the *Miami Herald*'s Tallahassee correspondent at the time, said: "I thought sure he wouldn't go through with it. I thought if he had to look Mrs. Spenkelink in the face, he would blink." Graham had not blinked, and voters had decided he was tough because he had delivered on a tough task. Over time, Graham translated that strength in the eyes of the voters into strength in the eyes of the legislature. In a very real sense, his stance on the death penalty enabled him to govern effectively.

And yet Graham wisely chose not to beat his breast over capital punishment. Though the vast majority of Floridians supported the death penalty, few took joy in it. True, there were some who protested the state's mandatory seat belt law by plastering their bumpers with strips proclaiming, "I'll buckle up when Bundy does," referring to the most infamous killer on death row. A Miami man even ordered vanity license plates that said FRY TED. But most people wanted the death penalty carried out with dignity; it was a grim but necessary business in their eyes, and they would not have approved of a governor who seemed to be gleeful about it. Bob Graham, with his tight-lipped, solemn determination, his refusal to discuss specific cases in public, and his way of ordering each execution with a reverent, even sorrowful "God save us all," struck the perfect chord.

Opponents of the death penalty recognized Graham's virtuosity. He was paving a road for liberal Democrats to the popular side of the issue. To Mike Mello, the cerebral young lawyer in Craig Barnard's shop, Graham was "a model for all the Southern, New Democrat governors" on the death penalty. "He signed enough warrants, but not too many; ordered enough executions, but not too many." Graham pushed hard for the death penalty and complained about the chaotic appeals process—but even when the breakthrough came in 1984, and Old Sparky cranked up for serious work, Graham never gloated. He stayed on key, his pitch was virtuosic.

Graham pushed, firmly but quietly; the Florida Bar was still nowhere in sight; and Scharlette Holdman kept dialing, pleading for volunteers. She talked Tom McCoun of Saint Petersburg into taking the case of Timothy Palmes when the inmate's death warrant was signed. McCoun knew what awaited him, having waged the losing battle for Anthony Antone. When Antone's first death warrant had been signed, McCoun had cobbled together an appeal in just ten days of nonstop labor and had won a stay. He had used the extra time to examine the case more thoroughly, and turned up some new issues. But after Antone's second death warrant, when McCoun had tried to raise the new issues he had found, the courts had refused to hear anything not contained in the first filing. Up and down the line, courts were getting tougher. They wanted "finality." No second chances—even if your first chance was only ten days.

But like any good death penalty lawyer, McCoun also knew that the only predictable thing about these cases was that they were impossible to predict. As he set to work for Timothy Palmes's life, McCoun figured his strongest option was Craig Barnard's challenge to the limits on favorable evidence—sooner or later, judges might begin to see the light on that. Same with the racial disparities. As for the specific facts of the Palmes case, McCoun didn't have much to work with. In 1976, Palmes and his friend Ronald Straight approached a Jacksonville furniture store owner, asking for work as bill collectors. The businessman, James Stone, declined. Palmes and Straight, who had met in prison, looked too tough to Stone—strong-arm tactics weren't good business. Weeks later, Stone's body was found in a homemade coffin, weighted with concrete, in the St. John's River.

At the trial, the store's bookkeeper testified that she had lured Stone to her home, where Palmes and Straight tied him up and stabbed him to death. Palmes and Straight were both sentenced to death; the bookkeeper went free in exchange for her testimony.

Graham signed Palmes's death warrant the day after John Dobbert was executed. Tom McCoun filed an appeal based on Barnard's theories about favorable evidence and racial disparities, and included a claim that the bookkeeper's testimony was unreliable because she had given it to save her own neck. Once again, the first two issues were denied. As for the third, well, the trial prosecutor offered the best answer. "You've got three rats and you've only got two bullets," he told a reporter.

"What are you going to do?" Palmes died in the electric chair on November 8, 1984, the ninth man executed in Florida in a year.

Across the country, twenty-two people had been executed in twelve months, almost half of them in Florida. At last, it seemed, the death penalty logjam was broken. As was customary, Florida took a break for the holidays.

Craig Barnard loved the law, and this love was his deep keel; it kept him on a steady course when he lost so many fights. His love kept him on track, and balanced, as people were melting down around him. The law, at its best, promised rationality in an irrational time, dispassion amid raging emotions, predictability in place of wanton chance.

Even many of his opponents recognized Barnard's devotion and admired him for it. At the attorney general's office, there was a lot of contempt for most of the lawyers who opposed the death penalty, but in general the prosecutors made an exception for Barnard because he stuck to the law. "Always on target, always compelling," said Carolyn Snurkowski, the rising star of Florida's capital prosecutors. One time the attorney general caught wind of two lawyers from the Miami public defender's office going outside their jurisdiction to aid a death row inmate and the prosecutors cracked down hard on the violation. But Barnard did the same thing all the time; he had a finger, at least, in nearly every Florida death case. Dick Burr, Barnard's assistant, had a capital appeal in North Carolina! The prosecutors let Barnard get away with such things because they respected him. As one explained, "We didn't feel the need to yank his chain."

Judges mostly appreciated him too, even as they complained about all the repetitive work he generated. Barnard was always cordial and well prepared; his demeanor was not fiery or confrontational. He argued cases lawyer to lawyer, as if the courtroom were a symposium where everyone had gathered to seek good answers to hard questions. And he was gentle with everyone, from chief judges to file clerks. Barnard felt so comfortable in the Florida Supreme Court that he often called it "my court," and folks in the white marble building on Duval Street liked him right back. Once, he flew from West Palm Beach to

Tallahassee to argue a last-ditch appeal, but his luggage wound up in Jacksonville. The only clothes he had were the jeans he was wearing, and he couldn't go to court in jeans. The stores were all closed for the night; he was due in court first thing in the morning. So while a friend in Jacksonville scrambled to find the bag, Barnard called Sid White, clerk of the state supreme court, and told him what had happened. The bag arrived in time, but forever afterward when Barnard showed up at the courthouse people would grin and say, "Hey, it's the guy with no pants!"

He was the rock. Yet as the strain accumulated, even Barnard began to show it. He smoked more, ate more, left the office less. He kept a coffeepot and a small refrigerator by his desk so he could save the time of walking down the hall. His epilepsy was under control—as long as he took his medicine—but the weight and the pipe smoke and the caffeine and the stress were making him look like a poster boy for the American Heart Association. Barnard had hired Susan Cary to represent his office at the state prison, and she began to worry about her boss and friend. Cary was into all sorts of esoteric philosophies, and one day, with Margaret Vandiver, she visited Barnard's office and secretly popped a New Age tape into his stereo. It was one of those subliminal-message productions—just soothing music, but supposedly there were urgent pleadings underneath that would curb the appetite. The tape played about three minutes before Barnard said, "Want something to eat?" and lumbered toward his refrigerator. "I'm starved!" Vandiver chimed in, reaching for a candy bar.

What bothered Barnard most, perhaps even more than the executions themselves, were the growing haste and impatience with which the courts were treating his appeals. This wasn't the law he loved. For more than a decade, courts had been cartwheeling and somersaulting and reversing themselves, reinterpreting the death penalty from one case to the next. The courts had said mitigation was limited in Florida, then turned around and said it was unlimited. They had imposed the "reasonable person" standard for overriding jury recommendations, then back-flipped to affirm death sentences where juries had unanimously recommended life. They had upheld Florida's procedure for determining an inmate's sanity, then about-faced and struck the procedure down. They had accepted evidence of racial disparities to block death sentences in Georgia and rejected the same argument across the border in Florida. The courts weren't being arbitrary on purpose. Craig Barnard respected the courts, he liked the judges, and he knew they were struggling with a uniquely slippery law. What frustrated him was the way they appeared to be throwing up their hands, blaming the chaos on defense attorneys, and angrily sending his clients to the chair.

Barnard had a grand plan in his head. Step by step, case by case, he wanted to lead the courts through the job of nailing down the law. Set a standard for the override and then stick to it. Admit the mistake about mitigation and then correct it. Define competent counsel and then guarantee it. Measure racial disparities and then face up to them. Compare death sentences to life sentences and make them balance. People could say that he was trying to thwart justice, to delay the inevitable forever. In his self-assured heart Barnard believed he was defending justice. The "inevitable" was not inevitable; he and his colleagues won half their appeals. Barnard's questions were genuine. Answering those questions was an arduous prospect, but he believed the law—The Law, his love—required that they be answered, and it was going to take patience and flexibility and candor from the courts.

And he believed ultimately the courts would conclude that the precision promised by the modern death penalty was impossible to attain. When that fact became clear, he trusted that the courts would abolish the practice forever.

Ray Marky had his own grand design, which was in many ways the opposite of Barnard's: Marky was trying to advance the death penalty while Barnard was trying to stop it. Marky wanted to narrow the appellate field; Barnard wanted to widen it. Marky wanted judges to say no to death row inmates on a predictable basis; Barnard wanted them to say yes. But they shared this yearning for consistency, and both men knew consistency was in short supply. Marky was becoming just as frustrated as Barnard was with the corrosive effect of the death penalty on the courts. They differed a bit on the cause of the problem, but they agreed on the result: The death penalty was making a mockery of the law, which was Marky's love, too.

"Look, I may be naïve," Marky once said, "but the Rule of Law means something to me. It's not just a Fourth of July speech that we all wink at and forget. From that perspective, the death penalty is an absolute abomination." This from one of America's leading death penalty prosecutors. "It's frustrating, it's incoherent, it's impossible. Because we don't have any rational, equal application of the law." Marky paused a moment, seething. "You can ask: Is that the result of the complexity of the system? Is it the result of somebody's social agenda? Whatever. It's irrelevant. The result is what matters, and the result is that we don't have the fair, even, principled application of a penalty for a class of cases. I look at guys who avoid the death penalty, and I look back at Spenkelink, and I say, 'This system is crazy.'"

It took a lot of knowledge of the law, and a lot of experience in the courts, to understand the feelings of Craig Barnard and Ray Marky, the sense they shared that capital punishment was disfiguring the legal process. For most people, feelings about the death penalty came from the gut. Murder rates soared. Local newscasts were ghoulish parades of sheeted corpses. Citizens could not be blamed for imagining a river of blood coursing through the land, the skies raining bullets, ravenous predators roaming the streets. Fear is visceral, and often overmasters reason. Horror trumps analysis.

America had become, in millions of people's minds, a place where their children couldn't walk to school, where they couldn't carry their groceries to their cars, where they couldn't sleep soundly without bars on the windows. Working the night shift in a convenience store was like going over the top at Gallipoli. It hit people hard, up under the ribs; it made them want to throw up, made them want to strike back, made them want to see the good guys win for a change.

And so inevitably the day came when more people journeyed to Starke to celebrate an execution than to protest. January 30, 1985—the brisk pace of Florida executions was continuing. The holidays were over, J. D. Raulerson was headed for the chair. Raulerson was a stick-up man, a rapist, and the killer of a young policeman. Some eighty lawmen from Jacksonville called in sick or took vacation to be there when he died. They awaited the moment in the pasture across State Road 16 from the prison.

Some wore T-shirts lettered "Crank Up Old Sparky" or "Raulerson, Make My Day." Some hooted and jeered at the handful of protesters keeping a candlelight vigil; one or two spit loudly in the direction of the prayer circle. "They ought to put a pot roast in his lap!" someone shouted. "The bacon's sizzlin' now," said another. They roared and guffawed. Someone was singing in a merry voice, "Turn out the lights, the party's over." A state senator from Jacksonville, worried about the way this might look, worked reporters in the pasture: "These boys have been waiting a long time for this. If they're a little jubilant, are you going to put that in the paper?"

One sheriff's deputy stood a little to the side of his rowdy peers and gazed in the thin light of dawn at a flock of gulls wheeling and diving over the prison grounds. His name was Jim English; it was his partner, Mike Stewart, who was killed by J. D. Raulerson in a gunfight. They caught Raulerson and a cousin robbing a seafood restaurant and raping a waitress. Under his shirt, English still bore the scars of a bullet he took in the battle; in his gut he still carried a mournful longing for his lost friend.

He watched the birds light in the empty space between pasture and prison. He watched them rise, like a cloud, back into the sky. "I was thinking of the time that Mike and I went out on a boat in the river and chased seagulls around for a couple of hours," he said sadly. "Seeing those birds over the prison reminded me of that."

Inside the execution chamber, a burly man with a deeply etched face sat expectantly on the edge of a small spectator's seat, his weight poised on the balls of his feet, his eyes fastened on the door behind the chair. When the door opened, Jack Stewart saw his son's killer: rangy, slack, bald head slathered with white goo. Stewart continued to watch grimly as Raulerson was strapped in, hooded, and electrocuted.

Nearly ten years before, Jack Stewart had stood over the grave of his dead son and sworn that he would see the killer killed. Through those long years he had often imagined what it would be like—imagined a struggle to strap Raulerson into the chair, imagined a writhing body at the end of the wire, imagined screaming and gore. He kept his graveside promise but it was not as he had imagined. "There was no force," he mused. "There was no fight."

When it was over, Jack Stewart emerged from the death chamber into the now-bright morning. "How do you feel, Mr. Stewart?" a reporter asked. "A little weak," Stewart answered, blinking away tears. The great yearning in his gut was not gone, not entirely. He yearned still and would yearn evermore for a son he had loved and lost. But the part of him that ached for justice was salved at last. "This puts some of it to rest," he said, and he spoke for aching millions.

WITT DIES IN FIRST "ROUTINE" EXECUTION, said the *Florida Times-Union* headline on March 7, 1985. The previous morning, Johnny Paul Witt—who had suffocated an eleven-year-old boy with a gag and mutilated the body—had gone to the electric chair without drama or significant public demonstrations. "Witt's eleven predecessors in Florida's oak electric chair since the death penalty ban was lifted had all received one-day court reprieves before their executions," noted the *Times-Union*'s Andrea Rowand. "But for Witt, there were no temporary stays, no last meal and no last words."

The dead were beginning to run together in the public mind, to become mere numbers. The press stopped thronging to the executions, their accounts shortened and slid to the inside pages. It might have seemed that, after a dozen years, the death penalty machinery was finally cranked up and cruising in the State of Florida. But that was not the case. Florida was now executing criminals at a rate unseen in a quarter century, but for every cell emptied by Old Sparky, another five death row cells were being filled. Despite the executions, death row was sprawling like a Gulf Coast suburb, gobbling up tier after tier of the state prison. Death row had turned into death town.

And Florida could not keep up even this insufficient pace. Just days after the "first routine execution," the death penalty machinery once again ground to a halt.

Scharlette Holdman had finally run out of lawyers. Two inmates were facing imminent execution; neither one had an attorney. And no matter how much she begged, charmed, and wheedled, Holdman could not get anyone to take their cases. James Rinaman's project for the Florida Bar was up and running by this time, but when reporters called him to ask about Holdman's crisis, he insisted that last-ditch efforts were not his line of work. "To ask a civil firm to jump in when there's a week or two left is just not appropriate for the lawyer or for the prisoner himself," Rinaman said. No help was forthcoming from that quarter.

For the first time, Florida faced the question: Would the State execute a man who had no lawyer? "It was bound to happen sooner or later," Holdman told reporters. "I long ago exhausted every person I knew." It seemed unlikely that James Agan, the first of the two inmates, would be allowed to slip through to the chair. Substantial mystery still clung to Agan's case, and surely some court somewhere would grant a stay until it was cleared up. While serving a life sentence at Florida State Prison (minimum twenty-five years), Agan had confessed to stabbing another inmate to death. But after he was sentenced to die, he recounted a curious tale: He said prison investigators, desperate to solve the killing, had offered him a deal. Agan was past fifty years old at the time, with more than twenty years to go before his first crack at parole. In all likelihood he would not live to see the end of his sentence. Agan said the investigators promised him another life sentence, essentially meaningless, and a transfer to a nicer facility if he would take the rap and close their case. Of course, the investigators denied any such deal was ever struck. But they did express doubts that Agan was actually guilty. "There are questions that need to be answered," prison sergeant Leonard Ball said. It was hard to imagine that Agan would be executed without a hearing.

Robert Waterhouse was another matter. From the record, he looked like an excellent candidate for execution. Paroled from a life sentence for murder in New York, Waterhouse moved to St. Petersburg, where he raped a young woman, bludgeoned her with a tire iron, and dumped her into Tampa Bay to drown. He was an archetype: the paroled killer who kills again. If anyone could be executed without benefit of an appellate lawyer, it might very well be Waterhouse. The shortage of volunteer lawyers had finally come to a head, and that head belonged to Robert Waterhouse.

Craig Barnard couldn't take the case himself; it was too flagrantly beyond his jurisdiction. As always, though, he was ready to consult. Panicky, Scharlette Holdman contacted Stephen Bright, a brilliant death penalty lawyer in Atlanta who had recently fought and lost the last appeals for J. D. Raulerson. With days left before Waterhouse was slated to die, Holdman begged him to take the case.

Bright argued that it would be ridiculous for him to plunge in so late in the game. He knew he could throw together an appeal, and he would almost certainly win a stay—the Waterhouse case had never been heard in federal court. But the trial transcript alone was 2,200 pages, and if he missed something important in his rush to win the stay, the courts might refuse to consider a new appeal later. It had happened to Tom McCoun in the Antone case, and to Barnard in the Adams case.

Bright had a proposal. What if he simply asked for a stay without filing his appeal? Just go to court and say, Look, Your Honor, I just got this case, I think there are issues, but there's not enough time to investigate. And I refuse to file an appeal just to give the appearance of fair representation. The strategy was essentially: We dare you to kill this man without a lawyer. On the other hand, this business of scrambling around wildly for last-minute volunteers had to stop. Now was the time, Bright argued.

They hardly had any choice. Scharlette Holdman was out of lawyers. Craig Barnard's team was handling fourteen cases and offering advice on dozens more. Millard Farmer was swamped, the Inc. Fund was swamped, the big firms in New York and Washington had reached the limits of their pro bono generosity. The Florida Bar project was not interested in last-minute undertakings. Florida's death row was pushing 230 inmates. If the lawyer shortage was not faced now, it would have to be faced soon.

On Friday, March 15—four days before Waterhouse was to die— Steve Bright stood before Judge Robert Beach in St. Petersburg and asked for a stay of execution. He told Beach he had taken the case because no one else would. He hadn't had time to read the trial transcript, let alone time enough to hunt down witnesses, study his client's past, schedule psychiatric examinations, dig up police records. He refused to file a hasty appeal.

Judge Beach granted the stay. "I think if the State is going to execute Mr. Waterhouse, it should be done with the same due process as all of those who preceded him." The grammar was awkward, but the significance was plain. When the Florida Supreme Court refused to overturn Beach's order—and upheld a similar order in James Agan's case—Scharlette Holdman's burden was abruptly shifted to the State of Florida.

The government's dilemma was simple: There would be no executions without defense lawyers, and there were no more defense lawyers. Florida voters demanded executions—so Florida politicians were going to have to solve the lawyer shortage. It was one of those weird ironies that democracy spits up now and again. To please pro–death penalty voters, Florida officials were forced to find anti–death penalty lawyers. The death penalty was turning out to be a whole lot more complicated than anyone had anticipated.

Attorney General Jim Smith, who was spending perhaps a million dollars a year or more trying to put men into the chair, now proposed a bill that would spend close to a million dollars a year for lawyers who would be trying to keep men out of the chair. When the Florida Supreme Court blocked the Waterhouse case, Smith went into overdrive, preparing a bill to provide state-paid lawyers to handle the death row appeals.

While Smith worked, another man was electrocuted—the last, it turned out, in 1985, and the last in the string of almost monthly executions that had started with Bob Sullivan. Marvin Francois had a lawyer, a gifted workaholic from North Carolina named Mark Olive. Olive had been recruited to run the Florida Bar's volunteer lawyers project; his appearance on the scene was a huge shot in the arm for Scharlette Holdman and her beleaguered troops. With help from the Barnard team, Olive plunged into the Marvin Francois's violent past.

The man's crime was enormous. In 1977, with three accomplices, Francois, a heroin addict, robbed a family of drug dealers in their suburban Miami home. When his mask slipped, exposing his face, Francois decided the witnesses must die. He lined them up—all eight of them—facedown on the floor and shot each one in the head. Miraculously, two survived to testify.

Olive pulled together a harrowing tale, "maybe the most tortured background I've ever seen," according to Barnard's colleague Dick Burr. But this potential mitigating evidence, unknown at the trial, came too late. Francois had already exhausted a full round of appeals, and on his second try the courts agreed that six murder victims outweighed any mitigation. On May 29, 1985, Marvin Francois was electrocuted. He died cursing white people: "If there is such a thing as the Antichrist, it is not one man, but the whole white race," he said as he sat strapped in the electric chair.

Francois had asked that his ashes be scattered in Africa. Susan Cary, the longtime activist who was Craig Barnard's intermediary at the prison, was determined that this last wish would be honored. But it was one thing to find bus fare for a condemned man's family, and quite another to raise the money for a trip to Africa. Cary collected the cremated remains of Marvin Francois and put them in a shoebox in her closet, where they sat for two years while she tried to figure out how to get them across the ocean.

In 1987, Michael Radelet, Cary's friend and fellow activist, announced that he was going to Senegal to visit a relative. Take Marvin, Cary suggested. Radelet was game, but there were rules—human remains can't just be toted from country to country. Uncertain as to the relevant legalities, Radelet contacted John Conyers, a prominent black congressman from Detroit; Conyers strongly opposed the death penalty, he was well known in Africa, and he had offered more than once to help Florida's anti–death penalty crusaders any way he could. The congressman pulled the right strings, and shortly before his trip Radelet received an official letter announcing that the Senegalese government would be happy to welcome "Brother Marvin" home.

Like Scharlette Holdman and Pat Doherty, Radelet had a darkly comic view of the world. Traipsing around Senegal, shoebox in hand, he would place the box on the opposite chair at restaurants and say things like "Marvin, would you like some water?" On sightseeing jaunts, he would take snapshots of the shoebox in front of important buildings and picturesque vistas. Finally, Radelet carried the box to a bluff outside Dakar, a lovely spot with the city in the distance and the Atlantic spread out below. He took one more snapshot—"Marvin at the seashore"—then opened the box and sprinkled the ashes on the sun-glittered waves. As he gazed into the oceanic expanse, it occurred to him that this very water might have rocked and sloshed all the way from Florida; now, the waves lapped the shores of Africa, bearing the remains of Marvin Francois to his dreamland.

Actually, as Radelet knew, not all of Marvin Francois made it to Africa. Radelet was an associate professor of sociology at the University of Florida, and one evening in 1985 he found himself talking about executions with a colleague from the psychiatry faculty. The man mentioned that his wife, a neurobiologist, had a collection of brain samples taken from the men who had died in Old Sparky.

This piqued Radelet's interest, to say the least, and he did a little digging. Back in 1979, some inmates had charged that John Spenkelink was beaten before he went to the chair, so the local coroner had begun performing routine autopsies after each execution. (The exception was Anthony Antone, who asked that his body be left intact for the afterlife.) Radelet learned that the coroner, without telling the families of the dead men, was making a practice of removing a piece of each brain —the amygdala, believed to be the seat of aggression—for a research project at the university. The idea was that head injuries in childhood might have damaged the amygdalas of these lethally aggressive men.

It is, of course, debatable just how much you can learn from a brain that has been cooked by two thousand volts of alternating current. In any case, the project never got very far because shortly after Radelet's chat with his colleague, he got carried away at his weekly seminar on the death penalty. A student posed a question about executions and Radelet countered: "Well, that's nothing. Right here at this very institution they are keeping the brains of these men in buckets." A reporter, Bruce Krasnow of the *Florida Times-Union,* was auditing the seminar. And as Radelet later observed, "There are some things a reporter just can't resist. Like the phrase 'brains in a bucket.' That really got Bruce's attention."

Krasnow's story led to front-page articles in Miami and St. Petersburg—even in *The Washington Post*. No one was ever able to say whether the practice was illegal or unethical, but it sure was creepy. That was the end of the project.

Attorney General Jim Smith made a personal appearance before the Florida Senate's Judiciary Committee in the late spring of 1985 to push his bill to solve the lawyer shortage. "Mr. Chairman and members of the committee," he began, "I'd like to take just a minute or two to talk with you about a catch-22 that, uh, relates to capital punishment in Florida. . . . We had our first execution in modern times in Florida in 1979. Since that time, death row inmates have been represented by essentially volunteer lawyers. We've got a lot of lawyers from out of state come into Florida and represent these people. . . . We're at a point in time now, though, where that category of volunteers is really running out."

Smith explained the recent state supreme court actions, and issued a warning: "I can see capital punishment in Florida coming to a grinding halt." That grabbed the senators like a python, and they listened intently to a proposal that would normally have struck them as outrageous. Smith outlined a request for more than $800,000 to hire lawyers, secretaries, and investigators to handle "collateral" appeals for condemned inmates—that is, the steps after the automatic review required by law. "I don't think we want to see this process stagnate," he said. "I think Florida, as we have been on this issue, should stay ahead of the curve and let's appropriate this money and get on with it."

One senator immediately recognized the problem with all this. "Now, how do you feel that the taxpayers are going to feel to have to pick up a second defense of these individuals?" he asked.

"Well," Smith answered, "I think that means executions will continue in Florida. . . . I don't think you have any problem."

"Can you guarantee that that's going to speed up the process?" the lawmaker persisted.

Having had five years of experience with the new death penalty, Smith answered carefully: "I can't guarantee anything." However, he could promise that without lawyers the process would slow down. This deflated the legislators a bit; they wanted to be able to tell voters that the money would be a down payment on a busier Old Sparky.

Smith moved to another tack, appealing to Florida pride. "You know, we're a big state," he said. "The people in this state want capital punishment and I think we ought to provide the resources to make it happen. As a lawyer and as attorney general it has been embarrassing that we've had these volunteers coming down here always making snide remarks about the legal processes of our state. Like we're trying to rush these people to judgment. That kind of thing, which is clearly not true."

The mention of these snide outsiders prompted a question from another committee member. "We're only going to permit members of the Florida Bar Association to defend someone?"

"We can't really, you know, do that."

Aghast, another member asked, "Some of this money would go to lawyers from, just as an example, New York?"

"No sir!" a horrified Smith responded. (Folks in North Florida hate New York lawyers.) "We're talking about hiring full-time attorneys to be there on a full-time basis to do this work," he said. Mollified, the senate committee approved the bill. Despite the blatant unpopularity of the concept—taxing death penalty supporters to pay lawyers for condemned inmates—the proposal glided through the legislature and was signed into law in June 1985. A new state agency was created, its name stupefyingly bureaucratic: the Office of Capital Collateral Representative (CCR).

Jim Smith was the key: Lawmakers knew he was gung ho on the death penalty. If Smith said this distasteful step had to be taken, then the legislature would take the step. And though he wouldn't "guarantee" more executions, he expected them. Eight men had been executed in 1984; once CCR was up and running, the annual number might be twice that, Smith predicted. "We haven't hit our stride yet," he said.

∴

The people who had fought so long and hard against the death penalty had mixed feelings about Florida's new state agency to defend death row inmates. Millard Farmer, for example, was strongly opposed. Farmer saw the state turning their cause into a bureaucracy; he saw the grinding pressures of popular political opinion controlling the purse strings, the caseload, even the hiring and firing at CCR. He urged Scharlette Holdman to resist, to keep her office open, urged her to wrest as many cases as possible from the hands of government lawyers.

But Holdman knew she had come to the end of her rope. "We have no choice but to believe people will be better represented with the state funding for this office," she said. The legislature had appropriated some $840,000, after all, for the first nine months of CCR's operations. Holdman, just a year before, had had to screw up her courage to speak of a mere quarter million. She loathed bureaucrats as much as Farmer did, but she believed that these unimagined resources would do more good than harm.

Her hopes would be greatly strengthened if Craig Barnard would head CCR. Barnard agonized over the prospect. In long conversations with colleagues, he acknowledged what they all knew to be true: He was the perfect person for the job. Nothing could be more natural than for Craig Barnard to become the official general of the death penalty defense. He knew the law better than anyone, and he knew how to manage a government agency. Barnard was confident he could have the job if he wanted it. The head of CCR would be appointed by the governor, but the governor would choose from a list submitted by the state's elected public defenders. Barnard was a legend among the public defenders, a shining star of their system. He could count on the strongest possible endorsement from them.

He disagreed, however, with the charter of the new agency. Barnard foresaw that once the state began hiring full-time lawyers to file death penalty appeals, private attorneys would stop volunteering to take cases. This, he believed, would be a disaster. In case after case, he had seen lawyers who were lukewarm on the death penalty—even lawyers who supported it—changed utterly by the experience of litigating a capital appeal. "We talked about this over and over," Dick Burr recalled. "Time after time, lawyers had seen the vagaries of the system, the lousy performance by trial attorneys, instances of incomplete investigations by prosecutors and police. And it was turning lawyers from some very powerful firms against the death penalty." Barnard strongly supported the Florida Bar's project to recruit and assist volunteers from the big law firms. Little by little, he imagined, this project might turn the power of the legal establishment to his side. CCR, he felt, could undercut that effort. "We couldn't afford to give that up," Burr said.

At last, Barnard said he would seek the job if Burr would come with him. Thus linked, each man's misgivings multiplied the other's, and they elected to stay where they were. The job of running CCR went to a man outside the inner circle, Larry Spalding, a Sarasota attorney active in the American Civil Liberties Union. Spalding had had experience with one death penalty appeal, on behalf of Howard Douglas, and Douglas was still alive. But it was hardly the most daunting case to appeal. Douglas's jury had voted unanimously to spare his life. He had had what was known in the business as "a strong issue." The inner circle was not terribly impressed.

Still, CCR was clearly the new focus, the new center of the action. Across the country, states had always watched Florida for signs of the future of capital punishment; Florida was the cutting edge, and now they watched this new agency. "If we do it right, we're going to be a model for other places in the country," Spalding told reporters. "They're already looking at us." The buzz enabled Spalding to assemble a distinguished team: Mark Olive left the Florida Bar project to be CCR's chief litigator; Steve Malone, a veteran of several difficult appeals, hired on; Mike Mello came up from Craig Barnard's shop. And, *mirabile dictu,* Scharlette Holdman—the thorn in Florida's side, the stone in its shoe, "The Mistress of Delay"—became a salaried employee of the State of Florida. She would be CCR's chief investigator. No one could coax painful information from witnesses like Holdman could. She was, in a sense, Spalding's most important hire, the ultimate proof that he would not be a bureaucratic sellout.

But this hiring took time, and Spalding had precious little. The day CCR opened its doors, in October 1985, he had only two of the ten lawyers allowed for in his budget. Two attorneys for the thirty-seven death row inmates known to lack a lawyer of any kind. And the thirty-seven were only the tip of the iceberg: Scores more inmates would lose their lawyers when the state supreme court affirmed their sentences. In addition, a new state-mandated deadline for filing appeals was about to expire for thirty inmates, many of whom were unrepresented. They needed immediate help. And the agency had scarcely started work when crates of documents began arriving from volunteer lawyers washing their hands of their clients.

Mike Mello had worked furiously, endlessly, alongside Craig Barnard through the string of executions from Bob Sullivan to Marvin Francois. But he had never seen anything like the workload facing CCR. And in the first eight days the agency was open, Bob Graham signed four death warrants. Six in the first month. Spalding dipped into his budget to buy roll-away beds so they could sleep at the office.

Craig Barnard, meanwhile, did what he always had: came to work early, stayed late, worked weekends to the sound of the radio. CCR did not significantly lighten his load. He still had more than a dozen death penalty cases of his own, and beyond that he remained the wise man of Florida's capital defense bar, and the calming older-brother figure.

The attorney shortage had forced Florida's execution engine into a spluttering stall. For the first time in a year and a half, Barnard had enough time between executions to breathe deeply, take stock. He had a lot of losses to reflect on; Florida led the pack in every category: most people sentenced to death, most people on death row, most executions. As the state's top anti–death penalty lawyer, Barnard had to feel the weight. And yet, you could flip the statistics: Florida's defense attorneys, with Barnard in the lead, had won far more than they had lost. Nearly 90 percent of Bob Graham's death warrants had ended in stays. They had managed it with few friends in high places: not in the legislature or in the executive branch; not in the trial courts, where judges imposed the death penalty with unanticipated frequency, or on the state supreme court; not in the regional federal courts; and certainly not in the U.S. Supreme Court, where death penalty conservatives held firm control.

Death penalty supporters often accused defense lawyers of employing devious tactics. The truth was something different. Barnard and his colleagues were simply holding the law to its promises. The law promised reliability, predictability, balance. The law promised heightened scrutiny of capital cases. The law promised to weigh every aspect of a defendant's crime and character. The law was staggering under the weight of its promises.

Thus, despite the losses, Barnard still centered his thoughts on victory. Above all, he focused on his favorite issues—racial disparities and limits on favorable evidence—even though appellate judges groused and chafed each time they saw these perennial losers. He was dogged, but he was also creative. Worried that the courts had flat stopped listening to his claims about mitigating factors, Barnard subtly shifted his line of attack. He went back to the Florida Supreme Court's 1976 ruling in Vernon Cooper's case. There, the court applied only the mitigating circumstances listed in the law, and declared that "we are not free to expand the list." Later, the court declared that it had not meant to set limits.

Barnard was getting nowhere by attacking the flip-flop directly, so he decided to try a subtly different approach, saying that no matter what the law *intended,* many trial judges and lawyers *believed* favorable evidence was limited. Maybe they were mistaken, but it was a reasonable mistake, especially given the *Cooper* case. The effect, he argued, was the same as if the law itself had placed intentional limits on favorable evidence. This was a contorted argument—straining beyond the words of the law to focus on the manner in which the law was interpreted. But Barnard hoped this new twist on the old argument would finally catch some appellate court's attention. He desperately needed judges to take a second look.

Barnard had a case, moving through the appeals process, that seemed a perfect test of this strategy. James Hitchcock was on death row for raping and strangling his brother's stepdaughter. Hitchcock had given various accounts of the crime. When he turned himself in, he told police that he had consensual sex with the thirteen-year-old girl, but afterward she threatened to tell her mother and started to yell. He carried her outside, and—trying to silence her—beat and eventually strangled the child. At trial, he again maintained the intercourse was consensual, but now claimed that his brother had discovered him in the girl's bed, and that his brother had killed the child in a rage. The jury believed neither story entirely: They concluded that Hitchcock raped the girl, and when she cried out, he killed her.

In the hearing to determine Hitchcock's sentence—life or death —the defense attorney had tried to present a wide variety of reasons to spare his client. There was evidence that Hitchcock was brain-damaged from sniffing gasoline fumes as a boy, and evidence that his father's early death, which forced him and his six siblings to eke out a living picking cotton, had left him scarred. Hitchcock had no record of criminal activity or violent behavior, had turned himself in, and was a young man, just twenty years old. Despite a terrible mistake, he might be rehabilitated during a life sentence that would last at least twenty-five years. The defense attorney urged the jury to "look at the overall picture" of James Hitchcock, "the whole ball of wax."

That was precisely what the U.S. Supreme Court, in 1978, had said courts must do in death penalty cases: Look at the overall picture of the defendant and his crime, consider the whole ball of wax. But Hitchcock's trial was in 1976, when the *Cooper* ruling governed Florida trials. Hitchcock's judge and prosecutor apparently understood *Cooper* to mean that only the favorable factors listed in the law could be weighed. The prosecutor told the jury to "consider the mitigating circumstances . . . by number," and he read through the statutory list. He told the jurors that of all the evidence raised by the defense attorney, only Hitchcock's youth was applicable. The judge gave the jurors essentially the same instruction: Stick to the list. The jury recommended death, and afterward the judge noted in his sentencing statement that "this Court is mandated to apply the facts to . . . enumerated 'aggravating' and 'mitigating' factors." In other words, only the factors on the list.

No one could say if the additional information would have changed Hitchcock's sentence. His crime spoke volumes against him. But it seemed clear that potentially favorable information had been barred from consideration because the judge and prosecutor believed it was supposed to be barred. Barnard presented this argument to the federal district court. As always, he added the claim that racial disparities made the death penalty unconstitutional. As usual, the district judge denied both claims. Barnard doggedly raised the issues to the Eleventh Circuit Court of Appeals. As usual, the circuit court denied both claims. Barnard appealed to the U.S. Supreme Court to take on these questions—questions the high court had refused so many times before. By the spring of 1986, he was waiting for his answer.

The men of death row often debate the proper way to go to the chair. Is it better to walk in with dignity, to sit calmly, to mask the panic and the horror? Or should they fight? Struggle, kick, twist, spit, scream curses, club with manacled fists. What is the more manly thing to do? The prisoner who sits erect and stoic—is he a man or a sheep? "A fuckin' sheep to the slaughter," one inmate says. "They'll have to take me, I ain't goin' easy." While another inmate says the opposite: "You can't let them get to you, you can't show fear."

Such conversations are a staple of the death house, and every man takes every position at one time or another—the vision of their final moments is one they rehearse over and over in their minds. Doomed men are not different because they are going to die; everyone will die, the good and the bad, saints and sinners, predators and prey. The condemned are different because they have their deaths described to them, they know the day, the hour, the place, the affliction, all in advance. If they read the newspapers, they know that they will die with a wet sponge on their heads, that every muscle in their bodies will spasm, their knuckles will pop. They know the last sound they will ever hear —the thunk of a circuit being opened. They experience it again and again and again, in daydreams and nightmares, and they alter every variable, ponder every option.

They often debate the right way to go to the chair, but through thirteen executions, the decision was always the same. All took the dignified approach, all tried to mask their fear and shame and anger. On April 15, 1986—after nearly eleven months without an execution —Daniel Thomas had to make that choice for himself.

Perhaps it is dull by now to say that Daniel Thomas was the product of a ghastly childhood, but he was. He was three when his father died; he watched as his mother was raped, he watched as she fried her brain on cheap moonshine, and he watched her taken away to the asylum, where she died insane. He and his brothers survived from a very early age by eating out of garbage cans and sleeping under houses. The older kids kept the younger ones in line by burning them with hot iron rods. At the age of nine, when Thomas came to the attention of the State of Mississippi, the boy had never been to school or even worn a pair of shoes.

"The childhood shows the man,/As morning shows the day," John Milton wrote. So many inmates on death row share backgrounds of deprivation and violence that this common theme becomes impossible to ignore. Such backgrounds don't excuse crimes. The crimes of Daniel Thomas were far beyond any excuse. He was part of a gang of unspeakably violent thugs who terrorized Central Florida for ten months in the mid-1970s. Known as the "Ski Mask Gang" on account of their disguises, Thomas and the others robbed, raped, tortured, and killed. He was sentenced to death for the crimes of shooting a man dead and raping the man's wife beside the bleeding body.

Thankfully, many strong people have overcome deprived childhoods to live admirable lives. But the inmates of death row are not strong people. They are weak and badly flawed people; yet, one has to wonder if many of them might have turned out better had they been faced with less to overcome. The children of bad homes commit a very great proportion of America's most hideous crimes. Death row teaches that. And many people, after a long look at the place, conclude that the best way to cut the number of grisly crimes in the future would be to cut the number of abused and deprived children today. That's the pool death row draws from, overwhelmingly. This isn't bleeding-heart stuff, just simple fact. Better parents would mean less violent crime.

When his time came, Dan Thomas entered the execution chamber passively, hands shackled in front, a prison official on each side. He sat in the chair, just as the others had done before him; experienced hands tightened the chest strap and moved to the straps on his forearms. Then he exploded. Straining against the chest strap, he lashed out furiously with his legs. Assistant Superintendent Hamilton Mathis tried to grab one leg and strap it; Thomas drove his shin into the man's groin and Mathis fell back. Al Martin, the electrician, grabbed for the other leg and caught a foot in the chest. "Get off me!" Thomas screamed. "Get off me!"

The guards regrouped. Four men fell on the prisoner, but still Thomas kicked and thrashed. For a man who had lived almost a decade in a tiny cage, his strength was tremendous. "Get off me!" he screamed again. Richard Dugger leaned over him, trying to pin a leg; Thomas chewed at the air, trying to bite Dugger's ear off. Lieutenant Don Gladish, monitoring the line to the governor's office, dropped the phone and seized Thomas in a headlock. Thomas squirmed and twisted, trying to sink his teeth into Gladish.

Finally Dugger got a firm grip on Thomas's right leg. He twisted it back behind the leg of the chair. Exhausted, choking in the headlock, reduced to kicking with one leg, Thomas gave up the fight. But as the panting guards pulled the remaining straps double tight, Thomas continued to writhe and curse.

The fight lasted seven minutes. When it was over, Dugger was trembling. Thomas's power had amazed him; more than that, the whole time they had struggled, Dugger had been worried about what the two dozen witnesses would say later. It was one thing to subdue a prisoner in the bowels of the prison. It was quite another to subdue a man in front of an audience. For a moment, Dugger felt a surging temptation to bash the prisoner's teeth in, but he suppressed the urge. Likewise, when Thomas gasped that he would like to make a statement, Dugger resisted the impulse to say, "Fuck you." Instead, the warden leaned close to Thomas, out of range of the microphone, and barked: "No more bullshit outta you!" He gave Thomas a cold look, then repeated: "You can make your statement, but there will be no more bullshit."

Thomas, struggling to catch his breath, gasped, "Governor Bob Graham . . . has opened up a new wave . . . of politicking." A reference, apparently, to Graham's campaign for the U.S. Senate. "He has made it perfectly clear to all that the best way to win a political race is to boast that he will carry out the execution of every prisoner on Florida's death row. . . . We are human tools for the people in this state who are running for political positions."

The last strap was fastened across the prisoner's jaw. The hood fell. The end came to Thomas as it had to all the rest.

Over the next few days, Richard Dugger granted an unusual set of interviews. If death-chamber struggles were to "become fashionable" among the inmates, the warden said, he would be forced to take them to the chair shackled and bound. "We could add other restraints and bring him in trussed up like a mummy," he told the *Gainesville Sun*. For the boss of a maximum-security prison, Dugger was a mild-mannered man. This was the toughest he'd ever talked in print. "They read the papers like everyone else," he later said of the death row inmates. "I was putting them on notice. If we had to, we would put them in leg-irons and make them crawl to the chair."

On death row, they got the message.

A week later, April 22, David Funchess went quietly. A group of Vietnam veterans had held a vigil at the war memorial in Tallahassee, asking Governor Graham for mercy. The killer was a decorated Marine in the Vietnam War; the traumas he faced during combat along the Laotian border left him deeply changed. Before the war, Funchess did well in school and abided by the law. After Vietnam—where he saw a comrade decapitated by a mortar shell and was himself badly wounded by a land mine—Funchess was fearful, reclusive, a heroin addict. He locked himself in a garage for days on end, cradling an imaginary rifle; he dug foxholes outside his mother's house and cowered in them through the night.

To several psychiatrists, Funchess was a classic example of post–traumatic stress disorder, a mental illness seen frequently in Vietnam vets. Its symptoms were known to include violent flashbacks. The doctors speculated that Funchess was flashing back to Vietnam when, in 1974, he stabbed three people while robbing a bar, killing two of them. But the disorder was not officially recognized as an illness until 1980, so the conclusions of the psychiatrists were of no use to Funchess when he was sentenced.

∴

Graham stepped up the pace of death warrants once again; he was now signing four a month. True, there were more people than ever on death row. But many people—including some strong supporters of the death penalty—believed the warrant torrent was part of Graham's U.S. Senate campaign. "Nine months of Bob Graham running for senator nearly killed me," Ray Marky later said.

The lawyers at CCR wondered if it might kill them, too. "We were the only operation of our kind going anywhere," Mike Mello later recalled, "and we were being hyped as this grand experiment. In reality, it was a place with four roll-out beds in the office because there was never a chance to leave. I don't know the words to describe just how hard the work really was—in terms of hours or complexity. We worked one hundred hours a week, never less, often more. That spring of 1986, I literally lived in the office. Our personal lives disintegrated into nonexistence. You might think about going to a movie, or hanging out for an evening with friends . . . but then you'd compare that to rereading a trial transcript that might turn up another issue to save a life. And you'd stay at work. I thought it was never going to end. I thought I would end first."

Among Mello's cases was the appeal of Ronald Straight, slated for execution on May 20. As a protégé of Craig Barnard, Mello read Straight's transcript with a careful eye for indications that favorable evidence had been barred from the sentencing. Straight's was not an especially strong case for mitigation: He was a career con who had murdered a furniture store owner (along with Timothy Palmes, who had already been executed). But Mello built an argument that Straight's lawyer could have done more to support a life sentence—if he had known how much latitude he really had. The death sentence was thus constitutionally flawed. As usual, Mello included a challenge to racial disparities in the death penalty.

The Florida Supreme Court reiterated its familiar, contorted position that it had never limited favorable evidence. The federal district court ruled that Mello was raising the issue too late. The circuit court of appeals agreed with the district court, but granted a "baby stay" for an appeal to Washington. Straight's execution was postponed from 7 A.M. until noon. At 11 A.M., Supreme Court Justice Lewis Powell extended the delay five more hours so the other justices could be polled.

James Stone, the uncle of Ronald Straight's victim, spent the long day waiting in the prison pasture. He had been there when Palmes paid, and he would be there for Straight. Stone wore a T-shirt he had bought after the Spenkelink execution: "One down—133 to go!" It was terribly out of date. Death row was now swollen to 244 inmates.

Once again, the high court justices declined to consider the claim that mitigating evidence had been limited by Florida law and also the claim that the law was tainted by racial disparities. At 5 P.M., Ronald Straight went peaceably to Old Sparky.

Days later, the same U.S. Supreme Court—the same nine justices, employing the same law clerks, interpreting the same Constitution—announced that they would hear Craig Barnard's appeal on behalf of James Hitchcock. Two issues warranted their concern, the justices said: racial disparities and limits on mitigation.

Barnard and his colleagues had been scolded dozens of times for bringing up those issues again and again, accused of "abusing" the courts, filing "repetitive" appeals, raising the same tired, settled questions. Racial disparities and limits on mitigation—these two issues had been boilerplate in scores of appeals, beginning with John Spenkelink's. Now the U.S. Supreme Court, in its magisterial inscrutability, had decided that these questions were serious enough for their consideration. Happy as he was to win the chance to argue his case to the high court, Barnard had to wonder: If the old death penalty had been "arbitrary and capricious," what was this?

Whatever else it was, it was a big issue. Until the Hitchcock case was resolved, the death penalty would be stalled again in Florida. Governor Graham continued signing four death warrants a month, but stays were routinely granted.

Hitchcock v. Dugger, argued on October 15, 1986, was not Craig Barnard's first appearance before the nation's highest tribunal. He knew the dark room where the U.S. Supreme Court holds its public sessions, knew the simple podium, knew the imposing dais backed by a mismatched melange of tall leather chairs (each justice chooses a personal favorite). He knew the musty curtain through which the Court disappears to exercise its awesome authority. He knew how grueling oral argument can be at the highest level—the justices rarely sit back and let you say your piece; they pepper you with questions, interrupt, dispute, sometimes scold. He was adept at this sort of exchange. He knew when to dodge and when to hold his ground. This was not his first case in that intimidating setting. Merely his most important.

If a majority of the justices sided with him on the issue of racial disparities, the high court might strike down Florida's death penalty forever. Barnard's brief contained evidence that in Florida, killers of white victims were five times more likely to get the death penalty than killers of black victims. The data were not perfect; it was impossible to control for every variable among the countless elements that make up a murder case. Still, there appeared to be a pattern.

Despite the high stakes, Barnard planned to say very little on this subject because his presentation was scheduled immediately after a Georgia case dealing with precisely the same question. Anthony Amsterdam had been working for a decade to make this attack; with the Inc. Fund he had put his full weight behind the Georgia case. The statistical analysis from Georgia was more sophisticated than Barnard's evidence—and more stark. In Georgia, killers of white victims appeared eleven times more likely to get the death penalty than killers of blacks. Blacks who killed whites were the most likely of all. Barnard knew he would not win on the race question if his friends lost in Georgia. For this reason, he deferred to the Inc. Fund lawyers.

But a victory on the question of mitigating evidence would be huge in itself. Barnard was prepared to tell the justices that a favorable ruling would affect about two dozen Florida cases. Two dozen was the minimum, though—he didn't want the justices to worry about crippling the state's power. The reality was that a victory in Hitchcock's case could significantly impede Florida's death penalty for several years. Lower courts would need at least that long to plow through every case tried under the flawed law, to identify every taint and to remedy each mistake.

The faces behind the imposing dais did little to quiet Barnard's nerves. It was a new court, with increased muscle on the Right. The previous month, William Rehnquist had taken the place of Warren Burger as chief justice. Burger had been a solid vote for the death penalty, but Rehnquist was every bit as solid and—in the view of most observers—a more formidable thinker than Burger. Filling Rehnquist's seat as associate justice was Antonin Scalia, an outspokenly dazzling darling of constitutional conservatives. On this day, the trend on the high court in favor of state sovereignty was stronger—in terms of dedication and intellectual firepower—than it had been in decades.

Barnard had thirty minutes to argue his case. "Mr. Chief Justice, and may it please the Court," he began in the time-honored style. "James Hitchcock was sentenced to death by a process that precluded the consideration of compelling mitigating evidence." As the law had been construed at the time of Hitchcock's trial, Barnard said, evidence in favor of a life sentence had been limited "to a narrow statutory list."

He got just that far before the conservatives began challenging him: "Mr. Barnard, the Court of Appeals for the Eleventh Circuit in this case I think made a finding that the State of Florida law at that time . . . was ambiguous. Do you disagree with that?"

Barnard knew when to dodge, and when to hold his ground. "I disagree with the Eleventh Circuit," he said bluntly.

"Ordinarily, of course, we take the view of a Court of Appeals as to the law of a state . . ."

"The same Court of Appeals had previously expressed the view that the Florida statute was limited," Barnard parried. And he launched into the convoluted history of this matter: The Florida Supreme Court had said in the Cooper case that the list of favorable evidence could not be expanded. That "clear and direct" language was later upheld by federal courts. But then, Barnard said, the courts had taken it all back, claiming that there had never been any limits.

Now Rehnquist interrupted. "Well, Mr. Barnard, in this case I take it the defense counsel did offer mitigating evidence that went beyond [the list]."

"Yes, that is correct," Barnard answered, but then he tried to explain that it didn't matter what Hitchcock's lawyer presented in court. What mattered was that the judge and jury believed they could consider only certain things. Rehnquist kept after him; Barnard darted and jabbed.

But as they sparred, Barnard began to lose his balance, his plain-spoken command. Other justices chimed in, peppering Barnard with esoteric questions about what lawyers might reasonably have believed about the law, what trial judges might have concluded about the law, what jurors might have interpreted their instructions to mean. Antonin Scalia, the newest justice, seemed puzzled by the progress of the argument. Once or twice he tried to pull the matter back to ground zero, back to the fundamental question at hand: Was favorable evidence limited? But the interrogation soon had Barnard spinning down legal alleyways, skidding on mumbo jumbo.

He had battled for seven years, through more than a dozen executions, in courts across the South, for the chance to make this argument. But now, under heavy questioning, his argument was collapsing into gibberish. The issue was so clear in his mind, but it was becoming mush in his mouth. At his lowest point, Barnard launched into an answer with no obvious point, no visible end: "I think the importance of the jury's role, however, in Florida, I think might distinguish that, and the Court didn't decide, but *in dicta* in *Baldwin versus Alabama* observed that that might be the case that where deference is given to a jury the constitutional principle . . ."

"Yes," Scalia broke in forcefully, impatiently—as if he was back at the University of Chicago, quieting a floundering student. Scalia, the new darling of the Right. Seated beside Barnard, Dick Burr braced for the worst.

"But in this case," Scalia continued, "is it not clear that we have both the erroneous jury instruction—and we also have the judge, in his sentencing order, saying that he based his decision on the statutory circumstances and that's it?" The justice looked mystified by Barnard's acrobatics. "I don't understand what the argument's about in this case, frankly."

"Well, the argument is . . ."

"That's the whole problem, yes?"

It was a stunning moment. Barnard's help had come from the unlikeliest corner. He had feared Scalia; now Scalia was coming to his rescue. Barnard later said of this moment: "I wanted to run up and kiss him." Instead, he let out a long breath, a grin creased his round face, and he declared: "I agree that it's that simple. But we haven't been able to convince other courts that it's been that simple."

The normally staid U.S. Supreme Court audience erupted into laughter. Barnard coasted home from there.

On April 22, 1987, the U.S. Supreme Court published two death penalty decisions. The first was the Georgia case, *McCleskey v. Kemp,* dealing with racial disparities. In the chambers of the justices, among the law clerks, this was considered the most important case of the entire term. If the Court found that the capital punishment process in Georgia was unconstitutionally flawed because of racial discrimination, the death penalty would quite possibly be scrapped in America. It had happened before. Years earlier, arbitrary, racially tainted death sentences in Georgia had moved the Court to wipe out all existing capital punishment laws in *Furman v. Georgia.* This time there would be no obvious repairs. It was the biggest of the big issues.

Given the Court's strong support of capital punishment, the vote was surprisingly close. Four justices—the stalwarts William Brennan and Thurgood Marshall, joined by Harry Blackmun and John Paul Stevens—were convinced by the statistics that Georgia's law was unconstitutional. Citing a long run of earlier Supreme Court rulings, Brennan argued that a "risk" or "pattern" of "arbitrary and capricious" death sentences is enough to invalidate a death penalty law. "The Court," he declared, ". . . acknowledges that *McCleskey* has demonstrated a risk that racial prejudice plays a role in capital sentencing in Georgia."

They fell one vote short. Justice Lewis Powell wrote the majority opinion, signed by Rehnquist, Scalia, Byron White, and Sandra Day O'Connor. Powell did not dispute the statistics. Instead, he declared that such general statistics were not relevant. Warren McCleskey and his lawyers had to prove that he, specifically, had been discriminated against—a tough thing to do, because McCleskey had killed a police officer in the line of duty, a classic capital offense. The defense had to show who had discriminated against the prisoner—which district attorney, which judge, which jurors—and how and when. It was not enough to show patterns.

The majority did not explicitly acknowledge what they were doing, but implicitly they were undoing a cornerstone of the historic *Furman* decision. In *Furman,* Anthony Amsterdam had not shown that death was an arbitrary or capricious penalty in one particular case. He had persuaded five justices that the whole system of capital punishment, viewed broadly, worked in an arbitrary way. He had not proven who was arbitrary—which prosecutor or judge. He had shown a pattern.

Now Powell, writing for the majority, rejected the broad view. The same sort of disparities shown by McCleskey might show up in sentences for car theft, or dope peddling, or purse snatching. The *Furman* ruling had been interpreted in other Court decisions to mean that "death is different," but now Powell suggested the death penalty was more like other punishments than it was different. This was, apparently, a very great shift. And if the majority had gone the whole nine yards and formally overturned *Furman,* the *McCleskey* decision might have meant great changes. The philosophy that "death is different" might have faded from judicial doctrine—and with it the barren, endless attempt to make capital punishment rational and consistent.

But the justices did not take that vast step. Instead, they left themselves in a chasm between conflicting strains of thought. Two incompatible ideas sat side by side in the law. Death was still different, because the earlier decisions enshrining that idea were not reversed. The law still promised a virtually impossible consistency, and condemned inmates could continue to demand it in court. But the failure of the system to deliver that consistency—in the broad view, which is the only way to judge consistency—would not be grounds for attack.

In the days when *Furman* had been decided, the Supreme Court had been horrified by the idea that some six hundred men sat on death row while only a handful were being executed. That fact, plus concerns about racial discrimination, had led the Court to scrap the old laws. Now the population of America's death rows was climbing toward two thousand. And still, the number of executions was a comparative handful. Nationwide, between fifteen and twenty men were being sentenced to death for every one who was executed.

And what could be said of the ones who died? Were they the worst, the most unmitigated, irredeemable of the lot? As Florida's experience showed, they were more nearly a random selection of the larger death row population. It was a sort of lottery—and a lottery is the very model of an arbitrary and capricious system.

The *McCleskey* decision appeared to say that it made no difference that the death penalty was a lottery, not as a general statement. Now every individual inmate had to prove that he, personally, had been screwed. Those would be the rules until the U.S. Supreme Court changed its mind again.

But the courts can change their minds very quickly. That was the message of the second death penalty ruling published on that April day in 1986, *Hitchcock v. Dugger*. Technically, the U.S. Supreme Court had never ruled on whether Florida's death penalty law limited a defendant's right to present evidence in favor of a life sentence. But the Court had been asked repeatedly to take the question under consideration, and repeatedly the Court had refused. And sixteen people had gone to Old Sparky. That suggests the majority had made up their minds. Now they changed them: The justices ruled unanimously—all of them, the conservatives, the moderates, the liberals—that the law had been "authoritatively interpreted by the Florida Supreme Court" to mean that mitigating evidence was limited.

Craig Barnard was right. The Florida Supreme Court had denied this for some eight years—sixteen executions—but Barnard had kept at it, kept hammering, despite scoldings and even ridicule from judges and prosecutors. The public had complained bitterly about lawyers like him, with their delaying tactics and technicalities. Politicians had proposed all sorts of bills to limit his access, and the access of his colleagues, to the appellate courts.

Now the U.S. Supreme Court said unanimously that Barnard had been right all along. Justice Scalia, the new conservative tiger, wrote the opinion. "We think it could not be clearer," he intoned, in his confident, definitive way, that the judge and the jury believed they could consider only a few favorable factors. It could not be clearer.

The Court's opinion in *Hitchcock* was brief, scarcely hinting at the years of litigation that had gone into Barnard's victory. In the end, the subtle shift Barnard had made in his argument was the fig leaf the justices grasped to cover their sudden change of heart. "The sentencing judge assumed . . . a prohibition [on favorable evidence] and instructed the jury accordingly," Scalia wrote. Therefore, "we need not reach the question whether that was in fact the requirement of Florida law." But Scalia did note that other judges in other cases had reached the same mistaken conclusion about the law. And he mentioned with obvious approval that Florida's legislature had changed the wording of its death penalty statute to make it clear that all favorable evidence should be considered.

The opinion was written to make it seem that a very small point had been decided, but Craig Barnard could see that a new generation of appeals had been opened for the men who had been on Florida's death row the longest. What was true for James Hitchcock was at least arguably true for all of them—dozens of them, and they were the men closest to Old Sparky. And *Hitchcock* had an even larger meaning for Barnard. After the ruling, he proudly told his troops: When people ask why we keep appealing, why we raise these issues over and over, why we never give up fighting . . . tell them to look at *Hitchcock*.

PART III

A FAILURE OF

EXECUTION

Some 230 people lived on Florida's death row by 1986—several had been there a dozen years. Their fate was the subject of political campaigns and judicial seminars and angry letters to the editor. But somehow the whole vast, chaotic enterprise of the death penalty boiled down in the public mind to a single man. Ted Bundy.

In a state that ranked, year in and year out, near the top of the crime statistics—a person could hardly shake the sand from a beach blanket in Florida without spraying at least a grain or two on a criminal —Ted Bundy stood out. During his 1979 murder trial, one poll found that his statewide name recognition was second only to the governor's. And his notoriety went far beyond state lines; if he was not, in early 1986, the best-known killer in all America, he would be when NBC devoted four hours of prime time to a movie version of his bloody career. Five books had been written about him, countless magazine and newspaper articles. Bundy could, if he wished, command an interview with any television network; even the staid *New York Times* sought an audience with him. In his infamy, he became an archetype—not one condemned man among hundreds in Starke, but the essence of death row itself. Bundy's enigmatic face became the face of evil, his undistin-guished flesh the embodiment of America's spreading dread.

A remarkable set of forces converged to make this happen. Fore-most was the enormity of his crimes. Over a period of at least four years, and perhaps nine, Ted Bundy abducted, raped, and murdered an unknown number of young women—at least two dozen, likely three dozen, maybe as many as fifty. His carnage spanned the country, from Washington and Oregon eastward through Utah, Idaho, and Colorado to an awful end in Florida. Covering thousands of miles in his beat-up old Volkswagen, carefully choosing his victims from widely disparate police jurisdictions, never harming anyone he might have met before,

Bundy epitomized the serial killer in rootless contemporary American society. He was not the first serial killer, but none before him had so completely exploited the grim advantages of contemporary America: the interstate highways, the footloose freedom of young women, the anonymity of the suburbs. Bundy was brighter than the average psychopath, too, and he made a study of investigative techniques, immersed himself in the nature of law enforcement bureaucracies, using this knowledge to stay ahead of the law—allowing him to kill twenty times or more before scattered detectives fully realized they were all looking for the same man.

His persona was a part of the mix: intelligent, charming, attractive. Bundy was capable, when he applied himself, of breezing through college courses; he was a promising volunteer in Washington State Republican political circles; he volunteered on a suicide-prevention hotline; he attended law school. All this made him compelling in ways most killers lacked—for it took him beyond himself into a realm of symbols. Bundy symbolized America's fear that violent crime had jumped the fence; the menace was loosed from the inner cities, from the biker bars and the psycho wards, and now it stalked nice subdivisions and sedate campuses looking just like a next-door neighbor. In all the books and articles about him, this was the dominant image: Bundy was "handsome," "brilliant," "charming"; he could have had a future as a senator or a millionaire. (In the TV-movie version of the Bundy story, the killer was played by Mark Harmon—*People* magazine's "sexiest man alive." Early in the film, someone greets him as "Ted! Ted Bundy! Seattle's answer to JFK!") This view was exaggerated. Even at his most "normal," Bundy was a petty thief, an alcoholic who haunted sleazy porno shops. But the hype was understandable. Among the addled, ignorant men who commit most of America's first-degree murders, Bundy was unusual. There were smarter, better-looking men just about anywhere in America—except on death row. There, he was a stand-out.

Among his talents was an actor's gift; like his other talents, this turned vile in his hands. Bundy often lured his victims to their deaths by playing a fumbling student, a solicitous police officer, an injured sailor in need of help. He could radically alter his appearance through

the simplest changes in costume, posture, hairstyle. When he was stalking women, tempting and trapping them, Bundy felt he was playing a
part in a movie. Playing a "role"—that's how he described his whole
life, his political activities, his courtroom theatrics, his romances. When
he went on trial for murder in 1979, he assumed his greatest role: the
suave young law student defending his own life. His trial was among
the first ever televised in Florida; he played masterfully to the lens.
Long before the invention of Court TV, Bundy's trial was a nightly
feature on public television stations across the country, and commercial
stations ran regular updates. The television coverage jacked up the
newspapers. Editors were so hungry for Bundy news that the Associated Press transmitted hourly dispatches.

What did people see when they tuned in the Ted Bundy show?
Not the face of a man broken by madness or consumed by guilt. They
saw a cold manipulator, arrogantly putting prosecutors and judges
through hoops; they saw a preening Narcissus, squeezing every drop of
pleasure he could find from the rights of the accused. Bundy became a
symbol not just of menace but of sneering menace. No shred of conscience shone through his performance.

All these elements and more, by some weird catalysis, made Ted
Bundy mythic. Like Jack the Ripper or Charles Manson, Bundy was
more than vile, more than deadly, more than a pervert. He represented
everything vile, all murder, every perversion. Of all the killers on death
row, Bundy was the one people hated and feared, and above all, he was
the one they wanted dead.

The story of his birth is a sad and mysterious tale, though how
sad, how mysterious, the world may never know. Theodore Robert
Cowell was born November 24, 1946, at a home for unwed mothers in
Burlington, Vermont. A bright, slight girl named Louise Cowell was
seven months pregnant when she arrived at a place known to gossipy
townspeople as Lizzie Lund's Home for Naughty Ladies. Louise was
quiet and studious, neither well off nor poor; she was a shop clerk from
Philadelphia living at home with her parents. Louise Cowell finished
second in her high school class. Had she finished first, she would have

won a scholarship to college; had she gone to college, she might not have become pregnant; had she not become pregnant, a very bad man might never have been born.

Hundreds of journalists, detectives, and shrinks would explore every aspect of the life of that child, but virtually nothing would be learned about his father. When Louise arrived at the home for unwed mothers, the staff asked, and she told them she had been swept off her feet by a smooth older fellow named Jack Worthington. This Jack Worthington, Louise said, was a Navy man fresh home from the great war, rich, educated at a posh prep school. He had seduced her, then vanished. It was a plausible story in those frenetic days. Depression and war were finally past; young people courted and mated and reproduced as never before in American history—and not all of these couplings were on the up-and-up. Decades later, investigators would search in vain for any record of a Navy man named Jack Worthington. Fruitlessly they combed prep school records for traces of the mystery man and they found nothing. This did not disprove Louise's story; this would not be the first time a man had lied to get laid. Actually, a man who puffed himself up to get what he wanted, then swept his tracks clean, would have been an apt father for Ted Bundy. Nonetheless, the fact that so many investigators could not find even a hint of Jack Worthington gave rise to Gothic speculations about the killer's lineage—speculations about rape, or even incest.

After the birth, Louise Cowell left her infant son in Burlington and returned to her parents' house, where she considered her options, which were few. She could give the boy up for adoption and begin again. Or she could press ahead on her fated path. Louise was a serious and responsible young woman; she met her obligations, faced the consequences of her choices. She also had a streak of naïve optimism that would, nowadays, be called "denial." She took the child home to Philadelphia, where Teddy Cowell learned to walk and then run in his grandparents' rambling old place. He went exploring across the lawn, enjoyed the doting caresses of his aunts, and passed happy hours in the humid warmth of his grandfather's greenhouse. Through the imperfect filter of memory, Ted Bundy later recalled those as halcyon days, and he remembered being upset when, not long after his fourth birthday,

Louise moved him across the country to Tacoma to make an independent life.

In Tacoma, Louise Cowell met a decent, hardworking hospital cook named Johnnie Bundy, and when they were married she gave her husband's name to her little boy. Ted Bundy was a shy child, good in school but not precocious (his IQ was about 120, on the borderline between "average" and "superior" intelligence). Louise and Johnnie did their best to make a wholesome home: They went to the Methodist church each Sunday; Johnnie worked with the local Boy Scout troop. Ted Bundy had a paper route, picked beans alongside his stepfather for a little extra money, ran the low hurdles on the junior high track team. He was, by all accounts, a loving big brother to the two sons and two daughters born to Louise and Johnnie.

Except for some periodic troubles applying himself and occasional difficulties getting along with his classmates, young Ted Bundy seemed like an ordinary boy. At least until puberty, when the pressure of sexual maturing exposed some of the flaws in his personality. Like most boys, Ted Bundy sought out naughty books and pictures of naked women. But his search was unusually heated. Bundy roamed the neighborhood digging for smut in the garbage cans. And he masturbated compulsively, not just under the sheets or behind a locked bathroom door. One story was that Bundy had been caught red-handed in a school coat closet. This humiliation, combined perhaps with some other experience, left the boy so shameful that he would endure any amount of ridicule rather than strip for the showers after gym.

Ted Bundy always traced his "problem," as he called it, to his masturbatory obsession with pornography. Most boys, by the time they reach high school, pour their energies into trying to touch a real young woman; for Bundy, there was no reality, only images. Over time, he found himself aroused by increasingly explicit and violent images— stories and pictures of women stalked, women chained, women raped. Bundy began to frequent the dirty-book stores in Tacoma's seedy section, where he found material catering to every sadistic fantasy. And while other young men went on dates, he spent his nights darting across lawns, hiding in shrubbery, peeping through windows as women undressed.

In spite of this worminess, or perhaps as compensation, Bundy cultivated a grand view of himself, massively self-centered and grossly covetous. He resented Johnnie Bundy for not being rich, and he envied the children of his more cultured uncle. He wanted things and he wanted them now; he had neither the self-discipline nor the patience to work and wait. And so, while still in high school, he embarked on a career of petty theft. Bundy stole ski equipment; he decorated his college apartments by shoplifting stereo equipment and houseplants. At least once in his youth he stole a car. When he got a part-time job at a yacht club—surely seething with resentment at the wealthy patrons— he rifled lockers for wallets and clothes. When Bundy desired something, he took it, and when he felt pangs of guilt, he trained himself to ignore them. After all, the world looked so bountiful to Ted Bundy. With so much stuff out there, why shouldn't he have some of it? Who would miss it?

Ted Bundy lived in a world composed of props and stage flats. Like the lewd pictures he groaned over, it was all a matter of manipulating images, of designing appearances to satisfy certain desires. He did not want to be educated, he wanted to appear educated; he did not want to work for success, merely to seem successful. Bundy was always lying about his pedigree and his achievements. In college he threw himself into politics and overcame his shyness to date a rich and beautiful young woman—not because he loved politics or loved this young woman, but because he liked the way these things made him look. He mastered his roles: the future lawyer, the political comer, the brilliant wit. In reality, Bundy was a two-time college dropout and a budding sex criminal, but reality was a concept Bundy did not comprehend. Events were his to control, and people were but actors in a drama of his own imagining. "Control and mastery is what we see here," he once said, speaking of his own pathology in a thinly veiled way. If Ted Bundy was a dark genius of any kind, it was as a manipulator, the man who steered the perceptions. "Sometimes he manipulates even me," a psychiatrist once admitted.

He took the things he wanted and felt little guilt because nothing was real anyway. Booze helped him maintain his shadow world, and he became a heavy drinker. As the years went by, Bundy found less and less pleasure in images of women raped and brutalized. He wanted something more—he wanted to become the master of those images. On his nighttime rambles through the shadows, Bundy stopped looking through windows and began watching women as they walked home, imagining what it would be like to leap out at them, grab them, take them the same way he took everything else he wanted. The world seemed so bountiful to Ted Bundy, there were so many women out there. Why shouldn't he take one? Who would miss her?

Bundy was always surprised when anyone noticed that one of his victims was missing, because he imagined America to be a place where everyone is invisible except to themselves. And he was always astounded when people testified that they had seen him in incriminating places, because Bundy did not believe people noticed each other. These weren't purely delusions. Bundy had spent many hours driving around with bound victims and dead bodies in his car; many times he had lugged corpses in and out of his apartment—no one had ever noticed. Bundy considered his crimes the consequence of a society without communities, without roots; where people are bound neither to one another nor to codes of behavior. As the archkiller said: "I mean, there are so many people. This person will never be missed."

But they were real. Lynda Healy worked in radio, announcing the ski conditions each morning. The morning of February 1, 1974, she never got to the station. In the dark hours of the night, Ted Bundy opened her bedroom door, slipped his hands around her throat, and squeezed. Before he carried her from the room, wrapped in her red bedsheet, he carefully remade the bed with hospital corners.

About a month later, Donna Manson disappeared as she walked across the campus of Evergreen State University in Olympia, Washington. A month or so after that, Susan Rancourt vanished from another college campus in Washington, on the same night that two other women had narrowly avoided the advances of a mysterious man with his arm in a sling. In each case, Bundy had asked the pretty young women for help carrying his books to his yellow-brown Volkswagen.

Another month after that, Kathy Parks disappeared from a college campus in Oregon. A few weeks later, Brenda Ball staggered out of the Flame Tavern in a bad part of Seattle and was never seen again. (Bundy had picked up Ball outside a rough bar because he wanted to vary his pattern.) Soon afterward, he struck on another college campus: Georgann Hawkins seemed to evaporate into thin air from the University of Washington. Witnesses later mentioned seeing a man on crutches, fumbling with a briefcase, near the place where she was last seen.

On July 14, 1974, the sun shone gloriously over the soggy Washington coast. People flocked to Lake Sammamish State Park, on bikes, pulling sailboats, wearing shorts and bikinis. A man who called himself Ted wandered through the crowd, his arm in a sling, asking young women to help him load his sailboat. Two of them—Janice Ott and Denise Naslund—agreed to help him. They vanished. A month later, Carol Valenzuela was gone.

Ted Bundy moved to Utah to enroll in the University of Utah law school. The abductions stopped in Washington and Oregon. Now young women began to die in Utah, Colorado, and Idaho.

Bundy was a killing machine, but of a specialized kind. If his only goal had been to avoid detection, he would have taken victims with cloudy pasts and small futures. But in the world he imagined, it wouldn't do for the suave and brilliant young Republican to possess a poor runaway or a tired prostitute. He stalked college campuses, high schools, and ski resorts. He took the things he wanted. And "the ultimate possession was, in fact, the taking of the life," he told an interviewer.

He thought of himself as a hunter, aroused by the stalking. The record indicates that only one woman got into the hunter's Volkswagen and lived to tell about it. On November 8, 1974, Carol DaRonch was shopping at a little mall in Murray, Utah, when a man who claimed to be a police officer approached. He smelled of liquor. He said someone had been seen trying to steal her car. Come with me, he said.

DaRonch was suspicious when the man fumbled at a locked door of the mall. Even more suspicious when he told her to get in his car for a ride to "the station." Her suspicion turned to horror when he pulled off the street and struggled to handcuff her to the steering wheel. Desperate, she freed herself from the car and ran screaming down the street. Bundy roared away. Later that night, a strange man appeared in the auditorium of a local high school during a performance of a school play. He appeared to be wearing a fake mustache. He invited at least one woman to step outside and identify a car. A girl named Debra Kent walked outside during intermission and was never seen again.

Ted Bundy was arrested in August 1975. The charge was evading arrest—he had been driving suspiciously through a darkened neighborhood; when a cop tried to pull him over, Bundy floored it. The officer eventually caught up to the VW, and when he searched the car he found, among other things, a pair of handcuffs and a pantyhose mask. That was the beginning of the end. Carol DaRonch picked him out of a lineup, which shocked Bundy because he had done so much to change his appearance. He had combed his hair a new way, hiked his belt up nerdishly, scrunched his chin into the folds of a turtleneck shirt. He was even more amazed when a judge found him guilty of aggravated kidnapping in the DaRonch case, after he had played the role of bright young law student with bravura. How could anyone call him a criminal?

But there he was, at the state penitentiary in Utah, awaiting extradition to stand trial for a murder in Colorado. Police were finally onto him, though Ted Bundy could not digest it. People had always seen him as he wished to be seen. He controlled the imagery, and the only people who saw the truth were dead.

In Aspen, Colorado, Bundy was charged with the murder of a vacationing nurse named Caryn Campbell. He demanded to serve as his own defense counsel, playing the part of the promising attorney. This performance earned him unusual access to the telephone, the mail, and the courthouse law library, where they kept the windows open on warm June afternoons. On June 7, 1977, Bundy hopped out of the window while his guard was taking a cigarette break.

In decadent Aspen, Bundy's escape was the source of great goofing: Local entrepreneurs hawked T-shirts declaring that "Ted Bundy is a One-Night Stand"; a bartender invented the Bundy Cocktail, made of rum, tequila, and two Mexican jumping beans. A local restaurant put

Bundy Burgers on the menu: The bread was there but the meat was gone. Hitchhikers held signs that said I AM NOT BUNDY. But surely even the ski-slope sybarites would have been less amused at the thought of Bundy loose had they realized exactly what he did to women. Ted Bundy kidnapped women, raped them ferociously (sometimes sinking his teeth into their flesh). He bashed in their heads with tire irons, strangled them with his bare hands, sodomized them with rods and bottles. He kept some of the bodies for days in his apartments, washing their hair, painting their fingernails. In ten cases, maybe more, he decapitated his victims. Even after he dumped the bodies on remote mountains across the West, Bundy sometimes returned to the sites to rape an exposed corpse.

But these things were not yet known, not fully, and so by the time Bundy was recaptured a week later he was a celebrity. And when, six months later, he escaped again by crawling through the light fixture in his jail cell, he became a regular John Dillinger. No jail could hold him. He made the FBI's Ten Most Wanted list. Over the next two months, people got a clearer sense of just how awful Ted Bundy really was.

From Aspen he took a bus to Denver, caught a plane to Chicago, rode the train to Ann Arbor, Michigan. There, he pored over maps, looking for a place with sunshine and college students. He chose Tallahassee, Florida. Bundy had once asked an acquaintance what state was most likely to execute a murderer, and that friend said Florida. Perhaps Old Sparky drew him toward its embrace, like a distant magnet, or maybe mere chance took him there, instead of to San Diego, say, or New Orleans. In any event, by January 7, 1978, Ted Bundy was living in a cheap rooming house on the campus of Florida State University.

During his time in prison, Bundy had convinced himself that he had mastered the urges that drove him to kill. He was wrong. A man who craved mastery, he was not even master of himself. He drank constantly in Tallahassee, stole everything he could get his hands on, including some thirty pairs of socks in a few days—Bundy was a foot fetishist, in addition to his more lethal perversions. He spent the evening of January 14, 1978, in a bar next door to the Chi Omega sorority house on the Florida State campus. He was drinking bourbon, which always had an especially poisonous effect on him. After the bar closed at

2 A.M., Bundy was seen roaming nearby in tan slacks, a dark Navy peacoat, and a stocking cap, accosting women in a slurred and mumbling voice. About 3 A.M., he slipped into the Chi Omega house, carrying an oak club.

Bundy went first to the room of Lisa Levy, a beautiful freshman with a passion for fashion. He throttled her with a pantyhose ligature, raped her, sodomized her with an aerosol can, sank his teeth into her breast and buttock. He stalked to another room and savaged the two young women there with his club, covering the room in blood. He moved on to Margaret Bowman's room, strangled her with another pair of pantyhose, clubbed her . . . then heard a sound. He bounded down the stairs, through the front door. As he ran, Nita Neary, just home from a date, saw his silhouette—the sharp nose and thin lips.

That same night, several blocks away, Cheryl Thomas was brutally beaten in her bed; the damage to her skull was so great she would never hear again in one ear. She was not raped, but a puddle of semen was found on her sheets. In two terrible hours, two women were dead and three were near death, and the depth of his depravity was now public.

But there was more. For three weeks after the sorority house attack, Bundy wandered drunkenly across the east-west highways of northern Florida, running on stolen credit cards and stolen cars. On February 9, 1978, he steered a white van through the quiet streets of Lake City in north-central Florida. That morning, a blossoming but fey girl of twelve, Kimberly Leach, left one class at Lake City Junior High School to retrieve her denim purse from another. Outside the school, a white van was circling the block. Kimberly collected her purse, then disappeared.

Bundy was captured six days later near Pensacola, driving a stolen Volkswagen bug. He loved VWs, he told police detectives shortly after his arrest, because you could remove the passenger seat. Made it easier to carry "cargo"—by which he meant bodies, sometimes dead, sometimes alive. In those first few days back in captivity, he walked to the edge of confession, asking for a deal that would return him to Washington to serve a life sentence close to home. But there would be no confession, and no life sentence.

∴

After his capture, one of Ted Bundy's first phone calls was to Millard Farmer in Atlanta. Bundy did not know much law, but he knew who the good lawyers were. For a man facing three capital murder trials, Millard Farmer was one of the best.

When Farmer took death penalty cases, he had one goal paramount: keeping his client alive. Pressed by guilt over his family's wealth and power, Farmer hated the system that used its power to kill. He had little doubt that Bundy was guilty of all the crimes he'd been linked to, but he would not give even this crumb to the system he hated.

There was one hitch: Farmer was a Georgia lawyer and Bundy was facing trial in Florida. Farmer would need the judge's permission to appear in a Florida courtroom, and Judge John Rudd of Tallahassee was not about to grant it. Rudd was aware of Farmer's genius for turning criminal trials into political statements, his mastery of delay, his monkey-wrench throwing. Farmer, the judge believed, would turn the Bundy trials into a carnival sideshow. As it happened, Farmer was facing a contempt of court citation in Georgia. (It stemmed from the case in which Farmer insisted that his client, a black man, be addressed as "mister," like everyone else in the court—and when this didn't occur, began calling the judge by his first name.) On the strength of this violation, Rudd denied Farmer's petition to represent Bundy. The job fell instead to a string of frustrated and overmatched public defenders and volunteers.

Things were not going according to Bundy's script, so he seized control by doing whatever he could to undermine his lawyers. They tried to keep him quiet; Bundy insisted on late-night conversations with police. They tried to lower his profile; Bundy demanded press conferences. Bundy threw tantrums, dreamed up bizarre defense strategies, and turned on any lawyer with the audacity to say what they all knew: He was guilty. In both the Chi Omega rampage and the Leach murder, the police had amassed a staggering amount of material—everything from microscopic comparisons of hairs and fibers to sworn statements from scores of witnesses. There was enough work to keep a whole law firm busy for a year or more. Yet Bundy demanded to run his own defense, suffering the help of his court-appointed counsel only at his own mysterious whim. The old adage—a man who serves as his own lawyer has a fool for a client—was never more true than in the case of Ted Bundy.

Though he was officially barred from the case, Farmer struggled to save Bundy from himself, and from Old Sparky. During the sixteen months it took to bring the first case to trial, Farmer, and his assistant Joe Nursey, kept in touch with Bundy, massaging his ego, calming his nerves, and gently steering him toward his only rational choice—a guilty plea in exchange for his life. Such a result was not out of the question. Although the prosecution was quite confident they had the right man, and though mountains of evidence had been gathered, the evidence was circumstantial. At the Chi Omega house Bundy had left no fingerprints; the semen stains could not be matched definitively to him; the one eyewitness, Nita Neary, had only a faint impression of the man she had seen darting through the door. A doctor was ready to testify that Bundy's teeth perfectly matched the bite marks found on Lisa Levy, but his expertise—"forensic odontology"—was a largely unproven field. Likewise, in the murder of Kimberly Leach, the prosecution could put Bundy in Lake City on the day of the crime, and had only a hazy eyewitness connecting him to the victim. The strongest physical evidence consisted of hairs and clothing fibers indicating that Bundy and the girl had been together in the stolen van. Fiber evidence is hardly as strong as fingerprints. And there were no fingerprints.

The horrible possibility that Ted Bundy might beat the rap led the prosecution to agree to a deal. Bundy would plead guilty in exchange for three consecutive life sentences; his earliest possible parole date would be when he was 107 years old. The deal came together in the spring of 1979, as the Chi Omega trial approached. Millard Farmer carefully maneuvered Bundy to take it, treating him like a peer. "Ted," Farmer said gently in his sorrowful drawl, "I don't like the way the prosecution against you is shaping up. You're not getting any play. You're not disturbing their pace." Farmer never hinted that he believed Bundy was guilty; he knew that would turn Bundy against him, too. Gradually, under Farmer's patient tutelage, Bundy began to see the plea as a sort of victory, and Farmer began to sense that he might be able to save even this monster from death row.

The drama of the plea bargain played out against the larger drama of John Spenkelink's execution. In fact, Farmer was in Tallahassee to nudge Bundy when he entered Spenkelink's case. He would wonder, later, if perhaps he had spread himself too thin, trying to pull off two miracles in one week. And he was spread very thin, for at the same time he was trying to sell Bundy, Farmer also had to persuade Bundy's mother and his girlfriend. Against all odds, these two women staunchly clung to the killer's innocence. Without their support, Farmer knew he could never convince Bundy. So he flew to Seattle, where the two women lived, and there he repeated his delicate dance. It didn't matter that Ted was innocent, he softly assured them. The wheels were turning against him, and unless he took the plea bargain, he would surely wind up in the electric chair.

Farmer won them over. Louise Bundy and Carole Boone flew to Tallahassee where, one by one, they met with Ted and begged him to plead guilty. Bundy seemed to agree. Perhaps he thought he could back out of the bargain later, and throw the prosecution for a loop. Perhaps reality fleetingly pierced the cloud of images that constituted his world. He said he would take the deal to save his life. But it did not last. On May 31, 1979, six days after the Spenkelink execution. Bundy went to court to plead guilty. He carried his confession—as well as an angry statement denying his guilt and firing his lawyers. In court that morning, he stood and held a document in each hand, as if weighing the real world against the world of his imagining. He chose his cherished images, blasting his court-appointed lawyers for believing "I'm guilty. . . . Now, Your Honor, if this doesn't raise itself to the level of ineffectiveness of counsel, I don't know what does," he said.

After the hearing, Farmer stopped by the killer's cell and said, "I've only got so much time and I'm going to spend it on people who want to live."

On July 25, 1979, Ted Bundy was convicted of the murders of Lisa Levy and Margaret Bowman at the Chi Omega sorority house, along with the beatings of Karen Chandler, Kathy Kleiner, and Cheryl Thomas. Judge Edward Cowart, a great, jowly, folksy man, imposed two death sentences and bade Bundy farewell. "You're a bright young man," he said. "You'd have made a good lawyer, and I'd have loved to have you practice in front of me. But you went the other way, pardner." Six and a half months later, on February 12, 1980, Judge Wallace Jopling sentenced him to die a third time, for the murder of Kimberly Leach.

Bundy was not a popular man on death row. He made a good impression on some of the black inmates with his skill in the exercise yard—"We were amazed," one remembered. "Here's a white guy who can actually play basketball!"—but mostly the other inmates resented his notoriety and, despite their own evil, abhorred his crimes. Doug McCray, one of the death row old-timers, recalled the night the news came over the television that Kimberly Leach's body had been found. He got on the bars and said to Bob Sullivan, "Sully, man, the individual who would do something like that—he deserves the death penalty." There was a lot of boasting around the prison, prisoners saying: Let Bundy out with us. We'll take care of him. From the security of his cell, the most infamous serial killer in America sniffed, "I have nothing for those animals out there."

Bundy mostly kept to himself. In a way, prison was a relief to him; he had always fared better behind bars than on the streets. The stress of maintaining his images out in the real world weighed crushingly on him; it was so much easier in the unreal world of prison. On death row, Bundy claimed to have shrugged off his past like an overcoat on a suddenly balmy winter afternoon. "It's just done! It's back there in the mists," he told an interviewer. "I say 'mists' because I don't think anyone actually touches the past the way they can touch the present or the future." For a time, Bundy joined the sect that was given vegetarian meals on death row. He popped vitamins and munched health foods. He built up a considerable collection of socks, and slipped into an occasional reverie about how delightful it would be to wear a brand-new pair every day of the year. He drifted on a cloud of smuggled marijuana and hashish.

All in all, with his dope and his socks and his mysticism, Bundy was a mellow prisoner. Now and then a guard would marvel: Bundy, you're such a nice guy. I can't figure it out. And Bundy would flash his Cheshire cat smile. He got an incredible amount of mail, hundreds of letters a year—many from young women who said they had fallen in love with him, but also letters from people who hated him, and from people who wanted to write books about him, make movies of his life, save his soul. When he answered a letter, he generally ended his response with the words, "peace, ted," all lowercase, like some blissed-out sixties poet. Visitors came often, and when they did, Bundy liked to discourse on liberal causes. He claimed to support women's rights and oppose global warming. And he was always dreaming up money-making schemes. "One time, he asked me for all the information I could come up with on children's gardening," said Michael Radelet, the University of Florida sociologist and foe of the death penalty. "He had this idea that you could make a lot of money selling ten- or fifteen-dollar gardening kits for kids. They'd have a little rake and a little shovel and some little gloves and some seeds." Bundy also enjoyed meeting with investigators chasing serial killers. This gave him a chance to play his favorite role: the master, as he explained what makes a predator tick.

In these ways, Ted Bundy passed his days, and each daily step toward execution was so tiny—microscopic, really—as to be imperceptible to the public eye. As year followed year, and Bundy remained alive and well on death row, he became Exhibit A in the fulminations of politicians, editorial writers, talk show hosts, and ordinary citizens who railed against the torturous appeals of death row inmates. If anyone should die, Ted Bundy should. Even many opponents of the death penalty agreed with that. So why wasn't he dead?

Contrary to popular belief, the courts moved Bundy as fast as they could. Never—not once—did any court, anywhere, decide a single issue in his favor. Even the prosecutors acknowledged that Bundy's lawyers never employed delaying tactics. Though people everywhere seethed at the apparent delay in executing the archdemon, Ted Bundy was actually on the fast track.

∴

Bundy's lawyers lodged their required appeals to the Florida Supreme Court within two months after each of his trials. Then Robert Augustus Harper (the lawyer who had saved Willie Darden when he was scheduled to be killed along with John Spenkelink) filed full briefs within the allotted time. Next, the State of Florida was given time to digest and respond to Harper's appeals. In spring 1982—two and a half years after the Chi Omega trial—the first of the two cases was put on the docket for oral argument.

Two and a half years may have seemed like a very long time, but in context, it was entirely understandable. The Florida Supreme Court was dealing with roughly one death case per week; nearly half the court's time and energy was being consumed by this tiny field of battle. Scores of condemned prisoners were ahead of Bundy in line, and each had a complicated appeal based on a large trial record. Each record had to be scrutinized, each appeal contemplated. And when the court finally got to Bundy, the justices were faced with the combined records of two trials comprising some twenty-eight thousand pages (roughly the expanse of the *Encyclopaedia Britannica*). Bundy's was the largest and most complicated criminal case in the court's history.

Even if the court just went through the motions, there were a lot of motions to go through. But the state supreme court did more than go through the motions. At least one of Harper's arguments deeply concerned the justices. Harper challenged the use of hypnosis to "refresh" the memories of witnesses. He presented scientific evidence to suggest that hypnotism is unproven and unreliable. Sometimes, a person will latch onto a belief while under hypnosis and subsequently believe fiercely that it is true—even when it isn't. Key witnesses at both of Bundy's trials had undergone hypnosis. Nita Neary caught just a fleeting glimpse of a man's profile as he rushed from the Chi Omega sorority house. A hypnotist drew out details that helped her identify Bundy on the witness stand. In the Leach murder trial, a witness was hypnotized twice before testifying that he had seen a man who looked very much like Ted Bundy leading Kimberly Leach into a white van.

Based on the Bundy trials, the justices decided to outlaw the use of hypnotically refreshed testimony in Florida courts, but after long contemplation they carved a narrow exception for Bundy himself. In

1984 and 1985, respectively, they rejected the Chi Omega and the Leach murder trial appeals, saying that Bundy's cases contained "sufficient evidence . . . absent the tainted testimony, upon which the jury could have based its conviction." Therefore, the erroneous use of hypnosis was, in these cases, "harmless." Technically, the court was applying an invalid test to deny Bundy's demand for new trials. The proper test for deciding whether an error is "harmless" is whether the "tainted testimony . . . might have contributed to the conviction." In the two Bundy cases, the hypnotically refreshed testimony provided the only eyewitness links; surely it "might have contributed" to the convictions. The Florida Supreme Court had bent over backwards to affirm Bundy's convictions—creating a "Bundy exception" to the law. Each appeal took five years to complete, but in keeping with a larger sense of justice, the court found a way to preserve the death sentences.

The governor's office scheduled Bundy's clemency hearing for December 18, 1985. Shortly before the hearing, Bundy fired Bob Harper—the latest in a long string of lawyers dismissed by the killer—triggering speculation that the old manipulator was trying to gum up the works. It didn't work. Governor Graham proceeded as scheduled.

Bundy wrote his own crude petition to the U.S. Supreme Court, asking for a review of the state supreme court's action in the Chi Omega case. This was filed January 15, 1986. Three weeks later, Graham signed Bundy's death warrant, scheduling the execution for March 4, 1986, and the result was pandemonium. Because Bundy was operating without a lawyer, his files were moved to the offices of CCR, the state agency charged with representing death row inmates. Just four months old, the agency was swamped with scores of cases, many of them much older than Bundy's. Into this madhouse came the biggest criminal court record in Florida history—the files filled an entire room. And the execution was a month away. There was no way the small team of CCR lawyers could handle such a case.

They went looking for help. Mike Mello knew some lawyers at the prestigious Washington law firm of Wilmer, Cutler and Pickering. He called one of them, who in turn approached a partner named James

Coleman. The decision to take on a case as massive and notorious as Ted Bundy's was not easy for the D.C. lawyers, but after "much free-form negotiation and soul searching" (as Mello later put it), Coleman agreed to step in. At first, his service was limited: He would simply try to block this warrant. Eventually, Coleman and his firm wound up taking on the entire case.

Meanwhile, Bundy continued to play lawyer. After his warrant was signed, he fired off a handwritten request to the U.S. Supreme Court asking for a stay of execution while the justices weighed his appeal. This was quickly returned by Justice Lewis Powell, with the strong suggestion that Bundy get himself a real attorney and try again. When James Coleman entered the picture, the petition was renewed, and the high court was faced with at least one strong issue—the loop-hole created in the state supreme court's hypnosis ruling—wrapped up in an enormous trial record. The U.S. Supreme Court was in the middle of a busy term and had less than a week to read all the material. Not surprisingly, they granted a stay of execution; no Florida inmate had been executed on his first death warrant.

Coleman now had some breathing room. A specialist in lawsuits over government regulation, he was accustomed to complicated legal wrangling, but he was also accustomed to the fairly leisurely timetable of the civil courts. With an associate, Polly Nelson, Coleman began combing the trial record for procedural flaws and reinvestigating the Chi Omega case from the ground up. But he was barely under way when the U.S. Supreme Court, having studied the record, formally declined to review the Chi Omega decision and lifted its stay of execution. In a scene straight from Hollywood, the news was announced during a station break in an NBC miniseries, "The Deliberate Stranger," the story of Ted Bundy's life.

Bob Graham signed a second death warrant, and the execution was set for July 2, 1986. For the next four weeks, James Coleman and Polly Nelson worked feverishly. The appeal they crafted claimed more than a dozen flaws in the Chi Omega trial. These claims were sum-marily denied in the state courts.

Coleman moved to the federal courts, but his client's infamy pre-ceded him. According to the law, if any of Coleman's claims might have a legal foundation, the federal court was supposed to stay the execution and hold a full-scale hearing. The only way a judge could make that decision was by studying the trial record. In Bundy's case, however, the federal district judge made no pretense of studying the record—the entire fifteen-thousand-page file never left the trunk of the prosecutor's car. So much for soft judges; the "Bundy Express" was rolling. But the federal Circuit Court of Appeals would not tolerate such haste. Reluctantly, they stayed the execution.

This time, though, Coleman knew he had no breathing room. Along with all his other work, he had filed a petition to the U.S. Supreme Court to review the other Bundy case—the murder of Kimberly Leach. Coleman had no illusions that the high court would take the case, and he knew that as soon as the justices formally declined, Bob Graham would sign another death warrant. Coleman had to repeat all the work he had done in the Chi Omega files for the Leach case. He dove into the thirteen-thousand-page record.

On October 14, 1986, the high court, as expected, refused to hear Bundy's appeal in the Leach case; a week later, Bundy's third death warrant in nine months was issued. Now the "Express" was running with a full head of steam. Coleman's pleas for Bundy were turned down by three different courts in a single day. Once again, the rush was slightly more than the Circuit Court of Appeals could countenance. Another stay of execution was ordered.

Never before in the modern age—and never since—had so much death penalty litigation been dispensed with so quickly. The death penalty is a balky and spluttering machine; a single case, relatively simple, can take years to move from one court to the next. Bundy had two hugely complicated cases, but both had been moved from near the beginning of the appeals process almost to the end in less than a year.

Politicians and the general public often complained that Bundy was "manipulating" the system, "endlessly" appealing, "abusing" the courts. In fact, the only delay in Bundy's case was the delay in the Florida Supreme Court's decisions. There, a badly overburdened court had stretched itself to its limit in order to preserve the death sentences. After that, the case went sledding on a steep, slick slope. Bundy had moved so quickly that his case leapfrogged those of forty or fifty inmates who had been on death row longer.

But nothing sold on the campaign trail like promises to speed up the death penalty. In 1986, Bob Graham—having completed the two terms allowed him as governor—was running for the U.S. Senate. His opponent was an incumbent Republican, Paula Hawkins. Ronald Reagan, who had carried Florida by a landslide in the 1984 presidential election, campaigned for Hawkins, trying to work his conservative magic. But Graham could not be pigeonholed as a liberal. More than any other issue, his stance on the death penalty bolstered him against the conservative tide, and he won.

In the race to succeed him as governor, the death penalty drove out all other issues. Tom Fiedler, political editor of *The Miami Herald,* saw it coming early, when he covered a group of candidates addressing a powerful agriculture lobby. The printed agenda dealt with such subjects as land use regulations and water rights, but the applause was strongest when candidates talked tough on capital punishment.

The whole campaign was like that. Barry Kutun, a dark horse, ripped the Florida Supreme Court for being too slow on death cases. "They should be burning the midnight oil," he declared. Another dark-horse Democrat, Joan Wolin, went him one better. "I'm not only for the death penalty, I'll pull the switch," she announced. "I'll go to Bundy's and pull the switch." State Senate President Harry Johnston, a bona fide liberal, appeared on television glaring intently into the lens. "I have always—always—supported the death penalty . . . not just at election time," he intoned. This was a not-so-veiled reference to the Democratic front-runner, Steve Pajcic, who had voted against the death penalty in the state legislature. Now, running for governor, Pajcic promised that he would sign death warrants in spite of his personal belief that capital punishment was wrong. "The public strongly supports the death penalty law and expects the governor to uphold it," Pajcic said. He hustled hard to protect himself on the issue, securing endorsements from twenty-eight Florida sheriffs and two major police unions. But as the campaign wore on, Pajcic watched his poll numbers sag, and political experts attributed much of his problem to his stand on capital punishment.

"They're killing us with the death penalty," Bradford County Sheriff Dolph Reddish announced when Pajcic paid a visit to the courthouse in Starke. The sheriff had some advice for his candidate. "I'd go out there and stand by the electric chair with one hand on it . . . I'd get as close to that sucker as I could."

Perhaps spurred by Pajcic's weakness, Attorney General Jim Smith jumped into the race—driving a wedge through the Democratic Party and blunting its chances to hold on to the governor's office. At first, Smith called the death penalty a "nonissue," but soon enough he launched a series of attacks on the front-runner. "Stop your whining!" went one radio ad. "Be a man, Steve!" By the time Pajcic won the painfully fought Democratic nomination, he was badly wounded. On the Republican side, Tampa Mayor Bob Martinez won the nomination over another candidate who promised that if he became governor, "Florida's electric bill will go up." Martinez was super-tough on the death penalty, and he mopped up Pajcic in the general election.

Martinez was sworn in as Florida's new governor on January 6, 1987. Less than a month later, he signed his first pair of death warrants. Both ended in routine stays of execution. It was easier to promise speed than to deliver it.

The Circuit Court of Appeals put the Bundy cases on an expedited schedule, with shortened deadlines for briefs and arguments. Hearings in both the Chi Omega and Leach murder cases were set for early 1987. The Chi Omega hearing was particularly intense; the appeals judges could not believe that a prosecutor had left the trial record in his car. Judge Robert Vance, a tough man on the death penalty, was incensed. "I can't understand your behavior," Vance lectured the prosecutor. "This case is going to be reversed and sent down . . . because of a stupid error. If you had called it to the attention of the judge at the time, it could have been corrected in four days. It's wrong. It's clearly wrong, counsel."

If not for that error, Bundy might have slipped through to the chair in 1986. Instead, the courts had to retrace their steps and go through the motions of examining the claims raised by James Coleman. In April 1987, the appeals court sent both cases back to federal district court for proper hearings. The "Bundy Express" was sidetracked. For reasons that never became clear, the district judge in the Chi Omega case did nothing, waiting almost two years to schedule a hearing. But Judge G. Kendall Sharp picked up the slack, moving the Leach murder case to the top of his docket and ordering the combatants into his courtroom six months hence.

Was there any point to all these repetitive reviews by courts state and federal, all this sifting and resifting? Or had the law simply gone haywire? The thugs of death row were guilty of ghastly crimes. They had snuffed out hundreds of victims, shattered thousands of lives. Why not get on with it and put them in the chair? One reason the law forbids the hurry-up approach is that decent society hates to kill an innocent man, and not everyone on death row is guilty.

Not far from Ted Bundy on Florida's death row lived a man named Earnest Lee Miller and his half-brother, William Riley Jent. They had arrived at Starke in late January 1980, about a month before their more notorious neighbor; compared to Bundy, they were nearly anonymous. For a time, whenever Scharlette Holdman heard people refer to "Jent-and-Miller," she assumed it was one man with an odd first name. Jentin Miller. Truth was, for brothers they were very distinct: "Wild Bill" Jent was dark-haired and stocky, outgoing, and funny; Earnie Miller was blond, tall, slim, and quiet. On the day they arrived at their death row cells, Jent was the one who made a joke of their situation. "Hey, Earnie!" his voice boomed down the corridor. "This is another fine mess you've gotten us into." According to the judge who sentenced them, Jent and Miller were guilty of "one of the most cold-blooded and heinous murders in the annals of Florida jurisprudence."

On a sultry Saturday afternoon, July 14, 1979, a rancher was riding his horse through the Richloam Game Preserve in north-central Florida, looking for stray cattle. As he passed through a popular picnic ground, he noticed—amid the scrub, garbage, and cypress roots—a corpse, horribly disfigured by fire. It was the body of a young woman, much of her face and torso burned away. The rancher sent a companion to summon the police. He stayed behind to shoo the buzzards.

Detective David Fitzgerald of the Pasco County Sheriff's Office was one of the first to arrive. He was a handsome young man, and moved with the confidence of a small town's golden boy; nearly everyone in nearby Dade City knew him either as the former baseball and tennis star at the local high school, or as the son of the popular proprietor of the Crest Restaurant across the street from the courthouse. This was the green young detective's first murder mystery, and he found precious little to go on. A plastic milk jug lay near the body, smelling faintly of gasoline. Two cheap rings were on the victim's fingers; a roach clip lay in the soot beneath the body. Clinging to the body were a few shreds of unburned clothing; nearby was a pair of sandals. The ground was crisscrossed with tire tracks from a dozen recent picnics. Plaster molds were made of the tracks nearest the crime scene.

Clouds threatened an evening rain, so the crime-scene investigation was rushed. Toward sundown the body was taken to the local morgue, where the following morning Dr. Rehana Nawab performed an autopsy. Nawab, too, was green, and this was her first autopsy of a burn victim. As she went about her work, she found a small skull fracture and a pocket of blood on the victim's brain. From this, she concluded that the victim had been beaten. She drew blood samples, which showed high concentrations of carbon monoxide. From this she concluded that the woman had still been breathing when she was set ablaze. Fingerprints were taken. The teeth were in bad condition, Nawab observed. There was little else to say. The doctor theorized that the killer or killers had clubbed their victim unconscious, poured gasoline over her from the plastic milk jug, then set off a fireball. Following standard procedure, Nawab preserved certain tissue samples, including the larynx, and classified the remains "Jane Doe."

Not much to go on. David Fitzgerald had an unidentified corpse, some jewelry, a pair of sandals. No fingerprints on the milk jug. All he knew was how the murder had happened. A beating. Immolation of an unconscious victim. Fitzgerald threw himself into the missing-persons reports that began to pour in from around the state, looking for a match.

Dade City, about a dozen miles from the crime scene, is the quiet seat of Pasco County, a town of neat lawns and cookie-cutter houses located in cattle and citrus country about an hour north of Tampa. North of town, up Highway 301, this Main Street idyll gives way rapidly to a world of beat-up trailer parks and grim migrant camps. Six miles up the highway is the tiny hamlet of Lacoochee. Before World War II, Lacoochee was a working town, home of a thriving cypress mill. But then all the cypress trees were cut, the mill closed, and Lacoochee was left with nothing but dirt roads, ramshackle houses, rough bars, and poor people. It was just outside Lacoochee that Jane Doe was found.

Jack Armstrong was a sheriff's deputy who loved working Lacoochee. Despite his all-American name, Armstrong was a bit of a rough character himself, the son of a Boston steamfitter, burly, happy as a clam knocking back a few beers in squalid Lacoochee bars while sopping up the local gossip. And after the body was discovered on the Richloam Game Preserve, gossip was plentiful around town. A good bit of it flowed from Bivian Bohannon, a local busybody. If a crime transpired along that tough stretch of Highway 301—and many did—it was a good bet Bivian Bohannon would talk about it. She was a thresher of gossip, which she dumped, without gleaning, in great bales on the police. A loyal informant, though not always reliable, Bohannon talked eagerly about the grisly crime at the picnic ground.

Around that time, a seventeen-year-old runaway named Carlena Jo Hubbard was staying at Bohannon's house. As she once testified, she was a tragic child, the daughter of two heroin addicts from Kansas City; she had grown up in foster homes and was an addict herself by the age of thirteen. She favored LSD and angel dust, and these ravaged her unstable mind, generating wild and vivid dreams. Psychiatrists had diagnosed her as a paranoiac. Hubbard listened intently to Bohannon's stream of gossip and speculation, and after several days of it, she had a horrific dream. She awoke screaming: "Don't burn her! Don't burn her!" Bivian Bohannon was convinced by those words that C. J. Hubbard held the key to the fiery murder, and she ordered the girl to call the sheriff's office.

Hubbard welcomed the chance to help. But try as she might, she could not remember a crime. Maybe, she offered, the victim was a woman she knew only as "Elizabeth," who liked to hang out at Howard's Bar. This "Elizabeth" was a friend of a local man named Earnie Miller, Hubbard said, and she added that she recalled overhearing Miller "talking about killing people." That was how it began.

Jack Armstrong knew all about Earnie Miller—he was a thorn in Armstrong's side, a giant pain in his butt. Miller lived in a run-down house in Lacoochee surrounded by a tall chain-link fence, and he kept a pair of Doberman pinschers in the yard. Earnie Miller made his living selling dope, and he did not welcome unexpected visitors. For months, Armstrong had been following Miller, staking out the house, trying to nail him on a drug charge. But Miller was always one step ahead. Sometimes, Armstrong got the feeling that Miller was gloating.

And in the tangled little underworld of north Dade City and Lacoochee, some people believed that Armstrong had a more personal grudge against Miller, as well. The deputy often enjoyed a few drinks at Howard's, and he was known to hit on the barmaid, a slender, long-haired woman named Robbie Larramore. According to Larramore, Armstrong would invite her out to breakfast or to "go for a ride," and she always declined. Armstrong would ask, "Why not?" Larramore recalled that she answered, "I'm real picky about who I go out with."

Too picky to date Armstrong, but not too picky to date Earnie Miller—Larramore had lived for a while with Miller in the white house with the chain-link fence. One day, not long before the fiery murder, Jack Armstrong ran into Robbie Larramore at the Lacoochee Shop 'n' Go. "And he said to me if I didn't stay away from Earnie Miller, I'd better watch my step," Larramore recalled. Samantha Carver claimed she had heard a similar threat. Carver, an exotic dancer with a tattoo of a mushroom on her left buttock, had been riding in Miller's rattletrap green Galaxie 500 along Highway 301 one afternoon when Armstrong pulled them over. As Carver remembered it, Armstrong walked up and leaned toward the driver's window. "Maybe we can't get you for the drugs you're selling," he told Earnie Miller. "But we're gonna get you for something."

Thanks to C. J. Hubbard's dream, Miller's name surfaced, however tenuously, in connection with the murder of Jane Doe. Armstrong prepared a composite sketch of the dead woman and took it around Lacoochee. He wanted to know if anyone had seen her, in the company of Earnie Miller, on the evening of Friday, July 13, 1979.

It was a stroke of luck, really, that Armstrong knew the exact date of the crime. Dr. Nawab's autopsy had not been able to pinpoint the time of death—she guessed that the body had been dead roughly twenty-four hours before she first saw it, but she said possibly several days had elapsed. Armstrong had done some investigating on his own. On Friday, July 20, 1979, six days after the discovery of the crime, he had taken a drive out to the crime scene and come across a family enjoying a cookout: Kenneth and Addis Taylor, with their grandsons Randy and Pat. The Taylors told Armstrong they had been in the same spot, cooking hot dogs, the previous Friday afternoon. They'd spent a good three hours, Ken and Addis enjoying the sunshine, the boys running and playing. They hadn't seen a corpse. Armstrong also learned that Freddie Hayes and Joe Nichol had spent the late afternoon that same day fishing in the nearby Withlacoochee River. They had parked their white Ford pickup a few feet from the spot where the body had been found. They hadn't seen anything unusual. Six people, tramping around the crime scene, and no hint of a crime. "Therefore," Armstrong wrote in his report, "writer believes that body would not have been deposited at that location until 6 P.M." or later. That's how the detective knew to focus his inquiries on the night of Friday the thirteenth.

Carrying his composite drawing and a picture of the dead woman's jewelry, Armstrong trooped from bar to bar. "I got a lot of responses," he later testified. "Most of them were not too good." But at El Caboose, he found an answer he liked, from bartender Alicia Valdez. She was eager to please: Valdez was an immigrant from Mexico with a criminal past; if she failed to make a favorable impression on the authorities, she could be deported at the drop of a hat. Obligingly, she identified the woman in the drawing. On the night of July 13, that woman had been in the bar, Valdez said. She was with Earnie Miller. A whole bunch of people were drinking together, and they all left in Miller's car. Valdez did not remember seeing Bill Jent.

Miller was not an ideal murder suspect. He was a longhaired doper, a no-account punk, but there was little in his background to suggest he was especially violent. Born in Dayton, Ohio, in 1956, Miller was five years younger than his half brother Bill. According to an aunt, neither Miller's mother nor his father wanted the boy; after his dad left, his mother moved from apartment to apartment, preferring places that didn't allow children. Miller grew up hard. At fifteen he drifted to Lacoochee to pick oranges, then tried a stint in the Marines. He went AWOL and drifted back to Florida. Miller was known to get drunk and hit his wife, a dark-haired Mexican named Maria; but then, Maria was known to get drunk and hit Earnie. They had two children and lived apart.

Bill Jent looked more like the murdering type. Jent had been to prison—ten months for breaking and entering. He, too, had washed out of the Marines; after that, he became a tattooed member of the Renegades, a motorcycle gang. On July 8, a few days before the murder at the game preserve, Bill Jent had roared into Lacoochee on his Harley, driving right up to Miller's front door. He was on vacation. Miller was waiting with booze, pot, and a couple of women. "Hey," he said, and he pointed to Samantha Carver. "I got something for you." Miller's date for the week was a strangely charming junkie named Glina Frye.

They had sex and got blasted for a couple of days. On Thursday night, July 12, Bill and Earnie, Sam and Glina rounded up some friends for a party at a burned-out railroad trestle over the Withlacoochee River. They drank Canadian Mist whiskey, swigged beer, smoked pot, and snorted angel dust. A rope swing dangled from a tree, and they took turns leaping from the riverbank, clutching the rope, then dropping into the dark water. C. J. Hubbard was there, as were George Mortola, Salvadore Velazquez, Ricky Camacho, and Patricia Tiricaine, who was so drunk she threw up repeatedly. Twice during the party, a sheriff's deputy cruised by to take a look. He saw nothing unusual. When he rolled up a third time, after 1 A.M., everyone was gone. Miller drove Tiricaine home, and when he got back to his house he found everyone else passed out.

The following night, Friday the thirteenth, Bill and Earnie and Sam and Glina drove into Tampa to meet one of Jent's fellow Renegades at the airport. They made quite an impression in the lounge where they waited—raucous, raunchy, and loud.

When deputies David Fitzgerald and Jack Armstrong learned that Earnie Miller had been hosting his Renegade half brother on the night of the crime, the pieces began to fall into place. Everyone knows that motorcycle gangsters are capable of mistreating women, raping and even murdering them. The deputies had an ex-con biker, Wild Bill Jent, visiting a known criminal, shiftless Earnie Miller, who in turn was seen at El Caboose in the company of an unidentified young woman. The following afternoon this woman was found dead. It didn't take Sherlock Holmes to add two and two.

The detectives started looking for the members of the swimming party. At El Caboose, Armstrong found Salvatore Velazquez. Though he spoke little English, Velazquez acknowledged having been there, but said he had been too busy playing on the rope swing to notice much of anything. Patricia Tiricaine was also at the bar. She readily admitted attending the party, but explained that the whole night was hazy. She had been so drunk. Armstrong did not believe her. He took Tiricaine down to the station.

Years later, Tiricaine would say in a sworn statement that she was threatened with five years in jail if she didn't give the detectives what they wanted. "They told me I was with some people partying at the trestle and this girl got killed. And they said Earnie and Bill had killed this girl," Tiricaine declared. "They kept telling me, 'Well, this is the way it happened.' And I, you know, agreed with them."

However it transpired, after several hours of questioning, Tiricaine confirmed the detectives' theory. She told them she was swimming when she heard muffled screams. Curious, she walked toward the noise. She saw Miller talking to Glina Frye. "I got her," Miller had said. Then Tiricaine saw a dead, nude body. And Miller threatened her: If you tell anyone, he had said, the motorcycle gang will come after you. A strange, sketchy story. Tiricaine did not say she had seen the crime; she gave no hint of a motive; she said nothing about how the body had gotten from the trestle to the game preserve.

But for Armstrong and Fitzgerald, Tiricaine's tale solved the puzzle. They began trying to find Glina Frye, George Mortola, and Ricky Camacho. Intriguingly, all three had skipped town the day after the murder was discovered. Miller and Jent were still in Lacoochee, but that meant nothing to the detectives. After all, Earnie Miller had always been smug. In fact, on July 25, Miller brought a friend to the police station to look at the composite drawing of the victim. He claimed he was trying to aid the investigation. Detectives arrested him on the spot, and an hour or so later they picked up Jent. The half brothers were charged with the murder of Jane Doe.

The other party-goers were tracked to Reedsville, North Carolina, where they were arrested as accessories. Glina Frye, George Mortola, and Ricky Camacho all insisted that there had been no murder at the railroad trestle and—though David Fitzgerald threatened them with prison—for nine days, they stood firm. On the tenth day, Frye started to talk.

In a sworn statement several years later, Frye said someone had sketched three electric chairs on a sheet of paper, then labeled them: "Bill," "Earnie," and, on the last, "Glina." However it transpired, Frye offered a story that fit nicely with the details emerging from Tiricaine's ongoing sessions with police. By now, Tiricaine was saying that she had seen Bill Jent leaning over the young woman, beating her with a stick. Glina Frye's account matched neatly, down to the stick in Jent's right hand. As the interrogations continued, Tiricaine added that she had also seen Miller strike the victim. Frye's account grew to match. (Frye later swore that she had changed her story because the detectives demanded that she incriminate Miller. "They said I had it all mixed up, that I was trying to protect Earnie.")

Precisely how many times the stories changed is impossible to calculate, because contrary to his ordinary practice, Armstrong made no tapes of the interrogations. Despite the alterations, though, the details from the two women never entirely meshed. The witnesses could not decide whether the victim was nude or clothed, standing or prostrate. They weren't sure how she had gotten to the swimming party, and disagreed about what had happened on the way to the game preserve where she was dumped. Perhaps that was to be expected, given the booze and the drugs.

One fact they eventually agreed upon was that the body had been transported in the trunk of Miller's car. So the detectives impounded the car, popped the trunk, and immediately saw that the space had not been cleaned in many months—if ever. This was good news. A badly beaten body had been stuffed in there, possibly after being raped. She should have left traces: blood, vaginal fluid, stray strands of hair. Miller's trunk could seal the case.

But they found nothing. Nor was that their only disappointment. In the course of grilling Glina Frye, the detectives discovered that she had been in Tampa with Miller and Jent on Friday night, July 13. They had registered at a motel, so there would be a paper trail. And they had made nuisances of themselves at the airport bar; someone would probably remember them. This was a problem: Armstrong had the statements of six people who had been at the crime scene that Friday afternoon and had seen nothing amiss. If those witnesses were right, then the body must have been dumped and burned later that evening, when the suspects were more than fifty miles away.

Regarding the car trunk, the detectives theorized that a blanket must have sopped up the evidence. It was a stretch to think that a couple of stoned thugs would have been so tidy, but it was possible. The alibi was more troubling. There was no solution but to move the date of the murder from Friday, July 13, to Thursday, July 12. And the existence of the six crime-scene witnesses had to be buried. Armstrong's report was not among the files that were given to the defense. When defense attorneys asked him, under oath, to recount each step of his investigation, Armstrong neglected to mention anything about the six witnesses.

With the killers in jail, David Fitzgerald apparently saw little need to keep plowing through the mountain of missing-persons reports. So when a man named T. B. Bradshaw turned up at the station one day, convinced that the dead woman was his daughter Linda Gale, Fitzgerald listened skeptically and sent the man on his way. If he had a dollar for every parent who wanted to claim the victim, he'd be a rich man.

One report did intrigue Fitzgerald, though. A woman told him that her daughter, Tammy, had run off with a motorcycle gang, supposedly in the company of a man called "Wild Bill." That was Jent's nickname. Fitzgerald asked Glina Frye about it. Frye was shaping up as the prosecution's star witness, a great talker, wonderfully cooperative when the police needed new details; she was helpful as usual. Yes, Frye told Fitzgerald, the victim's name was Tammy, though Frye was unsure of the girl's last name. Thus, when indictments were handed up charging Miller and Jent with first-degree murder, the victim was identified as "Tammy LNU," for Last Name Unknown. C. J. Hubbard's story about a girl named "Elizabeth"—the story that had originally linked the crime to Earnie Miller—was forgotten. (Police also quickly abandoned the "Tammy" theory. Only the name survived.)

Hubbard, meanwhile, was in protective custody, safe from the predatory motorcycle gang, trying desperately to be of assistance. She felt sure that she knew something about the crime, but she just couldn't remember. She met frequently with David Fitzgerald, who walked her again and again through the details reported by Tiricaine and Frye. These sessions continued for almost a month. Then Hubbard had another of her dreams. "I started dreaming where I could see what was going on," she later explained. She was at the party. She was making out with Ricky Camacho. She was swimming. From the water, she glanced down the darkened riverbank, and there were Earnie Miller and Bill Jent beating a woman with a stick. Things went hazy, but now everyone was crammed into Miller's car, riding through a forest. The car came to a stop. They all piled out. The body was on the ground, and flames were leaping. "The dream," Hubbard said, "came to life."

The detectives wrote up her statement, down to the last detail—all except for the fact that this was a dream. And suddenly there were three "eyewitnesses" to the ghastly murder of Tammy LNU.

But they had not a shred of physical evidence. The detectives had no fingerprints, no bloody clothes, no murder weapon; they didn't know where the gasoline had come from; they couldn't tie the milk jug to either defendant; the tire tracks near the body didn't match those of

Miller's car. Months passed. Jane Doe, the mysterious Tammy, was buried. Miller's trial, set for mid-November, approached. Still no evidence.

Then something marvelous happened. Fitzgerald produced a single strand of black hair, which he said he had found three days after the body was discovered, during a careful scouring of the crime scene. The hair had somehow clung to a cypress knee through a downpour, and miraculously Fitzgerald had noticed it amongst the scrub and litter at the site. At the state crime lab, an expert determined that the hair was very similar to Jent's hair. This was not conclusive, but it was the first, and only, physical link.

Why had this hair been produced so late in the game? The defense believed the detective was cheating. Bill Jent was a shaggy man, with shoulder-length hair and a bushy beard. Fitzgerald could easily have strolled into the prisoner's cell, plucked a hair from the pillow, and claimed that he had found it at the site. Normally, this question would be easily settled, because when evidence is discovered it is carefully entered into police custody, it is recorded, and a receipt is written. The receipt would prove that the hair had been found before Jent was arrested. Except Fitzgerald had never taken these steps. There was no receipt. Only the detective's word.

On the day Earnie Miller's trial began, November 12, 1979, rumors ran rampant in peaceful Dade City that hundreds of motorcycle gangsters were camped outside town, waiting to ride in, guns blazing, to free their friends. Security around the courthouse was at an all-time high. "We all believed that Jent and Miller were part of an enormous evil gang, because that's what the police were telling us," Judy Hinson later recalled. Hinson covered the trial for the local weekly, which ran pictures of the sullen, ponytailed Miller and his bearded biker brother. "In retrospect, I guess we went overboard. I've never seen a biker on the streets of Dade City." In truth, there was no encampment of bikers, and nobody came to the rescue of Miller or Jent.

Miller's trial unfolded simply. Dr. Nawab took the stand to explain her theory that Tammy LNU was beaten unconscious and died in the fire. Patricia Tiricaine, C. J. Hubbard, and Glina Frye testified to a beating and burning that fit the doctor's conclusions. But Frye gave her testimony a new twist. For the first time, she said that during a stop at Miller's house on the way to the game preserve, the half brothers had pulled Tammy's unconscious body from the trunk of Miller's car, stripped off her clothes, and raped her. Apparently unconcerned about the frequent police surveillance of the Miller place, the other men from the party joined in. Then the body was returned to the trunk, and everyone got back in the car for the ride to the dump site.

This was devastating for the defense, not least because the added felony of rape made the death penalty more likely, and Miller's attorney was aghast. Why, in her five previous sworn statements, had Frye neglected to mention this shocking scene? "I skipped over the rape part," Frye answered. "I just added a little bit more truth each time I told it."

Miller's lawyer, Larry Hersch, didn't realize just how many different versions of the crime had been recounted by the three eyewitnesses. Many accounts, with wildly conflicting details, lay undisclosed in police files and were never mentioned by detectives on the witness stand. Cross-examining the eyewitnesses, he could only hammer on the discrepancies in their formal sworn statements. All three women had given at least three different versions of the crime. They disagreed on who rode with whom to the party. They disagreed on who stood where. They could not remember whether they spent three minutes or ninety minutes at Miller's house. They were vague on the details of the beating, claiming only to have "glanced" at the murder in their midst. They were unsure who poured the gas, who struck the match. Hubbard said they partied by the light of a bonfire; Frye said they partied by candlelight. "Was [Hubbard] so drunk she thought that candle was a bonfire?" Hersch asked in his closing argument. "Or was Glina so high that she thought that bonfire was a candle?"

Discrepancies aside, an overwhelming fact remained: Three people said they witnessed a murder. That was enough. Earnie Miller was found guilty. The jury recommended a life sentence.

A month later, Bill Jent went on trial. The evidence was essentially the same, except for the mysterious hair and the fact that, once again, Glina Frye "added a little bit more." This time, along with the story of the gang rape, Frye described a hideous resurrection. As the victim was doused with gasoline, she awoke, and struggled to rise. Jent threw her back to the ground, and someone lit a match. This heinous new detail tipped the balance, and Jent's jury recommended the death penalty.

As they awaited sentencing by Judge Wayne Cobb, Earnie Miller and Bill Jent were kept at the Pasco County jail. During that time they were joined in jail by a sex offender named Elmer Carroll, another troubled denizen of Highway 301. He was in the cell next door to Miller, and listened for several days as Miller moaned that he had been railroaded for a crime he didn't commit. "He kept going on about how he wasn't guilty, he didn't do it," Carroll later recalled. "Finally, I said, 'I know. . . . I saw it happen.'"

In late June and early July of 1979, Elmer Carroll and Tina Parsons were living in an ancient Airstream trailer on the northern outskirts of Dade City. Eight feet away, in an identical trailer, a man named Charles Robert Dodd Jr. lived with his girlfriend, Linda Gale Bradshaw.

Bobby Dodd was twenty-three, a habitual felon from the dirt-poor hill country of North Georgia. Kind of a cute fellow, with dark, straight hair and piercing eyes, he romanced the ladies as a guitar player in a honky-tonk band; his signature tune was the theme from TV's *Batman*. Dodd made a little money working in the carpet mills of Dalton, Georgia, and a little more selling dope, and a little more— according to several ex-girlfriends—pimping prostitutes. He was a robber (though not always successful; he had scars on his back where a shopkeeper had blasted him with a shotgun). He kited checks. He had an explosive temper. Once, Dodd ran up on a friend who was working under a car, kicked the man in the groin, hauled him to his feet, and battered him with a wrench. He liked to talk about his skills in the martial arts, bragging how easy it was to kill somebody.

Gale Bradshaw was twenty, a school dropout at twelve, wife at fourteen, divorcée at fourteen and a half. A plain young woman, a little plumpish, with soft eyes, she had a sweet small smile, tight-lipped because she was ashamed of her rotted teeth. She lived across the border from Dalton in Cleveland, Tennessee, and one night, when she was sixteen, Bradshaw went to the Starlight saloon for a little drinking and dancing. There, she fell in love with the slight, cute guitar player who wailed on "Batman." It was a tempestuous romance because Dodd had so many women in his life. His wife, for example, and anyone else he could sweet-talk, and at least one girl whom he simply overpowered. In spite of it all, Gale Bradshaw was in love.

In the summer of 1979 they were both in trouble. Bradshaw had been writing bad checks; Dodd was wanted for the rape of a thirteen-year-old girl. They packed up their few belongings and headed south on Interstate 75, which took them down through the Georgia hills, through Atlanta, through the swampy borderlands into Florida, past the billboards advertising cheap tickets to Disney World. North of Tampa, they turned east toward Dade City, where Gale Bradshaw had kin. They wound up in a green-painted Airstream in a trailer park off Highway 301. Naturally, they struck up a friendship with their next-door neighbors; they had a lot in common, after all—age, class, problems with the law. Bobby Dodd and Elmer Carroll passed the hot afternoons drinking beer and smoking pot and cigarettes. Gale Bradshaw and Tina Parsons sipped tea made from hallucinogenic mushrooms. Dodd showed off his karate skills and played mumblety-peg with his switchblade. As the blazing day faded into humid night, Bobby Dodd sometimes took up his guitar and sang Gale Bradshaw's favorite tune, "Stairway to Heaven." And if he was angry at her (as he was, more and more often), he added a line of his own composing at the end: "And she's buy-uy-ying the stair-air-way to Heav-ennn (I'm gonna kill youuuu)."

Dodd was so often angry at Bradshaw because she was so often angry at him. Their life together on the run from the law had not brought them closer; Dodd was no more faithful in Dade City than he had been before. Some people remember him pursuing Glina Frye. Samantha Carver, Frye's roommate, recalled Dodd hanging around their trailer all doe-eyed and panting, trying to get Glina to go to bed with him. Carver said he brought Frye gifts of cheap jewelry, claiming to have stolen them from Gale. This Dogpatch Clyde was cheating on his Bonnie—and in the time-honored way of lovers on the lam, Gale Bradshaw apparently figured she might inspire fidelity by threatening to turn her lover in.

Dodd, according to the neighbors, figured differently. "He told me that Gale knew some things on him," Elmer Carroll said, "and every time he turned around she was saying that she was going to have him put in jail if he didn't straighten up." Tina Parsons recalled that Dodd "said he was going to kill her."

Sometime early in July, Gale Bradshaw got fed up and moved out of the trailer. She went to stay with a sister and telephoned her father in tears, begging him to come take her home. T. B. Bradshaw made the long drive down I-75, loaded his daughter's belongings into his car, and was ready to set off on the return trip when Gale asked if they could stop by the trailer to let Dodd know she was leaving. They stopped, and Dodd talked her into staying. Irritated, T.B. helped his daughter unload the car, then drove away. That was the last time he would ever see her. It was July 10, 1979.

When Elmer Carroll talked to Larry Hersch, defense attorney for Earnie Miller, he told this story: On July 12 or 13—"I don't keep up with dates"—"we were pretty high. And [Bobby Dodd] asked me if I knew any places that people camped out, and I said yes." Dodd, Carroll, and Gale Bradshaw climbed into Bradshaw's 1967 Buick, a blue jalopy with a leaky radiator. The car was always overheating; Gale kept a plastic milk jug in the back seat to replenish the water supply. They drove out Highway 301, through Lacoochee, across the Withlacoochee River, turned right on Clay Sink Road into the Richloam Game Preserve. "We got out of the car and smoked about ten joints. . . . And [Dodd] told me to get some gas." Carroll said he thought they might use it to start a campfire. He took the milk jug from the back seat and siphoned some gasoline from the tank of the Buick.

According to Carroll, Dodd began badgering Bradshaw for sex, and she demurred, saying, "You know, Elmer is here." Dodd persisted; Bradshaw resisted. Dodd said: "You've been talking about, you know, having me locked up. I don't like that." He pushed her to the ground, snapped out his switchblade, and said, "I'm gonna train you." And Bradshaw gasped, "Yes, Bobby, anything you say." Then he strangled her. He pounded her head on the ground as he choked her. "The bitch is still breathing," he said. Dodd took the milk jug, poured the gasoline over the still form, flicked his butane lighter, and said, "Burn in hell!"

Carroll said that later that night, he and Dodd sat drinking on the parking lot at the Lacoochee Shop 'n' Go. Dodd nudged the open car door. The door rocked gently, moving as if under an unseen power, and Dodd gestured toward it. "The bitch is haunting me already," he said.

Elmer Carroll's story appeared to have some holes in it—certainly one big hole. What was Carroll's own role in this gruesome crime? He was likely something more than a passive, frightened onlooker. Carroll's own legal problems stemmed from his sex drive, and Dodd liked his girlfriends to earn a little cash by selling sex. It is possible Dodd's temper was triggered by Bradshaw's refusal to have sex with Carroll, and that Carroll had altered the scene slightly to diminish his own role. Possibly, Carroll had an even more active role in the crime. His girlfriend, Tina Parsons, once said that Carroll admitted to her that he grabbed Bradshaw by the neck.

But in numerous respects, Carroll's story was more credible than the ones told by the three eyewitnesses at the trials of Miller and Jent. There was, first, the matter of personal interest. The Miller-Jent witnesses all knew that they could be charged as accessories to murder if they did not testify. Deputy David Fitzgerald acknowledged that he threatened the witnesses with prison; it was part of his "interview technique," he said. Elmer Carroll, on the other hand, was making what lawyers call "an admission against interest." His story didn't help him; it could, potentially, hurt him. He was walking into an accessory rap, not away from one.

Carroll also provided a specific identity for the victim, not some vague "Tammy," last name and origins unknown. He provided a concrete motive for the crime—the most familiar of all murder motives, a lover's spat—in contrast to the seemingly unprovoked outburst of Miller and Jent. He explained the means; that is, why a milk jug was handy for pouring the gasoline. His account meshed with the behavior of the various suspects after the murder. Miller stuck around town, driving the old Ford with the dirty trunk; he and Jent visited Tampa but returned to Lacoochee. Bobby Dodd, by contrast, hightailed it out of Pasco County, and when he turned up again around Dalton, he gave conflicting explanations of Bradshaw's disappearance. He told T. B. Bradshaw he had taken Gale to Tampa; he told Gale's brother Tommy that he left her by the side of the road; to another Bradshaw relative he said he was "too messed up" to remember what happened. In a letter to Gale's sister, he claimed that she left him.

But Armstrong and Fitzgerald nevertheless thought Carroll was lying because he said the victim was strangled, and the autopsy said she was beaten. Further, they believed the dead woman was Tammy LNU, not Gale Bradshaw. To be certain, they showed Bradshaw's picture to Glina Frye. Is this the victim? they asked. Frye said no. The detectives moved Carroll out of the Dade City jail to a jail in nearby Brooksville, where they interrogated him over the course of three and a half days.

Years later, Carroll would give one description of the questioning and the detectives quite another. They all agreed that Carroll was hooked up to a polygraph machine; the detectives said he failed this lie-detector test. (There was no way of confirming this, because the graphs were destroyed.) Carroll said he got a dose of Fitzgerald's "interview technique"—which is to say, he was threatened with prison. "They said, 'We're not even going to look for Bobby Dodd. We got you,'" Carroll recalled. Carroll said he directed the cops to the crime scene; the cops said he had missed by a mile. According to Carroll, when they reached the scene Jack Armstrong drew his gun, pointed it, and announced, "I'm an expert marksman. I could shoot you and say you were trying to escape." Armstrong denied this. However it transpired, Carroll reluctantly recanted his story, saying Earnie Miller had offered him a stash of dope if he would make it all up.

On January 30, 1980, Bill Jent was sentenced to death. Judge Cobb, saying that the sentences should be equal, overruled Miller's jury and dispatched him to death row, too. As the half brothers headed off to Starke, prosecutor Robert Cole dispatched a letter to Pasco County

Sheriff John Short, commending the good work of David Fitzgerald and Jack Armstrong. "As you know, Carroll's testimony was such that there was a good possibility that Jent and Miller would get a new trial," the prosecutor wrote. "The work of these officers in breaking Carroll saved our office and yours from enormous expense and aggravation."

Strangely, considering their good work, Armstrong and Fitzgerald never advanced at the sheriff's office. Just five months after the sentencing, Fitzgerald was busted back to patrol for reasons that are not clear. He quit the force and opened a restaurant. The following year, Jack Armstrong was also back on patrol—he had asked to be reassigned, citing family problems. On the day they sent two murderers to death row, however, the deputies were jubilant. They took Glina Frye, their star witness, out for a few drinks to celebrate. In one of the many conflicting sworn statements Frye gave over the years that followed, she recalled a snippet of their conversation: "I told them I thought it stunk that two guys could go to prison for a murder they didn't do."

After Bobby Dodd left Dade City and resurfaced in Georgia, he moved into a trailer on Jupiter Circle in Dalton, where his next-door neighbors were the Mocahbees: father Albert, mother Lucille, and daughter Ida Mae, a slender girl of seventeen with stringy blond hair. Ida Mae was thrilled to see Bobby again. Like Gale Bradshaw, she had fallen for him as he twanged his guitar one night at the Starlight saloon. For Ida Mae, it was a goofy girlhood crush. She wrote "Ida loves Bobby" on the flyleaf of her Sunday-school Bible.

On November 9, 1979—three days before Earnie Miller's trial was to begin—Lucille and Ida Mae Mocahbee watched *Dallas* from 10 to 11 P.M. Then Lucille went to bed, and Ida Mae quietly stole $259 from her mother's purse and took some tools from the family toolbox. A neighbor said she rode away from the house with Dodd, who was wearing a cast on his hand. Twenty days later, a local undertaker was out hunting ducks when he came across Ida Mae Mocahbee's decomposing corpse. Her body had been burned. A Miller beer can was beside the body, smelling faintly of gasoline. Her skull had been smashed—"blunt-force trauma," the autopsy concluded, the sort of injury a human hand might make if it was encased in a plaster cast. The crime scene was near a lover's lane, the very place Bobby Dodd had raped a girl half a year earlier.

When Pasco County authorities were informed of this strange coincidence—one man, two girlfriends, both dead in precisely the same way—they theorized that Bill Jent's Renegade cronies had paid a visit to Georgia to frame Dodd. It was an intriguing theory, though far-fetched. The bikers would have had to find Dodd, follow him, figure out whom he was dating. Then they would have had to entice the girl to rob her own mother and come away with them. And there was a larger flaw in the theory: If Jent and Miller had wanted to frame Bobby Dodd, surely they would have mentioned his name before sending their friends to murder an innocent girl. They would have told the police, or told their lawyers, Hey, you guys should be looking at Bobby Dodd.

But Ida Mae Mocahbee was killed before Elmer Carroll ever entered the picture. At the time, Bobby Dodd hadn't entered the picture of the Jent-Miller case. This greatly complicated the conspiracy theory: First, Jent and Miller killed Tammy LNU for no apparent reason. Then they hatched a fiendishly complex plan to put the blame on Bobby Dodd—but failed to mention him as an alternative suspect. Next, they dispatched Jent's biker friends some five hundred miles to stalk and murder Ida Mae Mocahbee, but still they said nothing about Dodd. Then, fortuitously, Dodd's old neighbor, Elmer Carroll, showed up in the next cell. Cleverly, they bribed Carroll to implicate himself as an accessory to murder . . . and only then sprang the case against Dodd. It was a plot worthy of Agatha Christie, engineered by two dopers with double-digit IQs.

Still, this was the scenario police and prosecutors believed—or said they believed. In fact, the Florida detectives never tried very hard to follow up on their theory. Nor did the Georgia police put much effort into solving the Mocahbee murder. When Dodd's parole officer, Morris McDonald, once asked why the investigation into Ida Mae's death had been so lackadaisical, he was told that Georgia authorities didn't want to interfere with another state's death row justice.

∴

Bill Jent seemed to make the transition to death row fairly easily—as easily as anyone can. He had done time before, and besides, he was such an easygoing guy, life just washed over him. He whiled away the hours watching cartoons on TV. Earnie Miller was in prison for the first time, and he worried endlessly about his sanity. He rationed his TV time, afraid the tube would ruin his mind. He slept fitfully, always with a towel over his eyes, because sometimes inmates, walking down the corridor, would fling bleach into a guy's face just for the hell of it. What sleep Miller managed was haunted by nightmares of the electric chair.

They deserved their mind-numbing captivity and their tortured sleep if indeed they had raped and beaten and burned Tammy LNU. The case for their guilt rested on three shaky legs. First leg: The crime had occurred on July 12 and not on July 13, the night for which they had an alibi. Jack Armstrong's report of six people who had not seen a corpse at the crime scene on the afternoon of July 13 was buried in undisclosed police files. Second leg: The eyewitness testimony of three women. The report indicating that C. J. Hubbard's knowledge of the crime had come from a dream was buried in those same files, along with many conflicting versions of the crime described by the three women. Third leg: The unidentified victim. As long as she was Jane Doe, or Tammy LNU, Elmer Carroll's story about Bobby Dodd was a mere sidelight, and so was the death of Ida Mae Mocahbee. The case against Dodd depended on the fact that the dead woman found at the game preserve was indeed Linda Gale Bradshaw. And for years after the trials, the Pasco authorities insisted that no fingerprints of the victim had been recovered.

The death sentences were sent to the Florida Supreme Court for automatic review, where they were affirmed in 1982. In June 1983, Bob Graham signed death warrants for the half brothers. The case moved into the next stages of appeals.

Miller and Jent were represented by Howardene Garrett and Eleanor Jackson Piel, and no clients have ever had a more dedicated and delightful team of lawyers. Garrett, who represented Earnie Miller, was an assistant in the Pasco County public defender's office, a young woman of grit and wit and an unassuming good nature. This was her first death penalty appeal, but there was expertise in her household; Garrett's husband, Austin Maslanek, was one of Scharlette Holdman's stalwarts. Piel, a tough but elegant woman of regal bearing from the Upper West Side of Manhattan, was a graduate of the law school at Berkeley, an old-school liberal who used her wealth to support dogged fights on behalf of the downtrodden. One day, while riding the subway to work, Piel had read a story in *The New York Times* about the shortage of lawyers willing to defend death row inmates. She was scandalized— to her, the death penalty was outright barbarism—and as always her commitment followed her heart. She telephoned a lawyer in North Carolina, who brushed her off; undeterred, she contacted Holdman, who never declined an offer of help. "For me, it was like she was calling to offer a fifty-thousand-dollar check," Holdman recalled. "I looked on my list and found a case for her. It was Bill Jent."

Even for skilled lawyers, death penalty appeals are a world unto themselves. Howardene Garrett could look across the dinner table if she needed advice, but Eleanor Jackson Piel lacked such handy resources. Holdman arranged for Millard Farmer to take her under his wing, well aware that Farmer could be a prickly teacher. One day, Piel called Farmer, enthusiastic about a strategy she had devised for Jent's defense. Farmer sighed in his world-weary way. "Eleanor," he said mournfully. "Why don't you just go out right now and buy a shovel?"

What do you mean? Piel asked.

"You obviously want to put your client in his grave," Farmer said.

Some lawyers might have given up right then, but Eleanor Jackson Piel never gave up. When the death warrants were signed and it was time to argue for a stay of execution before the Florida Supreme Court, she was there, alongside Howardene Garrett, in a display of female power that set Holdman's heart aflutter. "Howardene and Eleanor wore white linen, because they are both such ladies and can wear white linen," Holdman recalled wistfully. "It said that here were the forces of good!"

But the women in white were denied, and so they rushed to the federal district court. With sixteen hours left before the scheduled execution, U.S. District Judge George Carr decided there were questions that needed answering in the case of Bill Jent and Earnie Miller. In their death-watch cells, Jent and Miller had been measured for their funeral suits and had ordered their last meals. When the news came of the stay, Miller heaved a sigh of relief. Jent was watching cartoons and seemed unsurprised.

The following year, Judge Carr held a hearing on the appeals and denied all claims. Garrett and Piel challenged the decision in the Eleventh Circuit Court of Appeals. While this appeal was pending, the Jent-Miller team was making some discoveries. Roy Mathews had begun digging into the case. He was an interesting character, the sort of man the mystery writer Elmore Leonard might have invented if Leonard had gone to Woodstock: a successful yacht broker who had tired of the selling game and become a private eye. Loose, laid-back, and groovy, living in a bungalow on a bluff overlooking the Gulf of Mexico, Mathews did his sleuthing for the Volunteer Lawyers Resource Center, the death penalty project sponsored by the Florida Bar. That's where he picked up the Jent-Miller case.

He had begun by tracking down the purported eyewitnesses. When Mathews found Elmer Carroll at a medium-security prison in Central Florida, he discovered that Carroll had returned to his original story: Bobby Dodd killed Gale Bradshaw, and Carroll saw him do it. Carroll told Mathews he had recanted only because he was threatened with death in the electric chair. Mathews located Patricia Tiricaine, who also recanted her testimony. "They took me down to the police station. And they said I was with some people partying at the trestle and this girl got killed," Tiricaine explained in a sworn statement after Mathews had found her. "And they said Earnie and Bill had killed this girl." Tiricaine told Mathews she was retching drunk the whole night; she had no memory whatsoever. She had invented her story rather than face five years in prison. "They kept telling me, 'Well, this is the way it happened.' And I, you know, agreed with them."

Glina Frye was a tougher nut to crack. Mathews found her working at a fast-food joint in Dade City; he approached her several times, and each time she rebuffed him. But something about Mathews made people want to talk. Especially women. One day, he waited outside the restaurant until Frye got off work, and this time, Frye broke down. She said the detectives had told her that Bill Jent accused her of killing Tammy LNU. She said the detectives had claimed that scrapings taken from the victim's fingernails were matched to Jent's skin. (Jent never made any statement implicating Frye, nor were the scrapings matched to him.) The detectives, Frye said, had given her a choice: She could testify, or face murder charges herself. "I sent two guys to the electric chair for something they didn't do," Frye said later in a television interview. "I know they didn't do it. . . . [Fitzgerald] plainly told me that he would prosecute me for murder and . . . go for the death penalty."

One shaky leg of the case was crumbling. Eleanor Piel, meanwhile, had managed to interest a reporter from *The Washington Post* in the mystery. The reporter was Athelia Knight, and she dug extensively, roaming across four states, interviewing dozens of people, plowing through reams of old files. When she published her findings, in August 1985, Knight acknowledged that she was unable to "prove Jent and Miller's innocence" beyond any doubt. (It is almost impossible to prove a negative, that something did not happen.) But she did succeed in knocking another leg out from under the case. For years, Florida authorities had insisted that there were no fingerprints of Tammy LNU. Knight, digging through old records, had discovered that prints were taken at the autopsy. She also learned that agent Steve Cole of the Tennessee Bureau of Investigation had, as part of his investigation into the whereabouts of Linda Gale Bradshaw, recovered fingerprints from Bradshaw's Bible and photo album. Cole matched the prints from the photo album with the prints of the Pasco County murder victim. "Tammy" was, in fact, Gale Bradshaw.

Amazingly, however, the authorities in Pasco County continued to resist the identification. All it proved, they said, was that Tammy LNU, dead in Florida, had handled Bradshaw's photo album in Tennessee. This was too much for the long-suffering Bradshaw family to take. For six years, T. B. Bradshaw and his children had been certain that the body in the game preserve was Gale's—the shape of that horribly burned face was the shape of Gale's face; the distinctive flat thumbs were her thumbs; the recovered jewelry looked like the pieces she had purchased from the Avon lady. And there was the fact that Bobby Dodd could never explain what had become of Gale. For six years, they had waited to bring Gale home from her anonymous grave in Florida, to give her a proper burial under a stone with her name on it. For six years, the Bradshaws had listened with chagrin as politicians had talked piously about the victims of crime, their suffering. But now the State of Florida seemed so determined to preserve two death sentences that they could not see the torment of the Bradshaws, would not grant them the only gift they desired: the gift of closure, of resolution.

Gale's sister, Suzie Vaughn, went on a letter-writing campaign. She fired off letters to governors, congressmen, senators—anyone who might have the power to help—and at last she caught the attention of two U.S. senators, Sam Nunn of Georgia and Lawton Chiles of Florida. The senators turned up the heat, and finally Tallahassee officials sent an investigator to Tennessee to settle the matter once and for all.

Years earlier, Gale Bradshaw had worked at a gas station, where each employee was fingerprinted before starting to work. The Florida investigator went to the warehouse where the company's records were kept. In a dusty carton he found Bradshaw's application, along with a nice set of prints. The prints matched: The woman found murdered outside Lacoochee that July day in 1979 was Linda Gale Bradshaw. Just as Elmer Carroll said she was.

Carroll was right about something else, too. As the defense team went through the case, checking and rechecking each detail, they asked an expert to review the autopsy findings of Dr. Rehana Nawab, the inexperienced pathologist examining her first burn victim. The defense expert was Dr. Ronald Wright, chief medical examiner for Florida's Broward County, a veteran of more than seven thousand autopsies, including many burn cases. When Wright considered the skull fracture and the puddle of blood under Gale Bradshaw's skin, he recognized both as fairly common results of burning. He saw no reason to conclude they had been caused by blows to the head. The trial testimony of Glina Frye and Patricia Tiricaine had described a savage beating with a stick; Wright doubted that such a beating had occurred.

Next, Wright took the section of the victim's throat that had been preserved by Dr. Nawab—a standard procedure in cases of burning.

Unlike Nawab, Wright dissected the tissue. On the larynx, he discovered familiar signs of strangulation. In his experienced view, Gale Bradshaw had been strangled to death. Just as Elmer Carroll said she was.

Not only had the witnesses against Jent and Miller been wrong about the victim's identity; apparently they were also wrong about the way she was killed. Now they were recanting their testimony. One shaky leg remained to support the case: the date of the murder. Intrigued by the crumbling evidence against the half brothers, the *Tampa Tribune* filed suit to force police and prosecutors to open their records of the investigation. In 1986, the Florida Supreme Court ordered it done.

For the first time, defense attorneys learned just how many conflicting versions of the crime had been offered by the three purported eyewitnesses. They were able to watch, through the chronological reports of the detectives, as the details shifted and coalesced. To their amazement, they found a brief mention that Carlena Jo Hubbard's account was "possibly a dream." Even more critical was Jack Armstrong's report on his visit to the crime scene, in which he named the six witnesses who had seen nothing unusual the afternoon of July 13, 1979. "From where they parked and where they were fishing it would have been an easy view of the body had the body been there," Armstrong had written, putting the likely time of the murder later that evening.

Jent and Miller had been in Tampa that evening. After the report was discovered, seven years after the fact, Armstrong said he had been mistaken in saying "it would have been an easy view"; maybe, he offered, the view wasn't so easy. Asked why he had never mentioned this evidence, he said, "I didn't think it was important."

Faced with the new evidence, the Circuit Court of Appeals sent the case back to U.S. District Judge Carr, who had denied the appeals of Earnie Miller and Bill Jent in 1984. Carr convened a hearing in November 1987, more than four years after Jent and Miller had their close brush with Old Sparky.

Once virtually anonymous, the half brothers had become two of the best-known prisoners on death row. The case for their innocence had been laid out on the front pages of newspapers across Florida, and in Georgia and Ohio. The ABC magazine program *20/20* had profiled the case, complete with Glina Frye's on-camera admission that she had invented her damning testimony. But the State of Florida was not giving up. On the eve of Carr's hearing, prosecutors prevailed on Frye to reverse herself for the third time. When she had been arrested, she denied seeing a murder. Then she said she did see a murder. Then she said she didn't. Now she said she did. "I'm through running," she told the prosecutors—a strange statement from a woman who had been living in Dade City for years.

The long-awaited hearing never got past the opening statements. Sandy Weinberg, an intense young corporate litigator from a posh Tampa law firm, had joined the defense, and like a hungry dog he tore into the state's suppression of exculpatory evidence. Imagine, Weinberg told Judge Carr, what the defense could have done with the knowledge that C. J. Hubbard—the first witness to tie Earnie Miller to the murder—had testified based on a dream. "The dream would've become one of the major themes of the trial," he declared. As for the six witnesses at the crime site, they might have given the defendants an airtight alibi. Going to trial without that knowledge "was like the Bucs playing the Bears without linebackers," Weinberg said. (Judge Carr lived in Tampa; it was a good bet that he rooted for the Tampa Bay Buccaneers.)

The judge was clear on the law. According to the U.S. Supreme Court's holding in *Brady v. Maryland,* defendants have a right to know anything police have discovered that might help them. "There's no dispute as to the facts or the law," Carr said at the end of the initial presentations. The judge adjourned for the day, spent the evening in reflection, and the following morning—November 4, 1987—he vacated both death sentences. His summary judgment was blistering: "The Court finds the failure of the State to produce the material . . . deeply troubling: by withholding such favorable evidence, the State demonstrated a callous and deliberate disregard for the fundamental principles of truth and fairness that underlie our criminal justice system. . . . The physical evidence linking Miller and Jent to the crime was negligible." Carr continued, quoting from the Supreme Court's

Brady decision: "The Court would remind the State that 'Society wins not only when the guilty are convicted but when criminal trials are fair.'" He ordered the State of Florida to retry the prisoners within ninety days or turn them loose.

If Florida freed Jent and Miller, it would not be the first time the state had released men because of their apparent innocence. In 1975, Governor Reubin Askew pardoned two men, Freddie Pitts and Wilbert Lee, after *Miami Herald* reporter Gene Miller assembled an overwhelming case for their innocence—including a confession from the actual murderer. Pitts and Lee had spent nearly nine years on death row. In 1978, a divinity student named Delbert Tibbs was freed after nearly two years on the row for a rape-murder he had not commited; the trial prosecutor later said of the Tibbs case that "this was a tainted investigation and the people involved knew it." In 1987, Joseph Green Brown went free after thirteen years on death row. The gun he supposedly had used to kill a store clerk hadn't fired the fatal shots, and the only witness against Brown said he had lied because of a grudge. Prosecutors insisted Brown was guilty anyway, but they declined to press new charges.

Innocent people do wind up on death row. Between 1970 and 1993, forty-eight people were released from America's death houses with strong showings of innocence, according to a congressional study. Another analysis documented more than four hundred cases in this century, involving prisoners who were convicted and faced the death penalty, in which the case for innocence appeared significantly stronger than the case for guilt. Twenty-three of those men were executed.

The State of Florida was not going to let Bill Jent and Earnie Miller walk free, however. Not without a fight. Sending an innocent man to death row is a terrible thing, and understandably, police officers and prosecutors and judges don't like to believe that they might have been party to such a grave injustice. They have to be deeply committed to their case to demand a man's death. When their commitment is then ratified by various state and federal courts—as they were in the early decisions against Jent and Miller—they frequently dig in their heels. For the police and prosecutors to reverse field now, for them to free Jent and Miller and go after Bobby Dodd, would be admitting that their haste had put two innocent men within sixteen hours of Old Sparky. They could not admit that in public; it is likely they could not admit it even to themselves.

They went to work shoring up the original theory. Already, they had Glina Frye back in the fold, claiming once more that she had witnessed the murder. They returned to Patricia Tiricaine—a woman who, in the opinion of the defense attorneys, could be convinced to say almost anything. The defense team worried that Tiricaine, lacking an independent memory of the night in question, might decide to go along with Frye once more. The prosecutors also began hunting for jailhouse snitches who might recall incriminating statements from the half brothers. (It is an elemental truth of the criminal courts that prison snitches can be found to say almost anything. An inmate in Georgia, for example, claimed Bobby Dodd had confessed both the Bradshaw and Mocahbee murders to him.)

All this activity worried the defense team, and their worries multiplied when—as Judge Carr's ninety-day limit approached—a rumor circulated that the prosecution might bring Bobby Dodd to Florida to testify that he had been at the swimming party with Gale Bradshaw. Dodd would say, according to the rumor, that he pimped his girlfriend to Jent and Miller in exchange for money or drugs, and when Gale refused to prostitute herself, Jent and Miller killed her. Dodd would get a small sentence to run concurrently with a sentence he was serving for drug dealing in Georgia. Jent and Miller would go back to death row. Whether this rumor was true is unclear. The scenario had some awfully big holes in it; no witness had ever placed either Dodd or Bradshaw at the party. But the original trials of Jent and Miller were also filled with holes, and they had ended in death sentences.

A debate erupted among the Jent-Miller defenders. Sandy Weinberg, who had argued before Judge Carr, was itching for a fight, as was Eleanor Jackson Piel. But Piel was not licensed to practice in Florida state courts, and Weinberg had little experience in first-degree murder trials. To bolster the team, Scharlette Holdman had recruited her wisecracking pal Pat Doherty, a veteran of many capital trials and appeals, and Doherty had far less confidence that the courts could be relied on to see things their way. "It is a terrible thing to be convicted of a crime you didn't commit," Doherty once mused. "But it's worse to have it happen twice. In a courtroom, anything can happen." For this reason, Doherty was leery of a trial, though he considered it inevitable. The publicity was intense, and the elected prosecutor for Pasco County was giving interviews in which he promised to return the half brothers to death row.

Doherty was steeling himself for the new indictment when he ran into an assistant prosecutor named Bernie McCabe at the courthouse. "Listen," McCabe said, "does this thing have to go to trial?"

"What do you mean?" Doherty asked cagily.

"Walking out," McCabe answered. Doherty was shocked by this cryptic offer of a deal. Bill Jent and Earnie Miller could be "walking out," free men for the first time in more than eight years.

"You do that," Doherty told McCabe, "and we can talk."

The deal was this: If Jent and Miller would plead guilty to second-degree murder, they would receive sentences equal to the time they had already served. Doherty called Scharlette Holdman and outlined the offer. Both of them remembered John Spenkelink, who turned down a plea bargain and paid with his life. Death row was full of guys who didn't take the deal. "It's a fuckin' no-brainer," said Holdman.

But the others on the defense team were not so sure. Weinberg wanted to go to trial. "Sandy thinks all his clients are innocent, and now he had clients who actually were. It just added fuel to his fire," Doherty said. Piel was indignant at the thought of the State of Florida getting away with such an outrage. But the lawyers agreed that the decision could be made only by the defendants—their lives were in the balance. Doherty traveled to Starke and laid out the proposal.

The prisoners agonized. Goddamn—they didn't do it! Didn't that matter? And what about all the people who believed in them, who had worked so hard on their behalf? What about Gale Bradshaw's family? Their tireless efforts to identify the body had been the key to this whole sordid affair. The Bradshaws deserved justice.

Doherty listened patiently as the half brothers anguished. Then he reminded them that the State of Florida had put them on death row once. There were no guarantees it wouldn't happen again. Did they understand what was being offered—freedom? "When's the last time you guys got laid?" he asked.

And Jent said: "When can we get out?"

News of the plea bargain horrified the small band of activists who were fighting so hard against the death penalty. The possibility of innocent men being executed was one of their strongest arguments. Here they had a chance to prove in court that it could happen and the chance was being thrown away. Forevermore, the authorities would be able to point to the guilty pleas as proof that no injustice had been done. "How the hell can they plead guilty if they're innocent?" Michael Radelet demanded in a heated phone call to Scharlette Holdman. "You know, from the legal standpoint. What's the explanation?"

"From a legal standpoint," Holdman answered, "if you'd been sticking your dick in a hole in the mattress for eight long years, you'd do the same damn thing."

On January 16, 1988, the deal went down. It was a cold day, the wind was biting, and a train whistle moaned as the fireplug Jent and the gangly Miller stepped from a prison van outside the Pasco County Courthouse. They were wearing tattered prison blues and plastic sandals and stainless steel handcuffs. Inside, they changed into fresh clothes that Howardene Garrett and Eleanor Jackson Piel had bought for them: Levi's, plaid shirts, and crew-neck sweaters (off white for Bill, electric blue for Earnie). When the two men marched into the courtroom, a relative caught sight of them and cooed, "Oh, they look so good." Miller's new sweater was a rare point of color in the drab white room, where even the American flag was dull with grime. Sandy Weinberg and his associate, Alan Wagner, wore lawyerly gray; Piel, the white linen crusader of earlier years, wore black.

The brief proceeding was laced with sham. Prosecutors rushed around in the minutes before the hearing looking for a notary public to seal the agreement; they had arrived unprepared. Incredibly, the official papers still identified the victim as "Tammy." Judge Maynard Swanson called the half brothers to the bench. He asked their ages. Jent was thirty-six, Miller thirty-one. They had gone to death row kids and came back middle-aged. Swanson asked about their schooling. Jent had had nine years; Miller ten. Can you read and write? Yes. Are you in prison? Yes. In the mental wing? No. Any psychiatric problems? No. Under the influence of drugs? No. Any complaints about your lawyers? No. The answers were so soft they were inaudible to the audience of lawyers, reporters, and family members. "Are you pleading guilty at this time because you are guilty and for no other reason?" asked the judge.

"Yes," they answered.

The Miami Herald began its story in the next day's paper: "William Riley Jent and Earnest Lee Miller have argued for years that a pack of lies put them on death row. Friday, a lie set them free." In Cleveland, Tennessee, Linda Gale Bradshaw's sister burst into tears when she heard the news. "I was in total shock," she said. "All these years of fighting down the drain. Now they'll never go after Bobby Dodd."

She was right. Her fighting did go down the drain. Dodd—the violent boyfriend two victims shared—has never been prosecuted for the murder of Linda Gale Bradshaw or Ida Mac Mocahbee. But the family had one consolation. Gale Bradshaw came home, to rest eternally under a handsome gravestone. Not Jane Doe in the Florida sand, but herself, in her native loam. Small justice, but the only justice to be had.

Eleanor Jackson Piel persisted with the case. On behalf of Jent and Miller, she sued Pasco County for violations of their civil rights. Despite the guilty pleas, the county decided it did not want to defend its actions in court, and paid the half brothers sixty-five thousand dollars.

It was one more cost of the death penalty business, and in those terms, sixty-five thousand dollars was like a single snowflake falling on the Alaskan tundra. Many citizens held the mistaken belief that executing prisoners saved money, compared to the cost of housing them until their natural deaths. The direct costs of an execution were tiny. In Florida, prison officials budgeted $150 for the funeral suit from Jim Tatum's Fashion Showroom in Jacksonville (slogan: "We fit them all, big and tall"), $150 for the executioner's fee, and $20 for the last meal. The big-ticket item was the undertaker: $525, coffin included.

But the incoherent nature of modern death penalty law meant

that an ever-increasing number of cases was wrapped in an ever-complicated web of appeals. And this inescapable wrangling cost many millions of dollars. Capital trials were more expensive than other murder trials because of the higher stakes involved, and because of the extra evidence gathered to determine the sentence. The mandatory review of death sentences by state supreme courts added a step unknown in nondeath cases—at a cost of at least $70,000 per case. Further state and federal appeals cost at least $275,000 more. (That was the bargain-basement price; Ted Bundy's volunteer law firm estimated it had spent $1.4 million in the first two years the firm handled his appeals.) In 1985, James Rinaman, the former Florida Bar president, had swallowed hard when Scharlette Holdman asked him for $250,000. Three years later, he estimated that it would cost $12 million a year to hire enough prosecutors and defense attorneys to keep Florida's death penalty moving. "It boggles the mind," he said.

In 1988, a study by *The Miami Herald,* relying on the most conservative estimates available, calculated that Florida had spent at least $57 million on a death penalty system that had executed eighteen men—an average cost of $3.2 million per execution. (This did not include the millions shelled out by volunteer defense attorneys.) The average cost of keeping a man in prison until his natural death was one sixth that amount. The same year, the *Sacramento Bee* estimated that California was spending $90 million a year maintaining the death penalty. A 1993 study by *The Dallas Morning News* found that Texas—despite having the most streamlined death penalty in the country—spent three times as much for each execution as it would cost to jail a man for the rest of his natural life.

The most sophisticated examination of the cost of the modern death penalty was done by a team of scholars at Duke University. Their finding: In North Carolina, murder cases that end in execution cost an average of $2 million more than murder cases that end in life sentences. Though the figures are slightly different in each study, the conclusion is always the same. The death penalty is an expensive proposition.

∴

But the cost of the modern death penalty is not measured only, or even primarily, in dollars. There is the cost in human lives. Not the lives of murderers, who tragically are a dime a dozen in America, but rather the lives of the families and friends of murder victims. For most of them, capital punishment has turned out to be a cruel kind of hoax, exacting a heavy emotional price.

Elisa Vera Nelson was a ten-year-old sweetheart of Palm Harbor, Florida, a bighearted girl brimming with confidence, warm as the morning sun. Smart as a whip, she loved the local library, not just for the books but also for the people she met there. Ten is a glorious age for a girl, especially for a girl as pretty as Elisa Nelson, who had long hair with streaks of gold, a button nose, and her mother's big, bright eyes. At ten, the world belongs to a smart and pretty girl; she understands it, senses its possibilities, wraps it around her finger; the cloud of adolescence is still below her horizon.

Elisa was the light of Dave and Wendy Nelson's lives, whirling through her dance classes, tumbling across gymnastic mats, proud of her dark green Girl Scout sash. Dave and Wendy had been high school sweethearts in Michigan; they married and Dave worked as a shop manager while Wendy gave birth to two kids, first Jeff—a little athlete, made his dad proud—then Elisa two years later. When the kids were four and two, the Nelsons visited West Florida and were captivated by the place and its potential. "Entranced," Wendy later said. It was 1972, and a boom was on. They packed everything they owned into a U-Haul truck and moved to Palm Harbor, outside Tampa.

The Nelsons were people who took command of their own lives, charted their own course, gambled, as long as the bet was on themselves. Dave opened his own construction business to capitalize on the boom, and in the beginning it was a little scary. Dave Nelson worked long days building driveways and parking lots, and when he got home, he worked long nights keeping his machines in working order. Wendy pitched in as a secretary, as a cashier at the Publix grocery store, even worked at a pizza parlor. And when it was necessary, she climbed into the cab of Dave's dump truck and wrestled the rig through the sandy soil. She wasn't a great truck driver, but she worked for free. The

Nelsons took their fate into their own strong hands and began to bend it to their wills.

Then one awful day, Larry Mann snatched their fate away. It was November 4, 1980. That morning, Wendy drove Elisa to the orthodontist to be fitted for braces on her gap-toothed smile. She unloaded her daughter's pink bicycle at the curb and gave her a note for the teacher to explain her tardiness. When Elisa was through with her fitting, she began pedaling toward school. She never arrived.

About 1 P.M., Larry Mann—a burly, bearded ex-con—slashed both his arms from the wrists up toward the elbows. And as the news swept Palm Harbor that Elisa Nelson was missing, Mann's wife was seized by a sense of dread. Just before her husband attempted suicide and was rushed to the hospital, she had seen him carefully washing dirt from the tires of his 1957 pickup truck.

A search party found Elisa Nelson the next morning, her body crouched in an orange grove. She was clothed; her throat had been cut deeply. Near the body was a fencepost with a bloodied block of concrete on one end. This had been used to crush the child's skull. That night, a friend of Mann's wife called a local television station and revealed Mrs. Mann's suspicions. In the days that followed, police found the pink bicycle; it bore Mann's fingerprints. They found Wendy's note to the teacher in Mann's truck, which also contained strands of Elisa's lovely hair. The tires on the truck matched tracks at the murder scene.

Elisa Nelson's funeral at the Lutheran Church of the Palms was attended by some three hundred people, many of them children who, in the weeks to come, would require counseling to deal with grief and fear. "Almost as if out of nowhere, an act took place that has changed all our lives," Reverend Tim Nehls said from the pulpit. "I believe there can be no greater pain than this. None of our lives will ever be the same."

"It was a real foggy time for us," Wendy Nelson said many years later. Word of a suspect spread quickly though little Palm Harbor, followed by rumors that the suspect was being treated at the local hospital. As it happened, Dave Nelson had a construction job at the hospital, and when he set out one day for work, Wendy was gripped by the thought that he was going off to hunt the killer. She pictured her husband as a jailed vigilante, and prayed quietly: "God! We don't need that." But Dave Nelson controlled himself.

Instead, he battled, as Wendy did, the self-doubt that consumed them. Could they have done more to protect their child? What kind of parents had they been? "I was her mother," Wendy told herself. "It was my responsibility to get her to twenty-one alive." They felt, or imagined, the eyes of neighbors boring into them, neighbors who wanted to believe that somehow the Nelsons had brought tragedy on themselves. But how could they have kept Elisa cooped up? "She was lively and vivacious; she was a gad-about-town; she knew people we'd never met. If we'd confined her to the yard, it would be death to her," Wendy mused. "We restricted her route, we gave her a curfew—but this was ten in the morning; she was riding on a main street."

In losing their daughter, the Nelsons lost control of their lives; for the first time they felt helpless as they entered the maw of justice. Larry Mann stood trial but they could not even watch it; because both of them were called as witnesses, they were not allowed in the courtroom except to testify. They had to rely on Wendy's sister to take notes and repeat the testimony, and as they listened to her reports, they became convinced the entire proceeding was stacked in favor of the defendant. The jury heard everything about Larry Mann's troubled childhood and little about the girl he had killed. The jury saw pictures of the mangled body, but they didn't see the girl it had belonged to, for even Elisa's school picture was barred from evidence. "Lisa was a beautiful girl, with long blond hair she cared for herself," Wendy said later. "Not vain —but I know she wouldn't have wanted people to see her the way they did. She wasn't just a manila file folder. She was a little girl."

A compassionate prosecutor had taken pity on them. A week before the trial, he led Dave and Wendy to the courtroom, sat them down like two schoolchildren, and warned them about what was coming: Testimony would describe their daughter's agony, her brave attempt to flee even as the blood surged from her, the crushing death blow. Though the prosecutor meant well, his words robbed them of the

consoling images they had conjured for themselves. "We had told our-
selves that she probably was just hit over the head. Our hope was that it
was very antiseptic," Wendy remembered. Everything was out of their
hands.

Mann's defense attorney was Pat Doherty; Wendy and Dave Nelson had read in the papers that Doherty, an ardent runner, lived near
the crime scene and had jogged past it a million times. What kind of
person would take such an awful case, so close to home? How could he
separate himself? Nothing made sense anymore, nothing: After Mann
was found guilty, Doherty and his cocounsel admitted that their client
had confessed to them. Yet they had defended this guilty man. Who
had defended Elisa when she had faced death in that orange grove?

At the sentencing hearing, which the Nelsons were allowed to
see, prosecutors documented that Larry Mann was a repeat sex offender. In 1973, he had broken into a house where a young woman was
baby-sitting a toddler and, as the child screamed, forced the baby-sitter
to perform oral sex. Even earlier, as a juvenile, Mann had been charged
with abducting a seven-year-old girl from a church parking lot and
sexually assaulting her. (Key documents from that case were missing.)
The defense attorneys called to the stand a psychiatrist who testified
that Larry Mann was a pedophile who loathed himself for his sick
condition. The doctor theorized that Mann turned his loathing on
anyone who learned of his perversion—including a victim like Elisa
Nelson. The murder and the suicide attempt were mirror images of the
same self-hatred, the doctor said. It was all gobbledygook to the Nelsons.

And though they had braced themselves for the prosecutor's sum-
mation, still it was hell. "Over half the blood in that girl's body
pumped from her neck," the man told the jury. "There were blots of
blood ten, or twelve, up to eighteen feet away. . . . Let me suggest
that it indicates that at some point Elisa Vera Nelson was on the
ground, that her hair was pulled back and her throat slashed, and that
she tried to crawl away. . . . Let me also suggest that at some point
this man began to tie her up, and I think, given the testimony you have
heard in this case and the way this man is with children, that his inten-

tions were to sexually molest her. But she was able to resist. He abandoned his efforts, and when she tried to get away, he cut her throat."

Against that, Pat Doherty was able to say only that "there isn't one among us . . . who couldn't gladly forfeit this man's life if we could bring back this child." But that was not the point, not entirely. Elisa Nelson's death called out for a reckoning—not to undo the death, but to balance it. A world in which happy, pretty children die ghastly, violent deaths is a world out of whack, and the idea of blood atonement is an ancient and visceral way of restoring it to order. "Whoso sheddeth man's blood, by man shall his blood be shed." Basic stuff, the Book of Genesis, from a world that made sense, the world Dave and Wendy Nelson understood. By a 7-to-5 vote, the jury recommended death for Larry Mann, and Judge Philip Federico agreed.

The Nelsons had believed in the death penalty even before they lost their daughter. Wendy's mother had circulated petitions demanding the restoration of capital punishment after it was outlawed in Michigan. "We always had a strong sense of justice," Wendy recalled. "Certain forms of behavior deserved certain forms of punishment." Simple as that.

In May 1979, when Elisa was a sprightly nine-year-old, Wendy watched the news coverage of John Spenkelink's execution, and she was appalled by the sight of hundreds of people weeping and shouting in protest—hippies holding candles, wearing flowers in their hair—and just one or two citizens outside the prison supporting the governor's brave decision. Dave Nelson watched, too, and Wendy's sister Wanda, and they agreed this was a terrible display. It sent entirely the wrong message, so lopsided, so out of tune with the grass roots. They made a promise among themselves that the next time, they would go to the prison and make a stand for all the decent people who supported the death penalty.

By the time she could keep that promise, Wendy Nelson was no longer an ordinary citizen of the grass roots. Again and again, she made the trip to Starke, arriving at the pasture near the prison long before dawn—often to find that another execution had been blocked by the courts—but whenever she was interviewed by reporters as she stood vigil, she was always identified as Wendy-Nelson-whose-daughter-was-murdered-by-a-man-on-death-row. For some people, this constant public embrace of a private devastation would be unbearable. For Wendy Nelson, it was empowering. She seized her horror and bent it under her will. And she did more than stand vigil; she organized a support group for crime victims. She wanted to fight as hard for victims as Scharlette Holdman fought for killers. She called her group the League of Victims and Empathizers: LOVE.

It began very small, entirely within the circle disfigured by Elisa Nelson's murder. When, early in 1982, Governor Graham signed two death warrants, Wendy summoned the membership to Starke in support of the executions. Both death warrants were stayed at the last minute, but it was a beginning. Wendy and her five friends were featured in the *St. Petersburg Times:* GROUP LOBBIES FOR EXECUTIONS OUT OF CONCERN FOR VICTIMS, said the headline. In the accompanying picture, the six citizens stood behind five hand-lettered signs.

WE'RE FOR THE VICTIM, said one. And another, almost identical: WE CARE FOR THE VICTIM. Reverend Tim Nehls, the man who had eulogized Elisa Nelson, held a placard declaring WE SUPPORT GOV. GRAHAM. Wanda Vekasi, Wendy's sister, carried a sign that said PRAY YOU'RE NEVER THE VICTIM OF A VIOLENT CRIME. Wendy's own sign spoke volumes, tore your heart out: DO YOU KNOW THE ANGUISH?

No one could know the anguish, though, no one but Wendy's fellow survivors. Through LOVE, she spent hours talking with other crime victims, and gradually she learned that her experience with the courts—grim as it was—had been better than most. Many families got the cold shoulder from the justice system, as if their grief was an impediment to the machinery of the courts. Wendy Nelson began showing up at trials, a voice of experience for devastated families. She could take a victim's mother aside and say, "This is the medical examiner's testimony, you don't want to hear this." She could sit with a family in court, and when they wondered angrily why they weren't allowed to hear the huddled conferences at the judge's bench, she could explain it to them.

It was therapy, and she was the first to admit it. "There was a sense of extending a hand to people, and when they appreciate it you know you're doing something nice and you feel a little better," she explained. If there was a kernel of good to be mined from her tragedy, Wendy was going to find it. "I wanted my daughter's name to stand for something positive." She was trying to gain control again.

She came to the conclusion that the survivors of crime were unknown, unheard, and forgotten by the system. As her group grew and meshed with other victims' groups, Nelson poured her energy into a constitutional amendment to guarantee certain rights. "Informed, heard, and present"—these three words summed up her mission: Victims must know what's going on in the inscrutable world of the courts, they must have a chance to say what crime has cost them, and they must be allowed to watch justice being done for them.

In Tallahassee, crime victims were often mentioned in the speeches of blustering politicians, but they had little force in the back rooms where deals were cut. There was no PAC for victims; they staged no glitzy campaign fundraisers. Wendy Nelson had to find her support among ordinary people, gathering signatures to force the amendment to a public referendum. Though she hated public speaking, she made herself do it, pleading her case in tremulous voice to any audience that would listen. Meeting by meeting, town by town, she helped collect hundreds of thousands of signatures, but not enough to get the matter on the ballot.

A state senator from Miami, Dexter Lehtinen, took up the cause, encouraged by his legislative assistant, whose sorority sisters had been murdered by Ted Bundy. Lehtinen went to the legislature, brandishing the petitions, and warned his colleagues that they could no longer stand in the way of the amendment. Cowed, the lawmakers voted to put the question on the ballot, where it passed in a landslide. A state office of victims services was created, and Wendy Nelson was appointed to the governor's coordinating committee, which met quarterly and suggested changes in the legal system to better serve victims.

She published a LOVE newsletter, offering advice, tracking legislation, directing shattered survivors to counseling. In 1990, she waged a losing campaign to vote Chief Justice Leander Shaw off the Florida Supreme Court—Shaw was, in her view, too soft on criminals. In all these ways, she took her tragedy and tried to redeem it, turning her suffering into power, and the Florida courts were better for her work. She was brave and she was strong, but in the case that mattered the most to her, Wendy Nelson remained as powerless as the day her daughter had died.

Murder had always been her greatest worry as a parent—though not with Jeff. Jeff was a strapping kid, a talented soccer player, he could run like the wind. With Elisa, Wendy Nelson had worried more about murder than about sudden illness or freak accident. "The things that made her most appealing—her outer beauty, her inner beauty, her vivaciousness—were also the things that made her most vulnerable," Nelson mused. Elisa's grandmother shared the same concerns. After the murder, Wendy was going through her daughter's things and found a letter from Grandma. It mentioned that a little girl on the safety patrol had been abducted in Michigan. "Be careful!" Grandma wrote. It tore Wendy up. Of all the angers in the world, none burns more fiercely than the rage at a person who has found your most vulnerable spot and wounded you there. Wendy was so angry at Larry Mann that she hardly recognized herself. For a short time after her daughter's murder, she attended counseling with a crime survivor's group, but she had to quit when the therapist assigned her to make a list of the things she would like to do to the killer. "I couldn't do it," she said. "I was afraid of my rage."

The death penalty was her solace, because it channeled her fury. One day, she would get Mann out of her life forever, and it would be done in a lawful way. In her work with crime victims, she had met many people whose victimizers had received lesser sentences, and she saw what an ordeal it was to go year after year to parole hearings to plead with the State to keep a scourge behind bars. She would not have to endure that. The day would come when it would all be over. Year followed year in Wendy's life, however, and that day did not come.

On September 2, 1982, almost two years after Elisa Nelson's murder, the Florida Supreme Court vacated Larry Mann's death sentence because of missing documents related to his earlier crimes. The earlier crimes had been used as aggravating factors in support of the death penalty, so they had to be supported with proof. Returned to the trial court, Mann was quickly resentenced, and on May 24, 1984, the state supreme court affirmed the new death sentence. Governor Graham's staff added Mann's name to the long list of condemned prisoners awaiting clemency hearings.

The hearing was held November 20, 1985, five years after the murder. Attorney Frank Louderback, representing Mann, told the governor and cabinet that prison had changed his client for the good. Mann was off drugs, into the Bible, turning his life around. The lawyer read from a letter Mann had sent to the Nelsons, in which the killer called his remorse "the cross on which I'm crucified daily." Mann had written of his wish that he could restore peace to his victim's family. But the peace Dave and Wendy Nelson imagined was a peace that would come only after Mann's death. "There's really no such thing as life in prison," Wendy told a reporter. Unless Larry Mann was executed, the possibility of his release would always be "hanging over our heads." Bob Graham signed Mann's death warrant six weeks later.

By then, Wendy Nelson had had enough experience with the system to know that Mann was not likely to be executed on this first warrant. It was only a small blow when the warrant was stayed by a federal district judge days before the scheduled execution, and the judge moved quickly to hold a hearing on Mann's case, after which he promptly denied the appeal. But when Mann moved to the Eleventh Circuit Court of Appeals, the three-judge panel assigned to the case was troubled by a flaw in the trial record—small, but with constitutional implications involving the role of the jury in recommending death sentences. In Florida (and in other states where the death penalty was modeled on Florida's course-charting law), the jury's recommendation was "advisory." However, this advice carried "great weight"; in all but a few cases, the state supreme court had struck down death sentences where the judge had overruled the jury's recommendation.

By the time Larry Mann reached the federal appeals court, confusion over the jury's role had come to focus on the mind-set of the jurors themselves. Did they fully appreciate the importance of their recommendation? Or did they believe they were mostly window dressing, and that the real life-and-death decisions rested with the judge and the higher courts? In other words, did these twelve citizens—so intimately involved in deciding whether a killer should live or die—feel the proper weight on their shoulders?

It was a staggeringly subjective question, but the U.S. Supreme Court had raised it to lofty significance not long before Mann's case reached the Circuit Court of Appeals. In 1985, in a case called *Caldwell v. Mississippi,* the high court ruled that a death row inmate's constitutional rights were violated when his prosecutor and judge assured his jury that their recommended sentence would be reweighed on appeal. This promise that appellate judges would be a backstop for the jury's decision created a great risk that the jury would underestimate its own responsibility, the Court declared. Similar comments had been uttered during Larry Mann's trial and sentencing, admonishments to the jurors that their role was "purely advisory," and so forth. And so, on May 14, 1987—six and a half years after Elisa Nelson was murdered—the three judges of the Circuit Court of Appeals vacated Mann's death sentence and ordered another sentencing hearing.

The news devastated Dave and Wendy Nelson, and the fact that they heard about it from reporters rather than from the State only made it worse. For all their work to ensure decent treatment of victims, they were still the forgotten parties, watching their lives as if through a mirrored glass. The Nelsons could see the system as it probed and kneaded the bruises on their souls, but the system seemed blind to the Nelsons' existence. Their hopes rose when the prosecution persuaded the court as a whole to reconsider the panel's decision, only to be dashed again in 1988, when the panel's opinion was affirmed. They shifted their hopes to the U.S. Supreme Court, which they knew was increasingly hostile to death row appeals.

Of all the survivors of murder victims in Florida—and there are thousands upon thousands—none were stronger, more capable, more energetic than the Nelsons. Their fight for victims' rights had helped to change the nature of Florida's courts. But even the Nelsons weren't strong enough to cut through the confusion of the death penalty. Which is why, when the man from the attorney general's office called with news from Washington in 1989, he began by saying, "Wendy, you better sit down." Despite its pro–death penalty majority, the high court had declined to take the case.

Eight years had passed since Mann's death sentence had been imposed; almost nine since the death of their daughter. Through all those years, Dave and Wendy had waited for the system to deliver on the justice they had been promised. Now, they were back to square one. "I had been expecting the Supreme Court to take our case, rule in our favor, Governor Martinez would sign the death warrant, and the show would be on the road," Wendy said later. "Thank God for my family. I was at my wit's end. I couldn't have survived without them."

Dave Nelson was her rock through the ordeal that followed. He attended the meetings with prosecutors (including one where he had to sit across the table from the man who had killed his daughter). He strengthened Wendy through the two long weeks it took to empanel a new jury and hear once more the grisly story of their child's last moments. All those years spent trying to regain the reins of their lives, and now the Nelsons were reminded that their goal was out of their hands. As the hearing went on, the stress began to clutch at Dave's body, his chest grew tight, then came the shooting pains. There was no reason for such a healthy man in his prime to feel on the verge of a heart attack; no reason except that he was being crushed in the sputtering death penalty machine. The new jury, fully apprised of its considerable power in sentencing, recommended death even more strongly than the original jurors. The first vote was 7 to 5; this time, it was 9 to 3. Once again, the judge dispatched Mann to death row.

On a warm spring morning, not long after the new sentencing, Wendy Nelson sat at the kitchen table in her immaculate house in Palm Harbor, her hands wrapped around a cup of coffee. On a nearby wall was a picture of Elisa, a happy child frozen in time. Wendy's light-colored hair was swept back, framing her broad, scarcely lined face. There were traces of her daughter in her eyes, nose, and mouth. "If somebody had asked me years ago what I would do if all this happened, I wouldn't have thought I'd still be alive. I am amazed," she said, "to be functioning at whatever level.

"We were aware of all the delays. But I have to say I'm surprised we're this far back—ten years later and we're still at the first step. If things go well for us, it could be another three or four years . . ." She paused, and the silence in the house was enormous. "The bottom line," she began again: "If they're dead, they can't commit more crimes. I want a finality, I'm tired of hearings and court proceedings. I want him out of my life, and I really see only one way to do that."

The coffee was going cold, and she had work to do. The latest LOVE newsletter needed finishing, and she was putting the finishing touches on a conference for crime victims. "Everyone dies, I know that, even children," she said. "But when you know what her last hour was like, it's hard to think about her without thinking about that. It's almost as if I'm denied my memory of her. The violence is always there." She gestured toward her daughter's smiling picture. "Birthdays are the worst," she said. "Her sixteenth was really rough. We're coming up on twenty-one. And sometimes I try to imagine what she would be like . . . but I only ever knew the child."

At this writing, Larry Mann's death sentence has been reaffirmed by the Florida Supreme Court and he has initiated what might be his last round of appeals. "You know the process," an aide to Florida governor Lawton Chiles said. "It will be at least a couple of years." At the Nelson house, they're coming up on Elisa's twenty-fifth birthday.

The Nelsons' experience was typical of the ordeal friends and families of murder victims have endured under the modern death penalty. The rough numbers have gone like this: Twenty killers are dispatched to death row, twenty sets of survivors watch and wait as the legal system gropes along the slippery slope of the law. Eventually, one family gets the satisfaction of the promise fulfilled. Which family? It is a lottery. A child killer like Larry Mann remains alive after fourteen years on the row; John Spenkelink, the second-degree murderer, is dead; Anthony Antone, the brain-damaged middleman, is dead; James Adams, who convinced a veteran cop he was innocent, is dead.

After Craig Barnard's victory in *Hitchcock v. Dugger,* Florida officials never regained the pace of executions managed from late 1983 to early 1985, but even if they had, they would have delivered only a fraction of the executions promised by trial judges. As it was, only one man was executed in 1987—Beauford White, who had never killed anyone (he had stood lookout while six people were slain during a drug robbery in Miami; the actual killer, Marvin Francois, had been executed in 1986). White's jury had unanimously recommended life. Two were executed in 1988: Willie Jasper Darden, whose tangled passage through the courts had resulted in a record six stays of execution, and Jeffrey Daugherty, who—despite having murdered four women—had come within a single vote of a stay from the U.S. Supreme Court. In Florida and elsewhere around the country, judges and prosecutors began quietly lowering their sights, giving up on swift and sure justice, and learning to live with the wheezing system. "We'll just keep plodding along," said Carolyn Snurkowski of the state attorney general's office, while Parker Lee McDonald, a veteran justice of the state supreme court, said: "If I could figure out a way to make this better or easier or quicker, I would. But I can't. The old cases never really go away, and the new ones just keep coming." For supporters of the death penalty, there was just one bright spot by the end of 1988. Ted Bundy appeared to be nearing the end.

When Bob Graham signed three death warrants for Bundy in 1986—a single-year record that still stands in Florida—the shaken killer agreed to permit his lawyers to make a defense he had sworn he would never allow: that he was mentally ill, and that his illness should have rendered him incompetent to stand trial. This was a bitter pill for Bundy; in his world of images and appearances, he had stubbornly clung to his public persona of rationality, promise, and competence. Years earlier, before the Chi Omega murder trial, his lawyers had questioned his sanity and Bundy had taken the incredible step of demanding another lawyer to thwart them. But the death warrants had apparently cut through Bundy's vanity enough that he had agreed when his appellate attorneys suggested he cooperate with Dorothy Otnow Lewis, the Yale psychiatrist who often consulted on Craig Barnard's cases.

In her meetings with the killer, in her examination of Bundy's school records, and in interviews with his relatives, Lewis had discovered that the warm, peaceful boyhood Bundy remembered in his grandfather's home was just a figment. According to Bundy's aunts and uncles, grandpa Sam Cowell was "an extremely violent and frightening individual," Lewis reported, a man of awesome rages, so loathed and feared that his own brothers refused to invite him to the family Christmas party. They even wanted to kill him, Sam's sister Ginny had told the doctor. "I always thought he was crazy," Ginny said. Sam Cowell was a landscape gardener who screamed at workmen if they dug up a single wrong shrub, an oppressive father who pushed his daughter Julia down the stairs when she slept one morning to the unconscionable hour of nine o'clock. He kicked dogs and swung cats by the tail. In his greenhouse—the fragrant, humid hideaway Ted Bundy vaguely recalled as his favorite spot—Sam Cowell kept a cache of pornography, which Ted and an older cousin pored over when Ted was just three or four.

Lewis had also discovered that Sam's wife, Eleanor, was mentally ill for many years, agoraphobic—she feared leaving the house for any reason—and given to uncontrollable shrieking harangues. Eleanor Cowell was repeatedly hospitalized, and during at least one confinement she was treated with electric shocks. Though Lewis found no suggestion that young Ted Bundy was physically abused, the doctor theorized that spending his formative years in such an unstable home had surely traumatized the child. Lewis found evidence of such trauma from an early age: Bundy's Aunt Julia described a strange game that Ted played on her as a toddler. On "several occasions," Lewis recounted, the three-year-old boy collected butcher knives from the kitchen, stole into Julia's room as she slept, pulled back the covers, and put the knives in her bed. And then he stood there and watched her with "a glint in his eye."

Here, perhaps, were the roots of Bundy's evil: the identification of women with charged images on pornographic pages, the stealthy introduction of implements of violence into the bed of a sleeping form . . . and rich soil for speculation about flawed genes. But even if Dr. Lewis had drawn such a cause-and-effect conclusion (and she did not go that far), it would not have cut to the legal issue at hand. All that mattered was Bundy's competence at the time of trial. On this score, Lewis had delved into the roller coaster of Bundy's life from his late teens to his early twenties.

She found that, contrary to the popular image of the killer, Bundy had not been a young man of consistent achievement and rising promise. His fortunes had vaulted and plunged like an Alpine range. For a time he would pull A's and B's. Then, suddenly, he would become listless and drained, hardly able even to haul himself to class. He would drop out of school. Then another burst would come, a new school, a new major, a new political campaign. He had attended the 1968 Republican National Convention as a volunteer for Nelson Rockefeller. And then another trough, as he washed out of law school. Dr. Lewis diagnosed "bipolar mood disorder," known to most laypersons as manic depression, and in her interviews with Ted Bundy she traced these wild swings right up through his final capture and his two murder trials.

Lewis concluded that Bundy had been in a manic phase through a key period before the trials. This mania had been characterized by "inflated self-esteem and grandiosity . . . decreased need for sleep . . . attention drawn to unimportant, irrelevant external stimuli . . . excessive involvement in activities that have a high potential for painful consequences. And certainly his behaviors during his trials would constitute that," Lewis reported. "I don't even think Mr. Bundy was competent to accept or reject a plea," she concluded. "I think that he was high as a kite, he was grandiose, his judgment was impaired."

This had been the core of Bundy's last appeal. Death penalty cases often wait a year, two years, even more for a full-scale hearing in federal court, but Ted Bundy's case did not linger. After the Circuit Court of Appeals ordered a hearing, in spring 1987, U.S. District Court Judge G. Kendall Sharp moved swiftly to dispose of the matter, and scheduled presentations six months later. As he entered the courthouse in Orlando to begin the proceeding, Judge Sharp was asked by a reporter if he thought the hearing was a waste of time. "Absolutely," he replied.

One observer, author Ann Rule, described Sharp's handling of the hearing as "swift, impatient and firm." The judge listened as attorney James Coleman questioned witnesses about Bundy's behavior before and during his trials. Various lawyers and investigators who had worked on Bundy's trial defense testified that the killer flew into tirades, popped pills, and became fixated on the idea of marrying his girlfriend, Carole Boone, during a bizarre proceeding in open court. The judge heard the testimony of Dorothy Lewis, and also an earlier diagnosis by another psychiatrist, Dr. Emmanuel Tanay, who also believed Bundy was probably incompetent.

Against this evidence, the prosecution presented two psychiatrists who had briefly examined Bundy at the time of his trials and considered him fully competent. Their credentials did not quite match Dorothy Lewis's résumé—one, Dr. Umesh Mahtre, had failed the exam for a certificate in forensic psychiatry three times. More important than their testimony, though, was Bundy's own behavior before, during, and after his trials: He had plotted strategy, argued motions, questioned witnesses, analyzed verdicts. Just because these actions were grandiose, or hurt his cause, did not mean he had been incompetent. The standard of competence was straightforward: "Ability to consult with his lawyer with a reasonable degree of rational understanding," and "a rational as well as factual understanding of the proceedings against him." Ted Bundy's self-defeating actions in court stemmed from his own sense of images and appearances. "I screwed my life over, but I've always wanted to be an attorney," he once explained. "I want to show that a guy with a year and a half of law school can stand up there and let the air out of [the prosecutor's] tires. That I can . . . run these people ragged. That I'm not a fiend, necessarily."

Judge Sharp needed only a few weeks to dismiss the appeal, calling Ted Bundy "probably the most competent serial killer in the country . . . a diabolical genius."

With the required hearing completed, the case returned to the Circuit Court of Appeals, where Bundy's lawyers challenged Judge Sharp's decision. In ordinary capital cases, this step can take upwards of a year; in Bundy's case, briefings were expedited and an opinion was published within seven months. Earlier, when the circuit court had ordered Sharp to hold the hearing, the circuit court judges had mentioned "strong indicia" that Bundy had been incompetent to stand trial. Now, a three-judge panel declared that "what had appeared as 'strong indicia' prior to the hearing are happenings that are consistent with a determination that Bundy was competent." Sharp's decision was affirmed.

To be on the safe side, the circuit court panel went one by one through the fifteen issues raised by James Coleman, dismissing each challenge in great detail, closing the door on possible misunderstandings. In light of the hurry-up schedule, the panel's opinion was remarkable—sixty pages long, thirty-eight footnotes, with copious citations from the trial record. Every *t* was crossed, every *i* dotted, every loophole sealed.

The panel agreed with Bundy on only one point: Judge Sharp had insisted that the appeal was an "abuse" of the federal process, a charge the judge amplified a few months later in testimony to a congressional subcommittee. "If every death row inmate 'milked the system' as Bundy has done, then it would shut down the . . . courthouse," Sharp declared. But the higher judges, even as they dismissed Bundy's entire appeal, rejected Sharp's rhetoric. "This case does not represent an abusive situation," they wrote, and in a footnote they added: "We likewise find no basis to dismiss the petition as a 'delayed' petition. Similarly, the . . . argument that Bundy's petition presents frivolous claims . . . is without merit."

Carolyn Snurkowski, the chief prosecutor, echoed this judgment. "So far," she said, "we have not had a problem with delaying tactics." Bundy was back on the express track.

His lawyers requested a rehearing before the entire appeals court, which was promptly denied. Then they were given the standard ninety days to file a petition asking the U.S. Supreme Court to review the decision. Deadline day was November 15, 1988, a balmy afternoon in Washington, one of those glorious late-autumn days in the capital when the sweltering summer and drizzling winter seem equally avoidable errors. With twelve minutes to go, Polly Nelson—James Coleman's associate—rushed into the Supreme Court clerk's office, brushing stray strands of hair from her eyes, and filed Ted Bundy's appeal.

"You made it!" said the clerk.

"The word processor broke," Nelson explained.

The petition she presented proposed three questions for the Supreme Court's consideration. Had Bundy been given an adequate competency hearing before going to trial? Had the Circuit Court of

Appeals erred in approving the use of hypnotically refreshed testimony? Should a hearing have been held on Bundy's claim of ineffective trial counsel? The State of Florida responded thirty days later.

Now the massive record of the Bundy case, and the closely argued appeals, went to nine desks of nine law clerks in the chambers of the nine justices. These were some of the most promising products of the nation's best law schools, green but terribly bright. Their views tended to mirror, roughly, the views of the justices they worked for. In Thurgood Marshall's chambers, for example, the walls were decorated with political cartoons lambasting the death penalty; Marshall's clerks paid extraordinary attention to the progress of capital cases through the federal courts. Marshall opposed all executions, and he would oppose even this one. Among the clerks serving the conservative justices, the attitude was more thick-skinned; they often sent jokes through the Court's electronic mail about frying criminals, and when they studied death penalty pleadings it was generally with an eye toward narrowing access to the federal courts. Antonin Scalia's clerks, for example, adopted their justice's philosophy of seeking places to draw "bright lines" in the law, ways to add definition to the incoherent field of capital procedure. Scalia hammered home this philosophy in his famously affable way, often over dinner at his house, after which he liked to serenade his clerks at the piano as they poured liqueurs from a well-stocked cart.

Even in the conservative chambers, though, there was widespread unease over many death penalty cases, especially over the poor quality of many trial lawyers. The bright young clerks read through trial transcripts and were repeatedly amazed by the errors of commission and omission, stupid things said, smart things left unsaid—simple stuff they had learned in the first year of law school. Thus, even the clerks who made jokes about frying on the e-mail tried to give each death case a serious look, even Ted Bundy's. And when they did, they were impressed by the quality of the work done by James Coleman and Polly Nelson, especially on the question of pretrial hypnosis. The U.S. Supreme Court had never considered, head-on, whether a defendant could be lawfully convicted through the use of hypnotically refreshed testimony. This might be an opportunity to draw a bright line.

Under a different set of circumstances, some of the conservative clerks might have urged their justices to take up the hypnosis issue. Maybe if the killer was obscure, instead of being the most notorious murderer in America. If the petitioner had killed one person, maybe— but not dozens. When the justices took up the appeal at their weekly conference on January 13, 1989, they voted not to hear Bundy's appeal, and their decision was announced four days later. Within minutes of the announcement, Governor Bob Martinez signed Bundy's death warrant. Warrants lasting thirty days had become standard in Florida, but this one provided only a week.

Through his murder trials, Bundy's strongest supporter was a woman from Seattle, Carole Boone, who became his wife in a brief exchange during his sentencing for the killing of Kimberly Leach. When Bundy was sent to death row, Boone moved to Gainesville to be near the prison, and she visited him faithfully. It was a custom in those days, according to several prisoners, for inmates to put five bucks into a kitty before weekend visits. After they all put in their money, they drew lots. The money went to the visiting room guards, who would look the other way as the winning inmate joined his girlfriend in the bathroom. Carole Boone told friends that this was how she became pregnant by Ted Bundy. She bore him a daughter.

But over time they drifted apart. Bundy's decision to cooperate with the appeals challenging his own competency was a blow to Boone. She had always clung to the far-fetched belief that her "bunny" was innocent. In 1987, when her mother was injured in a car crash, Boone moved back home, taking Bundy's daughter with her.

Bundy had plenty of other visitors. Ann Rule, author of a book about Bundy's crimes, received scores of letters from young women pledging their love to the killer—especially after Bundy was portrayed on television by the hunky heartthrob Mark Harmon. "You're not in love with Ted," Rule counseled them gently. "You're in love with a movie star." Nevertheless, some of the women made their way to Starke. And mail poured into Bundy's cell by the boxload, not just from mixed-up women, but also from crime buffs and reporters and crusaders and thrill-seekers.

Among the people who befriended Bundy in his last years were a prosperous lawyer from Florida's Gulf Coast and an evangelist-turned-prosecutor from the opposite shore. John Tanner was the evangelist; in 1988, he was elected chief prosecutor for the region around Daytona Beach. He met regularly with Bundy as part of a prison ministry. They were an unlikely match, the archcriminal and the crime fighter, but they were united by Tanner's passionate opposition to pornography. Tanner devoutly believed that pornography corrupted youths and planted the seeds of violence, and he found in Bundy his greatest confirmation. Bundy always said that smut had been his downfall, and though many people found this oversimple, to Tanner it rang true. During his meetings with the killer at Starke, Tanner tried to lead Bundy to the Lord.

The lawyer was Diana Weiner, an attractive woman with long dark hair; more than one person commented that she looked like many of Bundy's victims might have looked had they lived to maturity. Weiner was ardently opposed to the death penalty, and she offered her support and assistance to several death row inmates, making the long drive to Starke in her black Mercedes. But her bond with Bundy was particularly intense, so strong that the friends of Carole Boone "never had the heart to tell her" about her husband's new friend. Weiner, in a conversation with death penalty opponent Mike Radelet, described her relationship with the serial killer as "spiritual."

As it became increasingly clear that Bundy's incompetence claim was not going to save him, Bundy and Weiner began to discuss the danger he was facing. By late 1988, the word among death penalty experts was that Bundy would probably be dead by springtime. He had to find a way to buy some time. But time was precious, and to buy time he had to offer something valuable in return. What did Ted Bundy—alone in a tiny cell with his pile of sweatsocks—have that people wanted? Only one thing: knowledge. Scattered from coast to coast were the families of dozens of missing young women. Only Ted Bundy knew exactly what had happened to their loved ones. Some of the remains had been recovered; only Bundy knew where the others were.

Locked in his mind were the answers that could put scores, maybe hundreds, of minds at peace. When a daughter or a sister or a niece disappears in the full bloom of youth and never surfaces, the mystery is an endless agony—attenuating over time perhaps, but never gone. And no matter how many years pass, the survivors never completely lose hope that their loved ones will reappear some fine day with a harrowing story of abduction or amnesia or a hidden stress that made them run away. Knowing that a loved one was murdered might seem like the worst thing in the world, but knowing nothing can be even worse. And even the survivors of victims whose bodies were found could benefit from Bundy's knowledge: He could confirm that he was the guilty one, that the real killer was not still loose, killing others.

Bundy had knowledge and he wanted time. Together with Weiner, he hatched a strategy: When the next death warrant was signed, Bundy would offer to make a clean breast, to start at the beginning and account for every victim. He would promise to pore over maps to pinpoint the location of each body. By telephone, he would direct search parties down the dirt roads and up the rocky hillsides of his deadly odyssey. He would offer, from the mind of America's most notorious serial killer, a windfall of material for investigators and psychiatrists. He would pledge to resolve the mysteries haunting all those grieving people. This would, of course, take time.

It's hard to keep a secret around a prison, and soon Bundy's plan became fairly common knowledge in the anti–death penalty circle. People called it "Ted's bones-for-time scheme." Word of the strategy quickly reached Bundy's official lawyer, James Coleman, who immediately recognized how damaging it could be to Bundy's faint remaining hopes in court. Any judge would see that Bundy had had nearly a decade on death row to give answers, if his desire to help was genuine. Watching him bargain over the bodies of his victims would surely horrify even the most open-minded jurist. Coleman contacted his client and begged him not to do it.

But when Martinez signed the death warrant, Diana Weiner put the plan into motion, over Coleman's objections. She telephoned Andrea Hillyer, the governor's chief death penalty aide. Bundy, Weiner hinted, was ready to "debrief" investigators from the state of Washington; he had important "information"—but he needed more time. John Tanner, Bundy's "spiritual adviser," made the same pitch in a call to the Florida Department of Law Enforcement. Again, the offer was vague: Bundy had information on cases in Washington and perhaps elsewhere.

How long does he need? Tanner was asked.

"Ted would probably like two or three years," Tanner answered, laughing.

Martinez replied quickly, via the press. "We have sent word back to each of those individuals that the rendezvous with the electric chair will be next Tuesday morning at seven," he told reporters. The governor's contempt for Bundy was evident on his dour face. "For him to be negotiating with his life over the bodies of others is despicable," he said. Clearly, Bundy needed more leverage.

He invited two investigators to meet with him at the prison on Friday morning, January 20. Bob Keppel was a Seattle detective who had tracked Bundy through his lethal ramblings in the Pacific Northwest. Bill Hagmeier was an FBI expert on serial killers. Both had spent many hours talking with Bundy in the past, and Bundy enjoyed their company. More important, they represented two kinds of influence that might be turned to his aid—the local lawman, representing the interests of traumatized families, and the G-man, standing for the national interest in better understanding the mind of the roaming sex killer. Bundy prepared scrupulously for his meeting with Keppel and Hagmeier, scripting his presentation on four pages of a legal pad. He numbered the points of his agenda by topic and subtopic, like a student preparing for a final exam.

Point one: The negotiations must proceed in secret though the weekend. "Anyone who leaks ruins for everyone else," Bundy wrote. Point two: They had to understand the pressure he was under, "where my head is at . . . how it is for me on death watch." Point three: He must butter them up. Why was he dealing with Bob Keppel and Bill Hagmeier? Because he knew them, they knew him, and he respected their abilities. Point four returned to Bundy's dire situation—how hard it was to "focus on the past" under the "pressure of execution four days away." He was "forced to focus on other things," like letters to family and meetings with friends. And he was getting "conflicting advice . . . close friends [and] family [were] strongly against this." He was "exhausted . . . no time."

Point five was the offer. "What I want to do," Bundy scrawled: "Tell the whole truth . . . nothing more or less . . . need time and less pressure filled atmosphere to do it." He would "give the complete picture of how I came to do what I did . . . how it was done . . . plus specific facts of cases." Point six: What did the detectives think about all this?

Apparently Bundy expected Keppel and Hagmeier to ask why he needed a reprieve to come clean. If they worked straight through, they would have close to a hundred hours to collect the confessions. In preparation for this question, Bundy jotted point seven, which he titled: "What makes it next to impossible under the circumstances." Here again, he emphasized the lack of time. Given the "passage of 10–20 years," he would need the leisure to wrack his brain. Investigators would need still more time for "verification & body location." A partial accounting would not be satisfactory. "Must be the whole story . . . something is not better than nothing." A partial accounting would only "hurt people closest to me . . . with[out] giving them my understanding of what really happened."

He moved to point eight: "What needs to be done." That was simple enough. The investigators had to convince the governor that Bundy was serious and "we all need time & more relaxed atmosphere to do it." Point nine was the clincher: "Will you take reasonable steps to give us time?" At this stage of the meeting he would ask Keppel and Hagmeier to "communicate" with Martinez and "persuade" him.

Once again, as he planned the crucial meeting, Bundy anticipated doubts from his visitors. He labeled point ten on his legal pad and scribbled: "Am I serious?" "That is [the] question," he wrote, and underlined it for emphasis. Bundy knew that people would think he was manipulating them again, so he outlined an argument in favor of his sincerity. He had never offered to confess and then reneged (except for his abortive guilty plea). He wasn't asking for executive clemency; "just time." The State would hold all the cards: "If I don't immediately begin to cooperate that's it, sign warrant," he wrote.

And he would "give a good faith demonstration." That was point eleven. The following day, Saturday, Bundy would show his good intentions by making a "disclosure" of "one case of buried remains." This was a "significant step," because he had "never done this before." That disclosure would be followed, under Bundy's plan, by a meeting on Sunday, attended by the detectives, a representative of the governor, and perhaps a survivor of one of his victims, or a person from a victims' advocacy group. Together they would arrange for his reprieve.

Incredibly, Bundy thought he might get the parents of Kimberly Leach to "speak out" in support of his scheme. (He felt this was "not manipulative.") At the Sunday meeting envisioned by Bundy, the various parties would prepare a "summary of allegations" that Bundy had the knowledge to clear up, and on Monday these would be presented to Bob Martinez. Surely then the governor would see the importance of more time. Only after Martinez had been convinced would they "go public."

The proposal was as audacious as it was impossible. Did Ted Bundy really believe that survivors of his victims would join with him to win more time, or that the governor of Florida would strike a deal with one of the most hated men on the planet? Apparently he did. He jotted point twelve on his legal pad. He would ask Keppel and Hagmeier: "Do either of you think a halfway decent job could be done in two days under [the] circumstances?" And if they answered yes, he would remind them how complicated it is to verify confessions and locate long-dead bodies. He added point thirteen: "We may not be able to put [this] together but it is worth a try. What do you think?"

Point fourteen of Bundy's outline was a rhetorical question. What, exactly, was he promising; what was the payoff? First prize was hilarious: "My promise and committment [sic]." A promise from Ted Bundy was like a child's chalked sidewalk drawing in a sudden summer rainstorm. It was, though, all he had. He promised to "work gradually from beginning to end" of his carnage, with the FBI present to "coordinate access" and control "release of information." He would take lie detector tests and submit to psychiatric study "for the understanding of why." That was the deal. Bundy added a final, fifteenth, point. He wanted John Tanner with him "if I go ahead with giving details," to provide "moral support." Having clung all his life to an image of normalcy, the reality "will be hard for me to reveal," Bundy wrote.

He was going ahead with his bones-for-time scheme, and this realization was a car door on the finger for his legal team. As decent citizens, Bundy's lawyers could only welcome the idea that the killer might bring some closure to the suffering he had caused. As lawyers, they knew that the plan was a disaster. On Saturday, January 21—after Bundy's meeting with the detectives—Mike Radelet called Mike Mello, saying Bundy wanted his advice. By then, Mello had left the daily grind of battling the death penalty to teach law at a tiny college in Vermont; having driven himself to the brink of nervous exhaustion at CCR, he was recovering amid snow-blanketed hillsides and fresh-faced young people in flannel shirts. Mello's advice to Bundy was blunt and simple: "Shut up, shut the fuck up, shut the fuck up right now."

Mello felt strongly that Bundy's slim chance of survival lay not with the governor but with the courts. While the prisoner had been meeting with the detectives, Mello had been on the phone with James Coleman, searching for a way out of the legal dead end. And as they talked, they had discovered that Bundy might have an untested appeal still available—the same appeal that had recently won Larry Mann a new sentencing hearing for the murder of Elisa Nelson. Had Bundy's jurors understood how important their recommendation would be in deciding the ultimate sentence? For all the hundreds of hours various Bundy lawyers had spent digging through the record, they had never raised this issue. Now Mello suggested they try it. The issue had won stays of execution for a number of Florida prisoners in recent months, and the central question was pending before the U.S. Supreme Court.

Coleman and Polly Nelson began ripping through the massive transcript of the Kimberly Leach murder trial in search of evidence that Bundy's jurors might have misunderstood their role. The lawyers found plenty. For example, one potential juror had been asked during jury selection: "Do you understand that the judge . . . in this case, as the trial judge, would have the ultimate responsibility for determining which punishment to impose?"

And the prospective juror had answered: "Yes, I do."

"In other words, the jury would render an advisory opinion only," the prosecutor had continued. "Just that, an opinion."

The truth was that Florida juries rendered more than an opinion: If they suggested death, the sentence was almost always death; when they recommended life, a judge was required to present extraordinary reasons for overruling that advice. This became the basis of Ted Bundy's last appeal.

Three days before the scheduled execution, Bundy met again with Bill Hagmeier to discuss the murders he had committed in Colorado. Desperate to prove that his confessions were real, Bundy wanted a phone link to the search parties that were trying to confirm his information. At the same time, however, he resisted saying too much. Bundy was trying to string the investigators along, tempt them, turn them into levers for his cause. It became a delicate dance: He walked up to the edge of full confession, then demanded more time. Always that theme: More time. He was getting ragged. "Must get it together today!!" he wrote on his legal pad, and he underlined this heavily.

Sunday brought more confessions. By the end of the day, Bundy had discussed about ten cases. Most were well known to investigators in Washington state; they had long before found the bodies. But Bundy supplied some details, especially about the baffling abduction of Georgann Hawkins in 1974. Hawkins had vanished from an alley behind a row of fraternity and sorority houses, a scant few feet from her own door. She had been out of view of witnesses for only a few moments. Bundy explained how he had approached on crutches, asked winningly for help, and—when he had lured her away from the houses—bashed her skull with a piece of metal. Bundy hinted darkly at his bizarre behavior with the bodies, his sexual compulsions that had continued even after his victims were dead.

He also discussed some murders in Utah, where most of his victims had never been found; Bundy pored over detailed maps covering much of the state, trying to recall where he had left the bodies. But always he pushed for the deal. Bundy wanted Bill Hagmeier of the FBI to contact the family of a Utah victim, Debra Kent, to enlist their support in his campaign for more time. The clock was running—Bundy wanted to know what Bob Keppel was doing to get more time. And what about Mike Fisher, the investigator Bundy knew best from Colorado? Bundy considered a personal letter to Governor Martinez, making the case for a sixty-day reprieve. Was sixty days too long to wait for his corpse?

As his next-to-last day drained away, Bundy was melting under the pressure. He needed a deal, but no one seemed to be lobbying on his behalf. Detectives began arriving in Starke from all over the country, each hoping to close a few mysteries—"too many cops," Bundy wrote on his legal pad—but this rush of interest was having no effect on the governor. "Must focus on Martinez now and families," he scribbled in a note to himself, and the families he targeted were the Leaches and the Kents. "Contact Kents . . . will find Debbie . . . need help to do so . . . and need time," he wrote. By day's end, he was down to pleading for a month's delay, to "talk & find bodies without pressure and distractions of [the death] warrant."

His plans went nowhere. The governor remained unmoved. In fact, aides to Bob Martinez were completing arrangements to have a film crew record the historic press conference where the governor would announce Bundy's execution. Footage from the event might make nice advertisements for a reelection campaign.

Ted Bundy's last trip through the courts was swift. On Friday, January 20, 1989, his appeal was denied by the Florida Supreme Court. The next morning, his lawyers were back before federal district court judge G. Kendall Sharp, who held a forty-minute hearing before dismissing their complaint about the jury's understanding of its role in sentencing. The next step up the ladder was the Eleventh Circuit Court of Appeals, which gave the lawyers a scant two hours to file a brief by fax machine. A three-judge panel—including the legendary liberal Judge Frank Johnson—held a telephone conference and unanimously denied the appeal later the same night. James Coleman and Polly Nelson spent Sunday rehashing the trial record, trying to buttress their final petition to the U.S. Supreme Court. That appeal was lodged Monday afternoon, just eighteen hours before the scheduled end.

Throughout the weekend, the pasture across from the prison was gradually transformed into a media center worthy of a small war. Dozens of mobile television studios parked on the soft grass and raised their satellite dishes like sunflowers to the sky. They had come from every major city in Florida and from points scattered to both coasts, from Washington State, from California, from New York and Colorado. Reporters arrived from the nation's great newspapers—*The New York Times, The Washington Post,* the *Los Angeles Times*—and from magazines like *Time, Newsweek, People,* and *Vanity Fair.* Network superstars scrambled for the story; Ted Koppel told Bundy's representatives that he would charter a plane at a moment's notice if the killer would appear on *Nightline.* Journalists came from publications in London, Paris, and Amsterdam. The local telephone company installed dozens of phone jacks on the wall of a weathered lean-to. A portable podium was placed on a relatively flat piece of turf for occasional briefings by the prison spokesman, and so many television and radio microphones were taped to it that the podium listed precariously. In America that week, there were three great media events: the inauguration of George Bush as president, the Super Bowl, and the execution of Theodore Robert Bundy.

Reporters tripped over one another trying to get their hands on the key detectives, Bill Hagmeier and Bob Keppel, and they slipped notes under Diana Weiner's motel room door. They huddled around Bundy biographers who had come to see the end of the story: Richard Larsen, author of *The Deliberate Stranger,* and Hugh Aynesworth, coauthor of *The Only Living Witness.* They shared the latest rumors—that Bundy's confessions numbered one hundred, or that Bundy was planning to feign insanity at the last minute. Hard facts were tough to come by. Only later did the truth of the confessions—that they were mostly unsatisfying—emerge. "I think he and his attorney-girlfriend, or whatever, virtually held us hostage for three days orchestrating what to say," Bob Keppel explained. "Bundy never sang like a bird." Bundy seemed to deny as many crimes as he admitted, and some of the denials made Keppel think he was holding out. They weren't "Bundy-type denials."

The prisoner's ragged emotions made the extraction of information even harder. "Scared and stressed-out, shaken and in tears," Keppel described him.

And the insanity ploy turned out to be nothing but fevered speculation, fueled by the arrival in Starke of Dorothy Otnow Lewis. She had come for a final interview with Bundy, and to help calm his nerves, but the governor took her presence very seriously. He assembled a team of three psychiatrists, as required by Florida law, and kept them on call near Starke. If Lewis pronounced Bundy crazy, the state shrinks were ready to conduct their own evaluations at a moment's notice.

As the hours evaporated, Bundy scheduled, then canceled, meetings with investigators from Colorado, Utah, and Idaho. (The fact that he had killed two women in Idaho was one of the few revelations that came from the bones-for-time scheme.) "We have three victims out there who have never been found," said Dennis Couch of the Colorado attorney general's office, after his meeting with the killer was canceled. "The hopes of the families were high. Now I imagine they're very disappointed. But that's Ted Bundy." Bundy also scheduled and canceled a press conference, choosing instead to grant just one interview. He had the world's media at his beck and call, but Bundy chose a California evangelist as his mouthpiece. This was James Dobson, head of Focus on the Family and host of a syndicated radio show. Dobson was one of America's leading crusaders against pornography. On Monday afternoon, from two-thirty to three-thirty, the prisoner taped the interview, looking haggard and drained as he described his juvenile obsession with smut, his search for harder and more violent images, and the awful translation from words and pictures to sexual savagery.

An old joke could be applied to most everything Ted Bundy ever said: How could you tell when he was lying? His lips moved. Nevertheless, there were reasons to think he was sincere when he said pornography was somehow integral to his "problem," as he often called it. Not as a cause but as an accelerant, gasoline on an ember. Every time Bundy had come close to a confession—and he had come close at least three times over the years—he had talked about smut and booze and their effects on him. But there was also something self-serving about his decision to talk with James Dobson. Among the anti–death penalty crowd, the interview was seen as "a fight for dignity." Said one Bundy intimate: "He truly saw the man who did all those killings as another person, not the 'real' Ted Bundy. The real Ted Bundy was, in his mind, a liberal, an environmentalist, a guy who cared about women and women's rights. The killer was someone else." Bundy wanted to display the self-image he preferred—thinker, victim, helper—and there was no more welcoming ear for this than Dobson, who greeted what Bundy had to say as confirmation of his own beliefs.

That night, January 23, 1989, Bundy dined on burritos with rice and salad, and met for the last time with his supporters. He was a slender, slight man, his skin pasty from years behind bars, his hair graying at the temples—yet an evil power still seemed to surround him. The dark roads snaking away from the prison seemed more menacing, the streets of Starke more frightening, because he was near, and the low fog clinging to the wet ground that night only deepened the sense of evil. He was a haunting force. Myra MacPherson, a tough veteran of years of reporting, slid a dresser in front of her motel room door before falling into a fitful sleep. It was crazy, she knew. But Bundy had that power. It drove deep rifts into the normally chummy comrades who fought together against the death penalty. Many of them were furious over the stagey confessions; one activist had snapped at Bundy: "Spare us the show—names, dates, and places!" Mike Radelet's name had been published as a confidant of the killer, so he had been besieged with telephone calls from "all over the country, from everyone with a missing daughter who ever got within a hundred miles of Bundy's itinerary. I was so angry with him for raising all those hopes." Some of the activists complained to Diana Weiner, who answered curtly, "Whatever Ted wants."

There was also a spat over funeral arrangements. Radelet suggested to Weiner, who was handling things, that she deal with a nearby undertaker who prepared the bodies of most executed inmates. The man was opposed to capital punishment, and he dealt respectfully with the bodies. "Besides," Radelet joked, "we get a bulk discount." Instead, Weiner chose what Radelet called "the most right-wing funeral home in Gainesville," and Radelet later blamed this choice for the appearance of a photo of Bundy's corpse in the pages of *The Weekly World News,* an especially outrageous supermarket tabloid.

Yet another fight erupted after Dorothy Lewis, the psychiatrist, spent part of Monday talking with Bundy about his "problem" and trying to calm him down. Several activists later said Bundy had asked them to send Lewis's notes of that session to Carole Boone. The killer hoped they would help his wife understand him. Lewis refused to part with the notes, saying that she had not been present when Bundy made the request.

Word came from the U.S. Supreme Court at 10:30 P.M. The last-minute brainstorm of Coleman and Mello—the question of the jury's understanding of its role in sentencing—turned out to be surprisingly effective. Bundy won four votes for a stay of execution. One more, and he would have lived.

When a man goes to prison, a lot of paperwork is prepared, many blanks are filled: height, weight, eye color, age. There is a blank marked Religion. When that question was asked of Ted Bundy, he had answered "Methodist," the church of his childhood. Florida State Prison had two Methodist ministers on call that night. Of the two, Bundy chose Reverend Fred Lawrence to pastor him through his last night on Earth.

A round-faced, pudgy, and unassuming man, Lawrence was surprised to be chosen by the nation's most infamous killer; though he was a frequent visitor to death row inmates, he and Bundy had never met. And he felt a strange touch of pride. "I don't know if one should be honored if Ted Bundy says your name," Lawrence said later. "But I guess I was." When he got the call, the reverend made a quick scan of his bookshelf and pulled down a small black volume, *The Minister's Service Book,* published by the Advent Christian Church. It contained orders of communion, weddings, funerals, and so forth, along with some inspirational poetry. He also grabbed his military Communion kit, issued by the Florida National Guard. Lawrence reached the prison by 1 A.M., when Bundy finished his last meetings with his lawyers, with John Tanner and his wife, and with Jamie Boone, Carole's grown son by another man. When Lawrence arrived, he talked briefly with the anti–death penalty crusaders Mike Radelet, Susan Cary, and Margaret Vandiver. They told him Bundy had been going through "a very public phase," and ventured that he would be emotionally drained by the time he returned to his cell. "They predicted it completely," Lawrence recalled.

Flanked by guards, Bundy and Lawrence left the visiting room and walked down the prison's long central corridor. A man on death watch was moving, so the rest of the inmates were locked in their cells. An eerie quiet filled the place, a weird vacancy, as the footfalls of the small patrol sounded dully on the buffed tile floor. The corridor seemed almost endless, but at last they came to the end, and turned from the wide central hallway into a narrower one that felt almost claustrophobic by comparison. On Q-wing, they descended a small stairway to the two cells facing the door to the execution chamber. Fred Lawrence settled onto a metal folding chair outside Bundy's cell. Two guards sat nearby. Bundy had no chair, so he took the pillow from his bunk for a cushion on the floor.

Ted Bundy knew he was about to die. Though his offer of confessions in exchange for more time had some supporters in unexpected places—like the Florida attorney general's office, where a number of prosecutors considered it a good deal—the governor was not buying. The courts were now closed. This was the end. Fred Lawrence wanted only to give the man a few hours of peace, which he considered his duty as a man of God. He spoke gently by way of beginning: "Ted, tell me something about your life in the church growing up."

Bundy closed his eyes and drew a deep breath; Lawrence soon realized the doomed man formed each answer in his head, shaped it from beginning to end, before he spoke the first word. When he spoke, it was in a low, sapped voice, and his memories were of Sunday services and potluck suppers and meetings of the Methodist Youth Fellowship. From Lawrence's beginning, Bundy took control of the conversation, presenting one last time the face of composure and keen intelligence. "It was as if he and I were two complete strangers who had bumped into each other and settled into a talk," Lawrence remembered. "He had complete control—I could recognize, could feel, this aura of great-ness around him. Diabolical greatness, like Hitler, I imagine."

They talked for more than an hour, but nothing Bundy said satis-fied the unspoken curiosity in the pastor's mind: What could make a man like this? "I don't think even he knew why he was who he was. I don't think he knew how many he killed or why he killed them. That was my impression, my strong impression."

A guard approached the cell and asked if Bundy needed anything. The prisoner shook his head and mumbled, "No." He was tired and withdrawn. About 3 A.M., he mustered the strength to place two tele-phone calls to the people who had supported him the longest. The first was to his mother. Her son's confessions had been a terrible shock to Louise Bundy. "Like a blow right between the eyes," as she put it. But now she showed only her customary composure. Over the phone line, she told Ted how much she loved him, and he answered that he knew how much he had hurt her. The confessions, he explained, had been his attempt to "make it right—to tell the truth."

During the ten-minute conversation, Bundy became a aware that someone was listening in on an extension. His anger flared: "Is some-body on this phone?!" he demanded. A guard's voice answered, "Yes, Ted. You know I'm on the phone." His temper passed as quickly as it rose.

He asked that his second call be placed to Carole Boone, and waited tensely as the number was dialed. A couple of minutes passed. Something was wrong. At last, the guard said, "That other call you wanted to make is not going to go through," and Bundy knew imme-diately what had happened—Boone had refused to speak to him. "His reaction was none at all," Fred Lawrence remembered. Bundy simply asked to speak to his mother again. During this call, Louise said, "You'll always be my precious son."

Lawrence opened his little black book to a favorite poem, "Some Easter Morn," and began to read:

We all must spend one lonely night
  In dark Gethsemane,

While others sleep, like Jesus weep
  In bitter agony!
We, too, must beg that God will let
  The bitter cup pass by,
And then—"Thy will, not mine, be done,"
  Like Jesus, we must cry.

We all must tread the lonely road
  That leads to Calvary,
The thorns must wear, the cross must bear
  In shame and misery;
And when, through gloom and darkened sky
  God's face we cannot see,
We, too, must cry like Jesus, "Why
  Hast Thou forsaken me?"

But oh, some glorious Easter morn,
  Perhaps not far away,
We'll see Thee come to roll the stone
  Of sin and death away;
And then, by garden and by cross
  Made pure and white and sweet,
We'll cast our lilies and our crowns
  Down at Thy dear feet.

A beautiful thought for a wretched sinner—the thought that, on some glorious morn, the stone of sin would be lifted from his soul. "Do you really believe God forgives?" Bundy asked.

"Yes, I do," Lawrence answered. "Because I have been forgiven."

Bundy nodded. "Do you mind if I listen awhile on the bed? I can listen better." And as Lawrence continued reading, the killer drifted off to sleep.

Seventy-five minutes later he awoke. It was almost time for Lawrence to leave. The pastor took his military Communion kit and blessed the wafers and wine. After the sacrament, they bowed their heads in silent prayer. "I don't know what Ted Bundy did, but I confessed my sins," Lawrence remembered.

Having witnessed the execution of Carl Shriner, Lawrence was able to describe for Bundy what would happen in the chamber: He would be strapped in, then offered a chance to speak, then the leather hood would fall over his face and the headpiece would be attached. He would hear the dull noise of the circuits being opened, and a second later the current would hit him. He should not fear pain.

Bundy listened with his elbows resting on his knees. Then he reached his hands through the bars, and Lawrence took them in his own. "And he squeezed for ten entire minutes," the minister recounted. "He never said a word. He held my hands tighter than anyone had ever held my hands. The last four minutes, he raised his head and gazed into my eyes—still not speaking—just gazed intently. I didn't see fear, or uncertainty. He just seemed to want to hang on a little longer before he disappeared. It was like holding on to a dead man."

In the predawn hours outside the prison, a macabre carnival assembled in the pasture. Hundreds of cars bumped and lurched into a makeshift parking lot, which was muddy from a weekend of rain. The cars disgorged people from across the state—police officers carrying sparklers, fraternity boys swigging from hip flasks, parents with their babies. They carried homemade signs, almost all of them in dubious taste. CHI O, CHI O, IT'S OFF TO HELL WE GO, said one, making a pun at the expense of the murdered and beaten women of the Chi Omega house. Another listed the ingredients for "Bundy BBQ"; another announced that SPARKS ARE GOING TO FLY! BUNDY: CATCH THE CURRENT, someone had written, playing off a Coca-Cola slogan, and someone else toted a sign saying, SOMETHING SPECIAL FROM FPL—a reference to Florida Power and Light. TEDDY IS DEADY. HAVE A SEAT, TED. A man carried a sign calling for PUBLIC EXECUTION NOW: I LIKE TO WATCH.

Other celebrants went to even more trouble. The members of the Zeta Tau fraternity from the nearby University of Florida wore professionally printed T-shirts, featuring a recipe for "Fried Bundy" on the back. They accessorized their outfits with frying pans, which they waved lustily. An entrepreneur had commissioned tiny electric-chair lapel pins, which sold quickly at five dollars apiece. There was a man in a rubber Ronald Reagan mask and a "Burn Bundy" T-shirt, carrying a child's stuffed bunny dangling from a noose. Two women strolled the pasture wearing homemade versions of Old Sparky's headpiece, which they had fashioned from Christmas gift boxes and lead stripped from a stained-glass window. An hour before the execution, a fourteen-car caravan pulled up, led by a flatbed truck bearing an illuminated sign: BUNDY, BURN IN HELL. In the bed of another truck was a life-size effigy: A handcrafted mannequin seated on a wired kitchen chair, a crown of sparklers on its head.

Diesel generators, powering the many television trucks, RVs and space heaters, rumbled a constant bass beneath the chatter and the shouting. The ground was crisscrossed with heavy electrical cables. The air was thick with exhaust, and through this foul cloud roving cameras shot brief patches of blinding light and hazy glare. The cameras, it was clear, were the reason so many people had spent so much energy on their signs and costumes—they wanted to be on television. The Zeta Tau brothers whooped and waved their frying pans whenever a camera-man ambled close. "The only one I'm talking to is Ted Koppel!" someone shouted above the noise. The crowd pressed hard against a temporary fence that had been erected to keep the party out of the road, shouting on cue and mugging for photographers. "We got cam-eras everywhere!" a reveler said excitedly. "We better watch for our-selves on TV!" With the choking fumes and the blinding light and the noisy, drunken throng, the scene had a surreal quality, flickering and sulphurous. The light seemed like fire, dancing through the crowd, and the fumes smelled like brimstone, and the noise could be mistaken for a wailing and gnashing of teeth. A Starke restaurateur did a brisk business selling coffee and doughnuts.

Wendy Nelson was there—Wendy, mother of Elisa, the victim of Larry Mann, who had won a new sentence on the same issue Bundy was denied. She stood apart from the crowd, but she understood the celebration. "They're certainly entitled," she said. "We're gonna once and for all get Ted Bundy out of the lives of his victims. I'm sure they've been through hell." The voice of experience.

Dawn was a faint hint of orange rind at the horizon, and as the minutes drew by, the rind shaded to rose and the sky turned deep blue.

The morning stars, long since obliterated by the television lights, evaporated in the rising sunlight like droplets on a griddle. A handful of death penalty opponents fell to silent prayer. Across the road, on the prison ground, the gulls flew up to meet the morning.

Witnesses to an execution are required to leave behind all pens, reporter's notebooks, tape recorders, cameras, and any extraneous items that might disturb a very sensitive metal detector. Beyond the scanner, they are patted down from head to toe. After the search, the citizen witnesses go to a small room where a modest breakfast buffet is waiting, while the media witnesses go to a stuffy room for a briefing.

The reporters are each issued two pencils and a legal pad, which they use to take down a stream of mostly useless information. This is primarily a way of killing time. The briefer informs them that they are at Florida State Prison. The prison is a quarter mile long. It is the only maximum-security prison in the state for men. There are X number of prisoners on death row (the day Bundy died, the number was 294). On it goes: The average cell is six by nine feet. The average death-watch cell is twelve by seven feet. The electric chair is made of oak. It was built in 1923 by inmates. The same chair has been used for all of the state's executions since 1923, excluding one performed under federal jurisdiction by hanging.

The briefing is interrupted when the little room goes dark—the whole prison goes dark, the fans stop whirring, the clocks stop humming, everything falls silent. The stillness lasts about twenty seconds, then the lights return—the prison has switched over to its own diesel generator to power the electric chair. Now the briefing moves toward the point: The spokesman notes that during the time he has been talking, the prisoner has been prepared. His head and lower right leg have been shaved, he has been dressed in dark blue trousers and a light dress shirt. He will enter the execution chamber at 7 A.M. in his stocking feet. A prison lieutenant will be on the phone to the governor. The director of maintenance, the prison medical officer and his assistant, and the executioner will also be waiting. (The briefer does not, of course, identify the executioner.)

The prison superintendent will lead the way; the prisoner will be flanked by an assistant superintendent and the prison's security chief. The spokesman asks the reporters to remain seated and quiet throughout "the procedure." The doomed man's last visitors are announced, the details of his final Communion—if he has taken one—and the menu of the last meal. The spokesman describes how much the prisoner has eaten.

Then the witnesses are taken to the chamber. Dead quiet reigns over the prison, not a soul in sight as they pass through the spine of the building and emerge in the rear yard. There, they are loaded into a prison van and driven past the tiny death row exercise yards with their high fences, volleyball courts, and rusting barbells.

Inside the little chamber, the citizen witnesses fill the first two rows of small wooden chairs. There are four rows of seats with six chairs in each row; the first row is so close to the glass, and the glass so close to Old Sparky, that witnesses sometimes feel like they are sitting in the prisoner's lap. There are twenty-four seats in all, but for Ted Bundy's execution, many more people jammed into the tiny spaces behind the chairs and along the walls. This was an Event; people pulled rank to be there.

The witnesses might expect a clock on the wall, ticking toward the fatal moment, but there is no clock. The white walls are bare except for two plastic speakers from Radio Shack, which are connected to the microphone in the death chamber.

Everything but the chair is hospital white. Behind the chair is a metal tool box, and on the box, neatly arrayed, are some straps, the headpiece, a white terry-cloth towel, and a pair of long leather gloves. The witnesses stare silently at the door behind the chair. The only sound is the *skritch-skritch* of a dozen reporters' pencils.

Time hangs suspended. Then the door opens and time begins to hurtle. The rhythm of "the procedure" is like a truck coming along a flat, straight highway. The truck is a distant dot, gradually looming and taking shape, moving, it seems, very slowly . . . but then at last it roars past, suddenly swift and furious. On that particular morning, warden Tom Barton was first through the door, a tall man with a craggy face and cropped iron hair. (His predecessor, Richard Dugger, had been promoted to preside over all Florida's prisons; he stood near a wall of the witness room, having come from Tallahassee to see the event.) Just behind the warden was Ted Bundy, drawn and wan, with his bald, gooey head and his stocking feet.

Prison officials on either arm of the prisoner steered him swiftly to his seat. Three sets of hands cinched the straps tight around him, doubling the strap ends back on themselves for a neat, almost stylish, effect. Barton stooped to lace the crude electrode on Bundy's leg, then resumed his full height and pulled roughly on each of the straps, checking the tension.

As they worked, Bundy scanned the faces through the picture window, pausing to make eye contact with Fred Lawrence, with James Coleman, and with Jerry Blair, the elected prosecutor who had directed his trial for the murder of Kimberly Leach. Lawrence tried to hold Bundy's gaze with the same intensity he had earlier applied to the doomed man's hands—but Bundy now seemed far off, already gone. His scan of the faces had the vacant quality of a drugstore surveillance camera.

Most execution witnesses have never met the man they are watching die, and for them these few moments when the prisoner studies the room are often the hardest. They feel a pang of voyeur's guilt. Strangers in the audience often secretly hope the prisoner's gaze will not settle on them; they dread being caught watching the utter humiliation of another human. They dread questions in the prisoner's eyes: Who are you, and why have you come? The nakedness and shame of a man in the electric chair is far more profound than mere nakedness of the flesh—his sins, his brokenness, his fear, his helplessness, all these are laid bare before the watching eyes of strangers. And the strangers are relieved if they are not caught staring, relieved when the fleeting moments of the prisoner's survey are brought to an end by the warden's demand: "Do you have any last statement?"

Often, the man has labored over a written text. Ted Bundy had not. For the first time in anyone's memory, this loquacious, expansive man had almost nothing to say. He looked at Coleman sitting next to Lawrence and murmured, "Jim and Fred, I'd like you to give my love to my family and friends." Then Bundy lowered his eyes and closed them as the last thick strap—wide in the middle, like a python with a rabbit half digested—was tightened around his jaw. The electrician, wearing the long leather gloves, fastened the headpiece, and attached the cable with a few firm twists, as if he were hooking up a VCR. The leather hood fell.

It all happened in a matter of minutes. Now the prisoner was immobilized but for the rising and falling of his last breaths. Tom Barton took the telephone from his assistant. There were no stays, of course. The warden nodded slightly to the executioner, who was invisible to the audience behind a thick wall. Two dull thunks sounded—the sound Fred Lawrence had advised Bundy to ignore. Then two loud snaps. Bundy's body stiffened.

The violence of "the procedure" is softened by the heavy straps and strong buckles, which prevent the body from moving much. Everything visible would indicate a sudden and violent shortening of every muscle in the body: Back pulled tight, head wrenched back, fingers clutching inward or splaying out. An enormous cramp. The current runs in a cycle, from very high voltage to more moderate voltage, and as the dosage abates, the body sags ever so slightly. Then— with a distinct *click!*—the cycle returns to the maximum current, and the body in the chair jumps again, like a man dozing on the sofa awakened by the doorbell.

This new surge of power flows only a few seconds before the mechanism reaches its failing point. That's the point at which the wet sponges covering the electrodes begin to boil. Steam rises, first in wisps, and then in small clouds. As the sponges boil dry, the flesh under the electrodes starts to burn, and smoke mixes with the steam.

The electric chair kills by a combination of massive shock and gradual cooking. At the flip of the executioner's switch, two thousand volts at fourteen amperes blaze almost at the speed of light across the short distance from the control panel to the headpiece. Some of the juice is deflected at the skull—human flesh is a poor conductor—but most of the jolt rips a ragged path of least resistance from the brain to the receptive electrode on the prisoner's leg. The cells of the brain, built for the tiny bursts of electricity that convey information through the body, are knocked senseless by this lightning bolt. At the same time, the prisoner's nerves light up with news of this fiendishly painful event, and the news surges toward the brain at about three hundred meters per second. By the time the pain arrives, though, the brain is already wiped out; the body screams into a dead receiver. Thus, doctors generally agree that the electric chair is painless.

But simply jolting the brain senseless is not necessarily enough to guarantee death, so the flow of juice is maintained. What happens over the next minute or two is that the prisoner is heated like the coils of an electric stove. Again, the targeted organ is the brain. Designed to oper-ate at around 98 degrees Fahrenheit, the typical brain shuts down for good at about 110 degrees. The wild card in the process is the heart, a cursedly stubborn organ, which tends to keep beating even after the brain is gone.

Some prisoners require more than one cycle to stop the heart, but Ted Bundy required only one. When the power was cut, his corpse sagged against the straps. A prison doctor checked his wrist and throat for a pulse, then unbuttoned his shirt—one button, very delicately—and placed a stethoscope on his chest. Then the doctor raised the hood, just a bit, and shined a penlight into the vacant eyes. At 7:16 A.M., on Tuesday, January 24, 1989, Theodore Robert Bundy—the face of America's death row—was dead.

"Please exit to the rear," a prison official said, and the witnesses stepped into the morning light. Some were first-time witnesses, and for many of them, the ritual had not been entirely what they had expected. It had been quieter, less violent, antiseptic—more like a magic trick, in a way, than a homicide. Magicians carefully bind their subjects, cover their faces, leave only the extremities showing—and then they do all sorts of violent things: Saw the subject in half, run her through with swords. And then—presto!—the subject is returned unharmed. The key is hiding the face. The soul of a person, the spirit, is in the eyes, as poets have remarked. When the face is covered, the person vanishes.

For witnesses to an electrocution, the event has all the trappings of a magic act. The subject is bound and gagged and strapped into place. Then a mask falls over the eyes. And everything thereafter has the quality of a stunt, culminating in that mystical, improbable cloud of steam. The whole dreadful thing has a quality of illusion. But the man who sat on the chair has not slipped through a trapdoor; the violence is not done to a dummy. A man is dead.

Following the custom in Florida, when the witnesses emerged from the death chamber a wire service reporter among them waved his yellow legal pad over his head. This was the signal to the people in the pasture that the deed was done.

Cheers erupted in the field. A group of off-duty cops waved sparklers and burst into song, "On Top of Old Sparky," the lyrics of the old campfire tune reworked for the occasion. "He bludgeoned the pooooor girrrrls, all over the heaaaaad. Now we're all ec-staaaa-tic, Ted Bundy is deaaaaad!"

"Whoooooo!" shrieked another cluster of revelers as they set off fireworks. From a group of fraternity boys came another song: "Na-na-na-na, Na-na-na-na, Hey-hey-hey! Good-bye!" People smiled and hugged and slapped each other on the back. Television reporters stood before their cameras to deliver the news to waiting viewers. Euphoria was general all over Florida. A Tampa-area disc jockey popped open a can of Jolt cola and put "Electric Avenue" on the turntable. In Tallahassee, a radio host cued a tape of bacon sizzling.

Most of the crowd in the pasture lingered a half hour, until a white hearse rolled through the prison gates and headed up the road toward Starke. As it passed, another cheer went up; one man rushed onto the blacktop to pat the hearse on the fender.

Then the people trudged to their cars, and soon there was a traffic jam there in the middle of nowhere, which had become, for that day, the center of the universe by the power of one terrible man. Horns honked, the exhaust cloud thickened, and one by one the happy citizens went home to put away their skillets, stow their death helmets, unwire their kitchen chairs. Ken Robinson of the Florida Highway Patrol, the man who had discovered Kimberly Leach's body more than a decade earlier, stood in the pasture as the cars streamed away and said,

"Justice has finally been done. Although it's a slow process, the process apparently is working."

As a symbol, the execution of Ted Bundy was the modern death penalty's greatest success, the highly visible execution of a plainly deserving criminal. Never before had the elements come together so perfectly. Only two previous executions in the modern era had been so publicized. One was Gary Gilmore's, the first under the new laws, and in that case, the symbol was flawed by the fact that Gilmore demanded his death—the criminal seemed to be driving the process. The other was John Spenkelink's, and in that case, too, the symbol was imperfect, because so many people familiar with the case weren't sure Spenkelink deserved to die. His death had a random and flukey quality, as if no one had been in control of the process. But it was often said that if anyone deserved to die it was Ted Bundy—and though it took nearly nine years of ferocious effort and a little rule bending, the justice system at last sent him to his death.

Bundy was such a powerful symbol that he lived beyond his physical death as a postmodern, suburban Lucifer. He became the quintessential killer in dozens of books, magazine articles, and newspaper stories. Supermarket tabloids resurrected him periodically. For example, one published a "seance-interview" with Bundy a year and a half after his death, in which the killer "told" a psychic that he had felt himself "sinking below the chair, through the prison floor and into the ground. I traveled through the rocks into the fiery lava at the center of the earth. Then I ended up in this icy wasteland full of demons and lost souls." He was immortalized in wax museums, and at least one pulp novel was based on the premise that he had faked his execution and escaped to kill again. On the high brow end, Bundy inspired a ballet in Seattle, and became the centerpiece of any number of scholarly papers, including a cover article in *Anthropology Today* in which his execution was compared to Aztec rituals.

But the highway patrolman's claim after the execution—that Bundy proved the death penalty "works"—was more complicated. At a cost of nine years and an estimated five million dollars plus, the death penalty machinery had succeeded in culling and killing one arch-criminal. But a broader question lingered after his death: Was the system delivering on its promises? By mid-1989 there were more than three hundred condemned inmates in Florida alone, more than two thousand nationwide; only a small fraction of that number had been executed. Bundy notwithstanding, most executed prisoners were impossible to distinguish from the condemned inmates who survived.

And the state and federal courts continued to reverse themselves, circling back on their own decisions. Three days after the Bundy execution, another Florida inmate received a stay of execution based on the jury's misunderstanding of its power in sentencing, the same issue that had just been denied to Bundy. Craig Barnard, during the last eighteen months of Bundy's life, had undertaken a scholarly assessment of the state of death penalty law in a single court. On top of his death penalty cases and consultations and duties at the public defender's office, Barnard had collected and analyzed every Florida Supreme Court capital case over a nine-month period from late 1987 to the autumn of 1988. As the Bundy execution approached, he was putting the finishing touches on a law review article summarizing his findings: In eighty-one cases, the only constants had been confusion and contradiction.

Barnard looked at the way the court had treated one of the simplest aggravating factors—"previous conviction for a capital or violent felony"—and noted that the court had not been able to decide on the meaning of "previous." In 1979, 1980, and a third time in 1984, the Florida high court had ruled that "contemporaneous . . . acts of violence on one victim" could count as "previous" convictions, meaning that in the rape and murder of a single victim, the rape could count as "previous." But in 1987, the court had reversed itself and announced that when two crimes arise from "a single criminal episode," one could not be considered "previous" to the other.

He looked at "great risk of death to many persons"—another aggravating circumstance. In 1980, the court had declared that a fire set to cover up a murder constituted "great risk" to "many persons" because the fire might have spread to neighboring homes. In 1987, the court had reconsidered the same case, and ordered a new sentencing hearing.

An aggravating circumstance added to the law in 1979 had said murders were more deserving of the death penalty if they were "cold, calculated, and premeditated . . . without any pretense of moral or legal justification." In the cases he had examined, Barnard had found the court to be flummoxed by its meaning. The justices had decided the factor applied to James Card, who robbed a store, abducted the clerk, drove eight miles to a secluded spot, and cut her throat. Robert Preston's case seemed almost identical: He also robbed a store, abducted the clerk, drove her to a remote spot, and cut her throat. In that case, however, the same court concluded that "cold, calculated" did not apply. The justices accepted the "cold, calculated" factor in the case of a man who shot his victim nine times, because they felt he could have reconsidered while reloading. But they rejected the factor in a case where the killer stabbed a robbery victim one hundred and ten times. (Eventually, the Florida Supreme Court threw up its hands and struck "cold, calculated" from the books, saying it was too vague to be lawful.)

The chaos was rampant as ever, Barnard concluded. The justices were still working with patches and baling wire. And the Florida Supreme Court was not alone in its confusion. All over the country, courts were consumed by legal gymnastics, and no state was managing to execute more than a handful of the people it sentenced to die. Even the U.S. Supreme Court could not settle questions; various justices gave speeches about the need for certainty, but the Court's own decisions remained inconsistent.

In 1987, the high court ruled that a victim's good character, and the suffering of the survivors, were not relevant at sentencing hearings. Capital punishment rested on questions about killers, not victims. A year later, the Court reversed itself. Justice Antonin Scalia, who had written the unanimous opinion in *Hitchcock v. Dugger* assuring the right to have favorable evidence heard, later backflipped and announced that the right to favorable evidence was groundless. Fourteen years and more than twenty executions after it had approved Florida's law with its aggravating factor for "especially heinous, atrocious or cruel" murders, the high court rejected that factor as unconstitutionally vague.

Though he limited his study to nine months in a single court,

Craig Barnard managed to suggest the vastness of the failure. He concluded with a plain statement of what he had learned over many years: "The purpose of capital sentencing is to select the few who must die from the many who will not. Even during this short survey period, criteria for that selection process changed, expanding and narrowing case by case; life-and-death distinctions were made on the basis of lines that were sometimes blurry and many times mobile. We, as a society, have asked our courts to put rationality into what is a subjective process involving some of the most highly charged cases and issues of our time. We should not be surprised if it is not always achieved."

Barnard finished writing in time for the 1989 hiring season at the nation's law schools. God, how he loved it—picking plums from the ranks of fresh young lawyers, boring into them with his probing eyes, seeking a glimmer of the future. Administrative work could be a terrible drag; the budgets, the worksheets, the office squabbles. But this was wonderful. Despite a ferocious cold, he went to a job fair in New York.

His plane touched down back in West Palm Beach the evening of February 26. Exhausted, Barnard drove home from the airport in his sporty little Dodge. He loved cars and coveted the newest features; this one had a computerized voice that said things like "Oil is low," or "The door is ajar." He liked talking back to the car. The fence outside his condominium was a jumbled heap, just as he had left it. But on his desk at work was a rough draft of the annual budget, and he expected a ruling any day that might put the next prisoner into the chair. Who had time to fix a fence?

He went inside, where he picked up the phone and dialed his father. Ronald Barnard was surprised to hear his son complaining of a cold. Craig was not a complainer. He listened as Craig said that he couldn't sleep, he had no appetite. "I thought I was gonna die on that plane," Craig said.

"Take a day off," his father counseled. "Stay home, eat some chicken soup."

Of course, Ronald Barnard knew that his son never took days off. They talked some more about this and that. A woman in the office owned a beagle that had just whelped a litter of puppies. Craig had loved dogs as a boy, but in recent years he had lacked the time and the energy to take on a companion. Now he was thinking about adopting one of those puppies. His father was pleased to hear it. He wanted Craig to settle down.

Later, Craig Barnard phoned his friend Susan Cary and his boss Dick Jorandby, and in both conversations he mentioned his cold and his exhaustion. Then he tried to get some sleep. As always, he was up before dawn, and when he rose he shut off the burglar alarm, collected the *Palm Beach Post* from the porch, stripped, and climbed into the shower.

By 9 A.M., everyone sensed something strange at the West Palm Beach public defender's office. Craig Barnard's office was empty, and there was no trace of his pipe smoke in the hallways. He was never that late. "Where's Craig?" people asked. Maybe his flight was canceled.

In Tallahassee, Scharlette Holdman was wondering the same thing. Where's Craig? She greeted every morning with a phone call to her counselor and friend, but when she called his house that morning, the phone just rang and rang. She called Barnard's office, and got no answer there, either. Her next call was to Susan Cary. As they talked, it dawned on them that Craig had once said cold medicine, combined with his epilepsy treatment, made him sick. Then came a more chilling thought. Could he have skipped the treatment in favor of a good night's sleep?

Holdman dialed Dick Jorandby, who immediately dispatched an investigator to Barnard's house. The alarm was off, the paper was inside. The investigator heard the shower running. Craig Stewart Barnard, thirty-nine, was dead in the tub, having drowned after an epileptic seizure. The calm eye of the capital punishment storm, the rock and rabbi, Florida's dean of death penalty law, was gone.

Dick Jorandby left Craig's office just as it was, a shuttered shrine above the sparkling blue of the Intercoastal Waterway. Barnard's estate collected $30,000 worth of forsaken vacation and unused sick days. Posthumous honors continued throughout the year: The old grand jury room of the Palm Beach courthouse was named in his honor, and the local Inns of Court chapter—a prestigious organization made up of judges and lawyers—became the Craig S. Barnard chapter. The annual award for distinguished service by Florida public defenders became the Craig Barnard Award. And so forth.

There might never be another figure like him—but he had developed so many other lawyers, each ready to fill a piece of the void; he had spread the knowledge, so another was not needed. Death penalty defense in Florida was no longer a matter of Scharlette Holdman's charisma and Craig Barnard's brains. It had been institutionalized. Building on techniques perfected by Barnard, the CCR office in Tallahassee was becoming a counterbalance to the bureaucratic weight and resources of the attorney general's office. Death penalty defense had, over the years, become as permanent as the prosecution. The lawyers weren't going away and neither were the flip-flops and confusion at the heart of death penalty law, so the fight would continue, case by case, issue by issue—forever, as nearly as anyone could see. The fight survived the loss of Barnard. And it survived the loss of Holdman.

Everyone had predicted it. Scharlette Holdman loathed working at CCR in the bureaucracy that had replaced her little office in the FOG Building. Coarse, flamboyant, and ferocious, Holdman hated bureaucracies when they tried to kill people, and now she hated the bureaucracy meant to save them. Bureaucracies were the bland face of authority; authority was Holdman's cursed enemy. From the beginning, she had battled with the agency's director, Larry Spalding, and eventually the battles had threatened to tear the office apart. Spalding was gas and Holdman was fire. Together, they made a conflagration. Holdman judged lawyers by their intensity, their audacity on the attack. Spalding was a pale figure by that standard. He followed the rules, and Holdman hated rules; he stuck by the budget, and Holdman hated budgets; he lacked charisma, and Holdman lived by charisma. Scharlette Holdman made no secret of her belief that someone else should be running the agency, especially when she had been drinking; at those times, she entertained anyone within earshot with her colorfully low estimate of Spalding's abilities. Some of the lawyers in the office sided with Spalding, and others (including the chief litigator,

Mark Olive) sided with Holdman. In one fiery encounter, Holdman got so angry she picked up a typewriter and threw it against a door.

Such a war of wills might be of small significance at a quiet bureau or commission, but CCR already had all the pressure it could stand from outside. Bob Martinez had adopted an approach to death warrants that perplexed even his predecessor, the vigorous warrant signer Bob Graham. Martinez churned out death orders at twice the pace set by Graham; at one point, nine warrants were active at one time, raising complaints not only from the defense lawyers but also from the pro–death penalty courts. The Martinez strategy seemed to be to squeeze the system until it cracked, hoping that some bad guys would fall through. Under such pressure, CCR could not afford internal rifts. In March 1988, Larry Spalding fired Scharlette Holdman. The last straw was, apparently, Spalding's discovery that Holdman had spent agency funds to pay travel expenses for volunteer lawyers and even funeral expenses for families of inmates. "This," Holdman later told investigators, "is my not-very-clever attempt to accomplish that which was prohibited." Several of the CCR lawyers left with her, including Mark Olive, the best of the bunch. Her departure soured some of the leading lights of the Florida legal community on Spalding, among them Talbot "Sandy" D'Alemberte, who would soon become the president of the American Bar Association.

In a single year, Florida's death penalty defense community had lost its twin headlights, Scharlette Holdman and Craig Barnard, but still capital punishment remained a quagmire.

Ten years almost to the day after John Spenkelink was executed, Aubrey Dennis Adams Jr. went to the chair for the murder of an eight-year-old girl, his first violent offense. Psychiatrists testified that Adams was brain-damaged, that he went into trances, that sexual frustration or humiliation could cause him to snap. The problem was somehow rooted in his childhood, the doctors believed: Adams was a fat boy, and his uncle often taunted him for having a very small penis. When he was eleven or twelve, his parents had taken him to a doctor who began a series of hormone injections. The hormone treatments fueled excruciating headaches that would last for days.

Adams married the first woman with whom he slept, and soon

she was taunting him for his inadequacy and openly pursuing other men. When she left him, he murdered a child. None of this excused him. But while Adams died in Old Sparky, men like Gerald Stano survived. Stano confessed to killing more than two dozen women. As of this writing, Gerald Stano is still alive. Thomas Knight, who murdered a prison guard while awaiting execution for two other murders, is still alive—twenty years after his first death sentence. Jesus Scull, who robbed and murdered two victims and burned their house around them, is alive. Howard Douglas, who forced his wife to have sex with her boyfriend as he watched, then smashed the man's head in, is alive. Robert Buford, who raped and beat a seven-year-old girl to death, is alive. Eddie Lee Freeman, who strangled a former nun and dumped her in a river to drown, is alive. Jesse Hall, who raped and murdered Susan Routt and killed her boyfriend on Dunedin Beach, is alive. Derreck Manning, who shot two deputies to death as they tried to arrest him for rape, is alive. James Rose, who raped and murdered an eight-year-old girl in Fort Lauderdale, is alive. Jimmy Lee Smith, who abducted a woman and her daughter and slaughtered them both, is alive. Robert Preston, who robbed a store and mutilated the clerk, is alive.

And so on, and on, and on. Twenty men have been sentenced to die under Florida's modern death penalty laws for every one who has been executed. Nothing but chance has separated those who live from those who die.

Barnard was gone, Holdman was gone. By 1989, Ray Marky had suffered a heart attack and left the attorney general's office. He took a less stressful job at the local prosecutor's office, where he watched dispirited as the modern death penalty—the law he had help write and had struggled to enforce—reached its soggy maturity. One day a potential death penalty case came across his new desk, and instead of pushing as he had in the old days, he advised the victim's mother to accept a life sentence for her son's killer. "Ma'am, bury your son and get on with your life, or over the next dozen years, this defendant will destroy you, as well as your son," Marky told her. Why put the woman through all the waiting, the hearings and the stays, when the odds were heavy that the death sentence would never be carried out? "I never would have said that fifteen years ago," Marky reflected. "But now I will, because I'm not going to put someone through the nightmare. If we had deliberately set out to create a chaotic system, we couldn't have come up with anything worse. It's a merry-go-round, it's ridiculous; it's so clogged up only an arbitrary few ever get it."

Marky had given the prime of his life to making the death penalty work. After all those years, the system was no closer to working than the day he started. "I don't get any damn pleasure out of the death penalty and I never have," he said. "And frankly, if they abolished it tomorrow, I'd go get drunk in celebration."

Bob Martinez signed more than 130 death warrants during his four-year term, resulting in only nine executions. In one, a schizophrenic named James Hamblen had pleaded to be killed; he said electrocution would be "spiffy." Another went very badly. On May 4, 1990, Jesse Tafero was strapped into Old Sparky fourteen years after he had murdered two police officers. In all previous procedures, the prison staff had packed a sea sponge into the headpiece, but over time the sponge had rotted. The electrician had gone to the supermarket and bought a new, synthetic sponge. When the switch was thrown, the sponge caught fire. Flames leapt from Tafero's head. At the end of the first jolt, he was still breathing; his head nodded after the second dose; only after the third cycle of current was the killer pronounced dead.

Despite Martinez's zeal, Old Sparky did not work its political magic for him. Though he campaigned hard on the death penalty—Ted Bundy was featured prominently in his television ads—Martinez lost his bid for reelection to the popular former U.S. senator Lawton Chiles. As governor, Chiles adopted a new approach to capital punishment: Instead of signing death warrants in a futile effort to speed the process, Chiles waited until an inmate's case appeared ripe. His first sixteen warrants produced eight executions—a far better percentage than that of any of his modern predecessors managed. A couple of times each year, one of the three-hundred-plus inmates on death row went to the chair; by autumn 1994, Florida had executed thirty-three prisoners, beginning with John Spenkelink, a total second only to Texas.

The defense bureaucracy at CCR burgeoned as death row expanded, tripling in size by the end of Chiles's first term. What Scharlette Holdman once had done with her ledger and phone came to require a state agency of twenty-two lawyers and thirteen investigators. The controversial agency was winning its war.

Some politicians and pundits still talked as if the confusion in the death penalty could be eliminated by a healthy dose of conservative toughness. Indeed, when Chiles ran for reelection in 1994 he was hit hard for signing so few death warrants—sixteen, compared to the hundreds signed by his predecessors Graham and Martinez. In the closing days of a bitterly fought campaign, challenger Jeb Bush attacked in the most visceral way. He turned to Wendy Nelson, the grieving mother of murdered Elisa Nelson, and put her in a television advertisement aimed at every screen in Florida.

"Fourteen years ago, my daughter rode off to school on her bicycle," Wendy Nelson told the camera. "She never came back. Her killer is still on death row, and we're still waiting for justice. We won't get it from Lawton Chiles, because he's too liberal on crime." The ad was widely denounced, and it backfired. In Florida, people were beginning to realize that no one—not even the governor—could control the execution machinery. On the same day the Nelson ad went on the air, Bush acknowledged that Chiles had no power to speed the death of Larry Mann, the murderer of Elisa Nelson. Even some pro–death penalty judges came to the defense of Chiles. The ad was "absolutely ridiculous, stupid, ignorant," said Raymond Ehrlich, a retired justice of the Florida Supreme Court. "Had the governor been silly enough to sign a warrant, the circuit court of the Supreme Court would have stayed the thing." The surging Bush campaign faltered, and Chiles was narrowly reelected. Among the people who knew the system best, the death penalty was no longer a matter of liberal or conservative. Twenty years after *Furman v. Georgia,* support for the death penalty crossed all lines. There was not a single guaranteed vote against the death penalty on any court, state or federal, with jurisdiction over Florida. And the same was essentially true everywhere in America. Courts and legislatures got tougher and tougher on the issue, but the results were negligible. The execution rate increased by tiny increments, while America's death row population swelled to three thousand. It made no real difference who controlled the courts, as California voters learned after they dumped their liberal chief justice in 1986. The court turned rightward, but seven and a half years later, California had executed just two of the more than three hundred prisoners on its death row. One of the two had voluntarily surrendered his appeals. No matter how strongly judges and politicians favored capital punishment, the law has remained a mishmash.

It is hard to see a way out. The idea that the death penalty should not be imposed arbitrarily—that each case should be analyzed by a rational set of standards—has been so deeply woven into so many federal and state court rulings that there is little chance of it being reversed. Courts have softened that requirement, but softening has not solved the problem. Proposals to limit access to appeals for death row inmates have become staples of America's political campaigns, and many limits have been set. But it can take many years for a prisoner to complete just one trip through the courts (nine and a half years for Ted Bundy, for example), and no one has proposed denying condemned inmates one trip.

The only way to make the death penalty work, reasonably quickly and reliably, may be to have a lot less of it. Broad laws, intended to weigh ineffable shades of evil, have proven to be failures. Possibly a narrow death penalty could work—for distinct crimes like serial murder or political assassination. If the crimes were better defined, and applied to fewer criminals, courts might find firm ground for judging. And under a lightened load, they might move more quickly.

Several polls have suggested that a majority of Americans might be willing to see the death penalty scrapped if they were sure that unmitigated and dangerous killers would spend the rest of their lives in prison. But most citizens lack much faith in the government's ability to keep bad guys behind bars. They have heard too many stories of murderers sent away for "life"—only to hit the streets in seven, ten, fifteen years and kill another victim. Support for the death penalty seems to flow in a cycle of cynicism: Jaded voters demand it because they don't trust the government to protect them; politicians call for more and stronger death penalty laws to please the voters; but the more death penalty laws there are, the harder it is to enforce them, which in turn makes the voters more jaded.

U.S. Supreme Court Justice Harry Blackmun was one of the four votes in favor of preserving the death penalty in *Furman v. Georgia,* and he voted with the majority to approve the new laws four years later. For two decades, he stuck to the belief that the death penalty could meet the constitutional test of predictability. But on February 22, 1994, Blackmun threw up his hands. "Twenty years have passed since this Court declared that the death penalty must be imposed fairly and with reasonable consistency or not at all," he wrote. ". . . In the years following *Furman,* serious efforts were made to comply with its mandate. State legislatures and appellate courts struggled to provide judges and juries with sensible and objective guidelines for determining who should live and who should die. . . . Unfortunately, all this experimentation and ingenuity yielded little of what *Furman* demanded. . . . It seems that the decision whether a human being should live or die is so inherently subjective, rife with all of life's understandings, experiences, prejudices and passions, that it inevitably defies the rationality and consistency required by the Constitution. . . . I feel morally and intellectually obligated simply to concede that the death penalty experiment has failed."

Also in 1994, an admiring biography of retired U.S. Supreme Court Justice Lewis Powell was published. Powell had been one of the architects of the modern death penalty. As one of the troika of swing votes in 1976, he had helped to define the intricate weighing system that restored capital punishment in America. Later, as the deciding vote in *McCleskey v. Kemp* in 1986, Powell had saved the death penalty from the assertion that racial disparities proved the system was still arbitrary. Now Powell was quoted as telling his biographer, "I have come to think that capital punishment should be abolished." The death penalty "brings discredit on the whole legal system," Powell said, because the vast majority of death sentences are never carried out. Biographer John C. Jeffries Jr. had asked Powell if he would like to undo any decisions from his long career. "Yes," the justice answered, *"McCleskey v. Kemp."*

∴

Doug McCray watched it all from his death row cell. When he arrived at Florida State Prison in 1974, nine men awaited execution and he made ten. He wept when his best friend, John Spenkelink, was executed, and wondered if he might be next. Instead, he watched Bob Martinez follow Bob Graham, just as he had seen Graham follow Reubin Askew. Death row grew to the size of a small town, and Lawton Chiles followed Martinez. He saw men cut, men burned, even saw a man killed on death row. He saw inmates carried from their cells after committing suicide, and others taken away after going insane. He saw wardens come and go; saw the seasons pass through a sliver of dirty glass beyond two sets of bars. While he watched, he became an emblem of the modern death penalty.

As a boy of eight, the son of good, poor parents, James Curtis "Doug" McCray had limitless dreams; he told everyone he met that someday he would be the president of the United States. Soon enough, he realized that poor black children did not grow up to be president, but still he was a striver. At Dunbar High School in Fort Myers, he was an all-state wide receiver on the football team, an all-conference guard at basketball, and the state champion in the 440-yard dash. He made the honor roll, and became the first and only of the eight McCray kids to attend college.

His was a success story, but for one flaw. McCray had a drinking problem. He washed out of college and joined the Army. A year and a half later, the Army gave him a medical discharge because he had been found to suffer from epilepsy. McCray married, fathered a son, tried college again; nothing took. He wound up back home, a tarnished golden boy.

On an October evening in 1973, an elderly woman named Margaret Mears was at home in her apartment, picking no trouble, harming no one, when someone burst in, stripped and raped her, then beat her to death. A bloody handprint at the scene was matched to Doug McCray. He insisted he had no memory of the night in question, and his jury unanimously recommended a life sentence. But McCray had the bad fortune to be tried by Judge William Lamar Rose.

To say that Judge Rose believed in the death penalty hardly does justice to his fervor. When he heard in 1972 that the U.S. Supreme Court had abolished the death penalty, Judge Rose protested by slinging a noose over a tree limb on the courthouse lawn. After the new death penalty law was passed, McCray's case was the first chance Rose had to use it. To him, the murder of Margaret Mears was precisely the type of savagery the law was intended to punish: committed in the course of another felony, and surely heinous, surely atrocious, surely cruel. Rose overruled the jury and banged the gavel on death.

McCray's case went to the Florida Supreme Court for the required review. In June 1977, the justices ordered Rose to certify that no secret information had been used in deciding the sentence. After the judge complied, the case rejoined the heap of death sentences awaiting review at the glutted state high court, and eventually it returned to the top of the pile. In October 1980, the Florida Supreme Court agreed that Doug McCray should die. The following year, the U.S. Supreme Court declined to review the state court's decision.

Through all this, McCray continued to insist that he had no memory of the murder. He passed a lie detector test, though such tests are not admissible in court. And there was another reason to believe what he said. It was possible that McCray's epilepsy, which had first emerged in several powerful seizures during his Army basic training, was the type known as "temporal lobe seizure disorder." This disease often emerges in late adolescence; it is known to cause violent blackouts; and it can be triggered by alcohol. The possibility had not come out at McCray's trial, nor was it properly researched for his clemency hearing, which was held on December 16, 1981, and went badly. An attorney, Jesse James Wolbert, had been appointed to represent McCray, and he did not bother to read the trial record, let alone prepare a compelling case for mercy. Perhaps he had other things on his mind: By the time McCray's death warrant was signed three months later, Wolbert had drained another client's trust fund and disappeared.

Wolbert's disappearance turned out to be a blessing, because Scharlette Holdman persuaded Bob Dillinger of St. Petersburg to take the case, and Dillinger was a damn good lawyer. He filed a hasty appeal in the Florida Supreme Court asking for a stay of execution. The result was amazing: Having affirmed McCray's death sentence eighteen months earlier, the justices now ordered a new trial. The sentence, they ruled, was based on the theory that the murder had been committed in conjunction with a rape. "Felony murder," this is called—murder coupled with another felony. The Florida Supreme Court, by a vote of 4 to 3, declared that the underlying felony, rape, was not proven beyond a reasonable doubt. Eight years after the original sentence, Doug McCray was going back to trial.

Except that something even more amazing happened next. The state supreme court granted the prosecution's request for a rehearing, and Justice Ray Erlich abruptly changed his mind. His vote made it 4 to 3 in favor of upholding McCray's death sentence. In the course of six months, Erlich had gone from believing McCray's sentence was so flawed that he should have an entirely new trial to believing that his sentence was sound enough to warrant his death. The court contacted the company that publishes all its decisions and asked that the first half of this flip-flop—the order for a new trial—be erased from history.

Governor Graham signed a second death warrant on May 27, 1983. By this time, Bob Dillinger had located his client's ex-wife in California, where she lived with her son by Doug McCray. The son was a chip off the old block; he was what his father had once been: bright as a penny, interested in current events, a devourer of books, good at games. The ex-wife, Myra Starks, was mystified by the course her husband had taken. They had been high school sweethearts, and she had married him certain that he was upward bound. When Mc-Cray left school to join the Army, Starks had clung to that vision, picturing a steady string of promotions leading to a comfortable pension. Then came the seizures and the medical discharge, and her husband's behavior had changed horribly. He drank heavily, and sometimes when he was drunk he struck out at her violently—though after each of these outbursts, he insisted he remembered nothing. Myra did not make a connection between the medical discharge and the change in her man; instead, she packed up their baby boy and moved out. Within a year, McCray was on trial for murder.

Bob Dillinger had also arranged for a full-scale medical evaluation of his client, and the doctor had concluded that McCray indeed suffered from temporal lobe seizure disorder. It all came together. The violent blackouts, triggered by drink. In prison, after a number of seizures, McCray had been put on a drug regimen to control his disease: Dilantin, a standard epilepsy treatment, in the mornings, and phenobarbital, a sedative, at night. When Dillinger arranged for Myra Starks to see her ex-husband, after a decade apart, she exclaimed, "He's just like the old Doug!"

But he was scheduled to die. Following established procedure, Dillinger returned to the Florida Supreme Court. It was the fifth time the court had considered McCray's case. This time, the justices concluded that the new medical evidence might be important in deciding whether death was the appropriate sentence. They ordered the trial court to hold a hearing, and stayed the execution while this was done.

Doug McCray had lived on death row nine years. Occasionally, a newly condemned prisoner would arrive on the row from the Gulf Coast with a vague memory of the once-famous name, and he would ask: Are you *the* Doug McCray, Dunbar High's Doug McCray? And he would beg for a chance to go one on one on the basketball court with the fallen legend. But nine years was a long time, and it happened less and less. In all that time, his case had not moved past the first level of appeals. The Florida Supreme Court weighed and reweighed his case, and with each weighing the justices reached a different conclusion.

The hanging judge, Lamar Rose, was gone, but in his place was another stern man who was no less outraged at the enormity of McCray's crime. At the new sentencing hearing, the new judge listened for several days as Bob Dillinger presented witness after witness in favor of mercy. Reverend Joe Ingle, a friend of John Spenkelink and many others on death rows throughout the South, testified to McCray's character in prison. He spoke of the Doug McCray who cried oceans of tears, who taught other men to read and write, who had a friend light candles in church each year to honor the woman he had killed. Dillinger called Myra Starks to the stand, and her testimony about her ex-husband's weird, wild blackouts meshed neatly with the doctors Dillinger called to testify about his dangerous epilepsy. Dillinger found an official of the local NAACP who testified that he had seen McCray drinking the day of the crime—alcohol was the trigger of the violent blackouts. Dillinger put friends, teachers, and coaches on the stand, and they all said how terribly unlike McCray this crime had been.

McCray had, over the years, become a favorite of death penalty opponents, because he seemed so gentle and redeemable. Frequently they argued that not all death row prisoners are like Ted Bundy, and McCray was the sort of prisoner they were talking about. The harshest word in his vocabulary was "shucks." He read every book he could get his hands on. There was a poignant vulnerability to him. Gail Rowland, the longtime assistant to Scharlette Holdman, liked to tell the story of McCray's Afro hairdo, which he maintained long after the style went out of fashion; he was on death row and didn't keep up much with fashion. For many years he smushed his hair down so the guards wouldn't see how long it was, and when visitors came he fluffed it up. Rowland recalled how heartbroken he had been when she had finally informed him: Doug, your hair is so seventies!

But the new judge focused, as the old one had done, on the crime: a defenseless, innocent woman alone, terrorized, apparently raped, then killed. He sentenced McCray to death once more. And the case returned to the Florida Supreme Court for a sixth time. In June 1987, the justices sent it back, with a reminder that the judge must consider all favorable evidence. To overrule a jury's recommendation of mercy, the court reminded, a judge must have justification no reasonable person would dispute. The judge's justification was an elderly woman savagely murdered—once again, he imposed the death sentence.

Doug McCray returned for the seventh time to the Florida Supreme Court. Did he deserve to die? Four times, the trial judge insisted that he did. Twice, the state's high court agreed. And four times, the same high court expressed doubts. A single case, considered and reconsidered, strained and restrained, weighed and reweighed. A prism, a kaleidoscope, a rune of unknown meaning. The life of a man, viewed through the lens of a complex, uncertain, demanding law. Should he live or die?

In May 1991, after weighing the case of Doug McCray for the

seventh time in seventeen years, the Florida Supreme Court reversed his death sentence and imposed a sentence of life in prison. For seventeen years, two courts had debated—the trial court and the state supreme court. No liberal outsiders had stalled the process, no bleeding hearts had intervened. Even the lawyers had added little to the essential conundrum, which was in the beginning as it was in the end: Doug McCray, bad guy, versus Doug McCray, not-quite-so-bad guy. The case was far from aberrant. It was one of hundreds of such cases.

On occasion, it is necessary to repaint the cells at Florida State Prison. Under the grasp of grimy hands, the onslaught of sweat and mildew, the alternating seasons of wet cold and wet heat, and the dust of the compound blown through cracked windows, the pale green or flat white or blanched yellow enamel slowly chips and flakes. Given the dangerous conditions of death row, the maintenance men have no time to strip the old paint down to the bare bars and raw concrete, so instead they just paint over the old grime and rot. The paint builds up, layer on layer, each coat slightly more corrupted than the one before. New paint does not solve the underlying flaws, it merely masks them.

Violent crime is a rot on the structure of American society, staining and flaking the face we present to ourselves and one another. Kids roam the streets with guns; maniacs and drugheads and perverts run rampant. Violence, and the fear that it causes, creeps through layer upon layer of our lives and culture. Our books are violent, our movies are violent, even our music and our games are violent. We live in fear for our children in their schools and even in their own bedrooms; in fear of panhandlers, loud youths on the subway, the guy at the next desk. Beeping your horn in traffic can be a daredevil act. And under the dangerous conditions in which we live, it's overwhelming to imagine stripping our culture down to bare structure and raw foundations.

The modern death penalty has become a sort of enamel we apply to mask these deeper corruptions. Not even the strongest proponents of capital punishment claim that a random few dozen executions each year will root out the rot where it grows. But after more than two decades spent tinkering with the death penalty, a random few dozen is still the limit of possibility. Would a perfect death penalty—predictable and swift—serve us better? It's an age-old question, but the question has become irrelevant to our times. As Florida and all other death penalty states have shown, perfection eludes our grasp.

America has a serious problem with violence. The answers are hard; we fear our society has gone soft. This is the story of the modern death penalty: Now and then, we buckle up a criminal and watch the smoke rise from his head and his leg. And when the rot shows through again, we add another layer of paint.

ACKNOWLEDGMENTS

This book would not have been written without the support, instruction, and encouragement of many people. First, my friends and teachers at *The Miami Herald.* In the pages and on the expense accounts of that fine newspaper, I was allowed to develop my theme; later, the *Herald* graciously gave me time for further research. My thanks to the late Janet Chusmir, a brave and comforting boss; also to Dave Lawrence, Doug Clifton, and Pete Weitzel; to my editors John Brecher, John Pancake, Chris Morris, Bill Rose, and Tom Shroder; and to the great Gene Miller.

When I joined *The Washington Post,* the sustenance continued. For this, I thank Donald Graham, Leonard Downie, Bob Kaiser, Karen DeYoung, Fred Barbash, and Bob Barnes.

Homes and hearts were opened to facilitate my work. I thank Jack Gordon and Myra MacPherson, Joel Achenbach and Mary Stapp, Steve Jennings and Monica O'Neil, Lynn and Greg Granello, Carol and Joe Robinson, Roscoe Hill, and Justin Gillis.

Friends and mentors polished and refined both book and author. Some have been mentioned already. Three others: Bob Richardson, Gene Weingarten, and Nancy Gibbs.

My editor, Henry Ferris, nurtured and improved this book from first glimmer to galleys, and it is very much a product of his talent and dedication. I wish to thank Peter Osnos and John Sterling for their confidence, and Esther Newberg for her faith in me.

Finally, my undying love and gratitude to Karen Ball and to my family for seeing me through.

SOURCES

GENERAL

INTERVIEWS

Several people deserve special mention, having given profoundly of their time, their insights, and their emotions. Dr. Margaret Vandiver patiently, meticulously, and scrupulously relived a number of experiences that were, for her, very ghastly. Ray Marky and Michael Mello, two walking encyclopediae of capital jurisprudence, patiently instructed me on the law from opposing viewpoints. And Dr. Michael Radelet, Florida's leading academic authority on capital punishment, was unstinting with his time, and, despite his dark speciality, hilarious in his reminiscences. In addition, I conducted interviews with the following subjects for this book—and for the newspaper articles that were the seed of this book—during a period ranging from 1987 to 1994 (a handful of sources asked not to be identified):

Ed Austin

James David Barber

Ronald Barnard Sr.

Trudy Barnard

Hugo Adam Bedau

Faith Blake

Irwin Block

Sandy Bohrer

William Bowers

David Brierton

Richard Burr

Bill Caldwell

Elmer Carroll

Samantha Carver

Susan Cary

Ramsey Clark

Robert Dillinger

Leigh Dingerson

Patrick Doherty

Richard Dugger

Martin Dyckman

Arthur England

Watt Espy

Millard Farmer

Reverend Tom Feamster

Howell Ferguson

Tom Fiedler

Deborah Fins

Howardene Garrett

George Georgieff

Steve Gettinger

Robin Gibson

Steve Goldstein
Arthur F. "Bud" Goode Jr.
Mildred Goode
Jonathan Gradess
Bob Graham
Richard Green
Robert A. Harper
Baya Harrison III
Larry Hersch
Andrea Hillyer
Judy Hinson
Scharlette Holdman
Warren Holmes
Steve Hull
Reverend Joe Ingle
Ralph Jacobs
John Jeffries Jr.
Bill Jent
S. R. Johns
Richard Jorandby
David Kendall
Gerald Kogan
Michael Lambrix
Robbie Larramore
Richard Larsen
Reverend Fred Lawrence
James Lohman
Doug McCray
Morris McDonald
Parker Lee McDonald
Ellen McGarrahan
Bob Macmaster
Doug Magee
Robert Mahler
Bob Martinez
Roy Mathews

Don Middlebrooks
Earnie Miller
Gene Miller
Ellen Morphonios
Polly Nelson
Wendy Nelson
Joe Nursey
Hudson Olliff
Jack Partain
Eleanor Jackson Piel
James Rinaman
Gail Rowland
Ann Rule
Dianne Rust-Tierney
Ron Sachs
Henry Schwarzschild
William Shade
Sam Shepard Jr.
Robert Shevin
Laurie Sistrunk
Neil Skene
Jim Smith
Carolyn Snurkowski
Larry Spalding
Bob Spangenberg
Eugene Spellman
Betty Steffens
Alan Sundberg
Ken Tucker
Paula Tully
Sue Tully
Bill Vaughn
Suzie Vaughn
Alan Wagner
Bill Wax
Sandy Weinberg

Bill White   Turk Williams
Art Wiedinger   Dr. Ronald Wright

ARCHIVES AND FILES

This account of events, many of them unseen by me, was possible only through the very thorough reporting of Florida's newspapers. I immersed myself in a quarter century's worth of clippings from papers including the *Tallahassee Democrat,* the *Gainesville Sun,* the *Orlando Sentinel,* the *St. Petersburg Evening Independent,* and the *Tampa Tribune.* Key citations appear in the notes. More generally, I drew heavily on the work of three papers:

First and foremost, the *St. Petersburg Times,* whose coverage of the death penalty has been unmatched in recent decades by any paper in America, to my knowledge. I must note the work of three *Times* writers in particular: Dudley Clendinin, who produced a series of remarkably intimate portraits of death row in the late 1970s, when it was still possible to get decent access to the place; Neil Skene, who comprehended and chronicled the intricacies of capital appeals better than any other reporter, anywhere, ever; and Martin Dyckman, Florida's preeminent editorial voice on this subject and many others. I was welcomed into the library of the *Times* with open arms, and found much of my book already there in the files.

The *Florida Times-Union* was invaluable because it has been the only paper to assign a reporter full time to Florida State Prison, resulting in a great deal of continuity and intelligence in its accounts of prison life and executions. Andrea Rowand Dickerson, Bruce Krasnow, and Bruce Ritchie, through their *Times-Union* clippings, were like eyes and ears on the past to me. (In this regard, I should also mention Ron Word of the Associated Press.)

And the files of *The Miami Herald* were not only a source but an inspiration; there, the reporting on this subject has often risen toward art in the hands of such writers as Carl Hiaasen, Barry Bearak, and John Dorschner.

Statistics regarding the number of prisoners on death row at any given time, the number of executions, and so forth were drawn from *Death Row, USA,* a periodic report of the NAACP Legal Defense and Educational Fund, Inc., and the quarterly summaries of the National Coalition to Abolish the Death Penalty.

A number of sources opened their personal files to me. The most extensive archive on the history of the death penalty in America belongs to Watt Espy of Headland, Alabama. Watt spent several days with me tracing through hundreds of years and thousands of executions. This was invaluable background. Leigh Dingerson allowed me access to clipping files of the National Coalition to Abolish the Death Penalty. Margaret Vandiver opened her substantial personal files to me and also arranged my access to the death penalty archive at Northeastern University. I received smaller caches from the personal papers of Ronald and Trudy Barnard, Sandy Bohrer, Susan Cary, Bud and Mildred Goode, Baya Harrison III, David Kendall, Reverend Fred Lawrence, James Lohman, Morris McDonald, Michael Mello, Wendy Nelson, Michael Radelet, and Gail Rowland.

I was aided in my research by the helpful clerks of the Florida Supreme Court and archivists at the Florida State Archives, both in Tallahassee. Court files can be accessed by the name of the inmate. At the Archives, the materials I studied relating to Bob Graham's handling of the death penalty are available at Tiers 30133 and 30134 (Boxes 2, 3, 5, and 10); Tier 30081 (Boxes 1–4, 5–13, 15, and 19); Tier 10883 (Boxes 1 and 2); and Series 918 (Boxes 2 and 4). Archive materials that I studied regarding Reubin Askew's handling of the death penalty and related matters are available at Tier 30861 (Box 3); Tiers 30828 and 30829 (Box 1); Tier 30842 (Box 60); Tier 30848 (Box 3); Tiers 30825–30828 (Boxes 5, 11, 21, 24, 25, 30, and 31); and Tiers 30818 and 30819 (Boxes 1 and 12).

BOOKS

An enormous amount has been written about the death penalty in America, and about death row, and about crimes that have led to executions. I can scarcely claim to have read this material exhaustively, or to have chosen from it systematically. But I offer this note both as a partial accounting of my sources, and to suggest directions in which interested readers might turn should they wish to read more.

Two books stand out as general introductions: *The Death Penalty in America*, edited by Hugo Adam Bedau (3rd edition, Oxford University Press, 1982), and *Legal Homicide*, by William Bowers (Northeastern University Press, 1984). Both Bedau and Bowers are committed opponents of capital punishment, but both are also scrupulous scholars, and their books contain much that is useful to persons of any viewpoint. Regrettably, neither of these landmarks of scholarship is entirely up-to-date. *Capital Punishment and the American Agenda*, by Franklin Zemring and Gordon Hawkins (Cambridge University Press, 1986), is another important work of rigorous scholars who oppose the death penalty; it brings the issue forward a few years. Welsh White's book *The Death Penalty in the Nineties* (University of Michigan Press, 1991) brings the subject still further. Bedau's book *Death is Different* (Northeastern University Press, 1987) provides additional light.

Amnesty International published, in 1987, a book-length report titled *United States of America: The Death Penalty*, which is essentially an indictment of the practice but nevertheless contains a sense of the important issues, and also several informative charts. AI produced another report, *When the State Kills . . . ,* in 1989, which details the status of capital punishment worldwide.

Much more has been written against capital punishment than in favor of it. To my way of thinking, the best book in support of the death penalty is *For Capital Punishment* by Walter Berns (Basic Books, 1979). Because Berns rests his case on timeless principles, his book suffers little from the passage of years. Ernst van den Haag is perhaps better known than Berns as chief spokesman on the pro side. He includes a summary of his views on capital punishment in *Punishing Criminals* (Basic Books, 1975). There is also a representative essay by van den Haag in Bedau, *The Death Penalty in America*. Van den Haag has made many spirited defenses of the death penalty on debating platforms through the years; you can get the flavor of his arguments in a book called *The Death Penalty: A Debate* (Plenum Press, 1983).

Among the books written against the death penalty, I would recommend several. *Facing the Death Penalty,* edited by Michael Radelet (Temple University Press, 1989), is a collection of essays from a wide range of perspectives: inmates, families of the condemned, scholars, attorneys. The contemporary legal objections to the death penalty are distilled in Charles Black's magnificent *Capital Punishment: The Inevitability of Caprice and Mistake* (2nd edition, W. W. Norton, 1981). Thorsten Sellin, the grand old man of anti–death penalty sociologists, summarized his work in *The Penalty of Death* (Sage, 1980). Albert Camus's "Reflections on the Guillotine" is a milestone.

Public Justice, Private Mercy: A Governor's Education on Death Row (Weidenfeld & Nicolson, 1989) is former California governor Edmund (Pat) Brown's highly personal account of his transformation from a supporter to an opponent of capital punishment, and provides a window on the pressures involved in ordering executions. The strain of executions on a prison warden is portrayed in Lewis Lawes's classic memoir *Twenty Thousand Years in Sing Sing* (Long & Smith, 1932).

In recent years, two religious figures dedicated to death row ministries have written passionately of their work: Joseph Ingle in *Last Rights* (Abingdon, 1990) and Helen Prejean in *Dead Man Walking* (Random House, 1993). I owe a personal debt to Ingle's book for its intimate portraits of several Florida inmates, and I admire Sister Helen's willingness to grapple with the awful pain and loss of the innocent victims of death row criminals.

The ardors and experiences of anti–death penalty activists are contained in *A Punishment in Search of a Crime,* by Ian Gray and Moire Stanley for Amnesty International (Avon, 1989). Many of the characters in my book can be found there, speaking for themselves. For young readers, there is a short primer against the death penalty by Kent and Betty Davis Miller called *To Kill and Be Killed* (Hope, 1989).

For a sense of what it's like to live, work, and die on death row, one might read Doug Magee's *Slow Coming Dark: Interviews on Death Row* (Pilgrim, 1980). Robert Johnson has written on this subject from two points of view. In *Condemned to Die* (Elsevier, 1981), Johnson describes the existence of inmates on Alabama's death row; in *Death*

Work (Brooks/Cole, 1990), he discusses the lives of prison authorities and death row guards. Johnson's *Death Work* is not to be confused with the ripping but unreliable novel *Deathwork,* by James McLendon (Lippincott, 1977), which has some interesting and well-informed atmospherics but should not be taken as reality. A better death row novel is Curtis Bok's *Star Wormwood* (Knopf, 1959). Steven Trombley wrote a book called *The Execution Protocol* (Crown, 1992) that rambles through the operations of Missouri's death row, lighting occasionally on an arresting detail.

The golden age of inmate memoirs was thirty or forty years ago, perhaps because in those days it seemed unusual to find a person who had survived a death sentence long enough to write a book. Two celebrated examples of the old vintage are Edgar Smith's well-written but unconvincing *Brief Against Death* (Knopf, 1968) and Caryl Chessman's self-indulgent *Cell 2455 Death Row* (Prentice-Hall, 1954). They are worth reading only as curiosities. The more recent memoir of Velma Barfield, *Woman on Death Row* (Oliver-Nelson, 1985), is vastly more honest and worthy than the older books.

There is an excellent, though highly academic, study of the early history of America's death penalty and its role in the culture called *Rites of Execution,* by Louis Masur (Oxford University Press, 1989). Jan Gorecki's *Capital Punishment: Criminal Law and Social Evolution* (Columbia University Press, 1983) covers more recent cultural developments. *The Penry Penalty* (University Press of America, 1993) is a scholarly look at execution of mentally retarded inmates. Similarly, *Death Penalty for Juveniles,* by Victor Streib (Indiana University Press, 1987), considers the issue as applied to another marginal subclass. The history of the NAACP Legal Defense Fund's attack on the death penalty and its victory in *Furman v. Georgia* is well told by Michael Meltsner in *Cruel and Unusual: The Supreme Court and Capital Punishment* (William Morrow, 1973).

On some more general subjects: For readers interested in the way criminal law becomes constitutional doctrine, the best book remains *Gideon's Trumpet,* by Anthony Lewis (Random House, 1964). Readers interested in the internal struggles of the U.S. Supreme Court over the modern death penalty should read *The Brethren,* by Bob Woodward and Scott Armstrong (Simon & Schuster, 1979), and *Turning Right,* by David Savage (John Wiley & Sons, 1992; expanded 1993). A vast library exists on the general topic of crime in America. *Crimewarps,* by Georgette Bennett (2nd edition, Anchor Books, 1989), is a deliberately provocative book that tries to get beyond the crudities of the nightly news to see what is actually happening. Despite the author's liberal interpretations, Bennett's underlying data might be of interest to readers of any philosophy.

A number of books have been written about innocent people sentenced to death. An excellent overview of this subject is *In Spite of Innocence* (Northeastern University Press, 1992), by Michael Radelet, Hugo Bedau, and Constance Putnam. Investigative reporter Gene Miller tells the story of a nightmare struggle to free two innocent men from Florida's death row in *Invitation to a Lynching* (Doubleday, 1975). *Adams v. Texas* (St. Martin's Press, 1991) is Randall Dale Adams's account of how he was falsely convicted, faced death, and won his freedom. This book is not as good, however, as Errol Morris's film on the same subject, *The Thin Blue Line,* which is widely available on video. I will also mention *Fatal Flaw,* by Phillip Finch (Villard, 1992), because it concerns a Florida case. Finch is an accomplished writer and *Fatal Flaw* is a good read—but it seems to me he falls short of making a persuasive case for Tommy Ziegler's innocence.

Plenty of books exist for readers interested in more on Ted Bundy; several stand out as generally accurate and highly readable: Ann Rule's *The Stranger Beside Me* (W. W. Norton, 1980); Richard Larsen's *The Deliberate Stranger* (Prentice-Hall, 1980); and *The Only Living Witness* (Linden Press/Simon & Schuster, 1983), by Stephen Michaud and Hugh Aynesworth. Michaud and Aynesworth benefited from a series of bizarre interviews they conducted with the infamous killer. After Bundy's execution, they published much larger chunks of their interviews in *Ted Bundy: Conversations with a Killer* (Signet, 1989). You have to be a dedicated student of Bundy's pathology to plow through these transcripts; on the other hand, they form the best available window on his rampant narcissism and bloviation. Bundy's last days are detailed from the perspective of one of his lawyers in *Defending the Devil: My Story as Ted Bundy's Last Lawyer,* by Polly Nelson (William Morrow, 1994).

An example of the way that Bundy passed from sordid flesh to a deathless symbol of evil is an odd paperback thriller called *The Stranger Returns,* by Michael Perry (Pocket Books, 1992). Here, Bundy becomes a sort of Freddy Krueger, a fictional predator virtually impossible to stop. Bundy's case is used more constructively in a number of studies of serial murder. *The Serial Killers,* by Colin Wilson and Donald Seaman (Carol Publishing, 1990), is one good example, and offers an inside look at the FBI operation devoted to tracking these criminals. *Serial Murder,* by Ronald Holmes and James DeBurger (Sage, 1988), takes a more scholarly look at the subject.

As I say, this list of books is idiosyncratic and perhaps contains important omissions. Fortunately, an exhaustive bibliography of modern writing on the death penalty—including essential journal and law review articles—is available: *Capital Punishment in America: An Annotated Bibliography,* by Michael Radelet and Margaret Vandiver (Garland, 1990).

SPECIFIC

Newspaper citations are abbreviated: the *Tallahassee Democrat (TD),* the *Gainesville Sun (GS),* the *Orlando Sentinel (OS),* the *St. Petersburg Evening Independent (EI),* the *Tampa Tribune (TT),* the *St. Petersburg Times (SPT),* the *Florida Times-Union (FTU),* The *Miami Herald (MH),* the Associated Press (AP), and United Press International (UPI).

PART I: LOOSE THE FATEFUL LIGHTNING

In recounting the battle over John Spenkelink's life, I have drawn primarily on interviews with David Kendall, David Brierton, Ray Marky, Robin Gibson, and Reverend Tom Feamster. My interviews with Kendall were particularly useful in establishing a precise sequence of events, because he consulted his detailed diary of that week as we talked.

Specific sources for each section:

The death warrant: The preparation of Spenkelink's death warrant was recounted by Betty Steffens. The reactions of Spenkelink and Willie Darden came from Brierton.

Notification of David Kendall: This material was derived from interviews with Kendall and from my own understanding of the history of the NAACP Legal Defense and Educational Fund, Inc.

Introduction of Bob Graham: The governor's political background, the context surrounding the death warrants, and the shape of the 1978 campaign were explained to me in interviews with Gibson, Steve Hull, Tom Fiedler, Martin Dyckman, and Robert Shevin, among others. I also consulted the clip files of *The Miami Herald* and the *St. Petersburg Times.*

For the history of the remarkable Graham family, I relied extensively on David Halberstam's book *The Powers That Be* (Knopf, 1979), and on a profile of Graham in the *Miami Herald*'s *Tropic* magazine by Michael Ollove (December 9, 1984). In addition, I drew on my own observations of Florida politics, The Washington Post Company, and the city of Miami Lakes.

For the account of Robin Gibson's preparations for the execution, I relied on interviews with Gibson, Hull, and Brierton primarily.

Kendall meets with Spenkelink: The description of North Florida came from my own observations. Kendall was the source for the conversation. Biographical material was drawn from my own reporting and also from profiles of Spenkelink by Barry Bearak (*MH,* March 27, 1979) and by Susan Taylor Martin and Charles Reid (*Tampa Times,* September 18, 1977). Letters quoted came from the Florida State Archives collection of the official papers of D. Robert Graham.

PAX protesters arrive: This account was drawn from interviews with Gibson, Hull, and Doug Magee; also from an article by Mike Jendrzejczyk in *Sojourners* magazine (July 1979), and from wire service accounts in the *MH* and *SPT* (May 20, 1979).

Georgieff and Marky: Here I have drawn primarily from interviews with George Georgieff and Ray Marky; also from the observations of Gibson, Steffens, Carolyn Snurkowski, Jim Smith, Ken Tucker, Gene Miller, and others.

SOURCES

Execution rehearsal: Quoted material came from *Execution Guidelines During Active Death Warrant . . . Effective May 1, 1979; Revised November 1, 1983,* a confidential document of Florida State Prison that I received from the files of Margaret Vandiver. Additional detail came from Brierton.

Spenkelink's clemency hearing: Quotations came from the transcript of executive clemency proceedings before the governor and cabinet on April 20, 1979, available from the Florida Board of Pardons and Paroles. Physical descriptions of Kendall and Lois Spenkelink were based on photographs published in the *TD* and the *OS* (April 21, 1979). In addition, Kendall shared his recollections of the hearing and provided a copy of his memorandum and appendices in support of his plea. Gibson and Steffens discussed Graham's view of clemency with me. Graham's violent physical reaction to the bloody pictures was recounted to me by two sources loyal to the governor who were in close contact with him during the period in question; these sources asked not to be identified.

In this section I have, for narrative purposes, described certain pauses and gestures that are not part of any available record. These are inferences based on repeated readings of the transcript. I have tried to make them neutral, and the reader is urged not to draw any conclusions about character, unsupported by the actual quotations, from such phrases as "Guarisco paused," or "A deep breath." (This technique was used sparingly throughout Part I; for example, describing Spenkelink as inhaling from a cigarette at a precise moment during a conversation, when my sources reported only that he was chain-smoking while he talked.)

Brierton described: Spenkelink's accommodations, his taste in cigarettes. The watchful guard came from Kendall, Feamster, and Brierton.

The profile of Brierton was drawn from my interview with him, supplemented by assorted newspaper accounts of conditions at Florida State Prison prior to Brierton's arrival and by interviews with Gibson, Hull, Feamster, and others.

Kendall meets again with Spenkelink: This passage was based on my interview with Kendall, who had recorded this and other exchanges in his diary. A number of sources shared letters they had received from Spenkelink, and still more Spenkelink letters (to Robert Mays of Frederick, Maryland) are among the Graham papers at the Florida State Archives. These were the source for my description of the smiling and frowning faces.

Spenkelink's maturation on death row: Here I drew primarily on interviews with Brierton, Kendall, Feamster, Richard Dugger, Doug McCray, and Reverend Joe Ingle (supplemented by Ingle's book *Last Rights*).

Kendall's speeding ticket: From Kendall.

Lois Spenkelink's protests: My sources for this passage were newspaper accounts and interviews, including a report by Matt Bokor of the AP in the *FTU,* a combined wire services account in the *SPT,* and a photograph in the *TD* (all May 21, 1979). The celebrity invitation list was published in the *TD* (May 19, 1979). The fears of Graham's aides were discussed by Gibson and Hull. The FRY JOHN SPENKELINK sign was described to me by Ingle.

Marky's confidence: My Marky interviews were the principal source. I found additional details regarding the frantic response to Kendall's 1977 appeal in the Florida State Archives collection of Reubin Askew's official papers.

I was never able to find, either in Askew's papers or in interviews with various aides, a conclusive explanation why he chose to sign only one death warrant as governor, and why Spenkelink was his choice. Anti–death penalty activists have long suggested that Askew chose Spenkelink out of revulsion at the homosexual overtones in his relationship with Joseph Syzmankiewicz. Whatever credence this theory has comes from Askew's extreme conservatism in areas of personal behavior: He was a Deep South Baptist who banned alcohol in the Florida governor's mansion and was no supporter of gay rights. It strains credibility, however, to believe that one of the first southern governors to embrace the civil rights movement would have acted from such a bigoted motivation.

Others have theorized that Askew was secretly opposed to the death penalty and chose Spenkelink because he was the weakest candidate for Old Sparky. In this version of events, Askew was trying to tempt the courts into overthrowing Florida's capital statute. The flaw in this speculation is that there was at least one case even weaker that Askew might have chosen: Clifford Hallman, whose victim died not of her wounds but of medical malpractice. Various interviews with Askew aides and reporters from that era suggest that Askew considered Hallman's case the weakest.

A third theory holds that Askew had qualms about signing a death warrant in any case where there was the slightest glimmer of doubt about guilt. Spenkelink had confessed to killing Syzmankiewicz. This theory is undercut by the fact that another candidate, Charles Proffitt, had also confessed.

The best explanation I found came from Ray Marky, who pointed out that in 1977, when Askew signed Spenkelink's first death warrant, Florida's death row inmates had filed a class action suit challenging the state's clemency process. Spenkelink was the only inmate who had declined to join the suit. Marky believes that Askew did not want to sign a death warrant in any case where there was pending litigation. That left Spenkelink as his only choice.

Askew has never publicly discussed his decision, and declined to be interviewed by me.

The governor's mail: This passage was drawn primarily from examination of the boxes of letters retained in the Florida State Archives. It was supplemented by an interview with Sue Tully and by material from the personal files of Margaret Vandiver.

PAX blockades governor's office: A copy of the letter from the PAX men to Graham is part of my files. The fact that legislators were advised to use the side door came from Jack Gordon. Gibson described his exchange with the protesters in our interview.

Kendall in Tallahassee: This was drawn from my Kendall interviews, supplemented by Steffens and Gibson.

Millard Farmer enters the case: Biographical material came primarily from Farmer and from a profile of Farmer in the *Atlanta Journal & Constitution*'s Sunday magazine (March 25, 1979). Farmer and Kendall both discussed their conversation with me.

Brierton under pressure: The superintendent's experiences and feelings as the execution approached were based on Brierton's own recollections. My account of his Tuesday morning meeting with Spenkelink's representatives was drawn from interviews with Brierton, Kendall, Ingle, Feamster, and Susan Cary—although Cary was circumspect about the details, wishing to preserve the confidentiality of her many negotiations with prison officials.

Kendall was the source for his phone call to Steffens and his sense that the prison was turning into a circus.

The Darden battle: Drawn from my interview with Robert A. Harper.

Spenkelink's Tuesday meetings: Impressions of the doomed man, and snippets of his conversations, came from Ingle (supplemented by his book), and from Kendall, who was also the source for the brief meeting at which Dugger outlined plans for the last hours. Kendall described his reaction to the denial of Spenkelink's appeals.

Marky senses victory: Drawn from my interview with Marky, supplemented by numerous sources who recalled Marky and his motorcycle.

The shouting match: Kendall and Brierton both described their heated exchange over Spenkelink's choice of clergy, agreeing on the tone and thrust. For the actual flow of the dialogue, I relied primarily on Kendall, because he was referring to his contemporaneous diary entry. The same holds true for my account of the later, calmer, exchange at which Brierton agreed to permit Feamster to stay with the prisoner. Kendall and Brierton were the sources, respectively, for my description of their thoughts and feelings.

Biographical material on Feamster came from my interview with him, supplemented by my own coverage of Jack Murphy's release from prison in 1986.

The prisoner protest: This account was drawn primarily from interviews with Brierton, Dugger, and McCray, who were inside the prison. The view of the protest from outside was described by Ingle (in my interview and in his book), and also in the *EI* and the *FTU* (May 23, 1979). Kendall described his own numb reaction, and, fleetingly, his last meeting with Spenkelink that night.

Farmer's appeal: This passage was drawn primarily from interviews with Farmer, Ramsey Clark, and William Bowers. My assessment of Judge Tuttle and the old Fifth Circuit was informed by Jack Bass's history of The Four, *Unlikely Heroes* (University of Alabama Press, 1990). I supplemented my Clark interview with material from his account published in *The Nation* (October 27, 1979). Kendall gave me a copy of the hastily drafted stay order.

Reaction to the stay: Kendall described his own response, and his recollection of the attempt to get word to the prison was supplemented by interviews with Ingle and Deborah Fins. Reactions of the protesters outside the prison were reported in the *Jacksonville Journal* and *FTU* (both May 23, 1979). Feamster was the source for Spenkelink's response. The relief and singing outside the U.S. Supreme Court was reported by Richard Cohen in *The Washington Post* (May 24, 1979).

Marky was the source for his own reaction, and for his demoralized conversation with Georgieff, and for his thoughts as he tried to sleep. He also described to me his decision to renew the fight, and the way his strategy emerged as he worked through the night. Jim Smith described his own background and attitudes in my interview with him. Both Marky and Smith discussed their actions on Wednesday as they flew across the country lodging their appeal, and their recollections were corroborated by various newspaper accounts, including one in the *FTU* (May 24, 1979).

Farmer's work continues: The views of the Spenkelink team as they celebrated the stay were described for me by Kendall, Fins, Ingle, Farmer, and others. Kendall was the source for his actions in Atlanta. Farmer and his colleague Joe Nursey were the sources describing the effort to assemble a team and a strategy to protect the stay.

The telephone conference: My account of the U.S. Supreme Court deliberations was based on published court documents, newspaper reports, and interviews with Marky, Kendall, Farmer, and others. Details of the conference call with the Fifth Circuit panel came from Marky, Georgieff, Gibson, Steffens, Smith, Tucker, Farmer, Kendall, and Clark (in an interview and in his article in *The Nation*). My assertion that Judge Rubin tried to persuade Judge Coleman to stand by the stay is my own conclusion, drawn from available facts: The two judges discussed the matter for several hours, and Rubin dissented from the eventual decision to let the execution proceed. There was no need for Coleman to try to persuade Rubin, because Coleman already had Judge Fay's vote to dissolve the stay. The obvious explanation for the extended discussion was that Rubin was trying to swing Coleman to his side.

Clark and Farmer each described their movements after the conference call. Howell Ferguson and Steve Goldstein recounted their entry into the case in interviews with me. Arthur England explained to me how he was notified of the final appeal, and how he arranged for the next morning's meeting.

Spenkelink's last meeting with his girlfriend was recounted by sources who asked not to be identified.

Spenkelink's last night: Drawn from Feamster interview.

Schedule for the last hours: Quotations were taken from *Execution Guidelines During Active Death Warrant . . . Effective May 1, 1979; Revised November 1, 1983* (see above).

The breakfast hearing: Clark's movements were based on my interview with him and his article in *The Nation.* Marky, England, Goldstein, and Ferguson discussed the hearing with me.

Inside the governor's office: This passage was based on interviews with Gibson, Hull, Steffens, Smith, Tully, Bill Shade, and others. Two sources close to Graham, both wishing to remain unidentified, reported that the governor had considered reversing himself.

The shot of whiskey: This episode was recounted by Brierton and Dugger.

Stays denied: The Florida Supreme Court's action was recounted in interviews with England, Marky, and Ferguson. The U.S. Supreme Court's action was described by Ramsey Clark in *The Nation.*

The Twenty-third Psalm: Kendall and Feamster described this exchange to me. The order in which Kendall recalled the lines of the psalm was based on Kendall's handwritten notes made as he tried to remember the words. These notes show Kendall inserting lines as they came to mind. The fact that the electric chair was powered by a generator because of the power company's fear of bad publicity or sabotage came from interviews with prison officials.

Lois Spenkelink's final efforts: Drawn from Ingle interview and book.

Spenkelink taken to the chair: Drawn from interviews with Brierton, Dugger, and others present who asked not to be identified. References to the subsequent investigation of the execution were based on newspaper reports, the Graham papers at the Florida State Archives, the findings of the governor's commission to investigate the allegations, and an interview with the commission's chairman, Irwin Block.

Inside the chamber: Based on interviews with Kendall, Feamster, and Brierton, supplemented by J. Paul Wyatt's report for UPI published in the *TT* (May 26, 1979).

The governor's order: Drawn from interviews with Gibson, Hull, and Steffens.

The execution: Based on interviews with Feamster, Brierton, and Dugger, and reports in the *SPT, MH,* and *TT* (May 26, 1979). My own observation of an electrocution in Old Sparky also informed the description.

Marky's reaction: Drawn from interviews with Marky, England, and Ferguson.

Conclusion: The description of preparations by news media to cover the event was based on interviews with a number of reporters. Magee, who had left the protests in Tallahassee to shoot pictures for *Newsweek,* described that magazine's plans to me. The actual play of the news, in comparison to the airplane crash, was evident from various archives and from the White House news summaries on file at the James Earl Carter presidential library in Atlanta. The T-shirt sale by the Jacksonville police softball team was reported in *Time* magazine (June 25, 1979). Spenkelink's funeral was described to me by Kendall, Ingle, and Feamster.

PART II: DANCING ON THE HEAD OF A PIN

A day on death row: This passage drew heavily on interviews and correspondence with a number of death row inmates, several of whom wished not to be identified. I had especially detailed conversations with Doug McCray and Michael Lambrix.

Here and elsewhere, my descriptions of men and conditions on death row owe a heavy debt to a remarkably detailed series of articles by Dudley Clendinin in the *SPT* (December 13 and 14, 1976; September 26–October 8, 1977), and to my interviews with Susan Cary.

My description of death row cells is drawn from interviews supplemented by photographs, especially those published in the *MH's Tropic* magazine (July 23, 1989) and the *SPT* (August 25, 1989).

Additional details came from interviews with prison officials, including David Brierton, Richard Dugger, and S. R. Johns.

Men of death row: This passage was shaped and informed by numerous interviews with inmates and death row activists. In addition:

My description of Vernon Cooper was based on correspondence with him; also on the judge's memorandum in support of Cooper's death sentence (case #74-185 in Circuit Court of Escambia County, dated July 1, 1974).

Johnny Paul Witt was drawn primarily from the Florida Department of Corrections' "case brief" on file at the DOC in Tallahassee.

George Vasil was drawn from an interview with Susan Cary, and from an article by Margaret Gentry of the AP (*MH,* February 21, 1977).

Jacob John Dougan was drawn from the "presentence investigation confidential evaluation" on file at the Florida State Archives collection of the official papers of Bob Graham. This was supplemented by the opinion of the Florida Supreme Court affirming Dougan's death sentence (case #49-260, dated March 17, 1977), by Andrew H. Malcolm's article in *The New York Times* (July 23, 1990), and by interviews with prison officials.

Sources on Anthony Antone are discussed below.

David Washington was drawn primarily from Doug Magee's interview with him published in *Slow Coming Dark,* corroborated by interviews and numerous newspaper reports.

Sources on Bob Sullivan are discussed below; the judge's quote regarding lack of remorse appears in the *MH* (November 13, 1973).

Joseph Green Brown was drawn from Barry Siegel's report published in *The Los Angeles Times* (May 10, 1987); Joseph B. White of Am-Law News Service in the *Palm Beach Review* (April 3, 1987); and Ed Dietz's report on the flap over Brown's eventual release (*TT,* March 7, 1987).

Joe Spaziano was drawn from interviews with McCray, Michael Mello, and Margaret Vandiver, and from the Clendinin series (see above).

Sources on Arthur F. Goode III are discussed below; the exchange with Ted Bundy regarding Goode was recounted by Joe Nursey in an interview with me.

Benny Demps was drawn from Ron Cunningham in the *GS* (January 9, 1981); Daniel Coler from wire service dispatches in the *MH* (December 4, 1980, and November 20, 1982); Steve Beattie from an interview with Michael Radelet.

The *MH* published photos of all death row inmates on May 27, 1979. The reaction of the governor's staff came from interviews with Robin Gibson and Steve Hull.

Scharlette Holdman: Throughout Part II, descriptions of Holdman were based on my interview with her; on interviews with Vandiver, Mello, Radelet, Gail Rowland, Susan Cary, James Lohman, Patrick Doherty, Baya Harrison III, and others; and on profiles by David Finkel (*SPT,* November 23, 1984), Joy Williams (*Esquire,* December 1985), Alfie Kohn (*Boston Globe,* April 21, 1983), John Dorschner (*MH*'s *Tropic* magazine, December 12, 1982), Peter Carlson (*People* magazine, August 1983), and Aric Press (*Newsweek,* November 16, 1981).

Craig Barnard: Throughout Part II, descriptions of Barnard were based on interviews with Cary, Mello, Doherty, Vandiver, Radelet, Ronald and Trudy Barnard, Richard Burr, Richard Jorandby, Richard Greene, Carol Wilson, Bill White, Laurie Sistrunk, Bob Dillinger, Carolyn Snurkowski, Ray Marky, and others.

History and early litigation of modern death penalty: For a sense of the pre-*Furman* history of the death penalty, I relied most heavily on the personal archive of Watt Espy. For the discussion of *Furman,* I drew on Michael Meltsner's book *Cruel and Unusual;* on *The Brethren,* by Bob Woodward and Scott Armstrong; and on the opinions themselves (*Furman v. Georgia,* 408 U.S. 238).

For the legislative response in Florida, I relied on interviews with Marky, George Georgieff, Robert Shevin, Jack Gordon, Don Middlebrooks, Martin Dyckman, and others; on "Florida's Legislative Response to *Furman:* An Exercise in Futility?" (*Journal of Criminal Law and Criminology* 64, 1973); and on the papers of the House Select Committee and the Governor's Select Committee on the death penalty, available among the Askew papers at the Florida State Archives.

My discussion of the Florida Supreme Court's early difficulties applying the law was strongly shaped by Neil Skene's "Review of Capital Cases: Does the Florida Supreme Court Know What It's Doing?" published in *Stetson Law Review,* vol. XV, no. 2. I corroborated Skene's analysis through my own reading of the relevant cases. Further reflection on the court's difficulties was supplied in interviews or conversations with justices Arthur England, Gerald Kogan, Parker Lee McDonald, Joseph Boyd, James Adkins, and Rosemary Barkett.

My account of the 1976 decisions reinstating the death penalty was drawn from *The Brethren* and from reading the relevant cases (*Gregg v. Georgia, Proffitt v. Florida, Jurek v. Texas, Woodson v. North Carolina,* and *Roberts v. Louisiana,* beginning at 428 U.S. 152).

Brown v. Wainwright: The long history of this lawsuit was written based on my interviews, and many facts were corroborated by newspaper articles, including: Kelly Scott, the *SPT* (August 1980); Barbara Malone and Ken Walton, *Miami News* (September 23, 1980); Scott, *SPT* (September 30, 1980); Walton and Malone, *Miami News* (September 30, 1980); Neil Skene, *SPT* (October 28, 1980); Peter Racher, *TD* (November 16, 1980); Skene, *SPT* (January 6, 1981); David Finkel, *SPT* (March 1981); Scott, *SPT* (November 3, 1981); Skene, *SPT* (April 20, 1982); AP (April 25, 1982); AP (April 29, 1982); Bill Rose, *MH* (June 16, 1982); Scott, *SPT* (June 16, 1982); Skene, *SPT* (January 8, 1983).

Murder of Richard Burke: This scene was based on interviews and correspondence with death row inmates who asked not to be identified. The description of Knight came from the Florida Supreme Court's decision affirming his death sentence (338 So. 2nd 201), from numerous lawsuits filed by Knight himself, from interviews with prison officials, and from the Clendinin series (see above). I drew also from Frank Dorman's coverage of Knight's trial for the Burke murder (*GS,* October 22, 23, and 27 and November 5, 1982). For the reaction to the killing, I relied on my interviews with Richard Dugger and various inmates, and on Matt Bokor's report for the AP (*SPT,* October 18, 1980).

Graham and clemency: This material was drawn from the files of the Florida Commission on Pardons and Paroles, and from interviews with Graham, Betty Steffens, Art Weidinger, and others.

"Operation Besmirchment": This was drawn from interviews with Lohman, and from material in Lohman's personal files.

Death penalty debate: George Georgieff's story about choking his wife was first reported in an article by Stephen Adler *(American Lawyer,* September 1981), and Georgieff confirmed it in his interview with me. The fact that domestic murders rarely get the death penalty is commonly remarked on by prosecutors and defenders alike; in the chambers at the Florida Supreme Court, people often refer to the "Adkins rule," named for Justice James Adkins, who felt no spouse murder qualified for the death penalty. Isaac Erlich's "proof" of the deterrent effect of capital punishment can be found in *American Economic Review,* vol. 65, no. 3 (1975), and in *Yale Law Journal,* vol. 85, no. 2 (1975); a detailed response by Lawrence R. Klein, Brian Forst, and Victor Filatov, originally published by the National Academy of Sciences, is reprinted in *The Death Penalty in America* (3rd edition), edited by Hugo Adam Bedau.

My references to execution witnesses who were later executed, to hangmen later hanged, and to Hubert Goddard were drawn from Watt Espy's archives.

SOURCES

Robert A. Sullivan: My description of Sullivan and the work of the RASLDF was drawn primarily from interviews with Vandiver and Ralph Jacobs, supplemented by the personal files of both. They provided copies of their correspondence with Sullivan as well as copies of the RASLDF newsletters.

For accounts of Sullivan's crime, I relied on coverage of the trial by Joe Oglesby and Charles Whited of the *MH* (November 1973), and on later investigations by Brian Dickerson (*MH,* November 28, 1983), Michael Matza (*Boston Phoenix,* September 20 and 27 and October 4, 1983), and John Harwood (*SPT,* November 27, 1983).

Details of the preparation of Sullivan's alibi came from interviews with Jacobs and Vandiver, from the RASLDF newsletters, and from the exhibits filed by Roy Black in the Circuit Court of Dade County (case #73-3236A) supporting a motion to vacate Sullivan's sentence.

My account of the hearing in Fort Lauderdale was based on interviews with Jacobs and Warren Holmes, and on coverage by Barry Bearak (*MH,* March 11, 1980).

Sullivan's bet with God was drawn from a journal he kept during his death watch, a copy of which was provided by Vandiver. Sullivan's testimony on behalf of James Hill came from his sworn statement in the files of case #80-5690-A in the Circuit Court for Hillsborough County. The stenographer's good wishes were written on a scrap of paper contained in Vandiver's personal files.

The details of Sullivan's execution, including the pope's plea, were reported by Carl Hiaasen and Brian Dickerson (*MH,* December 1, 1983), supplemented by my interview with Dugger.

Anthony Antone: This passage drew primarily from profiles written by Neil Skene (*SPT,* January 23, 1984) and Steve Doig (*MH,* January 23, 1984), and from interviews with Holdman and Doherty.

The attendance at various protests, and the question of whether executions were becoming routine, came from Wayne Snow of UPI (*SPT,* January 29, 1984). The Hollywood producer's visit was based on interviews with Holdman and Rowland. The fact that Bob Graham had a copy of *Deathwork* on his shelf was reported by Michael Ollove in the *MH*'s *Tropic* magazine (December 9, 1984).

Arthur Frederick Goode III: Descriptive material was drawn primarily from interviews with Bud and Mildred Goode, Vandiver, Brierton, Dugger, Radelet, and Phil Kuntz—supplemented, in many cases, by material from their personal files. I also drew from numerous reports in the *SPT* (especially March 18 and 21, 1977, and April 5, 1984); from an interview in the *FTU* (March 14, 1984), and from a tape recording of Goode's final press conference, provided by Kuntz.

Numerous examples of Goode's letters were provided to me by Bud and Mildred Goode, Vandiver, Kuntz, and others.

Sandy Bohrer's thoughts and actions were drawn from my interview with him. The description of Alvin Ford's insanity came primarily from interviews with Rowland and Vandiver.

Mildred Goode's poem was originally published in the *MH;* she provided a copy to me.

The account of Goode's execution was based on reports by Neil Skene in the *SPT,* Ed Deitz in the *TT,* George Bayliss in the *GS,* Michael Ollove in the *MH,* and Andrea Rowand in the *FTU* (all April 6, 1984); my own observations of the effects of electrocution also informed this passage.

My analysis of the Goode appeal (denied) and the Ford appeal (victorious) was based on readings of Bohrer's Petition for a Writ of Habeas Corpus in U.S. District Court of the Middle District of Florida (case #54-65-CIU-FTM-10) alongside the U.S. Supreme Court's opinion in *Ford v. Wainwright* (477 U.S. 398).

Barnard's new "big issues": This material was based primarily on interviews with Burr and Mello; my discussion of the Florida Supreme Court's flip-flop over mitigating evidence drew on many interviews, and on reading of the relevant cases (*Cooper v. State,* 336 So. 2nd 1133, and *Songer v. State,* 365 So. 2nd 696). Neil Skene's article in *Stetson Law Review* was also helpful (see above).

James Adams: This passage was largely informed by my interviews with Burr, Mello, and Greene; and by the Application for Executive Clemency, filed May 1, 1984, by Jorandby, Barnard, Burr, Greene, and Mello. The Supreme Court action, and Scharlette Holdman's reaction, were reported by Neil Skene (*SPT,* May 11, 1984).

Carl Shriner: This passage was based primarily on my interview with Reverend Fred Lawrence, and on reports in Florida's major newspapers (all June 21, 1984).

David Washington: Here I drew primarily from Laurie Hollman's report in the *SPT* (July 14, 1984), and on the U.S. Supreme Court's opinion in *Strickland v. Washington* (466 U.S. 668).

The attorney shortage: The passages recounting the rising crisis caused by a lack of lawyers to handle death row appeals were drawn primarily from interviews with Holdman, Rowland, Mello, Burr, Vandiver, Cary, James Rinaman, Doherty, Harrison, Dillinger, Millard Farmer, and others. These interviews were supplemented by numerous published accounts, especially Dudley Clendinin (*The New York Times,* August 23, 1982), David Finkel (*SPT*'s *Floridian* magazine, November 7, 1982), Brian Dickerson (*MH*, June 3, 1984), AP (*SPT*, June 4, 1984), Judson H. Orrick (*The Florida Bar News*, August 15, 1984), Paul Anderson (*MH*, December 13, 1984), *The Economist* (May 4, 1985), and Michael A. Millemann (*The Maryland Bar Journal*, September 1985).

The same interviews informed my account of the James Agan and Robert Waterhouse appeals. Also helpful in preparing that account were reports by William Cotterell of UPI (*TT*, March 12, 1985), Lynda Richardson (*SPT*, March 16, 1985), Margaret Leonard (*TD*, March 16, 1985), John D. McKinnon (*MH*, March 28, 1994), and an editorial in the *GS* (March 15, 1985).

Earnest John Dobbert Jr.: This passage was drawn from interviews with Doherty, Snurkowski, Dugger, Mello, Vandiver, Radelet, and others; and from a profile by Claire Martin (*Jacksonville Journal*, February 6, 1982), commentaries by Neil Skene (*SPT*, September 3, 1984) and Susan Cary (*SPT*, September 7, 1984), and reports of the execution by Lisa Getter in the *MH*, Thomas French in the *SPT*, Andrea Rowand in the *FTU*, and Jim Runnels in the *OS* (all September 8, 1984).

Thurgood Marshall's opinion was drawn from his dissent in *Dobbert v. Wainwright* (53 *Law Week* 3445); Laurence Tribe's view came from his book *God Save This Honorable Court* (Random House, 1985).

James Dupree Henry: This passage was drawn from interviews with Martin Dyckman, Tom Fiedler, Steve Hull, Robin Gibson, Mello, Radelet, and others; also from reports by Andrea Rowand in the *FTU* and Christopher Smart in the *SPT* (both September 21, 1984). Analysis of Graham as governor also drew from David A. Kaplan (*National Law Journal*, July 16, 1984), James Ridgeway (*Village Voice*, April 16, 1985), and the *SPT* editorial headlined GOVERNOR JELLO (June 11, 1981), among other sources.

Timothy Palmes: This account was based on interviews with Holdman, Burr, and others, and on reports by Andrea Rowand in the *FTU*, Richard Cole of the AP, and Denise Flinchbaugh of the *TT* (all November 9, 1984).

J. D. Raulerson: This passage was drawn from interviews with Radelet, Vandiver, Cary, and others; and from reports by Andrea Rowand and Roger Malone (*FTU*, January 31, 1985).

Witt execution: The quotation came from Andrea Rowand's account in the *FTU* (March 7, 1985).

Marvin Francois: This passage was drawn from interviews with Burr, Lohman, Mello, and others; the description of the execution was drawn from reports by Andrea Rowand of the AP and Larry Bivins of the *MH* (both May 30,

1985). My account of the handling of Francois's remains was based on interviews with Radelet and Cary. The "brains in a bucket" episode was drawn from interviews with Radelet and Vandiver, and from reports by Bruce Krasnow (*FTU,* October 6 and 8, 1985) and Greg Myre (AP, October 17, 1985).

Creation of CCR: Material in these passages was drawn from interviews with Jim Smith, Marky, Georgieff, Snurkowski, Holdman, Burr, Mello, Lohman, Cary, Rowland, Larry Spalding, Faith Blake, Millard Farmer, and others; also from transcripts of proceedings before the Florida Senate Committee on the Judiciary and Criminal Justice during the 1985 legislative session and the Senate Staff Analysis and Economic Impact Statement on CS/SB 616 (both provided to me by the Office of Capital Collateral Representative); and from Laurie Hollman (*SPT,* August 18, 1985), Mary Anne Rhyne (*GS,* December 4, 1985), Daniel Berger (*TT,* March 2, 1986), Jan Elvin (*ACLU Journal,* spring 1986), Jon Nordheimer (*The New York Times,* March 31, 1986), Larry King (*SPT,* November 15, 1987), Amy Singer (*American Lawyer,* January/February 1988), Barbara Stewart (*Florida Magazine,* April 23, 1989), and Mike Williams (*Atlanta Journal & Constitution,* August 13, 1989).

Daniel Thomas: This passage was based on interviews with Dugger, Cary, and various death row inmates; on a UPI report published in the *MH,* an AP report published in *The New York Times,* Bruce Krasnow's report in the *FTU* (all April 16, 1986), and an editorial in the *SPT* (April 17, 1986); also on an affidavit sworn by a witness to the execution, Douglas N. Duncan (April 20, 1986), provided to me from the personal files of Margaret Vandiver.

David Funchess: This passage was based on interviews with Lohman, Holdman, and Cary, among others, and on reports by Greg Myre of the AP (multiple Florida newspapers, April 23, 1986), Tom Lyons (*GS,* April 23, 1986), Tod Ensign (*Guardian,* May 7, 1986), and Lawrence Young (*Pittsburgh Post-Gazette,* March 23, 1988).

Ronald Straight: This passage was drawn primarily from interviews with Mello and Marky, and from a report by Bruce Krasnow and Mark Journey (*FTU,* May 21, 1986).

Hitchcock v. Dugger: This material was drawn primarily from interviews with Mello, Burr, Greene, Jorandby, Ronald Barnard, and others; from an AP report published in the *MH* (April 23, 1983); from the transcript of oral arguments held October 15, 1986, at the U.S. Supreme Court (case #85-6756); and from the Court's opinion in *Hitchcock v. Dugger* (481 U.S. 393).

McCleskey v. Kemp: My analysis was based on interviews; on *Turning Right,* by David Savage, and *The Brethren,* by Bob Woodward and Scott Armstrong; and on the U.S. Supreme Court's opinion in *McCleskey v. Kemp* (481 U.S. 279).

PART III: A FAILURE OF EXECUTION

Ted Bundy: My description of Ted Bundy and account of his execution spans most of Part III. This work was based in part on interviews with Millard Farmer, Joe Nursey, Michael Radelet, Michael Mello, Mark Menser, Ray Marky, Carolyn Snurkowski, Andrea Hillyer, Ann Rule, Richard Larsen, Gene Miller, Margaret Vandiver, Roy Mathews, Fred Lawrence, Doug McCray, and others.

I drew also on books: *The Stranger Beside Me,* by Ann Rule; *The Deliberate Stranger,* by Richard Larsen; *The Only Living Witness,* by Stephen C. Michaud and Hugh Aynesworth. More important to my assessment of Bundy was *Ted Bundy: Conversations with a Killer,* by Michaud and Aynesworth. I also viewed the made-for-television film based on *The Deliberate Stranger* (first aired in 1986 and now widely available on video) for purposes of describing this singular bit of publicity.

My view of Bundy was shaped in part by the findings of Dr. Dorothy O. Lewis, which I quote and paraphrase at length. These were drawn from her deposition filed in U.S. District Court for the Southern District of Florida (case #86-1421-CIV-WJZ), and from her testimony in the U.S. District Court for the Middle District of Florida on December 15, 1987 (case #86-968-CIV-ORL-18). I drew on that same transcript of the December hearing for other details of testimony from other witnesses.

For my assessment of the relative speed with which Bundy's cases were handled, I drew on interviews with prosecutors and defense attorneys mentioned above; a more complete analysis can be found in "On Metaphors, Mirrors and Murders: Theodore Bundy and the Rule of Law," by Michael Mello (*New York University Review of Law & Social Change,* vol. XVIII, no. 3). This scrupulously documented article was a key source for my chronology of events.

The Florida Supreme Court opinions which I discussed can be found at 455 So. 2nd 330 and 471 So. 2nd 8, 19. Judge Sharp's crucial opinion can be found at 675 F. Supp. 622. Sharp's dismissive remark to a reporter on the way into the courthouse was drawn from Kim I. Eisler in the *American Lawyer* (December 21, 1987). The conclusive decision by the Eleventh Circuit Court of Appeals can be found at 850 Fed. 2nd 1402.

My account of the delivery of the Bundy appeal to the U.S. Supreme Court was based on my own observation. My discussion of the thinking of the Supreme Court clerks was based on interviews, including two with clerks who wished not to be identified.

The birth of Ted Bundy's daughter was based on interviews with death row inmates and with friends of Carole Boone, and on an AP report published in the *TD* (November 5, 1981). My description of Bundy's relationship with John Tanner was based on interviews and a profile of Tanner by Mike Thomas in the *OS*'s *Florida Magazine* (July 1, 1990). My account of Bundy's friendship with Diana Weiner, and their plans to negotiate for more time, was based on interviews with Mello, Radelet, Vandiver, Hillyer, and Dugger; on my own observations; and on reports by Ed Birk and Brent Kallestad of the AP and Michael Moline of UPI (January 18, 1989) and dispatches to the *MH* filed by Tallahassee Bureau Chief Mark Silva (January 18, 1989). Weiner declined to be interviewed by me.

Direct quotations from Bundy's notes during his last days were taken from seven pages of his legal pad obtained by the State of Florida during the final hours of litigation and released by the State to the Florida media.

The final Bundy appeal was drawn from interviews and from Mello, "Of Metaphors, Mirrors and Murder" (see above). The last word—the U.S. Supreme Court's 5-to-4 vote to allow the execution to proceed—can be found at 488 U.S. 1036.

My account of Bundy's final hours was drawn from interviews, especially with Radelet and Reverend Fred Lawrence, and from my own observations. I was present at the celebration of Bundy's execution outside the prison. My description of what happens to an execution witness was based on my own experience.

The discussion of Bundy's symbolic value drew on a variety of sources (an exhaustive list is available in Mello, "Of Metaphors, Mirrors and Murders"), including *The Sun* (September 4, 1990), the *GS* (March 12, 1991), and Elizabeth Purdum and J. Anthony Paredes in 6 *Anthropology Today* 9 (April 1990).

1986 governor's race: Here I drew on my own observations, on interviews, and on reports by Diana Smith of the AP (*SPT*, February 22, 1986), a combined wire services account in the *SPT* (March 14, 1986), Martin Dyckman in the *SPT* (March 23, 1986), Tom Fiedler in the *MH* (April 25, 1986), Joe Bizzaro of Cox News Service (*GS*, August 25, 1986), Dan Sewell of the AP (*GS*, September 21, 1986), and Laurie Hollman (*SPT*, October 13, 1986).

Jent and Miller: My account of the Jent-Miller case was based primarily on interviews with Morris McDonald, Howardene Garrett, Eleanor Jackson Piel, Sandy Weinberg, Alan Wagner, Roy Mathews, Samantha Carver, Robbie Larramore, Bill Jent, Earnie Miller, Jack Partain, Judy Hinson, Larry Hersch, Dr. Ronald Wright, Suzie and Bill Vaughn, Elmer Carroll, Turk Williams, Patrick Doherty, Scharlette Holdman, and others.

I also reviewed the investigative files of the Pasco County Sheriff's Office (released under *Tribune Co. v. P.C.S.O.*, 493 So. 2nd 480), which were made available to me by the law firm of Carlton, Fields, Ward, Emmanuel & Smith in Tallahassee. Also, I reviewed the criminal records of Charles Robert "Bobby" Dodd at the Whitfield County Courthouse in Dalton, Georgia (Files 9522, 9537, 12,571, 13,335, 13,602, 16,080, and 20,504).

I drew extensively from sworn depositions—of Glina Frye, Patricia Tiricaine, Carlena Jo Hubbard, David Fitzgerald, Jack Armstrong, Dr. Rehana Newab, and others—filed in the U.S. District Court for the Middle District of Florida in *Miller v. Dugger* and *Jent v. Dugger* (cases #83-849-CIV-T-13; #86-98-CIV-T-13; #83-860-CIV-T-13; and #85-1910-CIV-T-13).

Morris McDonald provided access to his extensive investigative file, which he keeps at his home outside Dalton, Georgia. I also drew from articles regarding the Jent-Miller case by Bill Heltzel (*EI,* October 17, 1979); Daniel Berger (*TT,* July 14 and August 17, 1985); Mary Jo Melone (*SPT,* August 17, 1985); Athelia Knight (*The Washington Post,* August 25, 1985); Bob Jensen (*SPT,* June 23, 1986); Noreen Willhelm of Cox News Service (*Miami News,* November 15, 1986); Julia Helgason (*Dayton Daily News,* November 8, 1987); and David Finkel (*Esquire,* March 1989); and on the ABC News program *20/20* for August 18, 1986, produced by Daniel S. Goldfarb and reported by Stone Phillips.

My description of the hearing at which Jent and Miller were released was based on my own observations.

Cost of the death penalty: Much of this passage was based on my own reporting in a series for the *MH* (July 10–13, 1988), where the methodology is detailed. Since that appeared, a more complete catalogue of cost studies has been published by the Death Penalty Information Center in Washington, D.C., titled "Millions Misspent: What Politicians Don't Say About the High Costs of the Death Penalty." Though the tone of that document is contentious, the sources are objective and clearly identified for further examination.

The Nelsons: For this passage I drew primarily on my interview with Wendy Nelson; also on interviews with Doherty and Mello; and on *Mann v. Dugger* (844 Fed. 2nd 1446). I found additional material in reports by Patti Bridges (*EI,* March 16, 1981); the *SPT* (March 17 and 21, 1981); J. Paul Wyatt of UPI (February 2, 1982); Sandra Lane Rice (*SPT,* February 7, 1982); and Bettina Harris (*EI,* September 4, 1984).

Craig Barnard's last days: This passage was based primarily on interviews with Susan Cary, Margaret Vandiver, Mello, Richard Greene, Richard Jorandby, Ronald and Trudy Barnard, and Holdman; and on Craig Barnard's analysis of death penalty law in "The 1988 Survey of Florida Law" in *Nova Law Review* (vol. 13, no. 3, pt. 1).

I also drew on documents provided from the personal files of Ronald and Trudy Barnard, and on the obituary by Candy Hatcher published in the *Palm Beach Post* (February 28, 1989).

Scharlette Holdman's departure: This passage was based on interviews with Holdman, Larry Spalding, Faith Blake, James Lohman, and others; and on reports by Howard Troxler (*TT*, August 2, 1988); Dave Bruns (*TD*, August 17, 1988); Sandra Fish (*FTU*, June 30, 1989), and Bill Cotterell (*TD*, June 30, 1989).

Ray Marky's conversion: This passage was based on my interviews with Marky.

Jesse Tafero's botched execution: This material was drawn from interviews and from Ellen McGarrahan's account in the *MH* (May 5, 1990).

The 1994 governor's campaign: My description of Jeb Bush's ad featuring Wendy Nelson, and the reaction to it, comes from reports in various Florida newspapers during the last week of October and the first week of November 1994, and in particular from the *MH*, October 21, 1994.

Harry Blackmun's conversion: The material quoted came from Blackmun's dissent in *Callins v. Collins* (case #93-7054).

Lewis Powell's conversion: This material was drawn from John C. Jeffries Jr.'s biography, *Justice Lewis F. Powell Jr.: A Biography* (Charles Scribner's Sons, 1994), reported in *The Washington Post* (June 10, 1994).

Doug McCray: This material was drawn from interviews with McCray, Bob Dillinger, Holdman, Gail Rowland, Susan Cary, Doug Magee, Margaret Vandiver, and others; from McCray's case file at the Florida Supreme Court; and from reports by Dudley Clendinin (*SPT*, August 28, 1978); Kurt Anderson (*Time*, January 24, 1983); Anthony Lewis (*The New York Times*, October 21, 1982), and Neil Skene (*SPT*, May 27, 1984).

INDEX

mental problems of, 229, 236–38, 241
Ford v. Strickland, 198–200
Fortas, Abe, 148
Francis v. Resweber, 111
Francois, Marvin, 279–81
    execution of, 280, 286, 371
    last wish of, 280
Frankel, Marvin:
    and *Brown v. Wainwright,* 176, 181,
        184–86
    Ford's appeals and, 198–99
Frankfurter, Felix, 12, 230, 236
Freeman, Eddie Lee, 408
Frye, Glina, 343–44
    Bradshaw's murder and, 343
    Dodd's relationship with, 340
    Jane Doe murder investigation and,
        332–36
    and Jent's and Miller's appeals, 348–
        50, 352, 354
    Jent's trial and, 338–39
    Miller's trial and, 338
Funchess, David, 292
Furman v. Georgia, 5–7, 53, 55, 147–55,
    157, 162–64, 167, 217, 236, 238,
    298–99, 410, 412

Gacy, John Wayne, 125
Gans, Lillian, 182
Gans, Sydney, 182
Gardner, Daniel, 170–72, 238
Gardner v. Florida, 172, 185
Garrett, Howardene:
    and Jent's and Miller's plea bargain,
        356
    Miller's appeals and, 346–48
Georgia, 6, 98
    executions in, 219
    racial bias issue and, 250–51, 295, 298
    see also specific court cases
Georgieff, George, 260
    background of, 23–24
    and *Brown v. Wainwright,* 185
    conservatism of, 95
    and early litigation of capital
        punishment, 153–54, 164–65
    in justifying capital punishment, 208

and secret psychiatric evaluations of
    condemned inmates, 172
Spenkelink's appeals and, 53–54, 74,
    94–96
Spenkelink's stays and, 88, 94–96
Gerber, Bob, 205
Gibson, Richard Henry, 189–90, 202–3
Gibson, Robin, 13–15, 67
    death row tour of, 13–14
    execution schedules and, 26
    Graham's relationship with, 13–14
    naïveté of, 104
    and protests against Spenkelink's
        execution, 20–21, 60–61, 103–4
    Spenkelink's death warrants and, 14
    Spenkelink's execution and, 15, 112–
        13
    Spenkelink's stays and, 63, 94, 103
Gideon v. Wainwright, 147, 244
Gilmore, Gary, 23, 43–44, 401
Gladish, Don, 291
Glen (movie producer), 223
Godbold, John, 199
Goddard, Hubert, 209
Goldstein, Steve, 97, 101
Good, Margaret, 168–70, 172
Goode, Arthur Frederick, III, 48, 224–
    38
    appeals of, 228–30, 234, 236–38, 241
    attention craved by, 227, 231
    background of, 224, 226–27
    death warrants of, 224, 230–31
    execution of, 232–35, 237, 241, 252
    fellow inmates' dislike of, 135–36
    last words of, 234–35
    letters written by, 225–26
    mental problems of, 224, 227–31,
        235–38, 241
    monologues of, 225–27, 231
    pedophilia of, 224–27, 230–31, 233
    physical appearance of, 225
    press interviews of, 227, 233
    public opinion on, 227–28
    rapes, kidnappings, and murders
        committed by, 225–27, 232–33,
        235
Goode, Bud, 224, 227, 230
Goode, Mildred, 224, 232–33
Gottlieb, Karen, 92

St. Louis
at Meramec
LIBRARY

About the author

DAVID VON DREHLE is a senior writer for the *Washington Post,* having served the paper previously as a national politics writer and New York Bureau Chief. Educated at the University of Denver and Oxford University, he began his newspaper career as a sportswriter at the *Denver Post.* It was as a general assignments reporter at the *Miami Herald* that he began reporting on the death penalty. He is also the author of the award-winning *Triangle: The Fire that Changed America.*

St. Louis Community College
at Meramec
LIBRARY